Descartes's Concept of Mind

1941
Ɔ (A 319)

LILLI ALANEN

Descartes's Concept of Mind

HARVARD UNIVERSITY PRESS

Cambridge, Massachusetts, and London, England

2003

06- 553838 (6)

Library of Congress Cataloging-in-Publication Data

Alanen, Lilli.
Descartes's concept of mind / Lilli Alanen.
p.   cm.
Includes bibliographical references and index.
ISBN 0-674-01043-4
1. Descartes, René, 1596-1650.
2. Philosophy of mind—History—17th century.
3. Mind and body—History—17th century.   I. Title.

B1878.M55A43   2003
128′2′092—dc21   2003045298

Contents

Preface

Since the publication in 1641 of his *Meditations on First Philosophy,*
which argues for a real distinction between the human mind and the
body to which it is united, Descartes's mind–body dualism and its
problems have set the agenda for much of the theorizing in the West-
ern world about human nature and thinking. Cartesian dualism, also
called "Ghost-in-the-machine" dualism, is still being discussed in one
form or another in contemporary debates over how the mental should
be accounted for and how it relates to the physical. In defining soul or
mind in terms of thinking, and in arguing that the nature of thinking
is independent from that of corporeal, extended matter, Descartes
is often seen as having introduced distinctly modern notions of consciousness, subjectivity, and intentionality. In *The Concept of Mind*
(1949), Gilbert Ryle set out to bring some order in the logical space of
our discourse about the mental that "Descartes's myth" had messed up
and that distorts "the continental geography of this subject."[1] In spite
of Ryle, the confusion has spread over many continents, and Cartesian
myths or their descendants continue to distort contemporary theories
of mind and knowledge.

While recent discussions have centered around epistemological and
ontological issues raised by Descartes's arguments for dualism, less attention has been paid to the fact that the mind whose immaterial nature he is concerned to prove is the human mind that is also embodied, acting and suffering with the body to which it is intimately united.
This book articulates the views Descartes actually held on mind and
thinking and examines them in the context in which they were devel-

oped. Using Rylean metaphors, it purports to shed some light on the terrain and the conditions in which Descartes explored the logical geography of the concepts of mind, mental powers, acts, their representational functions, and their interrelations. Descartes's enterprise was not clearly restricted, as was Ryle's, to drawing logical maps of the location and interrelations of our concepts, and his philosophy of mind comes with a metaphysics of mind and body. My focus here, however, is on the former, and my ambition is to uncover Descartes's usage of the logical and conceptual maps available to him in trying to understand and account for our place as thinkers and agents in the infinitely extended universe opening itself to a new kind of strictly causal, mechanistic explanations. If Ryle's concern was to unveil the distortions in our mental geography caused by "Descartes's myth," this book seeks to redress the distortions of Descartes's concepts of human mind and thinking caused by the Cartesian myth that Ryle justly sought to correct, but that his gripping caricature has also helped keep alive.

Anyone who takes a serious interest in Descartes's view of human thought and nature must face the question of the consistency of his philosophy seen as a unified system. Since I do not address this issue directly in the book I need to indicate briefly my stand on it. Descartes's dualist worldview, which grants substantial reality to both thought and extension as really distinct and (so far as our knowledge is concerned) as having incompatible natures, is deeply problematic. His notion of the union between mind and body, each of which is intrinsically clear and distinct but conjunctively inconceivable, seems too tenuous and obscure to ground a coherent view of human nature. A choice is forced upon us: something has to go. Consistency? Dualism? The mind–body union and, with it, human nature as we experience it? All three perhaps? After more than three and a half centuries of wrestling with it, no clear way out of the dilemma has been found, other than the realization that there is something deeply misleading in the framework of substances and essential attributes in which the problem was posed in the first place. But even if we succeed in ridding ourselves of the excess metaphysical baggage accumulated over the centuries, we are still left with the mind and the world as we experience them and describe them in ordinary language, on the one hand, and with our scientific ideals and the methods we use in trying to explain those experiences on the other, and hence with the puzzle of how to relate these discourses to each other.

My discussion of Descartes's concept of mind is concerned with the minds of human thinkers, and hence grants his notion of human nature as constituted by both mind and body. Its guiding question is what, if anything, the wide variety of phenomena that Descartes includes in his broad definition of thinking—from intellect and reason to sensations and passions—have in common and how they relate to each other. It is about what separates mind from body, namely thinking, as much as about what unites them: the forms of embodied intentionality characteristic of the thoughts caused by and expressed in the body, whose function is to preserve the mind–body unity and which are constitutive for our experience as human, thinking, and corporeal beings. Unlike those who, starting with his arguments for dualism, are led to downplay the role of body-dependent mental phenomena or to treat them as purely accidental, I start—as Descartes himself does—from the idea of the mind united to the body (or, as he puts it in his early writings, of the mind informing the body), but find myself pushed in another direction that seems to undermine substance dualism. But since Descartes clearly defended dualism, either consistency has to go or dualism has to be reconceived, and I think the latter is by far the better alternative. That leaves us with what Descartes in his correspondence with Princess Elisabeth called three primitive and irreducible notions—thought, extension, and mind–body union—and the task of finding a way of relating and balancing them.

My aim is not to offer a theory about how that should be done. Descartes himself seems to suggest, in his correspondence with Elisabeth, that the three primary notions are on a par in being each legitimate within their own domain and so leave open the question of their respective weight and ordering. This obscures the fact that the third notion, that of the mind–body union, is not only the actual starting point and the final outcome of Descartes's *Meditations,* but also a presupposition of his other two primary notions to which he gives theoretical priority. Hence the instability of his dualism. I do not wish to defend that doctrine, but simply to examine and reflect on the ensuing views of the mind and its contents as they unfold in Descartes's thinking on this subject, from his earliest writings to his last.

My interest in Descartes's reflections on human nature and expe-rience was first stirred by Ferdinand Alquié, who introduced me to the study of Descartes at the Sorbonne. The decision to explore Des-cartes's philosophy of mind more systematically was made after a stim-ulating year as an American Council of Learned Societies scholar at the University of Pittsburgh in 1985–1986. It has been interrupted and set aside many times, and for different reasons, but never really aban-doned. My continuing to pursue it is due to the support, encourage-ment, and inspiration of friends, colleagues, and fellow scholars.

Erik Stenius, who was my first teacher at the department of philoso-phy at the University of Helsinki, passed on to me his interest in the classics and in making sense—in our terms—of their views. While owing my general way of reading Descartes to French scholars Jean Laporte, Henri Gouhier, Martial Guéroult, Geneviève Rodis-Lewis, and most of all to Ferdinand Alquié, I am deeply indebted to the work of Annette Baier, Alan Donagan, Harry Frankfurt, Anthony Kenny, Norman Malcolm, and Margaret Wilson, whose lucid and often chal-lenging discussions of various aspects of Descartes's views on mind, ideas, and action have kept my interest in the subject alive over the years.

The kind support of and discussions with Georg-Henrik von Wright, Lars Hertzberg, and Simo Knuuttila ever since I started to work in phi-losophy have been invaluable. Discussions about and around the top-ics of this book over many years with Calvin Normore and André Gombay have been a source of inspiration and instruction. Of the many persons to whose work on Descartes I am indebted and cite in this book, I want to thank in particular Jean-Marie Beyssade, Michelle Beyssade, Deborah Brown, John Carriero, John Cottingham, Edwin Curley, Harry Frankfurt, Marjorie Grene, Paul Hoffman, Hidé Ishiguro, Dugald Murdoch, Steven Nadler, Alan Nelson, Martina Reuter, Marleen Rozemond, Lisa Shapiro, and Mikko Yrjönsuuri for valuable and helpful discussions of various aspects of his philosophy. I have also learned and benefited from discussions about philosophy of mind and ethics, ancient and modern, with Tuomo Aho, Lisa van Alstyne, Julia Annas, Akeel Bilgrami, Robert Brandom, Arthur Collins, James Conant, Cora Diamond, Eyólfur Emilsson, Leila Haaparanta, John Haugeland, Sara Heinämaa, Timo Kaitaro, Marja-Liisa Kakkuri-Knuuttila, Heikki Kannisto, Peter King, Olli Koistinen, Juhani

Pietarinen, Hilary Putnam, Pauliina Remes, Gunnar Svensson, Gary Watson, David Wiggins, and Peter Winch.

I had the opportunity to teach graduate seminars on Descartes's philosophy of mind at Wayne State University in 1988 and at the University of California, Irvine, in 1998. I owe special thanks to Michael McKinsey and his students for the first occasion, and to Alan Nelson and all the participants in my seminar for the second, in particular David Cunnings, Larry Nolan, Alice Sowaal, and Andrew Youpa. The department of philosophy at the University of Uppsala has provided a friendly and research-supportive environment, and I am grateful to my colleagues, in particular to Krister Segerberg, Rysiek Sliwinski, and Sören Stenlund for the support they have given me, not least in granting leaves. Major parts of my work were funded by the Academy of Finland, and its completion was made possible by a grant from the Swedish Bank Tercentenary Foundation.

Above all I am grateful to Annette Baier, who showed that when doing philosophy as a woman, one need not feel bad in following one's own lights and interests were they to depart from those of one's male tutors and predecessors. Without her kind interest and encouragement I would hardly have embarked on this project. I would not have pulled it together without the companionship and support of Fred Stoutland, who not only endured discussions of nearly every aspect of it during the past ten years, but who has spared neither time nor energy in helping me straighten out thoughts and sentences, most recently by editing the whole manuscript in its last stage. The conversations with Annette, in Pittsburgh and later, and the continued dialogue with Fred have meant more to me than I could ever say.

Considerable improvements were made possible thanks to advice, in the last stages, from James Conant and Joseph Camp, and in particular to the insightful and extensive comments and criticisms on the whole manuscript by John Carriero and Paul Hoffman, who read the manuscript for Harvard University Press. I have also had the invaluable help of Auli Kaipainen in preparing the manuscript for the press and of David Bemelmans in the stage of its final editing.

My greatest debt is to my children Maija, Anna, and Harry, and to Fred Stoutland, to whom this book is dedicated.

*　　*　　*

Bits and pieces of the text have been published in separate papers. Chapter 2 started out as a criticism of the Rylean version of Cartesian dualism published as "Descartes's Dualism and the Philosophy of Mind" in *Revue de Métaphysique et de Morale* 3 (1989): 391–413. Revised parts of "Thought-Talk: Descartes and Sellars on Intentionality," which appeared in *American Philosophical Quarterly* 29 (1992): 19–44, are included in Chapter 3. Reworked passages from "Cartesian Ideas and Intentionality," which appeared in L. Haaparanta, M. Kusch, and I. Niiniluoto, eds., *Language, Knowledge and Intentionality, Acta Philosophica Fennica* 49 (1990): 344–370, are included in Chapter 4. Chapter 5 is an extended and revised version of "Sensory Ideas, Objective Reality and Material Falsity," which appeared in John Cottingham, ed., *Reason, Will and Sensation: Studies in Cartesian Metaphysics* (Oxford: Clarendon Press, 1994), pp. 229–249. Revised material from "The Intentionality of Cartesian Passions," forthcoming in Byron Williston, ed., *Beyond Dualism: Essays on Passion and Virtue in Descartes* (Humanities-Prometheus Press, 2003), is included in Chapter 6, and some sections of Chapter 7 contain material from "Descartes on the Will and the Power to Do Otherwise," in Henrik Lagerlund and Mikko Yrjönsuuri, eds., *Emotions and Rational Choice—Theories of Action from Anselm to Descartes* (forthcoming, Kluwer Academic Publishers).

Abbreviations

Alquié   *Oeuvres Philosophiques de Descartes,* ed. Ferdinand Alquié, 3 vols.
Paris: Editions Garnier Frères, 1963–1973.

AT   *Oeuvres de Descartes,* ed. Charles Adam and Paul Tannery, 12 vols.
Paris: Vrin, 1964–1976.

CSM   *The Philosophical Writings of Descartes,* ed. and trans. John
Cottingham, Robert Stoothoff, and Dugald Murdoch, 2 vols.
Cambridge: Cambridge University Press, 1985.

CSMK   *The Philosophical Writings of Descartes: The Correspondence,* ed. and
trans. John Cottingham, Robert Stoothoff, Dugald Murdoch, and
Anthony Kenny. Cambridge: Cambridge University Press, 1991.

NE   Aristotle, *Nicomachean Ethics,* trans. W. D. Ross, rev. J. O. Urmson,
ed. Jonathan Barns. In *The Complete Works of Aristotle,* rev. Oxford
trans. Princeton/Bollingen Series LXXI.2. Princeton, N.J.:
Princeton University Press, 1995.

OTH   William Ockham, *Scriptum in librum primum Sententiarum ordinatio,*
vols. 1–4, ed. by Gedeon Gál, Stephen Brown, Georg Etzkorn, and
Francis E. Kelley. In *Opera theologica.* St. Bonaventure, N.Y.: St.
Bonaventure University, 1967–1979.

ST   Thomas Aquinas, *Summa Theologiae,* ed. and trans. Thomas Gilby
et al., 61 vols. London: Blackfriars' Eyre and Spottiswoode, 1964–
1980.

Descartes's Concept of Mind

Introduction

The Cartesian concept of mind—or rather a certain picture of the mind attributed to Descartes—has set the stage for much of the contemporary discussion in philosophy of mind. This book reconsiders Descartes's concepts of mind and the mind–body union by a close reading of the texts, which attempts to examine them in a broad historical-*cum*-philosophical context without losing sight of the relevance of his views to present day issues in the philosophy of mind. My focus is on his philosophy of mind broadly construed, comprising his views about its nature as thinking and embodied, its cognitive capacities, as well as its volitional, moral, and emotional functions. Descartes's conception of mind or thought is remarkably broad—yet largely due to a long-standing interest in his epistemological views, attention has been almost uniquely centered on the intellect—on the mind as a purely thinking thing—and its role in the pursuit of knowledge. The ambition of this book is to correct the current picture of Descartes's view of the mental by drawing attention to aspects that others have largely ignored. Not only are they worth exploring in their own right but, given the role of Cartesian mind–body dualism in contemporary debates about the mental, it can be of interest to realize that his views are richer, more complex, and more difficult to classify than the usual dualism and anti-dualism dichotomies suggest.

The reading here offered is guided by the methodological assumption that the historical context does matter to our understanding of the doctrines of past philosophers and that, even if we have to work out our interpretation of their views in the light of contemporary

1

philosophical concerns, we need historical and exegetical research to ground it. Contrary to a view nurtured within analytic history of philosophy, my view is that the two enterprises of rational and historical reconstruction cannot be conducted independently.[1] Grasping the philosophical relevance of a text presupposes critical, historical work, while the latter would be of little worth if it were not philosophically informed, that is, if it did not address the philosophical ambitions and problematics central to the text.

In the case of Descartes, whose thinking is very much a thinking in progress, the central problems take different forms and directions at different stages of his career. These changes are reflected not only in his views of science and the nature of philosophical inquiry, but also in his views on mind and cognition—in the problems he poses and the solutions he proposes.

I begin by looking at the history of his intellectual ambitions as recorded in his earliest unpublished writings and correspondence. Retracing his own itinerary shows how Descartes was led, for reasons internal to his philosophical project, from his early interest in mathematics and in a mathematico-mechanistic science of nature to metaphysics. It also shows that Descartes had very early formed some distinctive views about the mind, which set the stage for his later reflections on its metaphysical nature and for the development of his mature philosophical psychology and epistemology.

This latter point needs some justification. All the canonical texts— the ones that have been considered philosophically relevant—are from the time he began to work on the foundations of his philosophy of nature in the early 1630s and consist mainly in his published work. The most important and most quoted of them are the *Discourse on the Method* published with three accompanying scientific essays in 1637 (hereafter referred to as the *Discourse*), and the *Meditations on First Philosophy,* with the Objections and Replies, published in 1641 (hereafter *Meditations*). It is also well known, however, that Descartes's first work of importance was in mathematics, that it was done somewhere between 1618 and the early 1620s, and that he spent more than a decade working mainly on the solution to problems in mathematics, kinematics, and optics and on an unfinished project of a universal method of science. As Descartes himself testified, he had outgrown his early interest in mathematics and the method of science by the time he turned to work on a systematic presentation of his philosophy of nature.[2] This accounts for the commonly held view that Descartes began his intellectual career as a mathematician and philosopher of nature and that his interests were directed to merely scientific and methodological matters until he was prompted to publish and defend his physics. According to this picture, his interest in mind, metaphysics, and the foundations of knowledge was a much later development motivated by various external, religious, or political concerns.

Some see a crucial change taking place after a presumed skeptical and perhaps religious crisis in the late 1620s, while others explain Descartes's new interests in metaphysics as a consequence of his reaction to the condemnation of Galileo in 1633, which resulted in the immediate cancellation of his plans to publish his *Le monde,* presenting his physical theory. Richard Popkin, who defends the first view, finds in the autobiographical part of the *Discourse* and in Descartes's letters evidence that "around 1628–29 he was struck by the full force of the sceptical onslaught, and the need for a new and stronger answer to it." According to Popkin, the philosophical revolution Descartes set in motion by his discovery of the cogito must be seen in light of his "awakening to the sceptical menace."[3]

Taking issue with Popkin, Stephen Gaukroger has recently argued for the latter view. Gaukroger finds many a crisis in Descartes's life, but none that show any concern with skepticism: "His interest in skepticism was relatively late, and took shape in the context of providing a metaphysical legitimation of his natural philosophy, a task which he never even contemplated before the condemnation of Galileo in 1633, and which was a direct response to that condemnation." Descartes's skepticism was purely instrumental, and served no other purpose than "establishing the metaphysical credentials of a mechanist natural philosophy, one of whose central tenets—the Earth's motion around the Sun—had been condemned by the Inquisition."[4]

Other commentators show little interest in this change of orientation. Whatever their account of his intellectual development, they agree that Descartes's philosophy represents one of those powerful doctrines that should be studied systematically and analytically, rather than historically, since only systematic analysis reveals the force of his arguments and the structure of his work taken as a whole. Martial Guéroult's *Descartes selon l'ordre des raisons* (1952) is an extreme representative of this approach in French scholarship, while Margaret Wilson's *Descartes* (1978) is an outstanding and influential example of it in Anglo-American scholarship. Both focus, not surprisingly, on Descartes's main philosophical work, the *Meditations,* and tend to read the other writings, to the extent they consider them, in light of their reading of the *Meditations.*[5]

While Wilson professes openness to many different approaches to the study of past philosophers, from historical exegesis to self-conscious analytic reconstruction, she also expresses some skepticism concerning the importance of historical consciousness to philosophical achievement. She points to Descartes and Wittgenstein as examples of important philosophers "who evince little or no direct concern with defining their positions in relation to the long history of philosophical thought" and goes on to note that "the depth of their implicit historical knowledge is at best controversial."[6] Those who take philosophical problems to be in some sense ahistorical and who measure philosophical achievement through contributions made toward the solving of those problems may take the alleged lack of historical awareness of philosophers like Descartes and Wittgenstein as evidence that the problems they address are independent of a particular historical context. They would welcome that as justification for treating these thinkers as "one of us," that is, as conversational partners whose historical roots can be ignored.[7]

But philosophical problems are to a large extent constituted by their historical context and can hardly even be identified apart from it. Understanding a philosophical problem—even in discussions with contemporaries—always involves some clarification of presuppositions, motives, commitments, and opponents of a thinker, none of which, when past thinkers are concerned, can be uncovered without detailed historical and contextual groundwork.[8] If it is true that Descartes avoids positioning himself explicitly in relation to his predecessors, he certainly knows the tradition he opposes well enough to formulate his questions and arguments with reference to their conceptual and philosophical framework. Descartes's relationship to his predecessors is complex. While it was his explicit goal to break with the reigning tradition of late Aristotelian Scholastic philosophy of nature, his thinking is deeply informed by Scholastic metaphysics, and it is from there that he takes over the conceptual apparatus in which his own views are stated.

It is well known that his use of traditional terms and distinctions in the framework of his new mechanistic theory of the physical universe stretches their meanings—sometimes even changing them beyond recognition. But this means that we need more, rather than less, knowledge of Descartes's background and the philosophical context of his positions. The more we know about the ways of thinking he departs from as well as those he aligns himself with, the better placed we are to make sense of his views in our own terms or, when that is not feasible, to realize how different they are from ours.[9]

For too long Descartes has been read as the starting point for a new way of thinking, a philosopher who should be interpreted in light of the changes his innovations brought about, with little or no attention paid to the historical background out of which his views developed. The task of unraveling his debts to the tradition from which he grew has barely begun, but as far as his metaphysics, philosophy of mind, and epistemology are concerned, it is already evident that, while in some ways his views represent new "modern" ways of thinking, he can just as well be considered one of the last great representatives of Scholastic thought, one deeply rooted in the medieval Aristotelianism that sought its Christian inspiration more from Augustine than Aquinas.[10]

This book contributes to that task by examining Descartes's philosophy of mind in the context both of his own intellectual development and projects and of the Scholastic philosophy from which it emerged. Cartesian scholars who have taken an interest in the Scholastic background of Descartes's thinking have contrasted it primarily with the doctrine of Aquinas or his followers.[11] Little attention has been paid to the rich tradition of philosophical psychology and epistemology developed in the late medieval period by thinkers in the Franciscan and Augustinian tradition, who anticipated many of Descartes's ideas that were long considered more or less Cartesian inventions. It is not my ambition to trace the historical antecedents of Descartes's philosophy of mind or to establish connections between his views and those of his predecessors. But I have tried to take note of some similarities and to discuss some ancient and late medieval views when doing so helps clarify Descartes's arguments and concepts, for example, his use of the term "intuition" (Chapter 1, section 2), his notion of "objective reality" (examined in Chapter 4), or his concepts of "assent" and "free choice of the will" (discussed in Chapter 7).

Descartes's philosophy of mind, in the broad sense used here, covers a range of questions—psychological, epistemological, metaphysical, and moral. My strategy is to follow, roughly, the development of his thinking about the mind and the order in which different kinds of concerns came to be addressed by him, taking note of the weight they were given at different times and the extent to which his basic views and terminology evolve. Chapter 1 examines Descartes's treatment of mind and cognition in his earliest unpublished texts, written when his physico-mathematical and methodological interests were dominant. It gives a brief sketch of his intellectual itinerary until the time he began more serious reflections on the nature of the mind and other metaphysical issues. Chapter 2 focuses on his mature view of the mind as distinct in nature from the body and yet at the same time embodied, and then on the different kinds of knowledge Descartes associates with his primary notions of thought, extension, and mind–body union. Chapters 3–5 deal with his notion of thought and its various aspects: its wide definition in terms of consciousness and its relation to language (Chapter 3), its intentional and representative nature (Chapter 4), and the status of sensations as mental phenomena (Chapter 5). These chapters center on the writings from the time he started to work on the *Discourse of the Method* published in 1637, until the publication in 1644 of the *Principles of Philosophy,* a time when he gives a systematic exposition and defense of his views on mind, matter, and mind–body dualism. The last two chapters deal with his treatment of emotions, of the will, of reason's mastery of emotions, and of related moral issues to which Descartes had given little serious reflection before his correspondence with Princess Elisabeth, starting in 1643, and the writing of his last published work, The *Passions of the Soul* (1649).

1

From Methodology
of Science to
Philosophy of Mind

Descartes's early interests were by no means exclusively scientific. Not only is the very distinction between science and philosophy hard to make in a seventeenth-century context, it is all the more misleading in the case of Descartes, whose earliest projects included *Scientia* in the classic sense of the word. *Scientia* means more than knowledge in the sense of a system of true, justified beliefs, and includes understanding based on intuitively grasped first principles. The knowledge sought by Descartes from early on is knowledge in the sense of complete and perfect *Scientia*. It has more in common with the traditional Aristotelian notion of *episteme*, which consists in the understanding of the explanatory order and the place of the knower within it, than with the conception of science as absolutely certain knowledge, where the focus is on the order of evidence and justification, so often associated with the Cartesian project.[1] In Descartes's early writings, *Scientia* is also closely connected to *Sapientia:* human wisdom in the sense of practical intelligence, the achievement of which is the goal of the universal method described in his ambitious and unfinished methodological project, *Rules for the Direction of the Mind* (*Regulae ad Directionem Ingenii,* hereafter *Rules*), to which major parts of this chapter are devoted. Against those who see the *Rules* as a mere offshoot of Descartes's mathematical interests, the project, I argue, is an expression of his early *philosophical* concerns—not of his scientific concerns in the modern, post-Cartesian sense of scientific.

If it is a mistake to think there is a sharp change in Descartes's interests from scientific to metaphysical or epistemological, it is equally mis-

7

taken to think that Descartes's mature philosophy is of one piece. His thinking is as much subject to evolution after he started to write about metaphysics as before he turned to it. His philosophy is very much a work in progress: his projects and his ambitions change over time, as does his articulation of fundamental positions. There is not one systematically spelled out view, but a number of core theses, which get revised as new difficulties, objections, and challenges turn up. Descartes's philosophy of mind is the result of an ongoing struggle to adjust some basic views about human nature, thought, and agency rooted in experience and tradition to the new picture of the universe, which had come to establish itself as the "Scientific Image," and which had lost all its intuitive ties with the former "Manifest Image."[2]

Read in this way, there is greater continuity in Descartes's fundamental views than most readings would allow for. The changes are more a matter of emphasis, subject matter, and perspective than of basic theses and convictions. Thus, if the questions concerning mind that Descartes first raised were questions of cognitive psychology, his treatment of them soon invited more general ones concerning the nature and status of the mind in a world of uniformly extended and mechanically moved things entailed by his mathematical-mechanistic physics. His philosophy of mind and epistemology grew from ideas outlined in his early work about the cognitive powers and their role in the search for *Scientia*. If his early conception of the mind was shaped by his thinking about the method and grew out of his effort to give a general account of rules for attaining certainty in science, his later work can be seen as the result of his effort to address the many problems that his early views left unanswered.[3] Questions about the nature of the mind and its status as a knower, but also about the reliability of clearly and distinctly intuited ideas of simple natures, which constitute the building blocks of true and certain science, and their connection to the world of extended things they are supposed to represent, all call for answers that Descartes was not in a position to give when writing the never-finished *Rules*. They seem however to have become important concerns for him already by the time he turned to working on his first draft of metaphysics (1629?) and promulgated, in correspondence, his original and radical theory of the creation of eternal truths (1630).

1. The Early Writings

Descartes was born at La Haye, in Tours, on March 31, 1596. Having completed by 1615 the curriculum at the most famous educational institution of the time, the Jesuit Collège de la Flèche, and taking a degree in law at the University of Poitiers a year later, Descartes described his disappointment with the sciences as practiced in the schools in Part 1 of the *Discourse on the Method,* written two decades later. After receiving his law degree he spent some years wandering through Europe, and, as his correspondence testifies, it was the fortuitous encounter in the late fall of 1618 with Isaac Beeckman, physician and amateur scientist—one of the earliest defenders of mechanistic theories—that awakened his slumbering intellectual ambitions to life again.[4] Although Descartes later minimizes and even denies any debt to his former friend and mentor,[5] it is clear that Beeckman played an important role in introducing Descartes to new scientific problems, principles, and doctrines—for instance his version of corpuscularianism—and, most important, to the general idea of a mathematical physics.[6] The discussions with Beeckman inspired Descartes to do some scientific work of his own but also gave him the grand idea of publishing "not an *Ars brevis* of Lullus, but a fundamentally new science, which will resolve generally all the questions concerning any kind of quantity, continuous as well as discontinuous, that one can ask." He describes the geometrical method he has in mind with great enthusiasm:

> And it seems to me that one could not imagine anything to which a solution could not be found with similar lines; but I hope to prove *(spero . . . ut demonstrem)* which questions can be solved in this manner and no other, so that there will remain nothing else to discover in geometry. The task, it is true, is endless, and cannot be accomplished by one person. It is incredibly ambitious; but I have discovered I know not what light in the obscure chaos of this science, and I think that it will help to dissipate the most impenetrable darkness.[7]

A year after the meetings with Beeckman, the idea of working out a new unified system of sciences began to take form, and Descartes reports his discovery of "the foundations of a marvelous science" (November 10, 1619). The vision of a unitary science interconnected with the idea of a unified method was to guide his work and activities for years to come, but it was not until nearly a decade later that he made his first serious attempt to state its main ideas more systematically.[8]

Throughout the next decade Descartes worked mainly, and successfully, on mathematics (he is likely to have worked out some of the main problems presented in the *Geometry*), on various problems in optics (for example, refraction) and other sciences, as well as on the project of a general presentation of his method. He wrote, probably in the early 1620s, a lost treatise *Studium bonae mentis*,[9] and in the latter half of the decade he composed the *Rules,* which includes some texts written at an earlier stage, but which he abandoned in 1628 a little more than halfway through. He never got back to it nor does he mention it in his later writings, but it was carefully preserved among his manuscripts found in Stockholm at his death.[10] Among the few other things known about his life and activities during this time is that he traveled a great deal, visited Paris, stayed there more permanently from 1625 to 1627, and got in contact with other contemporary scientists and mathematicians. Mersenne refers to Descartes in a letter from 1626 as "an excellent mathematician," but he seems soon to have impressed the circles around Mersenne not only with his scientific experiments and inventions, but also through his argumentative skills and philosophical method.[11] He withdrew to Brittany in the winter of 1627–1628, traveled to the Netherlands and back to Paris again, before moving in 1629 to the Netherlands, where he was to live until he accepted the fatal call to Stockholm by Queen Christina of Sweden in the fall of 1649. He died there from the flu a few months after his arrival, on February 11, 1650.

Let us now turn to Descartes's early thoughts on mind and cognition as recorded in the three sources we possess: some early notes preserved thanks to a copy made by Leibniz, the posthumously published *Treatise on Music (Compendium musicae),* and the *Rules.*

In the fragments of Descartes's writings from January 1619 copied by Leibniz, one finds the term *ingenium,* often translated in French as *esprit* and in English as *mind,* used in its primary sense of "human intellect" or intellectual ability; but it also occurs at least once in a more general sense in reference to strong affections or passions of the mind.[12] This is noteworthy because it shows the interest Descartes already took at this time in the passions, their effects and interrelations. He explains that the strong affections aroused by touching the relevant parts of the mind vary according to dispositions of character and the circumstances. He notes that though we pass from one passion (*passio*) to another gradually, it often happens that a passion can change more violently into its opposite, "as when sad news are announced in the midst of a joyous gathering" (AT X 217). We also find him studying his own emotional reactions: "I notice that if I am sad or in danger and preoccupied by some sad affairs, I sleep deeply and eat with great avidity. But if on the contrary I am full of joy, I neither eat nor sleep" (AT X 217, CSM I 4). That Descartes was himself prone to strong emotional reactions is clear from his correspondence. His letters to Beeckman, for instance, show him passing from enthusiastic friendship—almost devotion—to bitter contempt and scorn for one he once looked on with gratitude and affection as his intellectual mentor.[13]

The *Treatise on Music* that he wrote in the last months of 1618, rather hastily it seems, to present as a gift for the New Year to Isaac Beeckman, analyzes the effects of rhythms and other properties (*affectiones*) of sounds produced by musical instruments on our emotions (*affectus*).[14] Descartes states that the object of music is sound, and its aim is to please "and to stir various passions in us." Songs can be both sad and enjoyable at the same time. That they can have such different effects is not, he says, astonishing, for the authors of elegiacs as well as the actors of tragedies "please us all the more as they excite more pain (*luctum*) in us" (AT X 89). The variety of passions excited by music is explained through the variety of measures or rhythms: slow ones tend generally to produce "slow passions, as languor, sadness, fear, and pride, etc., and fast measures produce likewise fast passions, as joy, etc." (AT X 95). He also observes how the sound of music resonates through surrounding bodies, affecting the spirits "through which we are excited to move," creating a natural impulse to jump and dance. Thanks to this impulse, animals too can be trained to dance in rhythm. Descartes leaves the detailed explanation of all this to the "physicians," but the basic idea developed more than twenty-five years later in *The Passions of the Soul* is outlined here: mechanical movements and their variations, when affecting the senses according to certain measures and proportions, produce a variety of passions in the soul. The idea of some kind of natural correspondence between mechanical bodily motions and sensations is taken for granted.

2. The *Regulae ad directionem ingenii* and the Quest for Certainty

Even a brief look at the early methodological rules shows that the ambitions that guided Descartes from the start were philosophical more than purely scientific. For if Descartes started out with the specific ideal of a unitary science taking its inspiration from mathematics, the conception of the mind and its capacities that this ideal entails breaks with the most basic assumptions of Aristotelian philosophy. What emerges from the *Rules* is a new view not only of knowledge, but of the world itself, though that is not spelled out nor defended in any way, and all we get is a description (incomplete) of a method for attaining certainty in science. In presenting his new method, Descartes appropriates traditional terminology and distinctions without spending much time on clarifying the uses to which he puts them. Clarifying and justifying the general view in which his ambitious methodological and scientific project was embedded becomes increasingly important as he goes along, and eventually takes the place of the more particular goals of the practicing mathematician and natural philosopher. These early views are not much known or discussed,[15] but because I take them to be determinative for the whole Cartesian project, I spend some time presenting them, noting as I go along the problems that I take to be most important for the development of Descartes's mature views on the mind and related topics of interest.[16]

Descartes's goal from the earliest parts of the *Rules* is unity and certainty in the sciences.[17] The aim, as we read in Rule One, is to direct the mind to form "sound and true judgment about whatever comes before it" (AT X 359, CSM I 9). The mind, here a translation of the Latin *ingenium*, stands for our inborn mental or intellectual ability. It is also referred to as "good sense" *(bona mens),* "this universal wisdom," and at the very end of the first rule, as the "natural light of reason" *(naturalem rationis lumen)* (AT X 360). "Natural light of reason" and "good sense" are different names for an innate capacity each of us possesses but that needs to be trained and developed; it is what anyone seriously inter-

ested in investigating the truth of things should be concerned to perfect. The ultimate goal of perfecting the intellect is practical: "in order
that his intellect should show his will what decision it ought to make
in each of life's contingencies *(ut in singulis vitae casibus intellectus
voluntati praemonstret quid sit eligendum)*" (AT X 361). That Descartes's
interest in the right method for conducting one's mind also had a
moral orientation appears from the few remarks reported by Baillet
from the lost fragments of the manuscript *Studium bonae mentis*.[18]

The concern with certainty is prominent in the first twelve rules,
which are the only ones to be considered here.[19] Rule Two states
that we should be concerned only with objects of which our mind
(ingenium) can reach certain and indubitable knowledge (AT X 362,
CSM I 10). Three things are noteworthy here: intellectual ability is first
and foremost a power to distinguish the true from the false, something
that Descartes elsewhere calls judgment *(judicio)* and also reason *(rai-
son)* or good sense *(bon sens)*.[20] The second is that Descartes already
here sees true knowledge as a matter of voluntary control: one of re-
solving to accept only the beliefs one knows to be true. The third is the
insistence on limiting science to certain and indubitable knowledge
(AT X 362, CSM I 10).

Of all the sciences "so far discovered," only "arithmetic and geometry" would meet these requirements (AT X 363, CSM I 11). For they
"alone deal with an object so pure and simple that they assume nothing at all that experience might render uncertain; but consist entirely
in deducing conclusions by rational means *(consequentiis rationabiliter
deducentiis)*" (AT X 365). This rules out from *Scientia* any objects of
which "a certainty equaling the demonstrations of arithmetic and geometry" could not be obtained (AT X 366, CSM I 12–13). The certainty of mathematics is contrasted to current methods of dialecti-
cal reasoning, such as the probable syllogisms taught in the schools,
which, starting out from merely probable opinions, substitute probable conclusions for certainty and mere conjectures for truth.

Rule Three recognizes two ways to certain knowledge: evident intuition and deduction from evident premises (AT X 368, ll. 10–12, CSM I
14).[21] By intuition Descartes means "the indubitable conception of
a pure and attentive mind *(mentis purae et attentae non dubium con-
ceptum)*," originating from the sole light of reason which is simpler and

therefore more certain than deduction. Each of us can intuit "that she exists, that she thinks, that the triangle is bounded by just three lines, the sphere by a single surface, and the like" (AT X 368, CSM I 14).

The clear and distinct perceptions of the "pure and attentive" mind take precedence over both sense perceptions and common authorities as the only reliable sources of evidence, and are set up as norms for certain and indubitable knowledge. This obviously invites questions, and not only from commonsense Aristotelian empiricists. What kind of authority can the acts of the individual intellect have independently of the senses? Are contingent existential truths apprehended through the same kind of purely intellectual act as self-evident *(per se notae)* abstractive notions like "the sphere is bounded by a single surface"? Descartes may not have reflected on the implications of these views, and seems quite unaware of the problems his appeal to the light of natural intellect as the sole source of truth raises. Yet he clearly is aware of departing from ordinary usage, for he warns the reader that he will pay no attention to how "intuition" and other terms have been used "lately" in the schools, but will take account only of their meaning in Latin (AT X 369, CSM I 14). It is interesting, however, to compare his use of the term to that of his Scholastic predecessors. *Intueri* means seeing, and the metaphors of vision and light in accounting for the workings of the intellect loom large in the Platonic and Augustinian tradition that Descartes's use of the term evokes.[22] But intuition is not for Descartes only a matter of grasping simple self-evident ideas or propositions, for he also extends it to seeing the necessary connections between them:

> The self-evidence and certainty of intuition is required not only for apprehending single propositions *(enuntiationes)*, but also for any train of reasoning whatever *(ad quoslibet discursum)*. Take for example, this conclusion *(consequentia)*: 2 plus 2 equals 3 plus 1; not only must we intuitively see that 2 plus 2 make 4, and that 3 plus 1 make 4, but also that the third proposition follows necessarily from these two. (AT X 369, CSM I 14–15)[23]

It now looks as if deduction, "anything that can be inferred *(concluditur)* with necessity from certain other things which are known with certainty," would collapse into intuition. The difference, Descartes explains, is that deduction can cover a number of steps, each of which is individually intuited but all of which cannot be intuitively grasped at once. He thus distinguishes mental intuition "from certain deduction on the grounds that one perceives *(concipiatur)* a movement or a sort of sequence in the latter but not in the former, and also because actual self-evidence *(praesens evidentia)* is not required for deduction, as it is for intuition" (AT X 370, CSM I 15).

Intuition, here, is given a new and crucial role. Not only does it encompass the grasping of *all* truths that are evidently seen, including abstract notions that are self-evident by virtue of the meaning of the terms, it also seems to take the place of formal validation in a rational inference: it is not the logical *form* of the argument but the fact that its conclusion is *evidently seen* to follow necessarily from the truth of its premises that warrants the truth of the conclusion.[24]

Descartes, in associating intuition with certainty, self-evidence, and indubitability, uses terminology from a tradition that can be traced back to the Stoics, but more particularly to Duns Scotus and his late medieval followers, though he adapts it to his own purposes. Duns Scotus gave intuition a prominent place as a source of knowledge, but uses the term in the sense of Stoic kataleptic impressions: for evident, actual sensory impressions. Duns Scotus was also the first to contrast intuitive cognition to abstractive cognition as two different means to evident cognition. Intuition (whether sensory or intellectual) is primarily of things (external objects or internal, mental acts) acting on the (external or internal) senses, and it is invariably caused by the presence of the particulars acting on the senses, giving direct and indubitable knowledge of the actual existence of a particular thing. Abstractive knowledge, by contrast, abstracts from the *hic et nunc,* from the presence of particulars. Although it can concern present particulars too, abstractive knowledge does not presuppose their actual presence: it can be of past, absent, future, as well as of nonactual, merely possible things. Both give evident cognition, but intuitive cognition differs from abstractive cognition in providing evident knowledge of actual existence.[25]

Consider the standard examples of Cartesian intuition: they comprise intuitively known contingent propositions like "I think" and "I exist," and mathematical propositions like "2 + 2 = 4" and "The triangle is bounded by three lines" (AT X 369, CSM I 14). Whereas the evidence for contingent propositions was usually seen to consist in the immediate experience of the facts they describe, the evidence for the mathematical propositions is of a different kind—we might describe it as conceptual. For Descartes as for his medieval predecessors, evident propositions are propositions necessarily causing assent of the mind entertaining them. The propositions mentioned by Descartes are also standard examples of objects of evident and therefore indubitable assent among his predecessors. However, they make a distinction between them based on the grounds and the ways in which assent to them is caused. In the case of singular propositions like "I exist" and "I think," the evidence consists in my present perception of existing and thinking, which accounts for my unhesitating assent to these existential propositions. It is the *presence* or *actual fact* of my thinking and existing that is seen as immediately *causing* my assent and hence as constituting its evidence. For Descartes—according to the view of knowledge he was to spell out much later—this holds only in the case of first-person, present-tense singular statements: the only contingent propositions that are immediately self-evident are those that describe my own current perceptions and existence as a thinker. For the late medievals it holds for any actual perceptions of the external or internal senses. Thus I see the whiteness of Socrates, and immediately assent to the proposition "Socrates is white," or you see the house on fire, and the judgment "The house is on fire" forces itself on you. "I think," "I exist," and "Socrates is white" are all instances of true singular existential propositions that belong with standard examples of intuitive notions known through experience. By contrast, in the case of simple mathematical propositions, like "2 + 2 = 4" or "The triangle is bound by three lines," the evidence is based on the meaning of the terms. They belong to the class of notions described by Scotus and Ockham and by their followers as *abstractive* and *per se notae*—propositions immediately known through the meanings of their terms: as soon as the meaning of the terms are understood, assent is caused necessarily. Descartes, however, does not seem to distinguish these cases, but runs them together, listing the abstractive mathematical cognitions with "I exist" and "I think" as examples of direct intuitive knowledge. Unlike the Scholastics, therefore, who, following the tradition from Duns Scotus, Ockham, and Buridan, would treat the class of *evidently* known propositions as larger than that of evident *intuitive* notions, reserving the latter to actually present contingent things, Descartes treats *all evident* truths, including those known through discursive reasoning, as instances of intuitively known notions, blurring their distinction between intuitive and abstractive cognitions. At the same time he continues to describe intuition in terms that his Scholastic predecessors would have applied only to the former.[26]

Among the distinctions made by his predecessors that are at work in Descartes's account of intuition and judgment in the *Rules* is the one between having an intuition (entertaining a proposition) and affirming or denying it, which occurs explicitly in Rule Twelve, and reflects the distinction between notions that are merely apprehended (apprehensive notions) and those that are assented to, which they called judicative.[27] Questions that were standard matters of discussion in late medieval debates about cognition included: What, in a particular case, causes assent? When is it necessary—when can or should it be withheld? When does the assent given to a notion in forming a judgment qualify as evident and certain? How are certainty and evidence related—how do they differ?[28] None of them are at the surface in the *Rules,* yet Descartes cannot, having given intuition the place he does, ignore them for long. He may have attempted to dissociate himself from the tradition connecting intuition to sensory knowledge, by insisting that he does not use the term as in the Schools "lately,"[29] but this surely does not absolve him from dealing with the problems that usage raised. The same difficulties—in a more general and intractable form—having to do with the grounds and criteria of the evidence attributed to intuition as a source of certain knowledge confront his own views. They invite all the traditional skeptical questions concerning the criteria for perfect intuition and evident assent, or for the clear and distinct ideas that replace the notion of intuition in Descartes's later writings. His use of the notion of intuition as the source of evident knowledge also creates problems of its own. What, precisely, constitutes the object intuited in the case of mere conceptual truths and principles, or that of necessary connections between intuitions? Given, moreover, the extent Descartes accords to a mode of cognition restricted by his predecessors to the intuition of present particulars acting on the (external or internal) senses, the skeptical problems he had to confront are more general and intractable. For where the Stoics or the late medievals could appeal to the presence of the objects causing the intuitive notion and their action on the senses, such causal theories are not available to Descartes. Far from providing any solution to such problems, the account of perception suggested in Rule Twelve and developed later in the treatise *Man (L'homme)* and in the *Optics (La dioptrique)* renders them, as will be seen, even more pressing. If so, there is no need to invoke, as commentators often do, any extra-philo-sophical, political, or pragmatic reasons to explain the concern with skeptical issues that are given such a prominent place in the *Discourse* and the *Meditations.* They can be seen as arising directly from the epistemology outlined in the *Rules.*[30]

3. Intuition, Method, and Its Application to the Mind

Rule Four deals with the necessity of having the right method in the search for truth and stresses the dangers of proceeding without a method or, what is worse, following a bad one (AT X 371, CSM I 16). By method, Descartes means "rules so certain and easy" that by following them exactly one will "never take what is false to be true, . . . but by gradually increasing one's knowledge arrive at a true knowledge *(scientia)* of everything within one's capacity, [without ever] wasting one's mental forces" (AT X 371–372, CSM I 16).

The method will be helpful, first, by letting our natural intuition do its work properly of hindering us from taking the false for the true and hence falling into error and, second, by teaching us how to make the deductions that will lead us to the knowledge of all things. It guides intuition but cannot teach it, for the operations of intuition and deduction themselves are so simple and basic that "if our intellect were not already able to make use of them, it would not understand any of the rules of the method, however easy they might be" (AT X 372, CSM I 16).

Descartes appeals in this context to something "divine" within the human intellect, "in which the first seeds of useful thoughts have been sown" and which, even if neglected, can produce fruits, among which are the analysis of ancients (that they kept secret from posterity) and the currently flourishing algebra, both of which he describes as "spontaneous fruits springing from the innate principles of this method" (AT X 373, CSM I 17).

Whatever we are to understand by "innate principles" here, Descartes seems to think of them as prior to those of analysis and algebra.

The numbers and figures of ordinary mathematics are external garments rather than constituent parts of the method he has in mind, which contains "the source of all the others" and "should contain the primary rudiments of human reason, and extend to the discovery of truths in any field whatsoever." Descartes is convinced that it is also the most powerful of all cognitions naturally given to us, "as it is the source of all the others" (AT X 374, CSM I 17).[31]

I will not dwell on the commentary to this rule, which contains the first (and only?) mention of *mathesis universalis* and relates a story about Descartes's attitude to mathematics at the time when he first devoted serious attention to this subject (AT X 374, ll. 16–17).[32] Nor do I discuss Descartes's understanding of *mathesis universalis*, which he envisages as a general mathematical science of order and measure. I turn instead directly to the application of the method to the investigation of the mind, undertaken first in Rule Eight and then more fully in Rule Twelve.

Rule Eight commends us to stop whenever in investigating things in the order prescribed we encounter something we cannot intuit with sufficient clarity (AT X 392, CSM I 28). The commentary gives some examples to illustrate the application of this rule. The first is from Descartes's discovery of the anaclastic line in optics, and the second, described as "the most valuable of all," has to do with the examination of the mind or intellect itself.[33] Anyone who tries to examine all the truths the knowledge of which is within the reach of human reason *(humana ratio)*—something which everyone "who seriously studies to attain good sense" must undertake "once in her life"—will discover, by using the rules, "that nothing can be known before the intellect, of which the knowledge of all the rest depends" (AT X 395, CSM I 29–30). By emphasizing that the knowledge of the intellect comes before the knowledge of all other things, Descartes again marks his departure from the Aristotelian view, in which the knowledge of external, sensory things comes first. That Descartes had this doctrine in mind strikes me as obvious, given the context. He writes:

> After this, he will pass in examination everything that follows immediately upon the knowledge of the pure intellect, he will enumerate, among the rest, all the other instruments of knowledge that we possess in addition to the intellect, of which there are only two, namely imagi-

nation *(phantasia)* and sense-perception *(sensus)* . . . He will see that there can be no truth and falsity in the strict sense except in the intellect alone, although they often originate from the two others. (AT X 395–396, CSM I 30)

In examining carefully "these three modes of knowing," concentrating his attention on whatever might deceive him in order to avoid it, and "enumerating more exactly all the paths that can lead us to truth," he will find the most certain ones. By following this procedure, one can be assured on the one hand that whatever cannot be known by this means lies beyond the reach of the human mind, and on the other, that anyone who follows the method and uses his *ingenium* in the prescribed way is able to attain all the knowledge that is within its reach (AT X 396, CSM I 30).

It is striking that Descartes, in this passage whose interpretation has given rise to much speculation, should present the investigation of the human mind as a task anyone who cares about knowledge should perform "once in her life"—a task, as we know, the later *Meditations on the First Philosophy* urges the reader to undertake. The importance of thus examining human knowledge *(humana cognitio)* is stressed no fewer than three times in Rule Eight (AT X 395, 396, 397), but is its purpose to provide science with secure foundations that no skeptical argument could shake? I doubt that it is, in spite of ingenious arguments to prove the contrary.[34] There is, for one thing, no need to invoke any skeptical crisis to explain Descartes's concern with certainty and foundations; the role and certainty he ascribes to intuition are problematic enough in themselves to justify Descartes's later worries about the foundations of knowledge. There is, moreover, no necessity to appeal in this context to the kind of foundational issues with which Descartes later became concerned. Descartes himself does not reveal any concern with skepticism, and his interest in our cognitive faculties and certainty can be seen as arising out of purely methodological concerns.

The investigation of the human mind here called for is also presented as one required by the method itself—as part and parcel of the project of finding out and determining the nature of the method. Such an investigation is said to "contain the true instruments of science, and the entire method" and is thus subject to the goals of the methodological project of which it is part (AT X 398, ll. 4–5, CSM I 31). We need to know something about the cognitive powers themselves and the ways they work to see how they can be perfected by a method.

It is, admittedly, not very clear how this should be understood, and Descartes seems not to have been all that clear himself as to what he was up to. Several different assumptions seem to be at work. One is that the method he tries to formulate grows out of and reflects the natural working of the human mind, which bad habits of reasoning have corrupted. Examining how the natural (uncorrupted) mind works in acquiring knowledge is supposed to reveal the principles governing right reasoning. At the same time, and this leads to another assumption, this self-examination is also supposed to reveal the natural order of things themselves, insofar as they can be objects of knowledge. This is an epistemological order, an order of discovery from the simple to the complex—from what can be grasped in a single act of the intellect to what requires several different acts and faculties such as the senses, imagination, and memory.

The most straightforward answer to the question of what this excursus in cognitive psychology in Rules Eight and Twelve is supposed to achieve is suggested by Descartes's own presentation. The examination of our cognitive power and its limits is supposed to tell us something important about the *order* of discovery. It is only by reflecting on what the mind and its faculties are, how they work and relate to each other, that we can determine what is absolute and prior in the order of knowledge and what is relative.

To know the nature of the mind, we have to see how it *works,* just as to know what a tool is we must know what work it does. Only when we know what a tool is supposed to do and how it does it can we think of how to improve it. Descartes made this analogy in comparing his method to the mechanical arts, which need no other instruments than the ones they produce themselves (AT X 397, CSM I 31). The example teaches us that since at this preliminary stage we have "only been able to find some obscure or summary precepts which seem inborn to our mind rather than the product of any art," we should not try to use them to solve complicated problems of philosophy or mathematics but apply them first to "other things which are most necessary in the search of truth" (AT X 397, CSM I 31), namely, our cognitive capacity itself, its nature, and limits. The task at this point, however, is not to investigate the nature of the mind by raising general, philosophical questions about its nature, status, and relation to the body, but simply to describe the operation of the cognitive powers, their functions, interrelations, and limits.

Though the intellect alone is said to be capable of certain knowledge or "science," it can "be helped or hindered by three other faculties, imagination *(imaginatio),* sense-perception, and memory" (AT X 398, CSM 32). Having examined each of these faculties, we should look at the "things themselves," which are the objects of knowledge and are divided on the basis of their accessibility to intellect into simple and complex natures (AT X 399, CSM I 32).

Whether or not Descartes was clear about the philosophical implications of the views expressed in the commentaries to the rules, all the main themes of Cartesian epistemology are already in place in these texts: the concern with certainty, the insistence on the right order and method of inquiry, the primacy of the intellect over the senses, as well as the necessity to limit one's cognitive powers to what can be known with certainty, and consequently, to recognize the limited nature of human knowledge. To the extent that his examination of these issues leads Descartes not only to a reversal of the traditional order of knowledge, but to a redefinition of the objects of knowledge as well, it raises ontological questions that sooner or later he will have to address more explicitly.

4. New Suppositions in Cognitive Psychology and an Old Metaphor

Conforming to the plan sketched out in Rule Eight, Rule Twelve advises us to use all our cognitive faculties not only to "intuit simple propositions distinctly," but also "to combine properly what is sought with what is already known, in order to find the former, and to find out what things should be related with each other so that we make the most thorough use of all our human powers." The rule itself is anything but distinct. It is presented as summing up everything that has been said in the previous rules and as teaching in a "general manner" what is to be explained with more detail in what follows (AT X 410–411, CSM I 39).[35] It deals first with us, the knowers, and then with the things known.

Descartes now distinguishes four faculties of knowledge: the intellect, the imagination, the senses, and the memory. "The intellect alone is capable of perceiving the truth"; it needs however the assistance of imagination, the senses, and the memory (AT X 411, CSM I 39). Descartes does not pretend to give the full true story of "what the human mind is, what the body is and how it is informed by the mind, what faculties within the composite whole promote knowledge of things, and what each faculty does" (AT X 411, CSM I 39–40), but limits himself to a brief explanation of what "is the most useful manner of conceiving everything within us which contributes to our knowledge of things." The theory of sense perception, for example, is presented not as true but as a supposition that is convenient because it makes things "clearer" (AT X 412, CSM I 40).

This indicates that Descartes has an understanding of the nature of mind that anticipates his mature view in striking ways. While treating mind and body as two distinct natures, he takes the latter to be informed by the former so that they together form a "composite." He also takes the cognitive faculties to operate "within the whole composite," although the intellect clearly is thought to work also independently of the body. While these are traditional formulas, the view they express is certainly not. The mechanistic theory of perception sketched out in this rule shows that Descartes also held a mechanistic view of the human body, and that is not easy to combine with a traditional Aristotelian conception modeling the mind–body union on the idea of a substantial (hylomorphic) union of form and matter.

It is surprising to see Descartes so readily adverting to suppositions and hypotheses when it comes to presenting his own new theories. The psychological theory developed in Rule Twelve is not the only instance of this strategy. It is adopted also in the second part of the commentary on this rule, which deals with the things known. In both cases Descartes is aware of presenting a doctrine based on assumptions "which are perhaps not received by everyone," but which, whether one believes them or not, will help make things clearer and hence "distinguish cognitions that could be true from false ones" (AT X 417, CSM I 43–44). In the first case he compares his strategy to current practice in geometry, when assumptions are made about quantity that may not correspond to one's views of quantity in physics (AT X 412, CSM I 40); in the second he invokes the "imaginary circles" used by astronomers to describe their phenomena (AT X 417, CSM I 43–44). We would have no problems if these proposals came from a pragmatist—but from Descartes? Is he inconsistent, is this just a political strategy, or is our picture of Descartes as the proponent of a rigorously rationalist methodology and ideal of science in need of revision? There is something to be said for each of these views, but the one that is best supported by Descartes's practice as a scientist is the last.[36]

Here the suppositions are useful for his purposes, which is to outline a new doctrine that conflicts with the established views in physics and philosophy without having to defend it. They help him, first, to sketch out a mechanistic theory of perception without having to ground it in a general mechanistic theory of the physical universe, and second, to introduce a new epistemology without having to work out any of its metaphysical implications and give it a philosophical backing. The same strategy is adopted later in the *Essays* accompanying the *Discourse,* where Descartes argues from hypotheses in order to display some of his results without having to argue for the basic principles of his physics, which he knew were not approved by the Church.[37] But before discussing this further, let us look more carefully at the "suppositions" he rather carelessly presented in Rule Twelve.

The first is that the action of the external objects on the senses should be conceived in terms of local motion. Descartes reverts to the old metaphor of the seal and the wax, but stresses that it should be taken here quite literally: the external body really modifies the external configuration of the sentient body in exactly the same way as the seal modifies the surface of the wax (AT X 412, CSM I 40). This holds for all the external senses and all kinds of sensations: touch (including heat and cold), vision, sound, smell, taste. It is the most useful way to represent "all this," and no more falsity can follow from this supposition than from any other, because "the concept of shape (*figura*) is so simple and common that it is involved in all sensory perception" (AT X 413, CSM I 40). The reader is not asked to deny other features involved in perception but to abstract from them, because differences of shape alone are sufficient to explain all the differences there are between sensible things.

The second supposition is that we should think of this figure as instantly transmitted from the external senses to the common sense, without any "real entity passing from the one to the other," just as the letters are transmitted to the paper by the slightest movements of the pen (AT X 414, CSM I 41). The third is that the common sense should also be conceived as a seal, whose function is to form in the imagination, "here conceived as a real part of the body," "the same figures or ideas, coming pure and without body from the external senses." As we saw, the figures or ideas are taken to be transmitted without a real entity passing through. They are to be understood as configurations of extension (that is, as some kind of real traces or patterns) on the surface of the part of brain called imagination, "which has to be large enough for its different portions to be covered by many figures distinct from each others, and habitually retain them for some time, in which case it is the same as what is called memory" (AT X 414, CSM I 42).

The basic ideas of the mechanistic physiology are now in place, for Descartes indicates in the next paragraph how the nerves, originating from the brain, can be understood to move the members of the body just as we understand, with the help of the pen analogy, the common sense to be moved by the external senses. All the movements of animals lacking cognition, as well as "those operations that we perform without any direction from reason," can be explained in the same way, assuming the action of sensory objects on the "purely corporeal phantasy" (AT X 415, CSM I 42).

Although the Aristotelian seal–wax metaphor is taken literally here, when turning to the cognitive power itself, by contrast, it is used as a mere analogy, because "this force by which things are known properly speaking" has to be conceived as "purely spiritual, and no less distinct from the whole body than the blood from the bones, or the hand from the eye." The cognitive power can be active or passive. It is passive, like wax, in receiving figures from the common sense at the same time as the (corporeal) phantasy, and it is active when it "applies itself" to the figures preserved in the memory, or like a seal, forms new images. Here the seal and the wax work by "mere analogy, for nothing quite similar to this can be found in corporeal things" (AT X 415, CSM I 42). Nothing is literally impressed or transmitted; no positive account, on the other hand, is given of the connection between the acts of the intellect and those of the senses.

Depending on its different functions this power is called pure intellect, imagination, memory, or sense perception. It "is called mind (*ingenium*) properly, when it forms new ideas in the corporeal imagination, or concentrates on those already formed" (AT X 416, CSM I 42). It is said to see, touch, and so forth when it "applies itself with the imagination to common sense," it is said to remember, when it "applies itself to imagination alone" (without the common sense) and its figures, and it is said to "imagine or conceive" when it applies itself to the imagination to form new ones, and "if, finally, it acts alone, it is said to understand *(intelligere)*" (AT X 416, CSM I 42). The cognitive power when using the imagination is called *ingenium* properly, while the same power is called pure intellect when it acts alone, without the help of the imagination. It is not clear how consistent Descartes was about this distinction.[38]

By "applying itself," I take Descartes to mean the intellect using the cognitive powers depending on corporeal organs—in other words, whatever understanding or mental activity goes with the acts of the corporeal senses, which are passive in themselves, and receive mechanically impressed figures from the external objects acting on them, it depends on the intellect alone and not on the corporeal organs. There is nothing left of the doctrine of transmission of sensible forms from the sense object to the organ, and the image imprinted in the organ by the object, though it acts like a seal, is not connected to the object causing it by any resemblance.

Among the points to be noted here is that the operations of different cognitive faculties are all treated as functions of one power operating in different ways, depending on its function. The traditional faculty psychology as well as the division of the soul in three parts or different kinds of souls (the nutritive, the sensitive, and the intellective) are hereby abandoned and replaced by a monistic conception of soul or mind anticipating the broad definition of thought or mind in Descartes's later writings. That is, part of the functions of the animal or sensitive soul are merged with the intellective into one power, while the functioning of the sensory organs is explained by mechanistic models like the seal–wax analogy or the movements of a pen.

The enumeration of the various functions of our mental power sketched out here is supposed to teach us in what ways each can contribute to knowledge. In dealing with incorporeal matters, the intellect can only be hindered by the senses and the imagination: "But if the intellect proposes to examine something that can be referred to the body, it has to form an idea of it as distinctly as possible in the imagination; and to do this most conveniently, the thing itself that this idea represents has to be shown to the external senses" (AT X 417). If the senses and the corporeal imagination are of no use in dealing with purely intelligible things, they are indispensable for the knowledge of material things. But since only so many things can be distinctly represented at once, it is necessary to abstract from the ideas of those things anything that does not require immediate attention, so that what remains can be more easily remembered. For that purpose, one should not expose the things themselves to the senses, but certain abbreviated figures, which are easier to retain (AT X 417, CSM I 43). All of this is explained with more detail in the subsequent rules, on which I do not dwell here; but this view of representation that Descartes endorses is discussed in Chapter 5.

5. The Objects Known

The examination of the objects of knowledge undertaken in Rule Twelve is guided by three questions: (1) What is obvious by itself?[39] (2) How can one thing be known on the basis of another? and (3) What can be deduced from each of these? (AT X 411, CSM I 39).

The general aim is "to distinguish properly the simple notions of things from those that are composed of them, in order to see in both cases wherein falsity consists, in order to avoid it, and to see what can be known with certainty, so that we may concern ourselves only with that" (AT X 417, CSM I 43). The reader is warned that here too certain things have to be assumed that "may perhaps not be accepted by everyone." The classification of things into simple and complex is thus not going to be the usual one. The order invoked is that of knowledge, which need not be the same as that of existence. For instance, an extended body that has some figure is, considered in itself, one simple thing, but from the point of view of our intellect it is composed of three more simple ones: "corporeal nature, extension, and figure," which although they cannot exist apart from each other, can be distinctly understood separately. By "simple" here Descartes means "only those things of which our knowledge is so clear (*perspicua*) and distinct (*distincta*) that they cannot be divided by the mind (*mente*) into others which are more distinctly known, and such are figure, extension, movement, etc." (AT X 418, CSM I 44). Things that are simple from the point of view of our intellect are said to be either purely intellectual, or purely material, or common.

Purely intellectual things are those known by the intellect through a certain kind of innate *(ingenitum)* light that cannot be represented with the help of any corporeal images such as knowledge, doubt, ignorance, volition, and similar things, which are known "truly, and so easily, that nothing else is required for this than having our share of reason" (AT X 419, CSM I 44).

Purely material things are those that can be known only in bodies, such as "figure, extension, movement," and so forth; and common things are those that can be attributed without discrimination now to spiritual and now to material things, like "existence, unity, duration, and similar." To the notions lumped together as common belong those constituting "as it were links which connect other simple natures together, and on the evidence of which anything concluded through rational inference is based." The examples mentioned are "Things that are the same as a third thing are the same as each other"; "Things that cannot be related in the same way to a third thing are different in some respect" (AT X 419, CSM I 45). They can be known either by the pure intellect alone or by the intellect when it intuits images of things (AT X 419–420, CSM I 45)—presumably, the mathematical figures referred to above as simple and abstract "abbreviations." Common notions are not only purely intelligible and abstract, but also include the axioms of geometricians, which, falling under the domain of intuition, require the help of imagination and extended figures.

Descartes counts among the simple natures also "their privations and negations, inasmuch as we understand them, for the cognition, through which one intuits, what nothing, or an instant, or rest is, is no less true than the one through which I understand what existence, duration and movement is" (AT X 420, CSM I 45). Counting these nonthings among the simple ones makes it possible for Descartes to say that "all other things that we can know are composed out of these simple natures" (ibid.).

All the simple natures are said to be known through themselves, *per se notae,* and they never contain any falsity (AT X 420, CSM I 45). Can we have a true intuitive notion of nothingness? What leads Descartes to this unusual claim is his distinction between two faculties in the intellect: one through which things are intuited and known, and one through which one makes affirmative or negative judgments about them. The faculty of intuition is here, as later, presented as a passive power. Judgments are performed on notions that, when perfectly intuited—that is, known through themselves—are true.

Descartes is sometimes taken to claim that simple notions have no truth value in themselves. It is through judging, that is, affirming or denying something about them, that they acquire a truth value. To say that simple notions are without falsity is, however, not to say that they lack truth value; on the contrary, it is to say that they are perfectly known and hence in themselves always true. Judging, then, is more like a deliberate acknowledging of a simple notion that is true whenever it is perfectly intuited (AT X 420). This holds for any object of intuition, whether simple or composite: a thing that is perfectly intuited is always true. But if the intuition is imperfect, that is, when there is room for doubt concerning the truth or falsity of its object, we have what Descartes calls a question or problem.[40]

Judging is described as the joining or combining of notions: through judging, simple and self-evident true notions are combined together into complex ones, or combined with notions that have not been properly understood. In his later writings, Descartes refers judging to the will, which is seen as a separate power; here it is a function of the intellect. The conjunction of simple things is either necessary or contingent. It is necessary when one of two things is implied in the other so that we cannot conceive them both distinctly if we judge that they are separated, as the line and the figure, movement and time, and so forth (AT X 421, CSM I 45). To judge from these examples, Descartes has in mind things that can be distinguished only by a distinction of reason.[41] But he also mentions relations between numbers (3 + 4 = 7) and anything that can be demonstrated concerning numbers or figures. The necessary relations or connections between simples also include the following: "If, for instance, Socrates says that he doubts of everything, it necessarily follows that he at least understands that he doubts; and hence, he knows that something can be true or false, for there is a necessary connection between these and the nature of doubt" (AT X 421, CSM I 46; see also Rule Thirteen, AT X 432, CSM I 53). Examples of contingent connections are: a body is animated, a man is dressed, and so on. Examples of relations between propositions that are necessary, although they are not obviously thought to be necessary, are: "I am, therefore God exists" and "I understand, therefore I have a mind distinct from my body" (AT X 421–422, CSM I 46).

Descartes is talking now about things, now about propositions, now about figures and geometrical proofs. The basic point is that we can never be said, strictly speaking, to know or understand anything beyond the simple notions and the things composed of such simples on the basis of necessary relations. This is not to say that all knowledge is somehow a priori in the sense of being inferred independently of experience. Things can be composed on the basis of what we learn through experience, or through our own activity. Experience comes in three kinds: first, what is perceived through the senses; second, what is learned from others; third and more generally, whatever reaches our intellect, either from external sources or from the intellect's self-reflection. We read:

> It must be noted here that the intellect can never be deceived by any experience *(experimento)* if it intuits the object just as it is presented to it, either in itself, or in the imagination, and if it does not judge that the imagination presents the sensory objects faithfully, or that the senses convey the true figures of things, or finally that the external things would always be as they appear; for in all of this we are subject to error. (AT X 423, CSM I 47)

Throughout his writings Descartes remains faithful to the epistemological position expressed in this passage, the interpretation of which I discuss later (Chapter 5, section 1). As to the composite things, they can be composed in three ways: by impulse, by conjecture, or by deduction. Impulse here means that one is caused to judge and believe something on other than rational grounds without sufficient reason, either by "being only determined by some superior power, or by one's own freedom, or by the disposition of one's phantasy." While the first never deceives, the second does so rarely, but the third does it almost without exception (AT X 424, CSM I 47). We are dealing here with three different ways in which our beliefs are caused: by faith, by the intellect itself, or by the imprints in the imagination. Conjecture consists in judging on the basis of merely probable grounds, and it need not involve error as long as one judges the thing to be merely probable without affirming it to be true. Deduction, lastly, is the only way we have of composing things so that we can be certain of their truth—but for that it must be based on intuitively grasped necessary connections between (simple) things or notions, like the connection between figure and extension (AT X 424–425, CSM I 48).

All of this is presented in order to explain "distinctly" and "by sufficient enumeration" what was earlier shown only in a "confused and summary manner," namely, that there is no way to certain and true knowledge other than "evident intuition and necessary deduction." The ways to knowledge and the simple natures mentioned in passing in Rule Eight have now been presented methodically. Mental intuition is extended "to the knowledge of all these simple natures as well as to the necessary connections between them, and finally to all the rest that the intellect can experience exactly as being, either in itself, or in the phantasy."[42] True science, *Scientia,* thus consists in perceiving, clearly and distinctly, simple natures and their interconnections, which also includes "seeing" how, in what ways, the simple things contribute to the composition of all other things.[43] What can be known (with certainty) can be known through simple propositions and is contrasted with questions or problems that are unknown. The general idea seems to be that once a problem is perfectly understood and solved, it can be restated in terms of simple propositions and of what has been formed by such propositions by necessary deductions. This, I gather, is not just a matter of distinguishing the simple from the complex and seeing their interrelations, but also of understanding how, on account of the necessary relations that connect them, the former contribute to constituting the latter.

According to Descartes's plan, the first twelve rules contribute to the general task of helping us train and perfect our natural cognitive powers (intuition and judgment) to discern the simple propositions and their interconnections. The next set of twelve rules, which were never completed, deal with problems that Descartes describes as perfectly understood (even when the solution is unknown), which can be formulated in equations (for example, problems of arithmetic and geometry) and the means to solve them. Descartes obviously sees the training in these perfectly intelligible but "abstract" sciences as a necessary preparation for learning to use the last (unwritten) part of the method, which is supposed to deal with "all the other" sciences, the problems of which, unlike those of mathematics, are only imperfectly understood (AT X 429–430, CSM I 50–51).

6. The Method and Its Application

The interpretation of the subsequent rules—in particular the role of mathematics to physics and other subjects—raises many difficult questions beyond the scope of this book, which can only be mentioned. It is not clear, for instance, what Descartes in the end thinks his method of discovery is and in what sense, if any, one can speak of any common methodological procedures applicable in different scientific domains. Did he ever think that the "imperfectly" understood problems of physics could and should be reduced to "perfectly understood" mathematical ones? What view of the nature of proof and deduction does he commit himself to in stressing the role of intuition while criticizing formal syllogisms as useless for purposes of discovery?[44] Why did Descartes leave his methodological work incomplete and why is there so little mention of the method in his later writings? The *Discourse on the Method* (1637), as Descartes himself points out, is not a presentation of a method, but merely a discourse *about* a method. The scientific essays accompanying it, although they are supposed to illustrate the application and fruits of the method, do not display any general method; indeed, it is unclear just how they are supposed to illustrate the application of the method described in the *Rules* at all. How one answers these questions depends, of course, on what one takes Descartes's intended method to be.[45]

Clearly the mathematical method is essential to his thinking in the *Rules,* and it may be precisely because he thought of his algebra as the paradigm of his method of discovery that he abandoned the methodological project. He may have come to realize that it was not directly relevant to the subjects that he became more interested in: a general explanation of the physical universe, the nature and place of the mind in a world of extended bodies governed by universal mechanistic laws, the relation between the ideal object of mathematics and the external physical world that he had set out to explain. On the other hand, Descartes may not have had any "considered" view of the method as applied to the physical sciences when composing the *Rules,* and indeed, the third set of rules, which were supposed to deal precisely with that, were never written.[46] Or he may have come to see that the hypothetical methods he actually used in his physics did not fit the ideal of a strictly deductive method borrowed from geometry and arithmetic, by which his early methodological prescriptions were inspired, in which case the methodological project was bound to fall apart.

I take the configurational analysis presented in the essay on *Geometry*, which was published with *Discourse on the Method*, to be a paradigm example of the method anticipated in the *Rules* and described in very general terms in the *Discourse*. It can be seen as meeting Descartes's requirements of being rigorously deductive, intuitively evident, and genuinely informative. Descartes criticized syllogistic logic for being circular and useless as a method of discovery. It is, at best, a method of exposition, but useless as a method for acquiring new knowledge. He shows no awareness that these requirements on the method were difficult to meet—that the requirement of certainty provided by deduction from intuitively evident premises might conflict with that of informativeness and discovery.[47] Descartes is often taken to substitute intuition for formal validity and the methodological rules for formal rules of inference, on the mistaken ground that his criticism of syllogistic logic is a criticism of all formal logic. That the heuristic rules offered in the *Rules* or the *Discourse* do not form a logic in the sense of a theory of deductive inference should, however, not blind one to the fact that Descartes's mathematical method of discovery (algebra) was a strictly rule-governed and deductively structured method. Attempts to assess the epistemological descriptions of the rules offered in his methodological writings that do not take account of this fact are bound to misrepresent his ideal of method as well as his conception of knowledge.[48]

That Descartes abandoned the idea of a unified mathematical method can be granted without supposing any fundamental change in his general project. Descartes sought to bring about a general reform of the sciences, which included the replacement of Aristotelian physics with a mathematical-mechanistic science of nature, and this project involved an epistemological reform as well, the metaphysical implications of which had to be spelled out and defended. One can still see his methodological ideal at work, on a general level, in his metaphysics and metaphysical epistemology.

That Descartes did not complete the *Rules*, finally, is not surprising given that he gradually lost interest in the practice of mathematics, as his letters and the fact that he did not do much serious mathematical work after this time testify. The general physical and philosophical questions that he became increasingly involved with were simply not amenable to the formalization the application of his mathematical method of discovery would require. His new account of cognition and *Scientia* sketched out in the *Rules* had incurred a debt he could not ignore very long. The methodological project and its grand idea of a new universal deductive science were abandoned only to be replaced by a still grander project. I end this chapter by looking at some of the reasons for and main episodes of this development.

7. "A Little Grander Project": From Methodology to Metaphysics

In a letter to Mersenne of October 8, 1629, Descartes announces for the first time his decision to write a "little treatise" dealing with the rainbow and the meteors, and to publish it as "a sample of his philosophy" (while, he adds, hiding himself behind the painting to listen to what people will say about it (AT I 23, CSMK 6)). It is mentioned again six months later, still unfinished but expanding—his plan is now to have it completed in the beginning of 1633. Among the subjects he is studying, he lists chemistry, anatomy, and medicine. But he also confesses his reluctance to write the treatise, because he now sees it as "more important to learn what is required for the conduct of my life, than amusing myself to publish the little I have learnt." He also gives a reason for having abandoned working on "some other treatises" begun while in Paris, "for in the course of working on them I acquired a little more knowledge than I had when I started, and wanting to adjust myself accordingly I had to make a new project, a little grander(!) than the first: like one who having started to build a house to live in were, meanwhile, to acquire unexpected riches changing his condition, so that the house begun was now too small, and one would not blame such a person if one saw him start another one more suitable to his fortune." The project he has in mind seems to be even more general: he writes that it would serve for whatever new things he would learn "and even if I would not learn anything more, I would still be able to finish it" (letter to Mersenne April 15, 1630, AT I 137, CSMK 21). He declares in the same letter—referring to some mathematical problems Mersenne had questioned him about—that he is so "tired of mathematics, and thinks so little of it" that he could not bring himself to resolve the problems.

The treatises he refers to as having worked on in Paris may well have been part of the *Rules*. One wonders what fortune he had acquired that made him reconsider his plans. Taking as a hint what he says about his intense work in metaphysics during the previous nine months, it is not far-fetched to suppose that he had in mind the metaphysical demonstrations the certainty of which he prides himself later on in the same letter (AT I 144, CSMK 22). What, one may ask, motivated this sudden interest in questions of a purely metaphysical nature?

As noted above, in presenting his account of cognition and its objects as useful suppositions, Descartes takes on a heavy debt that he cannot ignore for long. Among the more pressing philosophical questions that his account raises, of course, is the nature of the intellect and its relation to the world of extended bodies perceived by the senses and pictured in the corporeal imagination. What is this cognitive power that is said to be wholly different in nature from the extended images and bodies it examines? How is it related to the corporeal organs that serve as its instruments of knowledge? What is the origin and nature of the principles and notions Descartes describes as innate and self-evident? What is the nature and the status of the objects that the (geometrical) patterns or "figures" drawn in and by the imagination are supposed to represent? How are these representations related to commonsense experience from which, on the standard Aristotelian account, the intellect derives its objects by abstraction? How are they related to the external things that they are taken to represent? Is their representational content explained causally, through the impression of patterns in the brain?[49] The account of sense perception suggested in Rule Twelve and worked out with more detail in the (unpublished) treatise on *Man (L'homme)* and *The Optics (La dioptrique)* gives us only a mechanistic, causal explanation of the workings of our cognitive powers, an explanation that is not meant to support or justify the veridicality of sense perception. In fact (as I argue in Chapter 5) that explanation undermines any confidence an Aristotelian empiricist could have in sensory perception, which was accounted for with the help of the theory of species ("likenesses") transmitted from the external thing to the sensory organ. If Descartes's new account of sensory perception is supposed to solve some of the difficulties related to the Scholastic theory of sense perception, it also creates new ones, which make it even harder to understand how sense perception contributes to the knowledge of things.

The question of the authority of intellectual intuition, once it is cut off from its basis in the sensory perception of empirical objects, seems particularly intractable. Appealing to the natural operation of the human intellect is not much of a defense for a theory that distances itself from currently held views (rooted in an Aristotelian account) about what the natural intellect is and how it operates. The accounts offered in Rules Eight and Twelve, if taken as arguments for the primacy of the intellect, are strikingly circular and hardly sufficient to persuade anyone committed to Aristotelian empiricism (backed up by the School and the Church) of the superiority of the abstract mechanistic and mathematical science of nature.

It is not surprising, therefore, that the question of the metaphysical foundations of physics already preoccupied Descartes by the time he quit working on the *Rules*. As he now declares to Mersenne, in the letter quoted above, the endeavor to know God and ourselves is the main office of human reason, and it is through the latter that he has come to discover the foundations of physics. It is a subject, he says, that he has studied more than any other, working on nothing else during the first nine months after leaving Paris and moving to the Netherlands. It is also one in which he prides himself on having obtained some satisfaction, for he thinks he has found "how to prove metaphysical truths in a manner that is more evident than the proofs of geometry," and yet, he says, he is not sure he can convince others of it! We do not know what the content of this metaphysical work was or which truths he had proved to his own satisfaction, but some version of the proofs of the existence of God and of the (immaterial) nature of the mind seems to have been part of them. Descartes says he plans to write something on the topic, but not to publish it, before he sees how his physics is received (AT I 144, CSMK 22). Descartes seems to think of his metaphysics as more controversial than his physics at this stage, which suggests that his early metaphysical arguments raised issues radical enough to be revealed only with some caution.

Is this to say that he had already worked out some version of the skeptical arguments introduced in their full force only in the *Meditations*, perhaps also including some version of the famous evil demon hypothesis? That is not altogether unlikely, since Descartes does not hesitate, in this same letter, to propound his infamous doctrine of the creation of the eternal truths, which shows him committed to the idea of a God with unlimited and unfathomable omnipotence, from which the step to that of an omnipotent, deceiving God—or demon—is not very long.

There is another hint that he had worked out some such arguments when he responds, in a letter written eight years later, to criticisms of the proofs for God's existence given in the *Discourse on the Method* (1637). Their unclarity is due, he explains, to his deliberate omission of certain arguments. "I had no better way of dealing with this topic than by explaining in detail the falsehood or uncertainty to be found in all the judgments that depend on the senses and the imagination, so as to show in the sequel which judgments depend only on the pure understanding *(l'entendement pure),* and what evidence and certainty they possess." This omission was due to his writing (in 1637) in the vernacular and hence being "afraid that weak minds might avidly embrace the doubts and scruples which I would have had to propound," and be unable to follow "the arguments by which I would have endeavored to remove them. Thus I would have set them on a false path and been unable to bring them back." He then refers to the beginnings of a treatise in metaphysics written eight years earlier in Latin "in which this argument is conducted at some length" and which, "if a Latin version of my present book is made, as is planned, I could have it included."[50] Instead of a Latin version of the *Discours de la méthode,* he eventually published the *Meditationes de prima philosophiae* (1641), in which the argument is indeed fully developed. But the only substantial addition in the *Meditations* to the arguments in the *Discourse* is precisely the hypothesis of the evil demon, or an omnipotent deceiving God, who could have created me so that even the most self-evident truths of mathematics—those clear and distinct ideas that are the criteria for true and certain knowledge in the *Rules*—could be false (AT VII 21–24, CSM II 14–17). The way from the *Rules* to the *Meditations,* of course, is long, and I do not want to claim that Descartes was in full possession of the arguments given in the latter at the time he abandoned his methodological project. But he obviously had already at this stage given serious thought to the questions that prompted him to turn to metaphysics.[51]

8. A New Foundation of Physics: God's Creation of Eternal Truths

Among the topics Descartes thinks fit to include in the treatise he contemplates publishing is the doctrine of the creation of eternal truths, first announced in the letter of April 15, 1630, to Mersenne. Indeed, he hopes "to put it in writing, within the next fortnight, in my treatise on Physics." He must have thought of it as less controversial than the other metaphysical arguments that he reserves for publication *after* the physics, and yet he clearly is aware that it is not going to pass without controversy. For, remarkably, he now tells Mersenne, whom he otherwise never fails to remind of his promise not to promulgate any news about his projects and writings, that he does not want him to keep this doctrine secret. He begs him, on the contrary, to tell people about it as often as possible—without revealing the name of its author—because he wants to hear the objections that can be made against it. It is worth looking briefly at this remarkable doctrine and new way of thinking about God, so much "worthier" than the usual, on which it is based, for it helps to explain Descartes's later concern with skepticism, and his other doctrines, both on objective reality and on freedom. This is how he first announces it:

> In my treatise on Physics I shall discuss a number of metaphysical topics and especially the following. The mathematical truths which you call eternal have been laid down by God and depend on him entirely no less than the rest of the creatures. Indeed to say that these truths are independent of God is to talk of him as he were Jupiter or Saturn and subject him to the Styx and the Fates . . . It is God who has laid down these laws in nature just as a king lays down laws in his kingdom. There is no single one that we cannot understand if our minds turn to consider it. They are all inborn in our minds just as a king would imprint his laws on the hearts of all his subjects if he had enough power to do so. The greatness of God on the other hand is something which we cannot comprehend even though we know it. (AT I 145, CSMK 22–23)

This sounds like another of those grand inspirational ideas not uncommon for its author, and although it was never discussed in the main parts of his published work, Descartes does not hesitate to defend it whenever the occasion arises (for instance, in the Fifth and the Sixth Replies). Why was he so excited about it and attributes such a crucial, foundational role to it, and how should it be understood? It is a highly controversial, not to say obscure, thesis, which raises numerous problems I cannot discuss here.[52] It cannot be seen as just another appropriation by Descartes of Scholastic doctrines, for the radical formulation he gives it seems to have no precedents, in spite of the fact that Descartes quotes Augustine himself to defend it.[53]

Descartes makes two interrelated claims concerning our cognitive powers that seem to be equally important for his project at this stage. One is that the mathematical truths—assimilated to the "essences of things"—are "inborn in our minds" and hence there is "no single one that we cannot understand if our mind turns to consider it." Since the fundamental laws of physics, which are mathematical and derivable from "eternal truths," are imprinted directly on our minds by God, the intelligibility of physical nature and the authority of human (mathematical) reason are hereby secured. The other side of the coin, and this must account for Descartes's excitement over it, is that it warrants the full intelligibility to our finite minds of the laws of nature without compromising the transcendent nature and immensity of God's intellect and power of creation. We can acquire a perfect science of nature by discovering the laws God has ordained for his creation, but the laws and "essences" of created things are not part of his eternal essence but posited and imprinted in our minds by him, and his nature transcends them. We cannot and need not see ideas in God's mind to understand the laws of physics. Moreover, his omnipotence is not constrained by the laws governing the world he has created, nor is his infinite greatness compromised by our science. As Descartes explains in his next letter to Mersenne,

> the eternal truths . . . *are true or possible only because God knows them as true or possible. They are not known as true by God in any way which would imply that they are true independently of him.* If men really understood the sense of their words they could never say without blasphemy that the truth of anything is prior to the knowledge which God has of it. In God willing and knowing are a single thing in such a way that *by the very fact of willing something he knows it and it is only for this reason that such a thing is true.* (AT I 149, CSMK 24)

The italicized passages occur in Latin in the French text, and reflect current formulations of the traditional Scholastic position endorsed, notably, by Suarez, to which Descartes explicitly opposes his own view. God makes the truths by knowing and willing them as a "total and efficient" cause, which is to say that they depend on him entirely and are produced, like other created things, *ex nihilo*. God in creating things does not merely give actual existence to eternal essences; he produces those essences themselves, some as actually instantiated (particular things), some as possible things. The latter are descriptions or formulas of things not actualized, of which existence can be predicated without contradiction.

The same point is repeated in the Sixth Replies, which is worth quoting at length since it is one of the fullest statements of this doctrine, one of the few, moreover, made in his published writings:

> If anyone attends to the immeasurable greatness of God he will find it manifestly clear that there can be nothing whatsoever which does not depend on him. This applies not just to everything that subsists, but to all order, every law, and every reason for anything's being true or good. If this were not so, then, as noted a little earlier, God would not have been completely indifferent with respect to the creation of what he did in fact create. If some reason for something's being good had existed prior to his preordination, this would have determined God to prefer those things which it was best to do. But on the contrary, just because he resolved to prefer those things which are now to be done, for this very reason, in the words of Genesis "they are very good"; in other words, the reason for their goodness depends on the fact that he exercised his will to make them so. There is no need to ask what category of causality is applicable to the dependence of this goodness upon God, or to the dependence on him of other truths, both mathematical and metaphysical. For since the various kinds of cause were enumerated by thinkers who did not, perhaps, attend to this type of causality, it is hardly surprising that they gave no name to it. But in fact they gave it a name, for it can be called efficient causality, in the sense that a king may be called efficient cause of a law, although the law is not itself a thing which has physical existence, but is merely what is called a "moral entity." (AT VII 435–436, CSM II 294)

It is precisely by insisting that God has freely made the necessary and the possible, as well as contingent actual existents, that Descartes goes beyond the tradition, to the dismay of Leibniz and other mainstream rationalists. Leibniz sees this as detrimental to the principles of rationality, to wit, to the presumption that there is a reason for everything—one, moreover, which is at least in principle intelligible to the human mind.[54] Descartes has been seen as committed to some kind of irrationalism because he questions this very assumption, notably in the passage just quoted, which continues by stressing the unintelligibility of God's power.[55] But this radical position need not be characterized as irrationalist. In fact, since God in creating the eternal truths also creates reason and the standards of rationality, reason cannot be used as a measure or standard of what God can or cannot will and make.[56] On the other hand, since reason, including its basic principles and notions, is created by God with all other things, we can trust that whatever we can clearly and distinctly understand has been made—possible or actual—by God in the way we understand it. Thus by his doctrine of the creation of eternal truths, Descartes can be seen as saving both the sovereignty of God and the intelligibility of the physical universe he created. He has also secured a place for God in the new unitary mechanistic picture of the world by rendering the latter totally dependent, for its laws as well as its actualization, on the former. We will see later the role it plays also for understanding Descartes's notion of objective reality (in Chapter 5) as well as his voluntarism (Chapter 7).[57]

As we have seen, Descartes abandoned mathematics in the early 1630, yet he did not give up his plan of a broadly mechanistic account of the physical universe nor the practice of scientific experiments to support it. His correspondence shows him intensely occupied with lenses, studying optics, discovering the law of refraction (before mid-1629, though he did not finish his treatise on *Optics* until 1632),[58] starting to work on the *Meteors,* studying medicine, anatomy, music and other subjects, and expanding his projects to an explanation of all of nature. It also shows him working on a draft of a treatise promised to his friend and regular correspondent Mersenne, presenting some of his discoveries, a project that he did not complete until 1637, when he published the *Discours de la méthode,* accompanied by three scientific treatises.[59] He worked out an algebraic solution to the problem of Pappus at the end of 1631, which he presented in his *Geometry* (*La géometrie,* published as a sample of his method with the *Discourse* in 1637), described by Stephen Gaukroger as Descartes's "last real mathematical innovation."[60] He also wrote his first general account of nature, *Le monde,* including the unfinished treatise on man, *L'homme,* both of which were to remain unpublished.[61] The incomplete *L'homme* is an application to human physiology of the general mechanistic principles of *Le monde,* aiming to show that the phenomena of life and sentience, traditionally accounted for by appeal to different kinds of souls (vegetative or sensitive) working in animal and human bodies, can be more clearly accounted for mechanistically. That explanation, again, is hypothetical; for we are presented with another supposition, "that the body is nothing else than a statue or machine made of earth" created by God to resemble us as much as possible (AT XI 120, CSM I 99). All the natural functions of this body are supposed to follow from the shapes, dispositions, and movements of its parts "as naturally as the movements of a clock or other automaton follow from the arrangement of its counter-weights and wheels," solely as a consequence of the movement of its "blood and its spirits, which are agitated by the heat of the fire burning continuously in its heart(!)" (AT XI 202, CSM I 108).

According to his correspondence, Descartes kept working on his physics from 1630 on and completed his *World* (*Le monde* or *Le traité de lumière*) in 1633, as he had promised his friend.[62] The unfinished *Man,* which is a part of the same work, was written at the same time, but both were to remain unpublished. Instead he decided, eventually, to publish the shorter treatise on *Optics,* together with the essays *Geometry* and *Meteors,* as samples of his new philosophy accompanied by the *Discourse on the Method,* in 1637.[63]

Among the reasons invoked for Descartes's changes of plans and projects during this time are, as noted above, the role of skepticism and the condemnation of Galileo in 1633.[64] Whatever the impact of these events, there are, as we have seen, enough internal reasons to explain the change of course that his writings take during the 1630s. Far from being, as some commentators like to speculate, a materialist philosopher of nature disguising himself as a Scholastic metaphysician,[65] Descartes strikes me, already in his earliest writings, as a thinker and practicing scientist with strong—not to say grand—philosophical ambitions and interests, among which the certainty of knowledge and the nature of the knowing mind occupy an important place from the start, and gradually become predominant.

The examination of Descartes's early, unpublished texts here undertaken shows that he held some (undeveloped) views on both the role of the intellect and other cognitive faculties before he turned to the questions of the nature of the self or mind and its relation to the body. Having worked out his metaphysics—and proved, to his own satisfaction at least, the existence of God, the immateriality of the mind, and the existence of an essentially extended material world—Descartes still faced the challenge of explaining the nature of the mind and its union with the extended, mechanically working body. This involves molding the apparently conflicting elements of his early cognitive psychology and mechanistic physiology into a more coherent view of human nature, one that can accommodate other important aspects of human nature and experience, such as the emotions, voluntary action, and the experience of a free will.

The rest of this book examines the view of the mind that results from his efforts to put these different elements and pieces together and to discuss, in particular, the ensuing notions of thinking and intentionality. My discussion in the following chapters thus grants both Descartes's dualism and his view of the mind–body union. I do not examine his arguments for these views given in the *Discourse on the Method* Part IV, and more fully in the *Meditations of First Philosophy,* nor do I dwell on the ways in which his thinking about these matters evolved.[66] Instead I turn directly, in the next chapter, to the account Descartes gives of the mind as embodied, and to the view of the knowledge of the mind he commits himself to in defining the mind as a thinking thing.

2

The Mind as Embodied: A True and Substantial Union

The previous chapter was devoted to what could be called the pre-history of Descartes's philosophy of mind. We saw that Descartes did not start to think seriously about questions of metaphysics before he moved to the Netherlands in 1629, but then he claimed in a letter to his friend Mersenne that he "worked on nothing else" during nine months. He also claimed that he worked out to his own satisfaction some arguments concerning the existence of God and the nature of the mind (AT I 144).[1] Yet he did not publish anything on this subject until the *Discourse on the Method* (1637), where he presented a summary of what is described as the "metaphysical" meditations, made shortly after his retreat to the Netherlands eight years earlier (see AT VI 31–40, CSM I 126). They are fully worked out only in *The Meditations on First Philosophy*, published in Latin in 1641. Descartes's arguments for the mind–body dualism are hence presented for the first time, in passing as it were, in the *Discourse*, but they are developed extensively in the *Meditations*, which also bear as their subtitle "in which are demonstrated the existence of God and the distinction between the human soul and the body."[2]

Those arguments are well known and have been widely discussed. They are notoriously problematic. Problems have been raised not only about their premises and cogency, but also as to what Descartes's argument for the mind–body distinction is supposed to establish.[3] Is it supposed to prove a real, actual separation of the two substances or merely a possible separation? It cannot be the former, for, as Arnauld pointed out, that would be to prove too much for one who claims to reject a Platonist view of the human being. On the other hand, if Descartes's argument, as his use of the Scholastic terminology of distinctions suggests, is meant to establish only the latter, a problem remains as to what kind of possibility it involves. Is it a matter of real possibility (and conceivability), one that could be actualized, at least by God's omnipotence, or rather some weaker, conceptual distinction, in which case Cartesian dualism as standardly understood would seem to be compromised? As I see it, Descartes has, at most, proved the latter, but I will not discuss this question here. I grant him at least a conceptual distinction: the notions of mind and body, as he defines them, are conceptually independent. The mind and the body are also mutually irreducible and logically distinct as subjects of predication: what can be predicated of the one cannot be predicated of the other. Granting him this much, I turn directly to the question of what view of human nature and mind he defends in the *Discourse,* the *Meditations,* and later writings, given that he takes the mind to be both distinct from and united with the body.

The view of man usually associated with Cartesian dualism in modern discussions is that of an immaterial soul or mind working "inside" an extended material body functioning according to the mechanical laws of nature. Gilbert Ryle, in *The Concept of Mind* (1949), labeled this the myth or the dogma of the "Ghost in the Machine." The true man, in this analogy, is neither identified with the human body nor with the composite of body and mind but with the mind alone. The human body is but a machine that the rational mind can manipulate in mysterious ways and that is also supposed to influence, mysteriously, the workings of the mind.[4]

In spite of its popularity in Anglo-American philosophy of mind, this Rylean version of Cartesian dualism has not much in common with the view Descartes actually held. It could be called the "myth of the Cartesian myth." This is not to say that the myth Ryle is fighting is a sheer construction. On the contrary, it has been immensely influential and still haunts philosophers of mind in the form of "homunculus" and other theories. But it is misleading to call this myth "Cartesian." As many scholars have noticed, Descartes's dualistic conception of man is closer to the Aristotelian than to the Platonist view and should therefore be distinguished from a crude "Ghost-in-the-Machine" dualism.[5] Even when the differences between "Cartesian dualism" and Descartes's dualism have been recognized, the nature of the latter remains a matter of controversy.[6] Moreover, mostly because of the influential status of the Cartesian myth, the epistemological and methodological implications of Descartes's views have been largely misconstrued or ignored.

My focus in this chapter is the notion of the mind–body union, which Descartes refers to in his later writings as a "primitive" notion, and the epistemological consequences of his distinction between three such primitive notions. I argue that they should be separated from some of the questionable theses concerning the nature and knowledge of the mind currently associated with Cartesian dualism.

1. Three Perspectives on the Mind and the Body

In discussing Descartes's anthropology—including the question whether he had any[7]—it is important to distinguish three different perspectives, dictated by different methodological and epistemological concerns, from which questions pertaining to the nature of man are addressed by Descartes.

The first focuses on the human body as an object of mechanistic physics and is at work already in Descartes's early accounts of the functioning of the sensory and other organs of living bodies.[8] Bits and pieces of his mechanistic physiology and theory of sense perception are presented to the public for the first time in the *Discourse* Part V (AT VI 45–60) and the accompanying *Optics*.[9] Its main points are summarized at the end of Part IV of the *Principles of Philosophy*. Descartes planned to develop but never completed a fuller account, as indicated by the unfinished *Description of the Human Body,* begun in the winter of 1647–1648. A last summary of his account of the functions of the human body is given in Part I of *The Passions of the Soul,* art. 4–16.

The second, most dominant perspective is on the mind or intellect as an epistemic subject. It is the perspective of the *Rules* (notably Rules Eight and Twelve) that do not, however, address its metaphysical presuppositions, and it is also dominant in the *Discourse* and *Meditations,* where Descartes spells out and defends his views of the metaphysical nature of the mind, its claims to knowledge, and its objects.

Although both perspectives deserve discussion, I do not treat them separately, but turn directly to the third perspective, which represents

Descartes's mature thinking on human nature and which, although it has received the least attention, is the starting point of my examination of the Cartesian mind. It is the conception of man as a *real* union between the mind and the body, which is briefly mentioned at the end of Part IV of the *Discourse* (AT VI 59, CSM I 141). In the first two Meditations, my body and the phenomena pertaining to the union of mind and body are listed as part of my nature (AT VII 18–19, 26, CSM II 13, 17). Since they do not pass the test of distinct conception, they are set aside as doubtful, to be taken up for examination again in the Sixth Meditation (AT VII 80–89), after the actual existence of the body and the external world has been proved. Here too they are discussed mainly from the special perspective of the *Meditations,* and the aim is to determine the role of sensory perceptions and feelings as sources of information about the external world. The mind–body union is at the center stage again in the later *Passions of the Soul,* where more general questions concerning moral agency and the mastery of the passions are addressed.

Descartes's notion of man as a union between mind and body comes under attack in the Objections accompanying the *Meditations* and is discussed more fully for the first time in the Reply to the Fourth Set of Objections (AT VII 227, CSM II 160). Arnauld has no objection to the view that the mind is a purely thinking thing and as such more perfect than and distinct from the body. He worries that Descartes's argument for the real distinction proves too much and commits him to the Platonist view that the human being is merely a mind accidentally lodged in and using the body (AT VII 203, CSM II 143). Descartes not only denies that the real distinction excludes a real union, since it merely shows that God, by his omnipotence, can separate the mind and the body, but he pretends that he has proved at the same time, with arguments "as strong as any I can remember ever having read," that "the mind is substantially united with the body" (AT VII 228, CSM II 160).[10]

This notion of a real union of the mind and the body is not introduced *ad hoc* to account for the unintelligible mind–body interaction. It represents Descartes's view of the human person as a conscious *and* embodied agent, which he took for granted already in the *Rules* but felt no need to explain until his proofs for the real distinction between the mind and the body forced him to defend also their union. He does not, as it turns out, have much of an account to give, but contents himself, when pressed (notably by the young Princess Elisabeth (AT III 661, 685)) on the question of how the immaterial mind can interact with the extended material body, with describing it as just another *primitive*, irreducible notion (AT III 665). The union covers such important features of human experience and action as sensations, passions, and voluntary movements, which are not intelligible in terms of the Cartesian notions of extension or thought alone. It is, as I will try to show, referred to as "primitive" (or primary) because it is on a par with the (simple) notions of extension and thought, each of which serves as a conceptual precondition for a distinctive domain of knowledge whose objects cannot be accounted for in terms pertaining to the other. This is not to say that it should be taken to represent—with thought and extension—a third principal attribute or that the mind–body union is a third kind of substance.[11] On Descartes's view, human nature is constituted essentially of a union between two different natures, which can be clearly and distinctly understood only when considered as distinct from each other.

I will not dwell on the ontology of this problematic notion, for I grant that it is, in the end, incoherent. Descartes himself recognizes as much in declaring that we cannot conceive at the same time the mind and the body as distinct and as constituting one single thing.[12] My focus is on the views of self-knowledge and the knowledge of mental phenomena to which Descartes commits himself in treating the mind–body union as a third primitive notion. Taking the union for granted, as Descartes does, and using it as a starting-point for examining his concept of mind, will help to put the other two perspectives, that of the mind considered purely as an epistemic subject and that of the human body as a piece of mechanically working machinery, in their proper perspective.

The question of the conceivability of the mind–body union is the topic of section 2 of this chapter. Section 3 discusses the epistemological theses associated with the Ghost-in-the-Machine version of Cartesian dualism. Section 4 looks at the differences between the "pure mind," whose nature is discovered in the Second Meditation, and the mind as embodied, which is the subject of the Sixth Meditation and which constitutes the mind of the true human being. Section 5 takes a closer look at the three primary notions of extension, thought, and mind–body union and the kinds of cognition associated with each. Section 6 discusses clear and distinct versus obscure and confused thoughts and the role of the latter in human experience. The question of what kind of knowledge of our mental states is possible is discussed in sections 7 and 8.[13]

2. The Mind–Body Union and Its Conceivability

Ryle's charge against Cartesian dualism is well known. It involves a category-mistake based on a false para-mechanical hypothesis: Descartes and his followers mistakenly conceived the mind as a thing, though of a different sort from the body. Mental processes were conceived as causes and effects, even if different from the mechanical causes and effects in terms of which the actions of bodies are explained.[14] The natural methodological counterpart of this dogma is the theory that the ways of knowing one's mind and its contents are analogous to the ways of knowing physical things, even though the latter are based on outer sense perception that is intersubjective and testable, whereas the former are based on nonsensuous "inner" perception, generally called "introspection."[15]

The metaphorical talk of "inner" and "outer" is connected with the view that the mind has privileged epistemic access to its own states. The contents of consciousness are perceived directly: they are, as it were, "phosphorescent" and, moreover, private (nonaccessible to other observers). The knowledge of the states and workings of one's own mind ("present thinkings, feelings, willings, perceivings, rememberings, imaginings") is therefore superior to the knowledge of "outer" things (bodies and "other minds"): unlike "outer" sense perceptions, consciousness and introspection cannot be mistaken and confused.[16] The somewhat weird consequence of Descartes's dualism, on this interpretation, is that statements describing mental states, although unverifiable because of their "private" nature, are more certain than statements concerning outer objects, the truth of which can be tested by intersubjective, scientific methods.[17]

Descartes clearly made use of metaphors very similar to the "Ghost-in-the-Machine" analogy in his early writings on man. Thus in giving his first crude accounts of the interaction between the rational soul and the body, he compared the body to a mechanically working statue of earth, the movements of which are controlled and regulated by the immaterial soul. In his later works he elaborated on this "para-mechanical" metaphor when giving a more detailed explanation of the mind–body interaction through the movements of the pineal gland and the animal spirits.[18] But it is important to realize that those are and remain metaphors for Descartes: mechanical accounts of something that, as Descartes clearly saw and recognized at a later stage, could *not* in fact be adequately represented by means of any para-mechanical model. In 1648, Descartes wrote to Arnauld:

> That the mind, which is incorporeal, can set the body in motion—this is something which is shown to us *not by any reasoning or comparison with other matters,* but by the surest and plainest everyday experience. It is one of those self-evident things which we only make obscure when we try to explain them in terms of others.[19]

Descartes rejected the Platonist view of man and conceived the union of the mind and the body as real and substantial on the model of the Aristotelian notion of an individual substance composed of form and matter.[20] But this traditional notion of an immaterial form inhering in a material body is notoriously problematic and obscure, and transposed into the framework of Descartes's radical dualism and mechanistic philosophy of nature, it appears totally unintelligible. When faced with this difficulty (raised, notably, by Elisabeth and Gassendi),[21] Descartes invariably replied that the union of the mind and the body *cannot* be understood by more clear and distinct ideas, but that it *need* not be explained at all. He claims that the notion we have of this union is a simple or "primitive" notion and insists that as such it should be plain to everyone. For it is the notion we have of ourselves as conscious agents, which is familiar from our daily experience and action.[22]

Can Descartes's answer to Elisabeth be taken seriously? The mind and the body, as Descartes defines these notions, can be clearly and distinctly conceived only when conceived separately from each other. But then they cannot without absurdity also be conceived as united, for this would be to conceive them at the same time as two different and one single thing, which, as Descartes admits, is impossible.[23]

Although he recognized the difficulty, Descartes did not give up the notion of a real union between the mind and the body, the natures of which are intelligible only when conceived separately from each other. Instead, he drew a distinction between different kinds of knowledge, depending on different primary notions, and insisted that the knowledge of the union belongs to a primitive notion distinct from other notions of the same kind. To Elisabeth he describes the primitive notions as "originals" or models according to which all our knowledge is formed. Some are general, like "those of being, number, duration, etc.," some particular to body, "like the notion of extension, which entails the notions of shape and motion," some particular to "the soul on its own," which can only be understood through "the notion of thought, which includes the perceptions of the intellect and the inclinations of the will." He continues: "Lastly, as regards the soul and the body together, we have only the notion of their union, on which depends our notion of the soul's power to move the body, and the body's power to act on the soul and cause its sensations and passions."[24] The soul's action on the body to cause voluntary movements, as that of the body on the soul in causing sensations and passions, are understood only through the notion of the union, whereas perceptions of the intellect and acts of the will that pertain to "the soul on its own" are understood through the notion of thought alone. While the latter can be clearly and distinctly understood, the former cannot, yet they can be clearly known through the senses and daily experience. To understand what this distinction between different basic notions and domains of knowledge amounts to, something has to be said about Descartes's scientific methodology.

We know, from the *Discourse on the Method* and Descartes's other programmatic declarations, that the general aim of his scientific reform was to gain clarity and distinctness where the Scholastics had achieved nothing but obscurity and confusion. What Descartes opposes, in particular, is the anthropomorphism of the traditional Aristotelian science of nature with its illegitimate use of notions derived from everyday experience and commonsense psychology in the explanation of physical events. The paradigm of such notions is that of an immaterial form or "real quality," for example, heaviness, which is supposed to inhere in a physical body and thereby explain its (natural) motions. Such notions are modeled on our own experience as conscious agents pursuing certain ends. Although we understand them clearly enough in applying them to ourselves, they become occult and unintelligible when extended to the description of changes in physical nature. To meet Descartes's requirements of clarity and distinctness, scientific explanations must be in strictly mechanistic and mathematical terms. Qualitative notions cannot be translated into quantitative concepts: they are purely subjective ("modes of thought" in Descartes's large sense of the phrase) and hence cannot represent real properties of external objects as the Scholastics mistakenly supposed. As Descartes explains in a letter to Mersenne, he rejects the assumption of real qualities added on to corporeal substances "like so many little souls to their bodies, and which are separable from them by divine power," but which in his view are nothing but modifications of substance (motions and shapes).

One reason for rejecting these so-called real qualities is that he does not find in the human mind "any notion, or particular idea, to conceive them by; so that when we talk about them and assert their existence, we are asserting something we do not conceive and do not ourselves understand." Another is that they were posited by philosophers "only because they did not think they could otherwise explain all the phenomena of nature; but I find on the contrary that these phenomena are much better explained without them."[25] This point is repeated with even more emphasis in a letter to Regius, where Descartes refers to the real qualities as "substantial forms":

> They were introduced by philosophers solely to account for the proper actions of natural things, of which they were supposed to be the principles and bases . . . But no natural action at all can be explained by these substantial forms, since their defenders admit that they are occult and that they do not understand them themselves. If they say that some action proceeds from a substantial form, it is as if they said that it proceeds from something they do not understand; which explains nothing . . . Essential forms explained in our fashion, on the other hand, give manifest and mathematical reasons for natural actions, as can be seen with regard to the form of salt in my *Meteors*. (To Regius, January 1642 (AT III 506, CSMK 208–209))

Although Descartes rejects the use of such obscure notions in the explanation of physical nature, he does not, interestingly, reject them altogether. The context within which they have an application is that of the mind–body union. Qualities, understood as modes of the mind united to the body, have a proper use and function, but this use is not relevant to physics or natural sciences. It is worth stressing that Descartes, unlike some contemporary scientific reformers, does not claim that we can do without qualitative notions or intentional concepts. He certainly did not believe that our concept of thoughts as caused by movements in the body would disappear once all their bodily causes were detected, or that we would be able, in some distant future, to consult brain scanners rather than our feelings to get reliable measures of our states of mind. The notion of a quality like heaviness, informing and moving a physical body, obscure as it is when used in the account of physical changes, is, in Descartes's view, derived from the notion we have of ourselves as conscious and acting beings. It belongs to the very essence of human experience and action and has no legitimate application outside this context.[26]

The moral to be drawn from this is twofold: not only are notions such as "real qualities" or "substantial forms" to be excluded from the scientific explanation of nature, but the phenomena to which they can be meaningfully applied elude, by their nature, scientific explanation. This is the consequence that Descartes in fact draws: there is no Cartesian science of human beings, only a science of the human body.[27] To qualify as an object of science in Descartes's sense, the body must be considered as mechanically moved extended matter. Important aspects of human nature and experience are thereby left outside the scope of scientific explanation when that explanation is limited to what fulfills the requirements of a mechanistic or physicalistic science of nature.

3. Privileged Access, Indubitability, and Introspection

According to the traditional two-story picture opposed by Ryle, Cartesian dualism allows both for a mechanistic science of the extended body and an independent psychological science based on introspection and phenomenological analysis of the mind and its inner states.[28] The belief in introspection as a legitimate and privileged method of knowing one's mental states is considered by Ryle to be part and parcel of "Descartes's myth": as the doctrine of Privileged Access it is supposed to be the "natural counterpart" of a dualistic view of the world.[29] As Ryle describes it, it is in fact a theory of twofold Privileged Access.

Its proponents are said to hold (1) "that a mind cannot help being constantly aware of all the supposed occupants of its private stage"; and (2) "that it can also deliberately scrutinize by a species of non sensuous perception at least some of its own states and operations." Both consciousness (the mind's direct awareness of its present states) and introspection (as described in (2)) are supposed to be equally exempt from error.[30]

Although Descartes undoubtedly held some version of a Privileged Access theory, he certainly was not committed to all the dubious consequences of the doctrine Ryle describes. He clearly did not hold thesis (1), which implies that only those beliefs and other mental occurrences that are the object of actual or remembered awareness count as "thoughts." For one thing, innate ideas and beliefs we are unaware of count as thoughts in Descartes's wide sense of the word (see Chapter 3). Moreover, innumerable thoughts occur without leaving traces in our memory—not only while we are awake but also while we sleep and maybe even before we were born.[31] It does not follow from the soul being essentially a thinking thing, and in this sense always thinking, that it must be aware of all its thoughts at all times. As to the second thesis (2), Descartes held it only with important qualifications.

Far from involving the kind of category mistake that Ryle, or his followers, impute to him, Descartes's distinction between the notions of the mind and the body takes account of the radical difference between the knowledge of the mind and its states on the one hand, and that of "outer" physical bodies on the other. The ways of knowing one's own mind and its states cannot be considered counterparts of the ways of knowing physical things.[32] Thinking, as Descartes understands it, covers not only acts of the reason or the pure intellect *(nous),* but all kinds of conscious and unconscious mental states, including acts of the will and the imagination, as well as emotions and sense perceptions. What is common to all these different modes of thought is that we are aware of their occurrence while actually attending to them: they are "thoughts" in Descartes's sense insofar as they are or *can be* immediately perceived.[33]

All objects of awareness that are immediately given to the conscious subject and that constitute indubitable data are modes of thinking in Descartes's sense of this term. I may have doubts concerning the nature, origins, or reality of the various objects of my actual thoughts, but *qua* actually perceived these phenomena are indubitable. The knowledge of the mind and its immediate contents can hence be said to be certain and "incorrigible," but this incorrigibility does not take us very far. It pertains to the mental only in the sense of actually occurrent conscious perceptions and the evidence this provides for the certainty that the subject having these thoughts or perceptions exists. It does *not* include any interpretations or judgments associated with these perceptions. I am probably mistaken in most of the interpretations or explanations I offer of, say, my present emotional state, but that I feel tense and unnerved or good and cheerful, whatever causes my present moods or states, is indubitable: no further facts could affect the evidence I have of being actually in the state I presently experience. I may be wrong in my description or account of it—it may even be impossible for me to correctly identify or account for it at all—but I cannot be mistaken in my certainty of having it. To speak of "knowledge" and "certainty" insofar as our actual awareness is concerned may be misleading, but it would be equally odd to claim that we could be mistaken about our having the present mental states or thoughts we are immediately aware of.

Appealing to the indubitability of these immediately given data of consciousness, Descartes in the Second Meditation infers that he exists as a thinking thing, and he considers this conclusion as evidently true. The Second Meditation is also where Descartes examines the nature of the mind and purports to establish the controversial claim that it is better and easier known *(notior; plus aisé à connaître)* than the body (AT VII 182, AT IX 18, CSM II 128). This knowledge, however, seems to amount to nothing other than the certainty that I think and exist, together with the fact (crucial for Descartes's argument for a real distinction between the mind and the body) that this certainty is acquired prior to the knowledge that any other thing, including my body, exists.[34] The indubitability of mental states is restricted to our awareness of their present occurrence and does not entail that all mental states are epistemologically transparent, that they can be known "through and through," by introspection.[35] When looking among one's own mental states for particular instances of thoroughly transparent thoughts, one will not find much beyond the present awareness of thinking that *p* or willing to *X* or understanding that "$2 + 2 = 1 + 3$" and the like. The knowledge of the mind in a wider sense will also include ideas classified as "innate" (AT VII 38, CSM II 26) and the "common notions" or "eternal truths" that are self-evident and undeniable but have no existence outside the mind. (They belong to what the Scholastics classified as abstractive notions, which are known by themselves, by mere inspection of the terms.) The discovery of their indubitability extends our knowledge of the mind and of what it is to be a thinker. However, as components and presuppositions of thinking, they are common to all rational thinkers and do not exist on some private mental stage to which its owner alone has privileged access.

4. The Pure Mind and the Embodied Mind

Descartes's arguments that the mind and the body are really distinct things are often quoted as evidence that he espoused a Platonistic view of man. For instance, in the *Discourse,* Descartes describes the "I" or the "soul" whose existence has been established by the famous "I think, therefore I exist" in terms which sound very Platonistic. It is not only said to be "entirely distinct from the body" and "more easy to know than the body," but it is also claimed that "even if the body were not, the soul would not cease to be what it is" (AT VI 33, CSM I 127).

It would, however, be a mistake to identify the "I" or the "mind," as described in similar passages in the *Discourse* and the *Meditations,* with the true man. Descartes's use of the term "I" is somewhat floating, but it is clear that the "I," whose existence as a purely thinking thing is established in the Second Meditation before any other knowledge, represents only a part of the "I" or the "Self" of a real human being, whose true nature is discovered only in the Sixth Meditation. It is only in the order of knowledge that the nature of the mind is more easily or certainly known than the body.[36] So although Descartes, having submitted all his former beliefs to the trial of doubt, first *discovers* himself as merely a thinking thing, he does not hold himself to be *only* a thinking thing. That he exists as a thinking thing is the only thing he can claim in the Second Meditation to know with certainty, given the standard of certainty in terms of indubitability that he has set himself. In concluding that the nature of the "I" is to be a thinking thing, Descartes has achieved a first fundamental certainty, but he has said nothing about the other properties the thinking thing might have in addition.[37]

It is not until the Sixth Meditation that Descartes is in a position to analyze the nature of his actual embodied self or mind. Of all the properties that were said in the Second Meditation to belong to his nature *qua* thinking thing, only those of the intellect and the will are now said to be necessary properties of the self. Descartes hence draws a distinction between the nature or essence of the mind in a strict sense and the nature of the mind in a broader sense: the latter includes modes of thinking (imagination and sense perception) that are not essential to the mind in itself but belong to it only as a consequence of its union with the body. The power of imagination, for instance, which is used to represent extended things, is said to depend "on something that differs from me" and cannot for this reason be said to belong to "the essence of my mind" (AT VII 73, CSM II 51). The same holds for the faculty of sensation (sense perception), which because of its passive and unpredictable character cannot depend on the mind alone (AT VII 79, CSM II 55). These faculties are modes of thought and as such belong to the mind, but insofar as they depend on the body they are, with regard to the mind alone, accidental properties. But if they are accidental modes of the mind when considered in itself, they are nonetheless necessary properties of the embodied, *human* mind that is, "as it were, intermingled" with the body.[38]

The ultimate contingency of the mind–body union is sometimes taken to imply the possibility of disembodied sensation. Although Descartes argues that the mind and the body are separable by God's omnipotence, and regards the intellect and the will as purely mental capacities, it is not very clear in what sense he thinks of them as separable from the other powers of individual thinkers, although it is clear that he regards the union as essential for human nature.[39] The connection between particular thoughts and particular bodily movements "causing" or accompanying them may be contingent. But Descartes denies that disembodied minds could have sensations or feelings like those human beings have, and he seems to regard the fact that they are connected with bodily movements as essential to those (confused) thoughts that depend on the mind–body union. If the latter is constitutive of the human being, the thoughts depending on it are constitutive for our human experience, not least for our experience as individual thinkers. The Cartesian Meditator may abstract from and even doubt the particulars of his present embodied position and circumstances—the dressing gown, the fire, his moving head, his open eyes, and his hands stretching out, for instance (AT VII 19, CSM II 13)—but he cannot even get started on his solitary meditations without granting both his individuality as a thinker and the particular things he now decides to call in doubt. He may bracket the question of his actual identity and existence, but whether or not he now wants to believe it, he is the same René Descartes, born in 1596, who put on his gown before he sat down with a piece of paper in his hand (!) to ask himself if he was dreaming or being deceived, and if any of his beliefs were true.

If Descartes rejects the Platonist view of man, it is precisely because it fails to do justice to the phenomena or modes of thought depending on the mind–body union and that he considers distinctive for our human condition. A pure mind accidentally placed in a particular body could at most move its members, but if it is supposed to have "sensations and appetites similar to our own, and thus form a true man," it is "necessary that it should also be joined and united more closely to the body" (AT VI 59, CSM I 141).

The union is not a matter of clear and distinct intellectual perception, but a brute fact of experience, something that our nature is said to teach us. The peculiarly "confused" character of the experience through which it is revealed, which Descartes stresses in many contexts, is illustrated by the following thought experiment. If I were lodged in my body (as a merely thinking thing), I would not feel any pain when my body is hurt, "for I should perceive this wound by the understanding only, just as the sailor perceives by the sight when something is damaged in his vessel." And if my body needs drink or food, "I should clearly understand this fact without being warned by confused feelings of hunger and thirst." Sensations and feelings like pain, hunger, and thirst are "none other than certain confused modes of thought which are produced by the union and apparent intermingling of the mind and the body" (AT VII 81, CSM II 56).[40]

The irremediably confused character of these thoughts is what marks the difference between human beings and purely rational beings—the difference between an embodied mind and a pure mind. If a pure mind—for example, an angel—were united to a human body, Descartes explains in a letter, it would not have feelings as we have. Instead of being affected with confused thoughts or feelings of the kind that the movements in the body produce in the human mind, the angel would perceive these movements clearly and distinctly. It would, in other words, see the damage caused to the body, without being in any way affected by it.[41]

The union between the mind and the body constitutes human nature. It is established by nature in such a way that movements in the body "produce" (confused) thoughts "in the mind," informing it thereby of the states and needs of the body (that the mind might otherwise forget). In spite of their confused and obscure nature, the thoughts caused by bodily movements (sensations and passions) always have "some truth" in them, and to this extent they also have their proper, important function: they serve the welfare of the body and hence the preservation of the mind–body union.[42] But they cannot be rendered clearer than they are actually experienced as being, nor are they intelligible outside the context of the mind–body union and those natural purposes for which they have been instituted. This means that they cannot be the objects of any special, direct, and infallible inner scrutiny. Introspection as a privileged method of psychology seems thus to be excluded.

5. Three Primary Notions: Extension, Thought, and Mind–Body Union

Let us look more closely at the distinction between different kinds of knowledge made in Descartes's later writings. As he wrote in the letter to Elisabeth quoted above, it is based on differences in the objects of knowledge and the primary or "primitive" notions through which they are known. Descartes insists on the importance of not misusing these notions:

> [A]ll human knowledge consists solely in carefully distinguishing these notions and in referring each of them only to the things to which it pertains. For if we try to explain some difficulty by means of a notion that does not pertain to it, we cannot fail to go wrong. Similarly, we go wrong if we try to explain one of these notions by another, for since they are primitive notions, each of them can be understood only by itself. (AT III 665–666, CSMK 218)

This is something we tend to overlook, because the notion of extension and others depending on this primary notion, like shape and motion, have become more familiar to us than the others (through the use of our senses!), "and the main cause of our errors is that we commonly want to use these notions to explain matters to which they do not pertain" (ibid.).

It is remarkable that in his letter to Elisabeth, Descartes holds our use of the senses responsible for having made the primary notion of mathematical physics much more familiar than the other ones. The *Principles of Philosophy,* written around the same time,[43] gives a different story. The primary notions, which he there calls "simple notions," are introduced to help us "correct the preconceived opinions of our early childhood." We read: "In our childhood the mind was so immersed in the body, that although it perceived many things clearly, it never perceived anything distinctly; yet in spite of this it made judgements about many things, which is the origin of many preconceived opinions which most of us never subsequently abandon." Descartes then proceeds to give a list of what he describes as "all the simple notions which are the basic components of our thoughts," distinguishing in each case "the clear elements from those which are obscure or liable to lead us in error" (AT VIII-1 22, CSM I 208).

The next paragraph gives a list of all the objects of knowledge (perception), which corresponds to the one given to Elisabeth, although the starting point here is the objects of knowledge themselves: the things *(res)* or their affections *(rerumve affectiones)*. The similarity to the list offered in the early *Rules* of "simple natures" is striking (AT X 419, CSM I 44–45). The things considered as simple fall under the simple notions, which are the same as those called "primitive" in the correspondence with Elisabeth. The most general, again, are substance, duration, order, number, and so forth, "which extend to all classes of things," and those that belong particularly to one or the other of the two main classes of things recognized by Descartes: the class of "intellectual or thinking things," which belong "to mind or to thinking substance," for instance, perceptions or volitions, and the class of material things, which pertain to extended substance, like "size, that is extension in length, breadth and depth, shape, motion, position, divisibility of its parts and the like" (AT VIII-1 22–23, CSM I 208–209).

That Descartes recognizes only two main categories of things comes as no surprise. What is surprising is that he acknowledges a third kind, which fits neither of these two:

> But we also experience within ourselves certain other things which must neither be referred either to the mind alone or the body alone,

which . . . arise from the close and intimate union of our mind with the body, as appetites like hunger and thirst etc., and further emotions, or passions of the soul *that do not consist of thought alone,* such as the emotions of anger, joy, sadness and love; and finally, all the sensations, such as those of pain, pleasure, light, colors, sounds, smells, tastes, heat, hardness and the other tactile qualities. (AT VIII-1 23, CSM I 209; my emphasis)

Such phenomena, which we "experience within ourselves," belong to what Descartes refers to, in the letter to Elisabeth, as the last primitive notion. In addition to general notions applicable to all kinds of things (substance, duration, and so on), we thus have three different simple or primitive notions: extension, thought, and the mind–body union. This means that whatever knowledge we have of things presupposes one or the other of these three simple notions: we can know particulars either as thinking, or as extended, or through experience as composites of mind and body. We also have common notions or axioms, too many to be listed, which form a separate group because they are not of *things,* but of eternal truths having no existence outside our thought (AT VIII-1 23–24, CSM I 208–209). Descartes writes to Elisabeth that all these notions are to be found in our soul, which contains them by its own nature, but does not "always sufficiently distinguish them from each other, or assign them to the objects to which they ought to be assigned" (AT III 666–667, CSMK 219).

But what is the status of the simple or primary notion of the mind–body union? Did Descartes hold, or was tempted by, the view that it represents a third substance? Should the notion of the mind–body union be understood as a third main attribute, of which sensations and other body-dependent thoughts are the modes?[44] If it were taken as another main attribute, like thought (through which we understand immaterial substances) or extension (through which we know material substances), would it not follow that our knowledge of the phenomena pertaining to the mind–body union would be comparable to our knowledge of the mind and of the body considered separately?

A principal attribute for Descartes represents the nature of a thing, that is, what we can perceive, clearly and distinctly, as belonging to the nature (or essence) of that thing (see *Principles* I, par. 48, 53–54, AT VIII-7 22–25, CSMI 208–209). If we had, innately, a notion of a separate main attribute for understanding phenomena pertaining to the union, then we could also know these phenomena as clearly and distinctly as we know those pertaining to the other two kinds of substance, provided we referred them to the correct main attribute. It could be tempting to interpret Descartes in this way, and some of the things he says in his correspondence and elsewhere may seem to support such a reading.[45] But though Descartes takes pains to stress in his letter to Regius that the human being should be described as a thing *per se,* and not *per accidens,* and that the whole composed of mind and body is a thing *per se* (AT III 493, CSMK 206), and also insists in his Reply to Arnauld that it is not an accidental but a *substantial* union (AT VII 228, CSM II 160), he nowhere describes the mind–body union as a third kind of substance, nor does he anywhere indicate that there are more than two principal attributes through which the human mind can have clear and distinct knowledge of things.[46]

The problem with the notion of the mind–body union is its hybrid nature. It is supposed to be a *simple* notion yet, from the point of view of the intellect—from that of clear and distinct perception—it is not simple but composite. Unlike the notions of thought or extension, which represent the two principal attributes of simple things or substances, it is a third kind of thing formed by the union of two simple and complete substances, which (as Descartes stresses to Regius and elsewhere) can exist apart.[47] That the union may be termed "substantial" does not make our notion of it a third kind of attribute. Because the two substances that compose it can be clearly and distinctly known only when considered apart, each through its own distinctive attribute, there cannot be a clear and distinct notion of their being united to one whole. There can be no intellectual conception of two distinct things as one.

But why, then, does Descartes characterize the notion of the mind–body union as simple or primitive? Presumably, because he wants to stress its irreducibility. Without representing a separate main attribute, it is like the notions of thought and extension in that it cannot be rendered more clear or distinct by further analysis. But since the notion or perception we have of the mind–body union, unlike those of extension and thought, is not in itself clearly and distinctly conceivable, we have to put up with something less than clear and distinct knowledge where the union is concerned. This, it seems to me, is what Descartes indicates in describing it as a fact of experience and in stressing that the notion is irreducible: it cannot be clearer than it is as actually experienced.

Thus, in characterizing his three notions as primitive, Descartes wants to emphasize that each of them can be known or understood only through itself and not by comparison to any other notion and, moreover, that each of them constitutes, in its proper domain, a presupposition for our knowledge of what belongs to that domain. All the concepts in terms of which physical bodies are understood presuppose the notion of extension, which cannot be analyzed: it is irreducible. The same holds for the notion of thought, which is presupposed in our knowledge of intellectual things. The third primitive notion, by which we are supposed to understand the mind–body union, is not a separate main attribute, but is irreducible in the same way. It is given with our experience of the mind–body interaction (of being affected by and affecting the body and its motions) and cannot be explicated in terms of more primitive notions, which means that it cannot be analyzed in terms of extension or in terms of thinking.[48]

As I understand it, Descartes's primitive notions belong to different and incomparable levels of description or contexts of discourse. They differ because they apply to different objects but also, I want to stress, by virtue of the different ways and contexts in which these objects are described and known. As Descartes explains to Elisabeth, the mind and purely intellectual things in general can be conceived only by the pure intellect, that is, by metaphysical thought and meditation. The body and extension generally can be clearly and distinctly conceived only by the pure intellect or by the pure intellect aided by the imagination (geometry). Both can be clearly and distinctly known because of the primary notions of thought and extension, which represent the main attribute of the substances to which they pertain. As to the union between the mind and the body and what belongs to this union, it can "be known only obscurely by the pure intellect or by the intellect aided by the imagination, but it can be known very clearly through the senses" (AT III 691–692, CSMK 227). This is to say that the mind–body union *cannot* be clearly and distinctly perceived by the intellect or the understanding, but that it is nevertheless clearly perceived by the senses: it is a fact of experience.

True knowledge or science requires that these notions should be carefully separated and applied only to their proper objects or in their proper domains. We should hence not try to use our imagination or the notion of extension to conceive the nature of the soul, nor should we try to "conceive the way in which the soul moves the body after the manner in which one body is moved by another" (AT III 666, CSMK 218). Scientific knowledge of nature is restricted to what can be accounted for in terms of extension and related notions, and metaphysical knowledge to the general natures of things, to their existence (for instance, the mind, God, bodies), and to the most general principles of knowledge.[49] As to our own nature and condition as embodied minds and agents, we have only our senses and common sense to rely on. Each of these kinds of knowledge is legitimate within its proper domain, but should not go beyond it: we go wrong if we rely on our sensory experience in trying to determine the true properties of physical things, as we go wrong in using quantitative methods or metaphysical investigations to clarify or explain our feelings, sensations, and motivations.

But can the experience we have of the phenomena pertaining to the third primitive notion really be regarded as a kind of knowledge? How can phenomena a characteristic feature of which is their confusion be clearly perceived? The various modes of thought and extension can be clearly and distinctly known only when regarded "simply as modes of the things in which they are located" (*Principles* I, par. 65 (AT VIII-1 32, CSM I 216)). Sensations, emotions, and appetites, these "confused" modes of thought depending on the mind–body union, are problematic not only because of our deep-rooted habit to refer them to things "located outside us"—to consider them not as modes of thought but as modes of extended things—but they are also inherently confused. This confusion, as will be seen, is due precisely to their "hybrid" nature: they are modes of thought, but caused by the body. Yet Descartes claims they can be clearly perceived "provided we take great care in our judgements concerning them to include no more than what is strictly contained in our perception—no more than that of which we have inner awareness."[50] The French translation of this passage has *connaissance claire et distincte,* where the Latin says "clearly perceived." Gouhier notes that the French translation sometimes renders *clare* by *distinct,* but that this latter term is used by Descartes only once, in *Principles* I, art. 68: "In order to distinguish what is clear in this connection from what is obscure, we must be very careful to note that pain and colour and so on are clearly and distinctly perceived when they are re-garded merely as sensations or thoughts" (AT VIII-1 33, CSM I 217).

Descartes, admittedly, did not give strict definitions of the terms "clear" and "distinct," and he uses "idea" and "perception" in a very broad sense.[51] The characterization and examples he gives of distinct perceptions or ideas seem, however, to imply that the things pertain-ing to the third primitive notion cannot, even when *clearly* perceived, be also *distinctly* perceived in any proper sense of the word. I am, for my part, inclined to follow Gilson, who argues that the notion of the mind–body union is not an idea of the same order as those of the mind and the body. The latter are innate ideas of the intellect or un-derstanding, the former is an "adventitious," sensory idea. It is not that the criteria of clearness and distinctness change with different kinds of ideas. The ideas are different because they do not meet these criteria in the same way, but vary with regard to their distinctness as well as their clearness.[52] I would not, however, go as far as Gilson, who charac-terizes the notion of the union, because of its sensory origin, as a "pseudo-idea." While it is true that it can be perceived only in sensory or affective experience, it remains an idea, albeit of a different kind from the clear and distinct innate ideas of the intellect.

6. Clear and Distinct versus Obscure and Confused Thoughts

Consider, again, the things listed by Descartes as belonging to the no-tion of the mind–body union that we are said to experience (clearly) within ourselves: appetites of hunger or thirst; emotions or passions like anger, joy, sadness, love, and so on; sensations such as pain, plea-sure, light, sound, and so on (*Principles* I, par. 48 (AT VIII-1 23, CSM I 208–209)). As modes of thought, they are states of the mind, but since they are states of the mind caused by bodily movements, they depend on the mind–body union. Their status is peculiar, for ontologically they belong to the mind, but causally and functionally they belong to the mind–body union and cannot therefore be known or understood without reference to this union,[53] which itself cannot be explained be-cause its notion is primitive and irreducible.

In modern philosophy of mind these things have been construed as "inner" and "private" mental objects that, on the view attributed to Descartes, can be known through introspection—by the mind's inward gaze. Does Descartes hold that they can be clearly and distinctly known, as modes of thought, by the conscious mind attending to its own thoughts?

There is, as we have seen, a sense in which any thought, in Descartes's wide sense of the word, is clearly known and indubitable. This follows from his definition of thought as anything of which we are immediately conscious. However, the claim that any thought, as an immediately given, indubitable *datum* is evidently known, does not entail the view that all thoughts are known or perceived with equal clarity and distinctness, or that all thoughts are always conscious in Ryle's "transparency" sense.

The fullest account of clear and distinct ideas in Descartes's writings is a brief paragraph in the *Principles*. A perception (thought) that meets the requirement of being both clear and distinct is there said to be "so separated and delineated from all others that it contains absolutely nothing except what is clear" (*Principles* I, par. 45 (AT VIII-1 21–22, CSM I 207)). A perception is called clear "when it is present and accessible to the attentive mind" *(praesens et aperta)*, when it is, as it were, in plain view and cannot fail to be noticed. For instance, mathematical propositions and other "self-evident" principles like "If equals are taken from equals the remainders are equal" or "What has been done cannot be undone" are examples of thoughts that can be clearly and distinctly perceived. As to sensations and emotions, they can be clearly perceived without being distinctly perceived. This is so because they are commonly associated with precipitated (unnoticed) judgments about their nature and origin. We tend to refer them, by a deep-rooted habit, to things "located outside us," that is, to consider them not as modes of thought but as modes of extended things. They can, however, be clearly perceived "provided we take great care in our judgments concerning them to include no more than what is strictly contained in our perception—no more than that of which we have inner awareness."[54] As the example of "pain" or other sensations show, a perception can be clear without being distinct, but the converse is not possible (*Principles* I, art. 46 (AT VIII-1 22, CSM I 208)). There are, needless to say, degrees of clearness: a perception can be more or less manifest, more or less carefully attended to. Likewise, there are degrees of distinctness: the more complete our knowledge of a thing is—the more of its attributes or modes we perceive clearly—the more distinct our perception of it is.

As I interpret this, Descartes seems to hold basically the same view as Leibniz, namely, that the clearness of perceptions involves merely an ability to recognize and distinguish one perception from another, whereas distinctness (although Descartes does not say it in so many words) requires that the content of a perception can be described and analyzed and hence that it is propositional and can be expressed discursively.[55] Pain can be clearly perceived, as can any sensation to which I attend: I can distinguish tickling from pain without being able to discern or detail the marks of the sensations through which I recognize the difference. The same applies to emotional states or moods. I can know more or less clearly that I am upset, in love, or tense without being able to explain what my emotional state involves, or account for why I am in this particular state. I can recognize without difficulty different shades of blue, as long as they are clearly perceived. If I cannot recognize them, for example, if I cannot tell the difference between dark blue and black, my color sensations are not clear but obscure. But even when I can recognize the differences, I may be unable to give a precise description of what accounts for them, no matter how clearly I perceive the sense qualities in question. Ideas of sensible qualities can be clear, but they cannot be defined, as Leibniz says. They can be known only through examples, and the best we can say of them, without having distinct knowledge of their inner structure *(contexture)*, is that they are *"un je ne sais quoi."*[56] Descartes, I think, would agree, and although he does not spend much time on what distinct knowledge involves in addition to a perfectly clear perception of all that an idea contains, nothing of what he says is incompatible with the criteria for distinctness given by Leibniz. On the contrary, Descartes's paradigm examples of clear and distinct ideas are mathematical propositions or common logical principles, the self-evidence of which can be accounted for by their being analytical truths—by our being able to analyze them.

What I said about sense perception is true of all the so-called mixed or confused modes of thought depending on the mind–body union. What distinguishes them from intellectual ideas or "pure" thoughts, which can be called "propositional," is not, I want to suggest, their lack of content, but rather that their content, even when they are clearly perceived, is to some extent confused and unintelligible. The immediately perceived clearness of sensations is nothing over and above their presence: they are clear insofar as they are actually perceived or had, although even then they are often obscured by being associated through habit or prejudice with false judgments concerning their origins, objects, and causes.[57]

They have a distinctive form by which they are recognized, and since they convey some information to the embodied mind about its own states, they have a content. But this content is not transparent—on the contrary, it is mostly obscure and confused—and has to be interpreted by the intellect. The clearness of a perception, that is, its mere presence and the force with which it actually manifests itself to the mind, is hence not correlated with its epistemological transparency and does not presuppose that the perceptual content is propositional.[58]

Such confusion, I want to claim, is inherent in thoughts that depend on the mind–body union and is related to its fundamental inconceivability. Not only is the human mind, because of its finite and embodied nature, so constituted that it cannot perceive all the bodily movements causing and accompanying its thoughts. (It is precisely because an important part of its content escapes our knowledge that a perception is obscure and confused (AT VII 147, CSM II 105).) It also lacks the conceptual resources for distinctly conceiving the mind–body union and interaction—its details are not only unknown but unintelligible (AT VIII-1 322, CSM I 285)—and hence it is not a confusion that could be clarified by empirical research, by brain physiology for instance. Nor is it a mere conceptual confusion that could be clarified by conceptual analysis.[59] It is rather a *distinctive* feature of the human mind, expressing its limited and imperfect nature as a created and embodied mind. But if the impossibility of eliminating the confusion in the body-dependent thoughts is an imperfection from the point of view of the rational mind and its claims to clear and distinct knowledge, it constitutes a perfection from the point of view of the union. For, as we are taught in the Sixth Meditation, these thoughts have a natural function that serves the preservation and welfare of the body and thereby of the mind–body union. What appears confused and mysterious from the point of view of the pure intellect, is natural and functional from that of the embodied mind, which uses its sensations and emotions as signs informing it of the state and needs of the body with which it is united and on the welfare of which its own well-being depends.[60]

This gives us a clue also to understanding the peculiar status of body-dependent thoughts and in what sense, precisely, they are essential to the union. It is not just that a disembodied mind does not have sensations because it would not, as purely rational, need them (as suggested by the examples given in AT VII 81, CSM II 56, and AT III 206, discussed above in section 4). Disembodied sensations are impossible not only because sensations causally depend on particular patterns of motions and reactions in the brain and body, but also because those motions could hardly be correlated with types of sensation without the sensory reactions they cause on the mental level—without being registered at some level of consciousness by the human being reacting to them. The individuation of sensations *qua* consciously perceived, on the other hand, presupposes a context of interaction between the conscious, sentient body and its biological environment. Sensations and the bodily motions causing them are interdependent in a way that makes their individuation impossible apart from each other and from the larger context defined by the natural ends of the mind–body union for which they have been instituted.

Marlene Rozemond has made pertinent criticisms of interpretations of Descartes's view of the mind–body union along the lines both of "interactionism," according to which they are mental modes of the mind differing from other thoughts only by being caused by the body, and "trialism," which construes them as a third type of mode (or modes of a third type of ontological category). It is not clear, however, how her own solution, that "sensations do constitute a new type of mode" resulting from the union, which should be construed not as a third type of mode but as a "special subspecies of thought," differs from the interactionist view.[61] I would go further and insist on the institution of the mind–body union as the only proper explanatory context for this subclass of thoughts. This goes beyond the interactionist view according to which they are produced by the interaction of two independently defined substances. Since the mind–body union, and hence the human body, has ends and goods of its own, sensations and other phenomena depending on this union presuppose this finality and cannot be constituted by mere causal interaction between independently describable bodily and mental states. What is particular about sensations, I would claim, is precisely their complexity as psycho-physiological states, which accounts for why they are not transparent to mental introspection. I return to this matter in Chapter 6 in discussing the status of emotions, another important subclass of body-dependent thoughts.

7. Knowing Our Mental States: Inconceivability or Indeterminacy?

Norman Malcolm, who attributes a crude version of substance dualism to Descartes, has argued that Descartes held that "an invisible, intangible, immaterial mind is that which thinks, wills and suffers" and that feelings like "joy, fear, surprise, regret, dismay are states of immaterial minds." Malcolm takes this theory to be as absurd as contemporary materialist theories opposing it, which claim "that the human brain, or even computational states of machines, are bearers of mental predicates."[62]

Malcolm is right that both theories are absurd, but he is wrong in attributing the thesis to Descartes. It is true that Descartes held that immaterial minds can think and will and that the acts of the pure understanding and will are in some sense independent of the body. But it is far from clear in what sense, beyond being different natures understood through mutually exclusive notions, they are distinct. For, as we have seen, Descartes considers the human mind as substantially united to the body and takes this union to be constitutive for human nature. He also seems to hold that all the thoughts of the embodied mind, even those that are said to depend on the mind alone, have some physiological correlates.[63] What Descartes's argument for a real distinction between the mind and the body proves, if anything, is—as Malcolm himself agrees—the logical possibility of their separability, not their actual separation.[64] But he argues, not implausibly, that once this logical possibility is admitted, the possibility of disembodied thought and sensation with all their disastrous epistemological consequences necessarily follow.

This comes close to the familiar charge against Descartes formulated already by Arnauld: his argument for dualism leads, by the force of its own logic, to a Platonic dualism that is incompatible with the view of man as a spiritual *and* embodied being Descartes himself defended.[65] His answer to Arnauld is a bit bewildering and indicates the difficulty Descartes has in trying to formulate his view in the traditional substance-attribute terminology, which his own brand of dualism seems to undermine. To read him as having an ontological two-substance view is to take essential forms and substances in a traditional way—to picture thinking as the form of a substance that, though it is obviously not taken as matter in the traditional sense, provides some kind of "metaphysical" matter or "stuff" for the form to inhere in. Once this picture is in place, we are unable to unite it to another, radically different kind of metaphysical matter whose essential form is extension. The underlying picture is the Aristotelian form–matter metaphysics, with its corresponding subject–predicate distinction and hierarchical order of being. This does not fit Descartes's view, however, for it is part of the asymmetry between thought and extension (considered as essential forms) that only the former, but not the latter, can fulfill the role of an individuating substantial form that his Scholastic predecessors ascribed to the soul. Descartes does not explain this but simply assumes that God has created this individual soul to inform and give unity to this body. Furthermore, Descartes insists that the underlying substances, which the essential attributes inform, remain in themselves unknown, and cannot be recognized independently of their main attributes. Even when his use of familiar metaphors, like that of the hand and the body, suggests it, the radical two-stuff view is not the way to think of Descartes's dichotomy of natures.

Instead of trying to understand how things we have no independent cognitive access to are united and interact, a better way (suggested by Descartes himself) is to read his mind–body distinction as a merely conceptual distinction. For its most important, but most neglected, consequence is the separation of two independent and mutually exclusive domains of knowledge pertaining to two incompatible main attributes, with the recognition that there is a domain of experience that belongs to neither of these but to a third primitive notion. This means, as we have seen, that the phenomena pertaining to the mind–body union cannot be understood in terms either of thought or of extension. The modes of thought depending on the mind–body union cannot, therefore, be clearly and distinctly known through any privileged nonempirical method (introspection or conceptual analysis). Nor can they be explained by empirical or scientific investigations in the narrower sense of the word. So we are left with the "primitive" notion of the mind–body union, by which we are supposed to understand these phenomena. But what kind of understanding could be obtained through such an obscure and problematic notion, and how could sensory experience that is inherently confused serve as the basis of any knowledge?

Such questions have led most of Descartes's commentators to reject his answer to Princess Elisabeth as totally unsatisfactory. Descartes, it is claimed, offers an unexplainable notion to explain an unintelligible fact of experience (the mind–body interaction).[66] Such assessments, however, usually assume that the third primitive notion should play a role, comparable to that of thought and extension, as an intellectually transparent basic notion, in terms of which the mind–body interaction could be distinctly conceived and explained. But as I have tried to show, it is a mistake to regard the notion of the mind–body union as a basis for an *explanation* of this fact.[67]

I here side with Henri Gouhier and those who stress the prephilo-sophical character of the notion of the substantial union and the experience associated with it. In taking over this Scholastic notion, Descartes should not be seen as trying to incorporate a piece of the old philosophy into the new one, because what Descartes "retains from scholastic philosophy is precisely what has nothing philosophical," namely, the (brute) fact of interaction as we feel and understand it without being philosophers, such as when we reach out for bread when we feel hungry,[68] and, I want to add, whenever we act intention-ally. Gouhier insists that this immediate experience of interaction, which he calls "psycho-physiology," necessarily escapes a scientific ac-count, but he still thinks that Descartes's theory leaves room for a sci-ence of the relations between mental and bodily states.[69] What could such a "positive science" be? What we would have at best is a scientific (physiological) account of the bodily changes and movements con-comitant to mental states—like the one sketched out in *The Passions of the Soul*. It is difficult to see how there could be, in addition, a positive psycho-physiology of lawful correlations between kinds of mental states and bodily states, each of which can be described only in mutu-ally independent and irreducible terms. There can be no lawful corre-lations because the phenomena to be correlated, belonging to entirely different domains or contexts of description, are picked out and indi-viduated in incommensurable terms. Descartes's dualism, as Donald Davidson has justly noted, is an anomalous dualism.[70]

But doesn't Descartes himself attempt to give, in the second and third parts of *The Passions of the Soul*, a systematic classification of the mental states caused by bodily movements? Here, it has been suggested, we have the outline of a genuine science—at least in the broader sense of *Scientia* used in the early *Rules*. This classification does depend, to a large extent, on the third primitive notion, because the passions are defined as functions of the needs and ends of the human being as a mind-body union, and the principles of classification take this union as their starting point. The third primitive notion would thus constitute the origin "of a science corresponding, in the Cartesian system, to the nature of man."[71] This would, however, be a different use of *Scientia,* which leaves room for cognitions that have pragmatic value though they are less than fully certain. Descartes's distinction between moral and absolute certainty at the end of the *Principles of Philosophy* indicates he does accept knowledge that does not fulfill the requirement of being absolutely certain.[72]

Merleau-Ponty thinks that the notions introduced by Descartes in discussing the union are mythical in Plato's sense of the word: their function is to remind the listener that the philosophical analysis does not exhaust experience.[73] If Descartes was tempted to give a systematic classification of passions based on an analysis of their effects and pragmatic function, his classification is neither exhaustive nor definitive. And while he undoubtedly considered it useful for the mastery of passions, it is far from satisfying the rigor of a strictly scientific classification. Moreover, it is just a classification: a grouping together of various kinds of emotional states accompanying bodily movements based on assumptions about their utility. As such it might serve as a tentative starting point for a future scientific psychology or phenomenology, but there is no indication that Descartes held such enterprises to be possible, and much to indicate that he did not believe it.[74] This is not to say that Descartes did not attach a great value to the utility of his classification and physiology of the passions. The point I want to make is rather that Descartes did not base this value on the presumed scientific character of his investigations, but recognized the importance of these phenomena for our moral life in spite of the fact that they could not be included within the domains of clear and distinct science.

Because of its prephilosophical and, one might say, commonsense character, the third primary notion should not be considered as the model or origin of a third kind of knowledge, which differs from the knowledge obtained through the other primitive notions merely by virtue of the kind of evidence on which it is based (the evidence of senses as opposed to rational argument or mathematical demonstration). Rather, the domain of the third primitive notion is that of the awareness we have of our actual states and the "tacit knowledge" involved in daily experience and action. In the same way as to "know" or "understand" a mental state is just to have it or to be in that state, so to understand the mind–body interaction or the abilities intentional action involves is just to have sensations, to do things, to move one's limbs, to act, and to interact with other people. Far from constituting a system of beliefs that could be made explicit and justified, the phenomena pertaining to the third primitive notion consist in large part in the sum of abilities and skills we exercise as agents and members of a social community and in our responses to the situations and beings we interact with—in our being agents and in being conscious of our actual states. We describe these phenomena in ordinary language, using the terms and expressions of everyday language and common-sense psychology, but we can neither individuate nor account for them at other levels of description, for that would mean abstracting from the context of daily experience and interaction in which they occur and are identified. Nor can we render them clearer than they are as experienced, by metaphysical, logical, or neurophysiological investigations.

Consider, once more, the answer Descartes gave Princess Elisabeth. Such understanding, he declares, is best achieved by those who never philosophize but use only their senses.[75] Instead of seeing that as an attempt to explain away a difficulty Descartes could not solve, it can be seen as a recognition that our notion of the union of the mind and body belongs to commonsense psychology and cannot, as such, be rendered any clearer by logical or scientific analysis. It is not a philosophical or scientific concept, but a nontechnical notion, which "everyone has in himself without philosophizing." Anyone can feel "that he is a single person with both body and thought so related by nature that the thought can move the body and feel the things which happen to it."[76] Thought and extension are technical notions, serving specific epistemological and scientific purposes, whereas the notion we have of ourselves as human persons is a nontechnical, natural notion that cannot be explained in terms of these technical notions. While the latter are clear and distinct to the philosopher, the former is not, for its meaning can only be understood in the context of ordinary language and the nonphilosophical, extrascientific purposes that it serves. Like other concepts of ordinary language it is, we might say, logically primitive: it cannot be translated into technical (philosophical or scientific) terms without losing its original meaning.

Is this to say that Descartes had no real philosophical solution to the famous mind–body problem? As stated before, I take the real problem to be not the interaction but the conceivability of a substantial union between two entities that are known only through logically incompatible notions.[77] The difficulty is to understand how the notions of mind and body, or of thought and extension, as used in philosophical discourse, are related to the mind and body of commonsense psychology and everyday discourse. Does it make sense to suppose that we are talking of the *same* things here, conceived first as distinct from each other and then as united? And if not, then it is not clear that the notion of a mind–body union does any philosophical work. The question can be put in this way too: What entitles Descartes to retain the philosophical concept of substance composed of form and matter, which he has rejected in his science, in the account of what he considers to be everyday experience? The Aristotelian notion of an immaterial form or soul informing matter is not a plain commonsense notion in itself, and in redefining the notions of mind and matter and showing their independence, Descartes undermines whatever commonsense intuitions the Aristotelian notion of a living, ensouled body may have retained.

Descartes, however, was lucid enough to admit the inconceivability of the mind–body union, given his definition of these concepts, and thereby to recognize the limits of the knowledge we can acquire in terms of clear and distinct concepts. This insight, I want to stress, is not merely negative. Recognizing the limits of rational knowledge and explanation, Descartes at the same time acknowledged the cognitive value and importance of the sensations, feelings, and tacit beliefs involved in daily experience and action too often neglected by philosophers. This experience has its own practical value and cannot be replaced by any other kind of knowledge. It differs both in its nature and purposes from scientific knowledge and can therefore not be judged by the standards of the latter. One should never, as Aristotle reminds us, seek more precision or clarity than the subject matter admits of.[78]

The notion of a mind united to a physical body may be crude, incomplete, and even incoherent when judged by the standards of scientific knowledge. But that need not bother us as long as this and related concepts have a legitimate use in those extrascientific contexts where they are ordinarily applied. What is important is to recognize that they cannot be torn out of that context and used in scientific explanation without absurd results.[79]

If mental terms are vague and indeterminate when compared to scientific concepts, we nonetheless understand them well enough to be able to use them meaningfully in our daily lives and our dealings with other people. Even philosophers master the use of these concepts, but, as Malcolm observes, when they step into their study, they become as it were bewitched: "They no longer understand what they have always known. They no longer see what has always been plain in view" (ibid.). For my part, I think Descartes's advice to Princess Elisabeth to abstain from meditations and the study of mathematics, to turn instead to the domain of ordinary life and conversation in order to understand the mind–body union, should be taken quite seriously. It was given in the same spirit as the remark by Wittgenstein that Malcolm also quotes: "God grant the philosopher insight into what lies in front of everyone's eyes."[80]

8. The Limits of Cartesian Dualism

My aim here has not been to discuss the ontological and conceptual problems posed by Descartes's notion of a mind–body union as much as to draw attention to some neglected consequences of his distinction between the two. Among these is the recognition of the very limited character of the knowledge obtainable in terms of the concepts of thought and extension that Descartes takes to be basic for all clear and distinct, certain knowledge. Only what can be clearly and distinctly conceived qualifies as true science in Descartes's view, and since the mind–body union is inconceivable *per se*, what pertains to this union necessarily falls outside the domain of a *vera scientia*.

A recent commentator, while recognizing Descartes's distinctive notion of the mind–body union and its role in his account of human nature, stresses the deep tension this creates for Descartes's philosophy between what our reason and what our everyday experience tells us.

He sees the recourse to this notion as an expression, ultimately, of a failure to account for human nature in a dualistic framework.[81]

Descartes's acceptance of the mind–body union as a third primary notion, and its confinement to the domain of common sense and everyday experience where it belongs, need not necessarily be a failure for his project of *Scientia*. It is a failure, certainly, for those who seek a unitary physicalist explanation of nature, but for those who are more skeptical of the pretensions of physicalism, in particular when it is taken to require, as Descartes thinks it does, the reduction of natural phenomena to events fully accountable by mechanical laws, it is not a failure. Instead his doctrine of three primary notions can be welcomed as a healthy admission of the inability of metaphysics and physical sciences to account for everything we experience and have to deal with, and thereby also as a recognition of the role and value of other equally important domains of properly human experience.

The distinction between the three primitive notions does not oppose reason to experience, but includes experience within the jurisdiction of reason. Reason itself leads Descartes to distinguish different kinds and domains of cognition, and hence to distinguish what can be the object of a science meeting the criteria of clarity and distinctness that certain knowledge requires, and what cannot. The distinction between these notions results from Descartes's recognition both of the limits of what can count as *Scientia* meeting his requirements of certainty, and of the importance of the phenomena of our "life world" and our experience of it, which no mechanistic and quantitative science can replace or render more accurate. If that experience falls short of metaphysical certainty, it is reliable enough to qualify for the moral certainty we as finite and fallible human beings have to put up with. We must rely on what our finite "nature" and experience teaches us and accept that uncertainty and fallibility are part of the very nature of this experience and our human condition.

Descartes's three primary notions can thus be seen as giving equal weight to independent areas of knowledge with objects, purposes, and standards of their own, none of which should be given ontological or epistemological primacy. When tensions arise, it is because these differences are not recognized, and concepts, techniques, and methods from one of the domains of certain science—metaphysics or mechanistic physics—are given prevalence over the others.

3

Thought,
Consciousness,
and Language

This chapter discusses Descartes's notion of thinking and the general criteria common to the various mental phenomena that he classifies as modes of thought. One of Descartes's most influential "innovations" is his redefinition of the notion of mind in terms of thought to cover not merely the acts of the pure intellect but any conscious states or acts, from the will and imagination to emotions and sense perceptions. The common and distinctive feature of these different "modes of thought" is the awareness accompanying them: they qualify as thoughts only insofar as they are consciously perceived.[1] "Soul" *(anima)*, "mind" *(mens)* and "thought" *(cogitatio)* are for Descartes different names of the same thing, and the generic feature that sets the soul or mind apart from nonmental or thoughtless things seems to be "consciousness" or "awareness."[2] Descartes, moreover, uses "idea" or "perception" coextensively with "thought" to refer both to the act and the object of awareness. A thought or idea in the widest sense can be anything from the acts and objects of intuition or pure intellect (which can be simple ideas or propositions) to sensations, emotions, and volitions.[3]

For better or worse, Descartes's emphasis on conscious awareness in defining thought or the mental has put a new topic on the agenda of philosophical psychology, which raises many problems that his followers—critics or allies—are still struggling to solve or eliminate. Although, as it turns out, consciousness is not prominent in Descartes's own discussions of the mental, I will start by reflecting on its role and relation to other general features which have been seen as central to his new concept of thinking. Sections 2 and 3 of this chapter take a close look at attempts to define Descartes's concept of thought in terms of propositional content and the problems this poses for treating (as Descartes clearly does) nonpropositional sensations as modes of thought. Section 4 discusses two proposals for taking the Cartesian notion of thought as a forerunner of computational views of thinking, and section 5 considers important aspects of awareness that the "computational" and "representational" views of mind leave out. My aim in these sections is to show that thinking, in Descartes's sense, involves many kinds of abilities and is too complex a phenomenon to be captured by any single property or cluster of properties. In the last section of this chapter I consider the analogy between thought and language and suggest that Cartesian thought, although it does not presuppose language, is like it in belonging to a logical and normative space of reasons. That space is essentially common and public even though Descartes, because of his focus on the individual thinker, notoriously neglects its social dimensions. If this is right, the properties most essential to thought—those that cannot be explained by the powers of matter—belong to a logical or conceptual order rather than to a psychological or metaphysical order: they are normative rather than descriptive. This also provides a more fruitful perspective for approaching the question about the intentionality of Cartesian thought discussed in Chapter 4.

1. Mind and Consciousness

Although Descartes's terms "mind," "thought," "idea," and "perception" cut across the distinctions of traditional faculty psychology, he retains the traditional division of psychic acts. The Cartesian mind, in other words, has the power to perform all those different functions that traditionally were explained by reference to different faculties (different kinds of soul). The faculties are replaced by a classification of modes of thought that corresponds to the traditional classification: intellect (or reason), will, imagination, memory, sensation, and passions (or emotions). The main difference between Descartes's philosophy of mind and medieval theories based on Aristotelian psychology is elsewhere, namely, in his redrawing of the border between the mental and the physical and in his insistence on the radical difference between what belongs to the mind and to the body. While Aristotelian dualists within the Scholastic tradition drew a line between the intellect and the senses, seeing the latter as directly dependent on the corporeal organs and having particular sensible things (not universal forms) as their objects, Descartes sees the acts of sensing, together with emotional states and passions, as modes of thought and hence as nonphysical. He holds that the intellect and the will alone count as "pure" thoughts, in that they depend on the mind alone, whereas the imagination, the memory, the sensations, and the passions are functions of the mind–body union and require the stimulation of bodily organs.[4] Although the latter depend causally on the mind–body union and on the action of animal spirits in the neural system and the brain, they are modes of thought and belong therefore to the mind, not to the body.

This means that Descartes rejects the traditional view that the pure intellect and the corporeal senses are separate faculties: sensations too, though inessential to self as a purely thinking thing, are modes of thinking and are said to involve some intellectual act in their very definition or "formal concept" (AT VII 78, CSM II 54). If the acts of the intellect or will are called "pure thoughts," all the others are mixed or composite body-dependent thoughts, which Descartes himself calls "confused thoughts." The question is what the so-called pure thoughts of the intellect have in common with the mixed modes of thought: Why does Descartes classify the body-dependent psychic functions as *thoughts* along with the pure thoughts of the intellect, which alone count as thoughts in the traditional sense of the term? His answer is that they involve some kind of intellection, but is this intellectual activity merely a matter of conscious awareness or is there some further feature by virtue of which a sensorial-*cum*-neural event comes to qualify as an intellectual (cognitive) act?

The short answer, which clearly will not do, is that it is an ontological matter: having thought is seen as a matter of being a thinking rather than extended substance, as if the ontological difference between two kinds of substance were *the explanation* of why mental phenomena are different from physical—as if dualism were the explanation for why thought is irreducible to matter! In fact it is the other way around: dualism imposes itself because the concept of body with which Descartes is stuck (given his definition of matter in terms of extension and his commitment to a mechanistic science of all nature) leaves no room for a coherent description or account of the phenomena he attributes to mind. It is because mind or thought cannot be explained by the powers of matter that he is driven to postulate another kind of substance. But if the appeal to a distinct kind of substance leaves room for phenomena that do not fit into the mechanistic pattern of explanation, it does not by itself explain anything and in fact creates more problems than it solves.

In considering the phenomena Descartes includes under his broad notion of "thought," I want to look at features they have in common other than being "attributed to the mind." Of these, consciousness or awareness is the first to consider because it is the one most generally associated with the so-called modern, Cartesian notion of mind or thought, and it alone seems broad enough to cover the whole range of phenomena characterized as thoughts. What, then, does awareness— being immediately conscious of something—involve for Descartes, and what is it about awareness that prevents it from being accounted for "by the powers of matter" alone (AT VI 59, CSM I 141)?

Consciousness is a notoriously obscure concept. In contemporary discussions, it is often taken to be *the* paradigmatic mental phenomenon and treated as the central subject matter of philosophy of mind. It is widely assumed that there is a clear distinction between intentionality and consciousness, where the former is a matter of propositional attitudes that, understood as functional states in the brain, can be handled by mechanistic models of explanation, whereas the latter cannot, and remain a mystery for the philosophy of mind and cognitive science. Consciousness, considered as inner, private experience, is problematic for any theory, and all the more so for materialist theories of mind that take the spatial metaphor of innerness literally and confine the phenomena of consciousness to events occurring in the brain. But, as argued in Chapter 2, this picture of an inner realm of consciousness offering itself to introspection belongs not to Descartes's own doctrine but to the "Myth of the Cartesian Myth" cultivated in the empiricist tradition.

The term "consciousness" as used in contemporary discussions of "qualia" or "what it is to be x" is only remotely connected to Descartes's use of the term "being conscious" *(conscius)* of something. The latter term appears in fact only once in the *Meditations,* though it is used, as we have seen, in the Replies to the Objections. The term "consciousness" *(conscientia)* does not occur in the *Meditations* at all and only rarely elsewhere in the Cartesian corpus, where it is mostly used in the sense of immediate knowledge or awareness. In Descartes's own view, awareness is a mark of thought or the mental but not constitutive of it. There are other more important and interesting features of Cartesian thought that (because of the empiricist fixation on inner experience) have been neglected: its connection with speech, its capacity for conceptualization, its intentional or representational nature, and its power of judging, where the last comes closest to constituting the very essence of thinking as Descartes understands it. It involves the capacity to distinguish the true from the false, but also the power to assent or deny, pursue or avoid, which the Fourth Meditation ascribes to the will and which is the basis of our commitment to truth and responsibility to avoid error. Consciousness may be a precondition for these capacities and powers, but they clearly go beyond it, and it is precisely what goes beyond immediate awareness that is interesting in Descartes's concepts of mind and thinking.

The question is frequently raised by interpreters whether Descartes wants to assert that the terms "thought" and "consciousness" actually are synonyms.[5] That would account for his extension of "thought" to include mental states that, like feelings and sensations, are conscious states but are not, in any ordinary use of the term, thoughts. The equation of the terms "thought" and "consciousness" is, however, problematic for more reasons than one. Thought includes innate ideas, which are plausibly understood as innate conceptual *capacities*. Though we are actually aware of the present acts of our mind, we are only potentially aware of its powers and faculties. Descartes clearly leaves room for thoughts of which we are only potentially conscious in declaring that people often do not know what they believe (AT VI 23, CSM I 122). Moreover, although he agrees that "it is self-evident there can be nothing in the mind, in so far as it is a thinking thing, of which it is not aware" (AT VII 246, CSM II 171), he immediately qualifies this by pointing out that "we cannot have any thought of which we are not aware at the very moment when it is in us," but since many thoughts are not retained in memory, we are not aware of them. We can have thousands of thoughts in an hour, and countless thoughts that occur while we are sleeping, or even at the fetal stage, that we cannot remember having ever noticed.[6] This seems to call for a very attenuated sense

of consciousness, one that has room both for perceptions that go unnoticed because they leave no memory traces, and perceptions that
are so slight and obscure that, even if they leave their traces and continue to affect us by association with other perceptions, cannot be
distinctly remembered or called to attention.[7] They have more in
common with Leibniz's *petites perceptions* than with the paradigmatic
clear and distinct Cartesian thoughts. Moreover, since the notion of
"thought" is a simple notion that cannot be defined, it is clear one
should avoid invoking consciousness as a definition of thought. I
therefore take "thought" and "consciousness" to have different meanings for Descartes, and will treat "consciousness" or "immediate awareness" as a mark by which mental acts and states qualifying as thoughts
are recognized and distinguished from other acts and states.

Taking consciousness to be a defining feature of thought would turn
thinking into a wholly private, hidden affair. If having thoughts is a
matter of "inner" or "private" experience, the recognition of thoughts
and hence of minds in other beings becomes problematical. So would
the distinction between different kinds of thought, because clearness
and distinctness, on which the distinction turns, would become a matter of mere inner, subjective awareness—a matter of how a thought is
immediately perceived by a subject.[8]

Although Descartes clearly thinks the various phenomena that he
ranges under his wide notion of thought are or can be matters of immediate awareness, it is not the only criterion for thinking. The surest
(external) sign that something is thinking, according to him, is the capacity of using speech or language; indeed, the capacity to use language is, in some contexts, presented as the *only* certain sign of thinking.[9] Whether and to what extent do these two criteria—the internal
and the external—overlap? Is what we are inwardly aware of always
something that could be expressed through speech acts? The question
of what awareness involves leads to the question of how language,
speech, and thought are related.

2. Propositional Thoughts and Sensations

It surely would be a mistake to conclude from the fact that language
is not explicitly mentioned by Descartes as a prerequisite of thought
that he does not regard thought and language as essentially intercon-

nected. The evidence that a thing is thinking is not only that it talks—parrots can talk—but that it has "real speech" of the kind humans have, which involves the capacity "of indicating by word or sign something pertaining to pure thought and not natural impulse."[10] The mere expression of their "natural impulses of anger, fear, hunger and so on" that even dumb animals can communicate by their voices or bodily movements is not sufficient. It is the capacity of using and understanding conventional signs that is the decisive evidence of thought or reason.

The movements occasioning sensations and passions occur mechanically in both animals and humans; it is only insofar as they are accompanied by thought that there are conscious sensations or passions, that is, modes of thought in Descartes's sense of the word.[11] But what is it that has to be, as it were, added on to the mere mechanical movements that account for life and sensation in animals in order for there to be conscious sensation and thought of the human kind? Does it make sense to suppose that there is some single feature or set of features that explains the difference between human and animal sensation and hence accounts for thought?

Descartes takes thought to be causally and logically prior to speech and considers the latter as the instrument or medium for expressing the former. Does this mean that the structure of language or speech reflects the structure of the thoughts it is used to convey?[12] Both involve representation, but in different ways: thoughts represent immediately, speech by means of external, public signs or symbols. It is difficult to account for what it is to think of something without using the analogue of speech and language. To what extent can the Cartesian notion of thought be clarified through such analogies?

The view that thoughts are propositional is popular in contemporary philosophy. It has also been attributed to Descartes, because like the defenders of this view he makes a distinction between two aspects of thought: the mental act or attitude on the one hand, and its object or representational content on the other. The distinction, in Cartesian terms, is between the idea taken materially, as an operation of the intellect, and the idea taken objectively, as the thing represented by that operation (AT VII 8, CSM II 7). This parallel has led some authors to suggest that a Cartesian thought or idea is a propositional content, which can be entertained in various modes. To think would be to have a propositional thought or, more properly, to have a propositional attitude. Norman Malcolm goes so far as to claim that Descartes's distinction between the mental and the physical is "*defined* by the presence or absence of propositional content."[13]

The suggestion is worth considering because it would explain, among other things, why Descartes defended the infamous and counterintuitive doctrine that brutes cannot think: lacking the capacity for real speech, animals also lack the capacity of thinking—that is, they do not have propositional thoughts. But Descartes's argument that brutes cannot think has also been taken to reveal a fundamental inconsistency in his use of the term "thought": the term, it is said, equivocates between two senses of conscious states—a wide sense covering both propositional thoughts and nonpropositional feelings or sensations, and a narrow sense restricted to the former—and it is because of this equivocation that Descartes failed to recognize that although they lack propositional thought animals have conscious feelings and sensations and hence some kind of mental life.[14]

But there are reservations to be made about such readings. First, it cannot be taken for granted that the distinction between act and object is applicable, at least not without strong qualifications, to all kinds of thoughts. Mental acts or states can be conscious thoughts without having any specific object at all—moods and some emotional states, for instance. Second, it takes for granted that Cartesian ideas (or the objective reality by virtue of which they represent) are propositional— but there is no textual evidence that the representative content of ideas is, for Descartes, always or essentially propositional. The definition of thought in terms of propositional content would, moreover, commit Descartes to an overly intellectualistic view of the mental that does not do justice to the complexity of his view of our mental life, which is best brought out by a closer inspection of the reasons he gives for why brutes cannot think.

The best and most certain evidence that there is a significant difference between humans and beasts is the human capacity for language. This, as Descartes explains in a letter to More, is not due to a difference in the organs, nor is it a matter of learning or of communicating natural impulses or feelings, which many animals can do without difficulty. The expression of feelings and passions can be achieved by the mere "machinery of the body," like the wagging of the dog's tail or, in humans, by the various facial expressions and gestures or motions of our limbs accompanying our passions (described in Descartes's late treatise of the *Passions*). It is a matter instead of "using real speech," which involves "a capacity of indicating by a word or a sign something relating to thought alone and not to natural impulse."[15]

It is worth noting that in writing this, Descartes is less sanguine about the claim that animals cannot think than he was at the time of writing the *Discourse* and the Replies to the Objections to his *Meditations*.[16] He is speaking, he stresses, of *thought,* of the functions attributed to the rational soul, not of those traditionally explained by postulating other, lower kinds of soul like life and sensation. "I do not deny life of animals, since I regard it as consisting simply in the heat of the heart; *and I do not even deny sensation, insofar as it depends on a bodily organ*" (AT V 278, CSMK 366, my emphasis).[17] He even admitted to Henry More that it cannot be proved that animals cannot think:

> [T]hough I regard it as established that we cannot prove there is any thought in animals, I do not think it is thereby proved that there is not, since the human mind does not reach into their hearts. But when I investigate what is most probable in this matter, I see no argument for animals having thoughts except the fact that since they have eyes, ears, tongues, and other sense-organs like ours, it seems likely that they have sensation *like us;* and since *thought is included in our mode of sensation,* similar thought seems to be attributable to them. (To More, February 1649 (AT V 276–277, CSMK 365), emphasis mine)

It is thus by analogy that we (wrongly) attribute thought and the human mode of sensation to animals. But, Descartes insists, we have strong (theological) reasons for believing that animals do not have thoughts,[18] and to the extent that they lack thought, whatever sensation they have is different from human sensation.

Many contemporary philosophers would agree that there is a sense of thought in which brutes cannot think, namely, thought as propositional. But they would also think it is a mistake to reduce, as Descartes has been taken to do, all forms of conscious or mental life to this restricted notion of thought. Zeno Vendler insists that there are other kinds of states that are mental although they do not have propositional content and do not qualify as thoughts in the proper sense of the word.[19] Sensations, feelings, imaginations, headaches, mental pictures, moods, melodies, and so on are, according to this contemporary use of the term, not modes of thinking; rather they are conscious, non-propositional states, some of which also occur in animals.

Descartes, undoubtedly, would agree that those mental acts that have a propositional structure are thoughts, though he did not use this terminology. The examples he gives of "pure thoughts" are either concepts, principles, or common notions, some of which are propositional while others are what we could call subpropositional thoughts, because, although expressed by a simple term (for instance, "triangle," "substance," "wax"), their content can be spelled out in propositions. I will hereafter speak of thoughts in this restricted sense as *propositional thought*. But Descartes would not agree that only propositional thoughts count as thoughts in the primary sense of the word, since he deliberately extends the term "thought" to all conscious acts or states.[20] (On the other hand he does not, as Vendler takes him to, identify thought with consciousness.)

In his discussion of the Cartesian notion of thinking, Norman Malcolm agrees with Vendler that only humans or language users are capable of propositional thought, but he does not think that propositional thoughts are paradigms of all kinds of thinking.[21] Nor does he think there is any ambiguity or confusion in Descartes's use of "thought." He criticizes Descartes for the generalization of an extremely narrow concept of thought to a paradigm of all thinking, arguing that Descartes failed to see that the verb "to think" is used in many ways and that it is wider than the concept to "have thoughts" in the propositional sense. Descartes's mistake lay in his deliberately adopted and consistently held view that all conscious mental events, sensations included, are propositional.[22]

It cannot be true, however, that Descartes distinguishes the animal mode of sensation from human sensation by the absence of propositional content, because he holds that human sensation is also a form of nonpropositional thinking. Descartes is not guilty of Vendler's charge that he confuses thought in the narrow sense of propositional thought with consciousness. Vendler may, however, be right that Descartes's *argument* that brutes cannot think equivocates between different senses of "to think," so that if it proves anything, it proves that animals cannot think only in a very restricted sense of thinking. I have no wish to defend that argument, but we might ask what it was supposed to prove? Showing that ants and flies have no reward or punishment to look forward to after this life was not, I gather, Descartes's main concern. What, then, *is* the point of it? To argue that animals are just mechanically moving devices is one thing. To say that the vital and psychic functions of animals can be mechanistically explained, whereas human thinking cannot, is another. Both claims are disputable, though there certainly is more to be said in defense of the second than the first.[23] Descartes, I take it, was more interested in defending the latter, and it is as such that his argument still is interesting. Before exploring his argument that the human capacity of thinking is not amenable to a mechanistic account, I want to examine more carefully what Descartes says about the human mode of sensation.

3. Sensory Awareness and Perceptual Judgments

What is it that has to be, as it were, added on to the mere mechanical movements that account for life, sensation, and instinctive reactions in animals in order for there to be *conscious* sensation (thought) of the human kind?[24] Let us look at a famous passage in the Sixth Replies, where Descartes gives an interesting account of sense perception and distinguishes three grades of certainty in the senses:

> The first is limited to the immediate stimulation of the bodily organs by external objects; this can consist in nothing but the motion of the particles of the organs, and any change of shape and position resulting from this motion. The second grade comprises all the immediate effects produced in the mind *as a result of its being united with a bodily organ which is affected in this way.* Such effects include the perceptions of pain, pleasure, thirst, hunger, colours, sound, taste, smell, heat, cold and the like, *which arise from the union and as it were intermingling of mind and body,* as explained in the Sixth Meditation. The third grade includes all the judgements about things outside us which we have been accustomed to make from our earliest years—judgements which are occasioned by the movements of these bodily organs. (AT VII 436–437, CSM II 294; emphasis mine)

Sense perception, at the third grade, includes judgment. But judgment, according to Descartes, depends on the intellect and the will, and judgments are carried out on propositions: they are "propositional attitudes." In order to involve judgment, therefore, sense perception has to be propositional: the act of sensing or its content must have propositional form. This is also assumed in Vendler's and Malcolm's interpretations. But at which stage does it become propositional?

Clearly not at the first grade, which includes nothing else but the mechanical movements of the nerves and the animal spirits resulting from the stimulation by the bodily organs. What about the second grade? What are these states of mind "intervening" between mechanical movements and judgment that are propositional attitudes?

This level includes nothing else than the immediate perception (or experience) of the affections or states of mind produced by the stimulation of the organs and nerves of the body and by the brain movements they cause. The objects of immediate perception are not corporeal movements, but sense qualities: colors, light, sounds, shapes, and the like. The states of mind caused by the movements in the brain are different kinds of states of awareness: sensations of various shades of light, of colors, shapes, smells, and feelings of cold, heat, pain, pleasure, thirst, hunger, and so on are produced by the bodily movements that result from stimulation of the sense organs, without there being anything in these movements resembling the different qualities or feelings perceived.

> When I see a stick, it should not be supposed that certain "intentional forms" fly off the stick towards the eye, but simply that rays of light are reflected off the stick and set up certain movements in the optic nerve and, via the optic nerve, in the brain, as I have explained at some length in the *Optics*. This movement in the brain, which is common to us and the brutes, is the first grade of sensory perception *(sentiment)*. This leads to the second grade, which extends only to the perception of the colour and light reflected from the stick; it arises from the fact that the mind is so intimately conjoined with the body that it is affected by the movements which occur in it. Nothing more than this should be referred to the sensory faculty *(ad sensum)*, if we wish to distinguish it carefully from the intellect. (AT VII 437, CSM II 295) [25]

The brain movements are described elsewhere as the last or proximate causes of the sensory ideas, which are their immediate effects and which Descartes takes to be affections of the mind. Strictly speaking, however, the relationship between physical movements and mental events cannot be causal—at least not an instance of mechanical causation—because no movement or form can be communicated from the physical body to the immaterial mind. Their connection, instituted by God, is that of sign to signification: thus the patterns or movements of animal spirits in the brain function as signals to the mind to which the mind responds by having certain sensations (AT VII 88, CSM II 60), and these sensations—we are now speaking of sensations in the strict sense, that is, sensations at the second grade—are themselves imbued with meanings. They convey information about the mind–body union, about how it is affected by and related to surrounding external bodies acting on its senses.[26]

Vendler reads Descartes's distinction between three grades of sensation as an account of three subsequent levels or stages in sense perception: physiological states, "raw" sensations or sense data, and judgments (objective or subjective) consequent to these sensations. He interprets the distinction between the second and the third level in terms of absence versus presence of propositional content.[27] But how, one wonders, can there be judgments about nonpropositional "raw" sensations or sense data? Such data, it would seem, have first to be somehow conceptualized in order to become objects of judgments.[28]

For Descartes, the immediate mental perception occasioned by a change of physiological state already involves some intellection or understanding that cannot be had by animals, which means that only the physiology of sensation is shared by humans and animals. Nevertheless, this immediate mental perception does not involve perceptual judgments, because judgment depends on the intellect and is referred to a separate, third grade of sense perception. While Vendler agrees that this third grade of sensation is lacking in animals, because they do not have the capacity of forming perceptual judgments, unlike Descartes he thinks that animals, as well as humans, have what he calls "raw sensations," which are mental or conscious insofar as they are felt or experienced. Thus, Vendler argues, the human mode of consciousness differs from the animal mode in involving the capacity to have propositional thoughts and form perceptual judgments, and this is what Descartes, if he were consistent, would have to say.

Malcolm, by contrast, takes Descartes's claim that the human mode of sensation includes thought to mean that "at the center of every sensation of ours there is a proposition." On this view, the propositional content of a sensation of heat in the second grade is expressed by the sentence "It seems to me that I feel heat," that of pain by "I feel pain,"[29] and the confusion involved in these mixed thoughts is a conceptual confusion, like that involved in attributing location to a sensation (for example, of pain) that properly should be viewed as a mode of thought, which cannot have any spatial attributes. Descartes held that "every 'mental operation' consists in taking an attitude towards a proposition," which Malcolm rightly characterizes as "an absurdly overintellectualized view of the life of man."[30] Such a view allows for no distinction between what belongs to the sense faculty strictly speaking and what depends on the intellect, and hence rules out an intervening second grade of sensation. It reduces sensations *qua* modes of thought to perceptual judgments. But Cartesian sensations can be reduced neither to propositional attitudes nor to mere "raw sensations."

The distinctions drawn in the passage I have quoted from the Sixth Replies should not be understood as a descriptive account of separate stages in the genesis of sensation. It is an analysis of grades of sense undertaken for epistemological purposes to separate the clearly known from the confused and uncertain in sensory perception. Sensations do not come to the mind as isolated raw sensations—as "pure sensations" in the strict sense of the word given above. They come in batches and are perceived in a context of many other sensations and habitual beliefs or opinions. They also come, at the third grade of sense perception, with implicit (unnoticed) "judgments" about their external causes that in fact depend on the intellect, not on the senses:

> [S]uppose that, *as a result of being affected by this sensation of colour,* I judge that a stick, located outside me, is coloured; and suppose that on the basis of the extension of the colour and its boundaries together with its position in relation to the parts of the brain, I make a rational calculation about the size, shape and distance of the stick: although such reasoning is commonly assigned to the senses (which is why I have here referred it to the third grade of sense perception), *it is clear that it depends solely on the intellect.* (AT VII 437, CSM II 295; emphasis mine)

There are two things to be noticed here. First, perceptual judgments—the judgments normally involved in sense perception—are judgments about *external* objects, about the things affecting our senses, not about the act of sensing itself. Second, they are generally unnoticed, which is why they are commonly attributed to the senses: they have been made long ago (in early childhood), and they normally occur so fast that we do not distinguish them from simple sense perception (ibid.). But they depend on the intellect, even when, as they usually are, unnoticed.[31]

Descartes holds that the linking of bodily movements with thoughts belongs to the second grade of sense perception, which therefore is lacking in animals. The movements of particles in the organs and the brain do not qualify as sensations unless they are linked with thoughts. But the thoughts they immediately trigger are not propositional: they are not of the form I hear or feel *p,* or that *p.* Descartes's view is that sensations affect the mind and are, automatically as it were, connected with unnoticed judgments, which do involve conceptual activity and are propositional. They are not, however, judgments about the sense perceptions themselves but about the external thing taken to cause those perceptions, and it is not their being linked with judgments that makes sense perceptions conscious, since judgments do not occur at the second grade. The perceptual judgments involved in the third grade are caused or occasioned by the sensory affections of the second grade. The physiological changes brought about by the stimulations of the senses, which belong to the first grade and are shared by brutes and humans, must first be brought to awareness by affecting the mind at the second grade—by affecting it so as to make it form various ideas and judgments. The judgments of the third grade are then the mind's immediate response to the felt affection.

Sensations (the colors, smells, sounds, and so on) are more or less clearly experienced states (ideas) of the conscious subject, which directly affect her behavior and thinking, triggering responses of various kinds, including the immediate perceptual judgments about their assumed external (or internal) causes. Their obscurity and confusion (their lack of distinctness) may cause but is not reducible to conceptual mistakes or false beliefs. On the contrary, the confusion of sensations and emotions is irreducible and belongs (as argued in Chapter 2) to their very nature as thoughts depending on the body. For although inessential to the mind as a purely thinking thing, they are essential to the human mode of thinking; they constitute our thinking as *human,* as opposed to the angelic or divine thinking of pure intellects, and they have their proper function in serving our needs as human beings. Instead of dichotomizing propositional thought and nonpropositional conscious states (like the sense data of empiricist theories), Descartes's account recognizes intermediate states between brute sensations and intellectual judgments, and what is common to these states is not the brute fact that they are felt but that they are felt thus and so, causing or, as Descartes says, occasioning determinate judgments.

The judgments triggered at the third level of sense perception are of various kinds—and calling them judgments may not be appropriate in all cases. Third-level intellectual activity includes automatic, habitual associations by which complex ideas and beliefs that are not the fruit of reflective judgments (involving voluntary assent) are formed.[32] Through their immediate association with earlier formed judgments and beliefs, sensory perceptions of the second grade give rise to spontaneous takings of something as such and so, takings that can also be expressed directly in behavioral reactions and dispositions without being noticed at the conscious level. Far from being discrete and brute raw feelings, human sensations are informed: they come to our conscious attention with and because of the informational content they carry. Descartes himself compares them to signs that we—as embodied minds—spontaneously interpret (a topic I return to in Chapter 5).

4. Human Thought and Artificial Intelligence

Because Descartes holds that thinking, unlike other functions of a living body, cannot be explained mechanistically, his argument that brutes cannot think is equivalent to an argument that machines cannot think. Although Descartes had no difficulty comparing animals and living organisms generally to machines (he introduced and vigorously defended the view that living organisms are machines and that life is a purely mechanical phenomenon),[33] the idea of mechanical reasoning or artificial intelligence was for him a nonstarter. The decisive difference between a machine and a real thinker is that only the latter has a capacity for speech or symbolic behavior of the kind humans are capable of. But what is so special about (human) language use and what does it show that the behavior of any mechanism fails to show?

Even if a machine could be constructed to utter words corresponding to bodily changes in its organ, it could "never use spoken words or other signs composing them as we do to declare our thoughts to others" because

> [I]t is not conceivable that the machine should arrange its words so as *to respond to the sense of whatever is said* in its presence, as the dullest of men can do. Secondly, even though such machines might do some things as well as we do them, or perhaps even better, they would inevitably fail in others, which would reveal that they were not acting through understanding *(connaissance)* but only from the disposition of their organs. For whereas reason is a universal instrument which can be used in all kinds of situations, these organs need some particular disposition for each particular action; hence it is morally impossible to have enough different ones in a machine *to make it act in all the contingencies of life in the way our reason makes us act.* (AT VI 57–58, CSM I 140; my emphasis)

The human capacities to which Descartes draws attention here and that he thinks no machine could have are: (1) the capacity to use linguistic and other signs to express thoughts and to give appropriate responses to meaningful speech, and (2) the capacity to act intelligently or rationally in all sorts of (new and unexpected) situations. The first could be called "symbolic behavior" and is, I take it, a special case of the second, more general capacity for rational behavior.

What does this capacity consist of? I will consider two interesting answers, both of which see Descartes's views of thought and reason as anticipating ideas that have been recently influential in artificial intelligence and cognitive science.

Noam Chomsky takes the quoted passage to show that the distinctive features of thought are those manifested in the "creative aspect of ordinary language use—its property of being both unbounded in scope and stimulus-free."[34] It should be noted that automatic behavior and animal behavior can be unbounded without being stimulus free and that it is the freedom from stimulus control that accounts for the appropriateness to new situations that Descartes stresses.[35] This creativity is characteristic of human language, and it is because he could not account for it mechanistically that Descartes was led to postulate a thinking substance.[36] According to Chomsky, modern studies of animal communication have not offered counterevidence to Descartes's assumption that human language is based on an entirely distinct principle, nor has modern linguistics dealt with his observations about language in a serious way.[37]

For Chomsky the main lessons to be learned from the "Cartesian" tradition in linguistics are the idea of an innate, universal grammar and the idea that the study of the structure of this grammar (the "deep structure") will reveal the structure of thought or mind.[38] Instead of appealing to a mysterious immaterial substance as the creative principle, modern "Cartesian" linguistics has proceeded to explore the deep structures of processes in the brain (transformational generative grammar and combinatorial semantics) that account for the creativeness of human speech. This idea of an underlying, predetermined, (and hidden) deep structure of the brain/mind has become the leading idea of what in contemporary cognitive science is known as the "representational theory of mind." It assumes that the exploration of the internal deep structure regulating the workings of the brain in producing symbolic behavior will ultimately answer our questions concerning the origin of linguistic meaning and linguistic creativity.

John Haugeland discusses Descartes's argument that brutes or machines cannot think in light of the general question of what makes an utterance or a symbolic structure meaningful. If linguistic and other symbols are meaningful insofar as they express thoughts, how is it that thoughts themselves come to have meaning or to represent? This is, roughly, the problem Haugeland calls the problem of "original meaning," and he takes the new model of representation introduced with Descartes's mathematical notation to provide an important and original answer to it.[39] Haugeland suggests that this new abstract model of representation can also be seen at work in Descartes's notion of thought—even though he may not have recognized it explicitly. Descartes extended the new mathematical model of representation to all scientific problems,[40] but it can be applied more widely, Haugeland argues, to *meaning in general.* The idea is that anything that can convey or have meaning, including in particular *thoughts in the mind,* represent basically in the same way as the terms and figures used in the solution of a mathematical problem represent the things they are taken to stand for. The representativeness or meaning of thoughts (what Haugeland calls "original meaning") could hence be understood in terms of problem solving or computation performed on a system of symbolic notation.

Perhaps Descartes did anticipate this new and important idea, which

frees the notion of representation from that of image likeness and resemblance. For what makes a given formal notation *symbolic,* that is,
what makes it suitable for *representing* a certain subject matter, is nothing other than the fact that it can be used to solve problems about it.
Not, of course, just any problems, for the notation in question has to
form an integrated system that can be used systematically and reliably
in a well-defined domain or area, which means that it has to include
also *rules* specifying which steps are allowed in the given context.[41] To
say something reasonable, or to respond appropriately to the sense of
what is said, would, in light of this reading, be to say something that is
determined by "the rules of reasoning." Haugeland concludes that
Descartes's test, in the passage from the *Discourse* quoted above, anticipates not only the talking Toyota but also the Turing test, and what he
says is essentially "that machines can't think (or talk sensibly . . .) *because* they can't manipulate symbols rationally."[42]

This conclusion, however, seems too quick. If we follow Haugeland
in interpreting the Cartesian notion of thought as essentially some
kind of rational, rule-governed problem solving, we must agree that
Descartes's pessimism concerning thinking machines has been proved
ungrounded. For what else is a Turing machine than a device capable
of automatic, rule-governed computation or problem solving? We
could then also praise Descartes (or blame him) for having inspired—
in spite of himself as it were—a leading idea of contemporary thought-
technology, which takes the computer analogy seriously enough to believe that thinking *is* a mechanical computational process and that it is
only a matter of storing the right amount of information and imple-
menting the right inference rules to have a machine that can pass the
test for thought, which Descartes did not believe any mechanical device could ever pass.

But such a reading, however ingenious, attributes a much too simplified and narrowly rationalistic view of thinking and representation
to Descartes. The kind of automatic, rule-governed computation or
symbol processing that a Turing machine instantiates and that can be
performed by electronic computers would not count as thinking in
Descartes's sense; nor would the mechanical operations of a computer
or robot, no matter how ingenious or intelligent, count as rational behavior as he understands it. Not only is such a view of thinking too narrow, it is based on precisely the kind of category mistake that Ryle at-

tributes to the Cartesians but that Descartes himself (as argued in Chapter 2) is not guilty of: explaining thought in terms of concepts and models analogous to those applicable only to extension and its modes.

Even if Descartes would not have accepted the idea of mechanical, artificial intelligence or reasoning, he may still be considered an important forerunner of contemporary cognitivist and computational views of the mind. A basic assumption of cognitivism is that the study of cognitive systems is a natural and relatively autonomous domain of research.[43] This assumption is rooted in the view that the essence of the mind is rational thinking and that rational thought or cognition can be studied independently of other phenomena, like sensations and emotions that Descartes classified as body-dependent mental phenomena, to which contemporary philosophers of mind refer as "consciousness," and which they do not consider as essential to thinking or cognition in their sense of the word.[44] Although Descartes's argument for the real distinction divides pure thought from body-dependent thoughts, it is not fair to trace the roots of the contemporary wedge between thought and consciousness to him. Cartesian thinking is reducible neither to a narrowly understood rational capacity nor to consciousness. Without identifying them, he clearly regarded consciousness—reflexive awareness—as a necessary condition for thought. Having proved the possibility of disembodied thought, Descartes showed no interest in the pure, angelic form of thinking, except for the purpose of contrasting it to the phenomenon of embodied, human thought. Sensations, feelings, and emotions are thoughts, and even though they are not essential to thinking in the restricted sense of the word, they are essential to human nature and, as I will argue, to human reason too. As body-dependent thoughts they connect the human thinker to the environment she needs in order to survive.

It may seem a short step from Descartes's metaphorical talk about thought hidden in the body or the mind acting in some particular location in the brain to contemporary literal talk about mental processes as computational activity (symbol manipulation) in the brain. But it depends on a series of moves that Descartes himself was hardly prepared to make. Descartes would not have accepted the mechanical application of rules on syntactic structures as a sufficient condition for *rational* symbol manipulation, or indeed, rational discourse. Even on the (unlikely) assumption that he would have subscribed to a generalized idea of meaning and representation in terms of rule-governed problem solving, the choice and application of rules still presupposes an ability to understand both the problems and what counts as a relevant solution in various meaning contexts, and that is not a mere matter of computational capacity.[45]

It comes as no surprise that the first among Descartes's followers to move in the required direction was the materialist Hobbes, who did not hesitate to identify thoughts with chunks of matter in the brain, and who anticipated contemporary computational psychology by declaring that reasoning is nothing but "reckoning," understood as mechanical operations in the brain.[46] For contemporary physicalists the mind *is* the brain, and hence the view that the rules of reasoning are rules "for manipulating thought symbols, in the notational system of the mind," as well as the assumption that the rules and the symbolic structures are somehow encoded in the brain, seems natural. Yet the issue here does not turn, as one may be inclined to think, on materialism versus dualism: it is not just because of his commitment to dualism that Descartes was not tempted by the Hobbesian move. Indeed, from the point of view of contemporary functionalism, it is irrelevant in what kind of medium—material or immaterial—symbolic structures, the rules governing them, and the operations performed on those structures are taken to be realized.[47] What separates Descartes's dualism from contemporary functionalism and identity theories, I venture to claim, is not so much his distinction between an immaterial mind and extended material body as his notion of the human being as a unity of mind and body, with properties that are not reducible to either mind or body but depend precisely on their "substantial" union.

It is important to notice that Descartes's argument contrasts *human* behavior (speech or rational behavior more generally) with automatic, mechanically performed movements. A machine could not use signs as "*we* do to declare our thoughts to *others*," or respond to the meaning of "*whatever* is said in its presence, as the dullest of *men* can do," nor is it "morally" possible that it would be so minutely disposed as "to make it act in all the contingencies of life in the way *our reason* makes us act" (AT VI 57, CSM I 140; my emphasis). He is concerned with human thought and rationality, not with some abstract, universal conception of reason. A real test for a Turing machine would not be just some episodes in an imitation game, but participation in a real conversation and performance in other real-life situations that can be seen as meaningful, even when it would fail to meet standard norms of rationality. Descartes, I venture, would agree with the critics of artificial intelligence who think that such capacities require not only some particular abilities to answer some questions and manipulate symbols rationally. They require a wide range of unspecifiable abilities and skills that come with being born as an *embodied* human being and growing up in some—at least a minimally—human environment. Among these is the ability to interact with the environment and fellow human beings, which involves the ability to grasp what in that environment is relevant—what does and what does not matter to a human inference maker in a given context, what counts as a problem and what makes sense as a solution. This allows for mistakes and irrational behavior that are not explainable merely by damage or mechanical irregularities in the workings of the bodily organs. A failure to meet the standards of rationality may occur for many reasons, including malfunction of the machinery of the body, but it does not count as a mistake unless it involves a grasp of what those standards are and what a right way of acting in the given situation would be.

A mechanical device, furthermore, lacks the power of free choice of the will that Descartes describes as the highest of human perfection, and that alone makes us responsible for all our acts, including our mistaken judgments. It is mainly thanks to this freedom of choice (which is the topic of the last chapter) that the human person counts as a rational agent capable of applying rules intelligently as opposed to an automaton that follows them mechanically.[48]

5. Transparency and Immanent Reflexivity

If there is more to the Cartesian notion of thought than rule-governed calculation, there is more to consciousness than sensations or qualia. Among the aspects of conscious thinking that the computational accounts ignore is the immediate certainty or indubitability accompanying any occurrent act of thought: as soon as I think of something, I am noninferentially aware of what I am presently thinking about. Contrary to post-Rylean orthodoxy, this certainty does not entail a full epistemological transparency and incorrigibility of thoughts. Descartes does use many misleading metaphors, among others that of what is immediately perceived *in* the mind, as if the object of immediate awareness was some inner idea, separable from the object represented and intervening between the thought and its object. What this talk about knowing what goes on in us means, however (as Alan Donagan perceptively points out), is that whatever an idea represents, it does so directly and immediately, so that I cannot be in doubt of what I am presently thinking of.[49] In thinking of the tower of the cathedral in Chartres, the tower is the immediate object of my awareness, not some internal idea or mental replica of it, which I would then have to compare with other ideas in order to be certain of which tower or thing I am actually thinking of.

As for transparency,[50] it is no doubt characteristic of *some* thoughts, notably of clear and distinct propositional thoughts. But clearness and distinctness represent a norm or an ideal, not a common property of thinking. A large part of our conscious thoughts are obscure and confused, yet we are aware of them and cannot doubt having one confused thought after another, even when, as may be the case with sensory perceptions, we are unable to tell what they are about. Awareness, like clearness and distinctness, comes in degrees, and the Cartesian notion of thought is broad enough to cover all sorts of mental states, from actually entertained distinct and transparent ideas to the most confused and even unconscious feelings.[51]

Of the various features discussed by contemporary philosophers as characteristic of the mental, the closest to the kind of awareness accompanying thought in Descartes's wide sense is the reflexivity that Harry Frankfurt takes to be distinctive of consciousness and that he describes as a secondary awareness of primary differentiating responses to stimuli. "To hear a sound consciously, rather than to respond to it unconsciously, involves being aware of hearing it or being aware of the sound as heard."[52] Like Descartes, Frankfurt insists that this does not involve any reduplication of acts of consciousness, with a distinct and secondary awareness having the primary awareness as its object. That would lead to an infinite proliferation of instances of consciousness. "Rather, the self-consciousness in question is a sort of *immanent reflexivity* in virtue of which every instance of being conscious grasps not only that of which it is an awareness but also the awareness of it."[53] This account suits many of the things Descartes says about thoughts and sheds some light, in particular, on his characterization of thoughts as immediately or directly perceived.

If one takes reflexive awareness in Frankfurt's sense to be what Descartes regards as distinctive of human thought, then his view of animals as nonthinking need not involve a denial of primary awareness in brutes. Thoughtless brutes can be aware of their environment as well as of their own states, and yet lack the reflexive awareness that involves awareness also of their responses to the latter. Being conscious, for Frankfurt, involves differentiating responses to stimuli together with an awareness of those responses, which is described as "a secondary awareness of a primary response." This reflexivity is a form of self-consciousness—not in the sense of consciousness of a self, or consciousness that there is awareness—but in the sense of "consciousness's awareness of itself."[54] This idea of self-reflexivity as awareness of one's immediate reactions or responses is presupposed in another feature that Descartes takes to be central to human thought, namely, the power to attend to, reflect on, and to some extent control one's thoughts.

Contemporary discussions of thoughts as computational, symbolic structures ignore this aspect of conscious thought, as it ignores, more generally, the complexity of the phenomena of consciousness. Its focus is almost exclusively on the propositions forming the content of these states, and on the syntactic structures encoding them. But Descartes's talk of immediate awareness (as of certainty, indubitability, and clearness of thoughts) qualifies the act as much as the immediate object of thought. Not only the acts of thought but the very *activity* of thinking—as in performing judgments or focusing one's attention—is self-reflexive, and renders itself, like the source of light in the metaphor Frankfurt uses, visible when enlightening other things.[55]

Thinking is essentially an activity, it never stands still, though the static character of the propositions and the metaphors we use in trying to account for it may make it look as if it did. It is misleading to think of ideas or concepts as pictures or of thoughts as propositions, as if the movement among them were merely accidental, or indeed, as if the inference or transition from one to the other could be caught up in a series of discrete, static propositions too. This way of thinking leaves little room for the phenomena making up most of our emotional and conscious life, nor does it leave room for what Descartes took to be the highest of human perfections (the one that makes the thinker an image of its infinite creator)—namely, the free power of choice of the will, which is unrestricted in its scope (AT VII 57, CSM II 40).

Descartes sees the will as superior to the intellect, as the active is superior to the passive; though this does not mean that the will could act without the intellect and its ideas. For Descartes, the talk of will and intellect as separate faculties is just talk: the mind is indivisible, and it is one and the same thing that in perceiving is passive and in judging or willing is active. The will is just the intellect acting. Ideas may be presented to or even imposed on the intellect, but the intellect is an active power able to determine itself, to direct its attention, and to choose at all times which thoughts to focus on and which to neglect, without other restraints than its own span of attention and memory. It is this very capacity of self-determination that Descartes has in mind when he writes in *The Passions of the Soul* that "the will is by its nature so free that it can never be constrained" and that the thoughts he calls "actions" as opposed to passions—that is, the thoughts depending only on the mind itself—are "absolutely within its power" (AT XI 359, CSM I 345). It is also through the exercise of this activity that the thinking thing discovers itself as acting or being acted upon. It is what makes Cartesian consciousness essentially a self-consciousness—an awareness of the self as a source of action, as an agent who in thinking and acting is responsible for what it does, for how it directs its attention, and for what it chooses to assent to or deny.

The question remains whether there is any descriptive characteristic common to the wide variety of phenomena included under the Cartesian term "thought." One of the most serious candidates, which has not been discussed yet, is intentionality—in Descartes's terminology, objective reality—which will be examined in the next chapter. Before that I want to return to the question of the connection between thought and language once more.

6. Thought, Language, and Normativity

Descartes, unfortunately, offers no account of the connection between thought and language. In his view speech presupposes thought, but would he hold, as Wilfrid Sellars does, that thought can be *explained* through language? Or would he agree with Donald Davidson that, although there is some similarity of structure between the sentences of a language and the thoughts expressed in that language, the parallel between them does not provide any "argument for the primacy of either," only "a presumption in favour of their interdependence"?[56]

Davidson defends the claim that "a creature cannot have thoughts unless it is an interpreter of the speech of another."[57] This is surely opposed to Cartesianism if one takes it to entail a "Robinsoe Crusoe" view of the mind. But the picture of a speechless person, growing up in the wilderness, and constructing a language and world out of his subjective and private sensations, belongs to an empiricist tradition foreign to the Cartesian thinker.[58] Cartesian thought—*cogitatio*—may not require membership in a linguistic community, but it certainly does require membership in a community of rational beings—no matter what the meditator wants to feign at the outset of his solitary meditations.

The emphasis on the isolation of the Ego in the *Meditations* may lead readers to neglect the fact that they belong to a given literary genre, and presuppose a real or feigned interlocutor, who may be God, or, as in the case of the *Meditations,* an alter ego and perhaps also a Superego representing Reason or Truth itself.[59] Descartes's solitary discourse is a dialogue between his anxious, imperfect, doubt-ridden, finite self and his ideal of a perfect, infinite thinker who never makes mistakes, whose knowledge is not limited but constitutes true science *(Scientia)* characterized by complete certainty. Like Augustine in his *Confessions,* but with a very different purpose, Descartes starts by revealing all his weaknesses—his lack of confidence in his epistemic powers, the specter of self-deception or, worse, of an omnipotent Deceiver—and he proceeds, step by step, to reinstate the faith he had lost, or had never possessed in a reflective way. He would, of course, get nowhere with that starting point were it not for his natural inclination to believe in reason, which he now tests and which passes the test only when activated by a light so great that it, as it were, compels assent:

> I have realized that from the very fact of my raising this question ["whether anything in this world exists"] it follows quite evidently that I exist. I could not but judge that something which I understood so clearly was true; but this was not because I was compelled to judge by any external force, but because a great light in the intellect was followed by a great inclination in the will, and thus the spontaneity and

freedom of my belief was all the greater in proportion to my lack of in-difference. (AT VII 58–59, CSM II 41)

The experience of necessity appealed to here must be seen against the background of a previous commitment to truth. It is not a matter of natural, psychological necessity, but of normative necessity: a recognition of a rational obligation to assent to what cannot be denied without contradiction and to the truth of what can be deduced from self-evident propositions. Descartes manages to work his way out of the whirlpool of doubts in which he had thrown himself solely by inspection of his ideas and beliefs, keeping a constant lookout for "what follows from this?" (AT VII 25, CSM II 16). From the undeniable fact that he is thinking, he concludes that he exists, having already by the reasoning leading to this first step discovered that thinking is rule governed, and that it presupposes some external reality greater and more perfect than the individual thinker, which is experienced as the source of the concepts and normative restraints regulating his thinking.[60]

The Cartesian thinker thus finds herself equipped from the start both with concepts and a capacity to discover the relations of compatibility and incompatibility between them. Descartes calls them innate, self-evident, common notions—they are "common" because they are natural and shared by all rational minds. They are a mixed bag, including both logical and metaphysical principles that Descartes held to be self-evident. Some of them, the eternal truths, are mere principles of reason, while others are of real things.[61] The latter are "ideas" in the strict sense, whose distinctive feature is to *represent* things (ideas are said to be representative by their very nature), though it turns out (to the exasperation of commentators) that some ideas fail to represent anything properly and are therefore called "materially" false ideas.[62]

Davidson's prelinguistic featherless biped, by contrast, needs to encounter another creature who can react to the same kind of stimuli from the same external source and thus discover, by triangulation, the concept of objective truth and that of true beliefs about a shared external world, all of which Davidson counts as necessary for interpretation and hence for talk and thought.[63] Descartes's starting point is different: instead of taking the external physical world and his sensory reactions to it for granted, he assumes what Davidson thinks has to be proved, namely, that he doubts and thinks and hence already has the concepts of thinking and doubting, and with them a whole battery of inferentially linked concepts. Not only does he find himself equipped with tools for thinking,[64] but most important, he starts out, at the very beginning of his solitary *Meditations,* with an appeal to reason and a commitment to truth: "Reason now leads me to think that I should hold back my assent from opinions which are not completely certain and indubitable just as carefully as I do from those which are patently false" (AT VII 18, CSM II 12).

That the Cartesian thinker is equipped with these concepts must be taken with a grain of salt. Unlike Locke, Descartes does not understand this to mean that they are fully formed in the mind at birth (or before); he holds rather that the mind comes to the world with an innate disposition to form them. Ideas are not entities separate from the faculty of thinking, but are innate in the way dispositions like generosity, or diseases like gout or stones, are said to be innate in some families: "It is not so much that the babies of such families suffer from these diseases in their mother's womb, but simply that they are born with a certain 'faculty' or disposition to contract them" (AT VIII-1 358, CSM I 303–304). Post-Hegelian thinkers know that it takes more than just minds and innate dispositions to think, learn, or discover anything, and they also understand, in a way Descartes did not, the role of the historical and social settings in which the mind is embedded, not to mention the practices that give it its distinctive human shape. It is good to remember, however, that the Cartesian thinker too discovers herself as embodied and thus born to a world of other thinkers and extended bodies, with all the limitations and challenges that imposes on her. Furthermore, the limits of what can be clearly and distinctly conceived are set for her—not by historical or psychological necessity, nor indeed by any eternal and unalterable logical necessity, but by an omnipotent and infinite God who has created the true and the possible and hence determined the boundaries of what finite minds can conceive.[65] For Descartes, thinking is essentially a rule-governed, normative activity.

This is not to say that the Cartesian mind has at birth a set of explicit rules that must be heeded: thinking is not, any more than meaningful speech, like a game of chess, the rules of which determine every admissible move and must be mastered in order to play. My point is that reason and thought, for Descartes, involve a commitment to truth and to laws of thinking, which are not psychological laws—laws that as a matter of fact govern our thinking—but laws of a logical order. They are not formed through our own activity, but are decreed by God, and constitute preconditions of rationality and hence of thought. They are laws that we must follow if we want to be rational, to understand, and to know—Descartes sees attending to them as a matter of reflective, *voluntary* commitment. This makes Descartes a pre-Kantian thinker, rather than a prenaturalist of a Humean kind: the necessity that constrains thinking is not one of causal regularity or habit, but of obligation and commitment to norms constitutive of rationality.[66]

The very light of reason to which Descartes appeals already in his early rules is a light that can compel only those who are already willing to follow it and who, by deliberate choice, keep their eyes closed and turn their mind away from the senses—who, as it is put in the *Meditations* (AT VII 131, CSM II 94), look inward, focusing on what reason or intellect alone can grasp. This inward turn is not the substitution of introspection for sense perception, not the inner sense taking the place of the outer. Readers influenced by modern empiricism may often understand it that way, because they mistakenly take the immediacy of what is given to reason as endowing it with epistemological priority over the deliverances of the external senses, leaving the Cartesian mind trapped in its private subjective experiences. But Descartes's appeal to the natural light of reason is more like Augustine's appeal to the inner light, the objects of which are accessible to all rational beings, and which corresponds to the role given to intellectual intuition (described already in the *Rules*) as the only source of true and certain knowledge. By looking into yourself when withdrawing from the external world, you are not left with subjective, private impressions, but with the resources required to discover what is common and universal, like the laws of number and reasoning, which are evident to all rational beings.[67]

The inner light does not, however, shine all by itself, automatically, and it takes more than opening one's mind's eye and turning it inward for it to work properly. It requires constant effort and practice; and learning to use it properly, so as to keep the truth rule constantly in mind and never assent to anything that is not perceived with perfect clarity and distinctness, can be a life-long struggle.

If Descartes describes this in the language of Platonists, as turning away from the senses that obscure or weaken the light of reason, he does not follow them in postulating a "third" realm of independently existing, immaterial essences, to be fully seen only in another form of existence. He appeals to a *natural* light, one that shines here and now for anyone who seriously attends to it and uses it in the right way. Its objects, the "truths" (which are too numerous to be listed but of which examples are mentioned in various contexts, notably in the *Principles of Philosophy*), are neither "things" nor "properties of things." They are said to "have their seat in our thought," but have no existence outside it, yet they are "eternal" and "common" to all.[68] They are fully intelligible to the human intellect, and are called "common" precisely because they can be clearly and distinctly perceived. Not as well by everyone, however, not "because one man's faculty of knowledge extends more widely than another's, but because the common notions are in conflict with the preconceived opinions of some people who, as a result, cannot easily grasp them" (AT VIII-1 24, CSM I 209). We seem to grow up as Aristotelians, fed and blinded by our spontaneous takings-to-be and habitual beliefs of which so many turn out to be in conflict with the common notions of true Cartesian science. Only those who have managed to rid themselves of preconceived opinions—false beliefs about the external world—can perceive them with "utmost clarity" (AT VIII-1 24, CSM I 209). Since habitual opinions and precipitated judgments of the senses keep presenting themselves, it takes great determination and attention to reach that point.

To the extent that the metaphors of light and seeing may suggest Platonic idea-entities as their objects, they surely are misleading. What the light is supposed to disclose, ultimately, are truths about objects in this world as they present themselves to human knowledge, once the right order and nature of things have been grasped. The light itself, Descartes insists, is natural too, just as is our innate capacity to think, with the laws or rational principles that govern it. The laws and principles presupposed in thinking—for instance, law of noncontradiction—are not listed in any mental manual, but are gradually discovered in learning how our concepts work and in grasping the inferential commitments and entitlements that structure their rational use.

The use of contemporary idiom, taking its inspiration from the writings of Wilfrid Sellars, in my reading of a text so often seen as a paradigm example of internalism needs to be justified. The evidence as well as the standards appealed to (the clear and distinct ideas) in the *Meditations* are "internal," and hence not at the measure of those of rational discourse, which according to contemporary requirements must belong to an essentially public and social "space of giving and asking for reasons." But Descartes too, after all, exposed his arguments to public discussion and approval (even if he was not very gracious in answering some of the objections of his contemporaries whom he himself had invited). Without neglecting any of the crucial and undeniable differences between a view of mind and thought created by God *ex nihilo* and one that sees it as constituted by social practices, there are in fact some interesting features shared by an externalist approach to meaning and intentionality of the Sellarsian kind and the Cartesian notion of thinking.

What Wilfrid Sellars calls "the logical space of reasons" is essentially a social space, one which presupposes a social context and a language as the framework of conceptual thinking. It belongs to what he calls "the manifest image of man-in-the-world"—roughly, "the world we know to be in ordinary experience." The distinctive features of persons in this framework "are conceptually irreducible to features of nonpersons, e.g., animals and merely material things."[69] This seems to echo Descartes, though for Sellars, to be a thinker, is to be a conceptual thinker, and a conceptual thinker is essentially a member of a social group.[70] It is through his Hegelian emphasis on the social group that Sellars differs from Descartes: no thinking can occur outside a "framework of conceptual thinking in terms of which it can be criticized, supported, refuted, in short, evaluated." Hence the irreducibility: the ability to think comes with the possibility to use external standards of correctness, truth, relevance, and evidence by which thoughts can be measured. Such standards can exist only in a complex and diversified framework, which constitutes a whole that is prior to its parts, which already are conceptual in character.[71]

Descartes too thinks of language as given and grants that the thinker needs concepts in order to think, and that concepts come in complex and diversified holistic structures. But he is not sensitive, in the way Sellars is, to the social and historical origins of language and the conceptual capacities of the thinker. Interestingly for Sellars, this is not just a matter of belonging to a group and learning language as part of growing up as a member of some community: being a member of a community has an irreducibly ethical dimension. To think of someone as a person is to think of her as "a being with which one is bound up in a network of rights and duties." From this point of view, he claims, the irreducibility of the personal is the "irreducibility of the 'ought' to 'is.'" The basic point is that thinking of someone as a person is construing her behavior "in terms of actual or potential membership in an embracing group, each member of which thinks of itself as a member of the group."[72] I have to see myself and be recognized by you as a person—a potential member of some group we both are part of—in order for me to count as a person.[73]

This approach is echoed in Robert Brandom's recent work, where the responses and behavior of a being are counted as beliefs and actions because and insofar as "it is proper to offer and inquire after reasons for them," which means that they must have "an intelligible content," that is, be "inferentially articulated" or "caught up in a web of reasons."[74] Actions differ from mere behavior because reasons can be given for them and because they can appear as the conclusions of practical inferences.[75] Reasons and inferences belong to the sphere of conceptually structured activity, which is distinguished from other spheres of activity not only by its propositional contentfulness, but notably by its normative character, by the fact that we are in a special way responsible for the reasons we endorse and the inferences we make. This view of understanding as "the faculty of grasping rules—of appreciating the distinction between correct and incorrect application they determine"—is attributed by Brandom to Kant, and it is sharply contrasted to the Cartesian "descriptive" and "naturalist" approach. "Being in an intentional state or performing an intentional action . . . has normative significance. It counts as undertaking (acquiring) an obligation or commitment." This, as Brandom sees it, is the Kantian version of the demarcation criterion, which picks us out as distinctly normative or rule-governed creatures, and his own work aims at spelling out the conditions and significance of the "rulishness" involved in language use. In calling the Cartesian way of conceiving cognition, action, and intentionality *descriptive,* Brandom wants specifically to contrast it with the Kantian account that he characterizes as *prescriptive.* The former connects intentionality to the possession or lack of certain properties, or to a nature, or a mental *substance,* whereas the latter focuses on "the special sort of *authority* one becomes subject to in applying concepts." Kant is also said to have shifted the focus from *certainty* to *necessity*, from Descartes's concern with the kind of grip we have on our concepts to the attempt to account for their "rulishness," to understand "their authority, bindingness, or validity," which Kant calls "necessity," and by which, as Brandom reads him, he means "in accord with a rule."[76]

Whether or not Brandom is justified in giving Kant the honor of being the first to make necessity thus understood the subject of systematic investigation, and thereby to make explicit the kind of governance by rules that he takes normativity of concept use to involve, will not be discussed here. Kant himself, as Brandom also points out, saw the concern with responsibility, and thus with normativity, as fundamental to the Enlightment.[77] Some may want to go much further back and see that concern emerging already in the Stoics—in their preoccupation with rationality and assent, or in Augustine's and his late medieval followers' concern with free choice, voluntary consent, and commitment. Whatever its ancestry, it clearly comes to the surface in Descartes, and even Brandom seems to recognize as much in writing: "Thus the *Meditations* is to be read as motivated by the demand that the meditator take personal responsibility for every claim officially endorsed—be prepared to answer for it, demonstrate entitlement to that commitment by justifying it." Yet he thinks this theme—explicit in Cartesian methodology—remained merely implicit in Descartes's account of "us," that is, in his account of thought, which remains "naturalistic" in a broad sense.[78]

Things are not, however, quite so simple. A lot hangs on how the difficult notion of normativity is spelled out. The very notion of nature in ancient philosophy, where the true and the good are seen as converging, is deeply normative. If there seems to be no room for normativity (and certainly not for final ends or tendencies to the good) in Descartes's conception of physical nature, this is because the normative is moved by him to the realm of the mental. The source of the norms is God, who institutes them and inscribes them in the human minds, who as free agents are responsible for subjecting themselves to those laws and for following them. The order of causes and the order of reasons, as distinct and irreducible realms, is thereby each in place. If what demarcates the latter is normativity, and if the necessity regulating the order of reasons differs from the mere regularity of the order of causes in being mediated by attitudes of acknowledgment and commitment expressed in our conduct and speech as autonomous agents, then all the important elements for a normative account of human nature seem to be in place too, or at least importantly prefigured, in the Cartesian account of mind.[79]

What the dialectics of the *Meditations* show, as I read them, is not that we can take our clear and distinct perceptions as true because they as a matter of fact compel our assent, but because we recognize their binding, normative force on us: their authority depends on this recognition or acknowledgment, which for Descartes is a matter of voluntary commitment. If thought, like language, belongs to the logical space of reasons, then the notion of intentionality itself—the relation of thoughts to their objects—should be, like linguistic meaning, accountable only within that same normative space.

Intentionality and the Representative Nature of Ideas

The previous chapter examined some general features of Descartes's notion of thought and its relation to consciousness and speech. This chapter takes a closer look at his concepts of "idea," "representation," and "objective reality" and the way he uses them in accounting for the objects or contents of thoughts: what they represent. To represent or be about—so-called intentionality—is a common and plausible candidate for what distinguishes thoughts or mental phenomena from the physical—at least, so we have been taught by Franz Brentano and his followers. Descartes too (as Brentano knew) held that the mental acts he referred to as "thoughts" had in common that they "represent," or as he sometimes expressed it, "signify" something to the mind. Unfortunately, as soon as one asks what "to represent" might mean and what the different thoughts that are said to represent something have in common, the troubles start again. My aim here (and in the next chapter) is to track Descartes's various uses of the terms "idea" and "representation" to see if he had a coherent account of intentionality.

The first section presents his distinction between two senses of "idea"—as act and as object—and places these concepts in a broad historical context. Section 2 analyzes Descartes's concept of idea as the object thought of and the metaphor of "image" used in the Third Meditation to describe it. Sections 3–5 discuss the nature of ideas as objects or contents of thought and their relation to the things they are of, and then defends an interpretation of Descartes's concept of objective reality in terms of his notion of possible being. Section 6 argues that Descartes's notion of intentionality does not commit him to the thesis of ideas as copies of external things intervening between the act of thinking and the thing thought of. The last section considers some of the problems that Descartes's account and terminology carry over from the Scholastic tradition in which they are rooted.

1. Ideas as Acts and Ideas as Objects

Descartes often uses "thought," "idea," and "perception" coextensively to cover both acts and objects of thought.[1] It is clear, however, that he does distinguish these two different senses of the term: idea taken materially, as an act or operation of the intellect, and idea taken objectively, as the thing represented by that operation (AT VII 8, CSM II 7). It is only when taken in the latter sense that ideas can be said to have reference to the truth or falsity of their objects; when considered simply as acts, ideas involve no error (AT VII 232, CSM II 163).

Do all ideas or thoughts represent something or other? Are ideas taken materially, as acts, in themselves representational? Is the representative content of an idea always propositional?

In the Third Meditation, where Descartes gives his most extensive account of ideas, he takes the term objectively and restricts it to a subclass of thoughts: thoughts "which are, as it were, images of things." An idea, in the strict sense, is hence a thought that includes some kind of "likeness" of the thing of which it is an idea—a man, a chimera, the sky, an angel, God. Other thoughts are said to have "various additional forms":

> [T]hus when I will, or am afraid, or affirm, or deny, there is always a particular thing which I take as the subject of my thought *(semper quidem aliquam rem ut subjectum meae cogitationis apprehendo)*, but my thought includes something more than the likeness of that thing. Some thoughts in this category are called volitions or emotions, while others are called judgements. (AT VII 37, CSM II 25–26)[2]

To say that some thoughts are, "as it were, images of things" is to say that they represent something: they have an object or content by which they are individuated as an idea of this particular thing or being. Considered apart from its content or object, any thought actually perceived has a definite form and can therefore be called an idea: "I use the term idea for whatever is immediately perceived by the mind, so that when I will and fear, since I at the same time perceive that I will and fear, the same volition and fear are numbered among my ideas" (AT VII 181, CSM II 127).

The distinction between thought as act and as object is clearly made in the first passage quoted above: "idea" here is restricted to what is said to be the proper sense of the word, namely, thoughts representing things that are somehow like images *(imagines)*. In the second passage, however (as in the one quoted below), "idea" refers to the "form" of *any* actually perceived thought. Whatever we perceive is perceived by way of an idea, and to everything we say there corresponds some idea of what we talk about:

> I understand the term to mean the form of any given thought, the immediate perception of which makes me aware [Latin: *conscius;* Fr. *connaissance*] of the thought. Hence, whenever I express something in words, and understand what I am saying, this very fact makes it certain that there is within me an idea of what is signified by the words in question. (AT VII 160, CSM II 113; AT IX 124)[3]

We have ideas, Descartes explains in a letter, not only of whatever is in the intellect, but also of whatever is in the will, because "we cannot will anything without knowing that we will it, nor know it, except by an idea," although this idea is *not* different from the action of willing itself.[4] Idea is here identified with the act of thinking itself.

Anthony Kenny, who devotes a whole chapter of his book to show the inconsistencies in Descartes's use of "idea," takes this as an instance of "the ambiguity of 'idea' as between act and object."[5] It surely is confusing, I agree, to read that ideas, when taken materially—that is, not objectively or formally—have forms of their own, to be distinguished from their formal and objective reality (AT VII 232, CSM II 163).[6] The confusion arises from Descartes's generic use of "idea" as a synonym of "perception" or "thought" to cover all kinds of acts and states of consciousness, in addition to its strict use, which covers only the contents of these acts or states. I don't think, however, there is any real ambiguity if one keeps in mind the distinction between idea as act and idea as content. In its strict and primary sense, "idea" applies only to the latter: to the object or content of thought represented in some imagelike way.[7] In its wider sense, "idea" applies to the act by which a given object is thought of.[8]

Descartes's distinction between act and object is basically the same as Brentano's, which was systematically developed by Husserl and is reflected in contemporary distinctions like John Searle's between the content of a mental act and the psychological mode in which it is represented.[9] Both the content (or object) and the psychological mode have their distinctive forms: both are thoughts or ideas in Descartes's general sense. But only ideas taken objectively (as objects) are representative and exhibit what Descartes (following the Scholastic tradition) calls a "similitude" or "likeness" with the thing represented. "Idea," when applied to the form of the mental act (to what is described by Husserl as the act mode or act quality, by Searle as the psychological mode), is not itself representative: it *is* the mental act that is perceived as a distinctive kind of mental act. It can, of course, on reflection, be made the object of another mental act in which it is represented. For instance, in desiring a unicorn I know (perceive) immediately that I desire a unicorn, and here it is the unicorn, not the desire, which is the object of my mental act. I can reflect on this desire, however, and make it the object of my attention, in which case the content of my mental act is my-desire-of-the-unicorn. This act is now directed to that same mental act (idea in the large sense) that, before reflecting on it, I perceived directly.

Husserl states the distinction more explicitly. He uses the verb *cogitare* to embrace all *acts* of consciousness, whereas he uses the term "consciousness" to comprehend "*all* mental processes."[10] In the *Cartesian Meditations*, Husserl uses the term *cogitatum* for the intended object or content.[11] This distinction corresponds to what he elsewhere calls *noesis* (the intentional or noetic act), on one hand, and the *noema* or the intentional correlate of this act, on the other. He also makes explicit the further distinction (which Descartes also makes) between the immediate object of awareness and the act itself as an object of reflection: "When living in the cogito we are not (actionally) conscious of the cogitatio itself as an intention Object; but at any time it can become an Object of consciousness . . . In other words, any 'cogitatio' can become the object of a so-called 'internal perception' and in further succession the Object of a *reflective* valuation."[12] Husserl calls acts of thinking that are themselves objects of consciousness "immanent objects," as distinguished from extramental objects of consciousness that, with respect to the mental act, are called "transcendent."[13] The unicorn, in the example given above, would be a transcendent object of thought, whereas the desire-of-the-unicorn would be an immanent object.

Descartes's notion of thought as covering both the mental act and its object can be seen as anticipating later accounts of conscious phenomena as complex processes or acts with correlative intentional objects. The act and the object are two *aspects* of one and the same conscious process or thought: idea as act and idea as object are two inseparable sides of the same phenomenon that necessarily occur together—although they can be considered apart for purposes of analysis. Like Husserl's acts of consciousness, Descartes's thoughts have a complex structure: they are acts of a distinctive form or character, and they also have a specific content or object, and hence are representations of something, whether the latter is some existing extramental thing or some merely thinkable thing. Once the act form is given, the thought (perception, idea) is identified by its content or object: it is what distinguishes, say, my desire of the unicorn from other desires of mine. Conversely, the same thing—the unicorn—can be thought of in various ways—desired, remembered, or feared. The whole act (the desire-of-the-unicorn), finally, can be the object of what Descartes would call a reflective act, the latter being what the Scholastics called a secondary intention and Husserl an immanent object. Like Husserl, moreover, Descartes takes consciousness and intentionality to be matters of degree.

There is controversy regarding what exactly Brentano and Husserl took intentionality to be and, in particular, how they differed in their conception of the object of the intentional act. They agreed, however, in taking intentionality to be a main characteristic of the mental and to involve meaning or representation—a phenomenon describable as representing something to a subject, as being "as if of" an object. Intentionality in this broad sense is central to Descartes's concept of thinking too. Whereas the idea of mental states as propositional attitudes is fairly recent (the terminology, at least, is that of Bertrand Russell), the idea of intentionality has old roots: Descartes and Brentano learned from the same sources. As Brentano put it, in an often quoted passage, "every mental phenomenon is characterized by what the Scholastics of the Middle Ages called the intentional (and also mental) inexistence of an object," and which he describes, somewhat hesitatingly, as "the reference to a content, a direction upon an object (by which we are not to understand a reality in this case), or an immanent objectivity." Thus a mental act, for Brentano, always includes something as an object within itself, which can be included in various ways: it can be hated, loved, feared, affirmed or denied, wanted, and so forth. This doctrine, as Brentano notes, stems ultimately from Aristotle's treatise *On the Soul,* and is central to his account of sensation and intellection: the form of the external object is actualized in the soul, without the matter by which it is individuated. The object thought is actualized in the intellect as an intelligible form, and the object perceived by the senses is in the sense organ as a sensible form (as shapes, smells, sounds, and the like).[14]

The term Descartes uses in referring to what Brentano calls intentional inexistence is "objective being" *(esse objective),* which in the Scholastic vocabulary is the same as "intentional being" *(esse intentionale).* Descartes's use of the term, however, goes beyond the Aristotelian-Thomistic terminology of intelligible forms or species, and his concept of objective being (or reality) cannot be unproblematically translated in those terms. Precedents closer to the Cartesian notion can, however, be found in another tradition, that of the Franciscan theologians and philosophers—like Henry of Ghent, Duns Scotus, Ockham, and their followers—whose views are also reported and discussed by Suárez.[15]

To trace the origins and background of Descartes's notion of objective reality is beyond the scope of this study, and so is a more detailed comparison of Descartes's view of the structure of thought with either Brentano's or Husserl's views of intentionality and of the object or content of the intentional act. Husserl developed his theory of intentionality, with its threefold distinction among the intentional act, its content (noema), and its external object in response to difficulties in Brentano's theory.[16] The problems encountered by Brentano and, before him, by Descartes have their roots in difficulties in the Aristotelian and Scholastic theories of cognition, some of which are mentioned in the last section of this chapter. Descartes's application of the Scholastic notion in the framework of his dualism poses difficulties of its own, which can only be briefly noted, but let us first consider Descartes's notion of ideas and how they are related to the things they represent.

2. Ideas and Images

In classifying his thoughts into "definite kinds" *(certa genera)* in order to determine in which of them truth and falsity properly are to be found, Descartes observes in the Third Meditation that some of them are, "as it were, images of things" and that the term "idea," strictly speaking, should be restricted to these (AT VII, CSM II 25). Thoughts are about what ideas, in this strict sense, represent, but ideas are also described as likenesses of things, which are somehow contained in my thoughts, along with whatever other form the thoughts happen to have.[17] Ideas in this strict sense are further classified in three kinds with respect to their apparent origin: innate, adventitious, and factitious. The first "seem to derive simply from my nature," as when I understand what a thing, truth, or thought is. The second are taken to come "from things located outside me," as when I hear a noise, see the sun, or feel the fire. The third, finally, seem to be "made by me" on the basis of the former, freely invented like sirens, hippogriphs, and the like (AT VII 37, CSM II 26).

What should be noted is that ideas here are kinds of thoughts, and are *also* what the thoughts are about: as it were "images" of things contained in thoughts. Insofar as ideas are what thoughts are about, they are bearers of truth and falsity. The problem is how these two metaphors, that of an image and that of containment, by which Descartes accounts for the representativity of ideas, should be understood.[18] A related problem is that truth and falsity, as usually understood, pertain to propositions not ideas, but Descartes insists that ideas considered in themselves have no falsity, and that ideas, to the extent that they are clear and distinct, are always true.[19]

The originality of Descartes's use of the term "idea" has often been noted, but also exaggerated and misinterpreted.[20] Most of the Scholastics, following the Augustinian tradition, restricted the term to divine exemplars, the purely intelligible forms or models in God's eternal intellect through which he knows all things.[21] Descartes clearly was aware of using "idea" in a new way in applying it to the contents of the human mind, and what made the term attractive to him was precisely the purely intelligible and representative nature of ideas as objects of the divine intellect.[22] Ideas are not forms abstracted from particular instantiations or from impressions received through sensory perception; they are forms of *possible* things (individual essences) like the divine archetypes on the model of which actually existing things are created. Thus, when Descartes describes human ideas as a kind of images, he insists on the immaterial and nonsensory character of such images. Ideas in the human mind are *as it were* images because, like the divine exemplars, they represent real or possible beings: in both cases their representative function is explained through some kind of likeness between the thing and the idea. But it is not, Descartes insists, a pictorial likeness that could be copied materially, as Hobbes takes to be the case:

> [M]y critic wants the term "idea" to be taken to refer simply to the images of material things which are depicted in the corporeal imagination; and if this is granted, it is easy for him to prove that there can be no proper idea of an angel or of God. But I make it quite clear in several places throughout the book . . . that I am taking the word "idea" to refer to whatever is immediately perceived by the mind . . . I used the word "idea" because it was the standard philosophical term used to refer to the forms of perception belonging to the divine mind, even though we recognize that God does not possess any corporeal imagination. And besides, there was not any more appropriate term at my disposal. (AT VII 181, CSM II 127)

That images depicted in the (corporeal) imagination are not called ideas at all is stressed explicitly in the definition given of "idea" at the end of the Second Replies (AT VII 160–161, CSM II 113).[23]

It is worth reflecting on the difference between an image depicted in the corporeal imagination (the part of the brain where the causal effects of sensory objects are impressed) and the idea informing the mind when "applying" or "directing" itself to what is pictured there. This image, according to Descartes's neurophysiology, is a pattern on the surface of the brain formed by the effects of neural motions and caused, in the last instance, by the action of external objects on the sense organs. The idea, on the other hand, is the actual sensation or sensory form (quality) as perceived by the mind. It is not transmitted to the mind through the sense organs but is actualized in it on the occurrence of certain patterns in the brain. As is well known, Descartes has no account of how this actualization comes about; he just accepts it as an unexplainable fact established by nature. The relation between the idea in the mind and the external object that prompts it cannot be causal in Descartes's sense of mechanical causation, nor a matter of pictorial resemblance.

Descartes's account of visual perception in the early *Rules* has been said to involve a visual metaphor of the mind as "a spiritual pair of eyes within the brain, there to attend to patterns delivered upon the corporeal screen of the brain loci."[24] Descartes, however, rejects such a metaphor in *Optics:*

> Now, when this picture thus passes to the inside of our head, it still bears some resemblance to the objects from which it proceeds. As I have amply shown already, however, *we must not think that it is by means of this resemblance that the picture causes our sensory perception of these objects*— as if there were yet other eyes within our brain with which we could perceive it. Instead we must hold that it is the movements composing this picture which, acting directly upon our soul in so far as it is united to our body, are ordained by nature to make it have such sensations. (AT VI 130, CSM I 167; my emphasis)

As Descartes wants to show in *World* and in *Optics*, there need be no more resemblance between an idea (for instance, a sensation of color) and the object causing it, than between a sign (for instance, a spoken or written word) and the object signified, or between tears on a face and the sadness they express (AT XI 4–5, CSM I 81–82). Nature could use corporeal movements as signs to make us think of certain things, in the same way as the words of a conventional language can make us think of things to which they bear no resemblance. Nature uses a language that the mind understands and interprets. The actions of external bodies on the sensory organ are signs whose meaning is represented by the mind. There are explicit references to this sign theory in the later work, not only in the Sixth Meditation, but also in *The Passions of the Soul*, which notes how emotional states can evoke representations without any resemblance between the representations and the objects giving rise to them.

Linguistic signs can be perceived and identified as physical tokens independently of their signification, but what about the signs of this "language" instituted by nature? The action of light (corpuscular movements) that, in touching our eye, signifies "light" to the mind is not *perceived* as a sign to be interpreted. It is an unconscious cause that automatically brings certain representations to the mind by natural institution.

One suggestion is that the relation between the physical stimulation and the sensation should be understood as semantical rather than causal. But this is not helpful if one does not have an account of what a semantical relation is.[25] The prior question, what Descartes understands by representation, given that it is neither a matter of mechanical causation nor of pictorial resemblance, needs to be answered first.

3. Likeness, Similarity, Identity

Calvin Normore traces Descartes's remarks about the image-likeness of ideas to the Scholastic tradition that explains images as involving two relations: "one of similarity and one of being produced with that similarity."[26] Without being images literally, Cartesian ideas are like images in being both similar to and causally connected with what they represent or are ideas of.[27] Thanks to this double relation, Cartesian ideas succeed in playing the Janus-like role of having both (causal) reference and (nonreferential) meaning.[28] In trying to spell out what these two relations involve, Normore presents some interesting suggestions that I would like to explore.

Ideas in the Scholastic tradition are exemplars in the divine mind to which God is supposed to look in creating. How is it, Normore asks, "that when God looks to the horse-exemplar and creates, the creature is a horse and not, say, a goat?" Part of the answer is the conceptual point that looking to the exemplar of a kind is the way this kind of particular thing is created. But there is also a story about the causal connection: God can be compared to an artist working from a model, and artistic production can be understood after the paradigm of organic reproduction. The artist's model plays a role comparable to a parent in organic reproduction, where the effect (in the absence of defects obstructing the normal process of reproduction) is of the same kind as the cause, just as in artistic production the work of art resembles the model—unless the skill is defective or obstructed. Since God is an artist whose skill can be neither defective nor obstructed, His products are of the same kind as the exemplars from which He works.[29]

Descartes holds human ideas to be innate—imprinted by God in the human mind—and as much creatures of God as other things. It is plausible, therefore, to conclude with Normore that, however the causal relation preserves resemblance, our ideas resemble the divine ideas and hence the objects of which they were models.[30] For Descartes, it should be stressed, the divine ideas or exemplars are themselves creatures of God, because God, in making things, also makes, *ex nihilo,* the models or ideas of things.

But Arnauld, in defending what he—as a faithful Cartesian—takes to be Descartes's theory of ideas against Malebranche, insists that the way ideas in the mind represent things is so particular to it that it cannot be explained by anything that is not mind or thinking: ideas, notably, do *not* represent in the way images represent what they portray, or in the way signs represent thoughts.[31] Like Arnauld, Descartes seems to have held the representativeness of ideas to be more fundamental to all other relations of representing or picturing, and hence not explicable through them.[32]

But Normore's story provides a kind of explanation of how ideas represent, that is, in what the image-likeness or similarity by virtue of which they represent consists, namely, in that the idea, exemplar, and object are identical, although they have a different ontological status. The divine idea (exemplar) of a particular thing and the innate copy of this idea in the human mind are identical with the particular, but differ in ontological status—they have another kind of being *(esse)* or reality. The particular horse running in the field has actual or formal being, and the same horse as thought or represented has objective being.[33] To appreciate the force of this suggestion we must take a closer look at the Cartesian notion of objective reality and some of its historical antecedents.

4. Objective Reality and Possible Being

By the objective reality of an idea Descartes means "the being of the thing which is represented by an idea, insofar as this exists in the idea" (AT VII 161, CSM II 113–114). The idea, taken objectively, is a kind of real being: without being real in the sense of an actually (formally) existing mind-independent thing (as, for instance, the sun or the people out there), it has *some* degree of reality *qua* conceived by an intellect. How should this be understood?

There are two features of the Cartesian doctrine of objective being to be noted here. The first is the independence of ideas, taken objectively, with respect to the act of mind conceiving them. The second is Descartes's application of degrees of perfection to the objective being of ideas.

In attributing some kind of reality to ideas taken objectively, Descartes ascribes to them a certain independence from the act of conceiving them. An idea, *qua* form of thought, has a nature that is not arbitrary and whose reality cannot be reduced to the (material) reality of thought or of the mind that actually perceives it. Ideas as representational forms in the mind have some kind of thought-independent *reality*. This is a feature not only of the eternal truths, but of any idea in the strict sense of the word. Caterus, who agrees on the immutable nature of ideas, does not think they involve any real being requiring a cause. He writes in the First Objections: "I take the same general view about all ideas as M. Descartes takes of a triangle. He says: 'even if perhaps no such figure exists, or has ever existed, anywhere outside my thought, there is still a determinate nature or essence or form which is immutable and eternal'. What we have here is an eternal truth, which does not require a cause" (AT VII 93, CSM II 67). Caterus also thinks ideas or concepts require no cause: conceptual entities may have some sort of reality as conceived, but "since it is merely conceived and is not actual, although it can be conceived, it cannot in any way be caused" (AT VII 94, CSM II 67–68). Caterus, like his predecessors, understands eternal truths to be mere logical or conceptual necessities, without ontological foundation in nature or in the divine intellect. They are eternally given transcendental conditions for intelligibility to which any intellect, infinite or created, is bound.[34]

Descartes departs from this view on two central points. Against the view that eternal truths are uncreated, he claims that they are freely posited by God: although unchangeable and hence necessary once they have been posited, they are not necessary independently of God's willing them so.[35] Against the view that eternal truths are merely conceptual or logical, Descartes holds that they have a special kind of being *qua* actually conceived by a created intellect, which requires a real being as its cause. Any distinctly conceivable idea has some degree of objective reality that must be caused, whether the thing represented by the idea is an existing mind-independent thing (the sun) or a possibly existing thing (a conceived machine of a highly intricate design) (AT VII 103, CSM II 75). That our ideas have a mode of reality of their own—which is lesser than the actual (formal or material) reality of thought and lesser than that of the objects represented by them, but nevertheless greater than pure nonbeing—is, on this view, a general feature of ideas. Ideas are *things* thought of or conceived, *res cogitata*.[36]

Now this latter view was certainly not unheard of in Scholasticism, contrary to what many modern critics assume.[37] The distinction between subjective (or formal) and objective being was a current one, which, as noted by Gilson, was used by Ockham and his followers.[38] He also notes the Scholastic origin of the distinction between the idea taken formally as a mental act and the idea taken objectively as representing an object.[39] One should not, however, be misled by the Scholastic origin of this terminology, for as Gilson warns us, the view it expresses is not Scholastic. In Scholasticism *objective being* is not a real being, but a being of reason, which requires no cause. In Cartesianism, on the contrary, objective being, although less than the actual being of the thing, is real being whose existence must have been caused.[40] Gilson takes the astonishment of Caterus and Father Vatier as indications of the novelty of Descartes's view on this point.[41]

But we must also take into account the testimony of Arnauld, who was the most penetrating and one of the most learned of Descartes's critics. The fact that Arnauld has no objections against Descartes's use of this notion should warn us not to make too much out of the astonishment of Thomists like Caterus or Vatier. The notion of objective being is, in fact, central to Arnauld's own theory of ideas, and he introduces it as completely self-evident, requiring no special explanation, although it takes some explaining to distinguish it both from corporeal images by which it is sometimes explained, and from alleged representative beings distinct from our representings or ideas.[42]

Early precedents for the Cartesian use of the notion can be found, for instance, in Henry of Ghent, who took Avicenna to assign not only a distinct intelligible content to essences or natures when considered in themselves, but also a distinctive kind of *esse*. Henry refers to this being as a thing's *esse essentiae*, which John Wippel has translated, with some hesitation, as essential being. The distinction between a thing's essential being and its existence is, for Henry, an intentional distinction, which lies somewhere between a distinction of reason and a real distinction. The essences of creatures, as objects of God's knowledge, depend on the divine ideas as on their formal cause, but Henry does not, according to Wippel, identify their *esse essentia* with their *esse intentionale*.[43]

Henry's view concerning the ontological status of nonexisting possibles is not easy to grasp. Without having actual existence, they are distinct from the divine essence. Wippel writes that they "seem to fall into a kind of metaphysical 'no-man's land' between purely intentional being, on the one hand, and actually existing being, on the other." Henry's division of being, he argues, can be represented by three levels: (1) that of "purely intentional or mental beings" (*entia rationis* or chimeras); (2) that of essential being (*esse essentiae*) enjoyed by nonexistent possibles *(res a ratitudine);* and (3) that of actual existence, enjoyed by actually existing entities. The second and the third level both fall under Henry's general heading of *ens reale* or real being.[44]

A similar notion of intentional objects with real being without actual existence reappears in Duns Scotus, who does not, of course, adopt it without criticisms and further distinctions.[45] Interestingly, as Normore points out, Scotus makes use of this notion also in his account of human knowledge.[46]

There is thus a sense in which things can be objects of thought or cognition without having actual existence. Things *qua* known or conceived have a kind of *esse* or real being that Scotus also calls *esse intelligibile* and that he qualifies as diminutive being (*esse diminutum*). Moreover, the distinctive *esse* attributable to ideas as things *qua* conceived is caused by God. Although Scotus's view on the ultimate origin of possibility and necessity seems different from the radical position defended by Descartes, it is interesting to note that Scotus too takes some kind of causality to be required for the being pertaining to things *qua* cognized. Without presupposing their actual existence, the essential being pertaining to things as objects of cognition and described as diminished is something that requires a cause.[47] Speaking of what it is that requires a cause in ontological terms as some diminished amount of being is not very helpful. But one can also think of the being a thing acquires in being thought of as having to do with the ways it meets the (transcendental) conditions of cognition in general. To be cognized, a particular must have some structure of properties and relations by virtue of which it is individuated as this particular thing of which existence can be predicated without contradiction (logical possibility). When it is cognized (understood), its (possible) being is actualized in the understanding.

5. Degrees of Objective Reality

While Descartes's use of the related notions of objective reality and possible being, disregarding his radical view of modality, appears well rooted in the Scholastic tradition influenced by Henry and Duns Scotus,[48] his application of the Platonist doctrine of degrees of reality to ideas taken objectively is a more controversial "innovation." What sense does it make to compare (as Descartes does in the Third Meditation) the contents of human thoughts with respect to their degree of reality? Can merely possible beings have more or less reality depending on their nature? This is how Descartes states his view:

> Insofar as the ideas are simply modes of thought, there is no recognizable inequality among them: they all appear to come from within me in the same fashion. But insofar as different ideas represent different things, it is clear that they differ widely. Undoubtedly, the ideas which represent substances to me amount to something more and, so to speak, contain within themselves more objective reality than the ideas which merely represent modes or accidents. Again, the idea that gives me understanding of a supreme God, eternal, infinite, <immutable,> omniscient, omnipotent and the creator of all the things that exist apart from him, certainly has in it more objective reality than the ideas that represent finite substances. (AT VII 40, CSM II 27–28)

The doctrine of degrees of reality applies primarily to natures, not to objects, which means that the nature of a self-subsisting thing, God, has the highest degree of reality (or perfection), and that the natures of created substances, which require only God for their subsistence, have more reality than that of modes, because they can neither be nor be conceived without the substance in which they inhere. In the Cartesian ontological hierarchy, modes occupy the lowest degree of reality or perfection.[49]

Granted this structure, we may still ask how it follows that our *ideas* of the different kinds of natures have a corresponding degree of reality. In asking this question we join those whom Descartes contemptuously declares to have such a weak natural light that they do not see that it is a primary notion that every perfection objectively present in an idea must exist really (formally or eminently) in some cause of the idea (AT VII 135–136, CSM II 97). Anyone ever so little familiar with Scholastic philosophy ought to know that it is a primary principle, manifest to natural light, "that there should be at least as much being [*esse*] in an efficient and total cause as in the effect of that cause" (AT VII 40, CSM II 28). But whoever thought of applying this principle to the intentional being of ideas existing merely objectively? Descartes is not content to affirm that the cause must contain as much objective reality as the idea that it causes. His claim is that the cause must contain at least as much reality actually (or formally) as the idea contains objectively: "inasmuch as this objective mode of being applies to ideas from their nature so the formal mode of being applies to the causes of the ideas, at least the first and principal one from their nature" (AT VII 42, CSM II 29).[50]

If Descartes is the first to apply the principle of causality in the context of ideas taken objectively, his successors seemed to have no difficulties in accepting it. Arnauld took it to be self-evident, and so did Spinoza, who described it as "acknowledged by everyone."[51] The principle is clearly indispensable to Descartes: there seems to be no other way for him to reach beyond the realm of merely possible existence presented by the various ideas in his mind. The way out is provided by the idea or concept of a supremely perfect being:

> Existence is contained in the idea or concept of every single thing, since we cannot conceive of anything except as existing. Possible or contingent existence is contained in the concept of a limited thing, whereas necessary and perfect existence is contained in the concept of a supremely perfect being. (AT VII 166, CSM II 117)

To say of something that it is contained in the concept of a thing is to say that it is true of that thing, according to a definition laid down in Descartes's exposition, *more geometrico*, of the argument in the *Meditations*. Since necessary existence is contained in the concept of God, it may be truly affirmed of God that necessary existence belongs to him, or, in other words, that he exists (AT VII 167, CSM II 117).[52]

Objective reality entails possible existence; indeed, the objective reality of an idea is the possible existence of its object. This connection of Descartes's views on objective reality with his views on modality explains, as Normore notes, why Descartes thinks of objective reality as requiring a formally real cause.[53] But the degree of objective reality (possible existence) is also connected to the conceivability of a thing: "possible existence is contained in the concept or idea of everything that we *clearly* and *distinctly* understand" (AT VII 116, CSM II 83; emphasis mine). Since ideas vary with respect to the degree of clearness and distinctness with which they can be conceived, this raises the question whether all ideas contain some objective reality, and if not, how those that have none could represent, which is discussed in the next chapter. First some other problems related to Descartes's view of representation should be considered.

6. Objective Reality and the Veil-of-Ideas

Cartesian ideas are representational acts or modes of the mind, and they represent by virtue of the objective reality that they contain or display *(exhibeat)* to the mind. But if objective reality simply is the thing in its intentional being—the thing itself as thinkable—then it seems misleading to speak of *ideas* as having objective reality, or of ideas, taken objectively, as contained in the mind. The idea represents because it is the thing thought of, not because it is some entity in the mind signifying the object and standing, as it were, between the thought and the external object. The immediate object of thought is the thing, not the idea (representation) of the thing. My thought of, say, a particular goat is identical with the particular goat though having a different ontological status. The goat as an object of my thought has objective (intentional) being; if it exists in actual reality, it has also formal (or subjective) being. What I am thinking of is a goat, which may not exist formally but which in my thinking of it acquires intentional being as an actual object of my thought. The goat as actual and the goat as thought of is the same entity but with different degrees of reality. The thing as thought of, *qua* object of thought, has a kind of being, which reflects on another level the degree of formal reality it would have as actually existing.

On this view, there is nothing between the representation and the thing represented. Nevertheless it is frequently said that Descartes's view of ideas involves intermediate representational entities between the mind and the object of thought. Anthony Kenny, for instance, writes that "for Descartes the res cogitata that exists in my mind when I think of the sun is not the sun itself, but some proxy for the sun," so to think of the sun would be to think of the idea of the sun.[54] What misleads here, of course, is the spatial metaphor Descartes uses when speaking of ideas being *in* the mind, but for an idea (the object *qua* represented) to be in the mind is simply to be thought of. The act of thinking (the representing) is a mode of the mind, but nothing can be literally *in* the mind since the mind lacks spatial extension. To Caterus's question what the idea of the sun is, Descartes answers that "it is the thing which is thought of, insofar as it has objective being in the intellect."

> By this I mean that the idea of the sun is the sun itself existing in the intellect—not of course formally existing as it does in the heavens, but objectively existing, i.e., in the way in which objects normally are in the intellect. Now this mode of being is of course much less perfect than that possessed by things which exist outside the intellect; but . . . it is not therefore simply nothing. (AT VII 102–103, CSM II 75)

Kenny sees in this passage "a certain reduplication taking place" because he takes Descartes's statement that "when I have an idea of the sun an idea of the sun has objective existence in me" to mean "when I think of the sun I think of the idea of the sun," and he concludes that an extra entity has been spirited into existence.[55] It should be clear by now, however, that Descartes does not claim that to think of the sun is to think of an idea of the sun.

There is, however, a natural source for this misreading other than the unfortunate metaphor of ideas being in the mind. Descartes often stresses that ideas are what we are immediately aware of—for example, in the *Meditations* where he states that the term "thought" is used to "include everything that is within us in such a way that we are immediately aware of it" (AT VII 160, CSM II 113). This suggests that in thinking of something, say this table, I am immediately conscious of my idea of the table, not of the table itself, and that ideas can immediately represent only other ideas. But Descartes's view is rather that I'm not thinking of an idea of the table but of the table. It is, as Alan Donagan stresses, "fundamental to Descartes's concept of an idea that, whatever it represents, it represents immediately," and this means nothing else than I can be in no doubt whatsoever about what I am actually representing or thinking of.[56]

Husserl agrees on this and concludes that consciousness and its contents can be the objects of an apodictic science, whose objects are immediately given and can therefore be studied without existential commitment to anything other than the thinking subject—indeed, without even raising the question of what else exists in reality. But Descartes had other ambitions: he was less interested in the structure of consciousness (thought) than in that of the world, and his problem was to find out which of his ideas are of real, that is, possible things, and among the latter, which are of things existing in actual reality "outside me" (AT VII 40, CSM II 27). On his view, there is nothing in an idea of a thing, no matter how distinctly perceived, to warrant the (actual) existence of its object, with the exception of the idea of God, which contains necessary existence (*Principles* I, art. 14 (AT VIII-1 10, CSM I 197)), or that of myself, since I am immediately aware of my existence as an individual thinker. It is this and not the notion that ideas stand between us and reality that renders the question of the truth of falsity of ideas—their correspondence to actual reality—such a crucial one for Descartes and forces him to rely on the veracity of the author of his clear and distinct ideas as the ultimate warranty of the truth and certainty of the science founded on them.

7. The Problem of Representation in the Aristotelian Tradition

The talk of ideas as *having* objective reality, even though Descartes is occasionally guilty of it, seems inappropriate if objective reality is a form of being of the things thought of or represented. Objective reality is the represented reality of the thing itself and cannot, therefore, belong to ideas as representational acts, that is, to ideas taken materially as acts of the mind. If the objective reality of the sun is the reality of the sun as an object of thought, then it cannot also pertain to *my* idea of the sun when I conceive it: in thinking of the sun it is not my thought that has objective reality but the sun when thought of.[57]

The difficulty here, however, is part of the deeper one of how ideas, considered in their objective reality—that is, as the things they represent taken "objectively"—can at the same time also be modifications (concepts) of the mind.

One traditional model for understanding this, not without problems of its own, is the Aristotelian notion of ideas as forms inhering in matter. Ideas are forms of things: they inform matter when actualized and they inform the mind when being thought of. The same form occurs here in two different manners of being. The form is the nature of the thing itself that can be actualized in various ways: it can be instantiated as a particular thing or it can be actualized in the mind, which conceives it by abstracting the form from its particular instantiations.[58]

Descartes too speaks of ideas as forms in this sense (Fourth Replies) and of ideas informing the mind (Second Replies). "Form" here should not be confused with "formal" in the sense of actually existing, which Descartes used before when contrasting formal reality with objective reality. The *formal reality* of an idea applies to the idea taken materially, as an occurrent act or operation of mind. But the idea *taken formally* is the idea taken objectively. Thus in answering Arnauld he stresses that ideas as representations (taken objectively) are ideas "taken formally": "Since ideas are forms of a kind, and are not composed of any matter, when we think of them as representing something we are taking them not materially but formally" (AT VII 232, ll. 11–15, CSM II 163). Since according to the traditional Aristotelian view, the form of a thing is its nature and hence as such remains the same whether we think of it or not—it is mind-independent—Descartes's view so far conforms broadly to the Aristotelian view.

Things get more complicated, however, if we ask what it is for an idea to inform a particular mind. The very notion of form or "species" ("intentions" in the Latin translations of Aristotle's Arabic commentators) carries with it an ambivalence that subsequent accounts accentuate.[59] Descartes is often accused by modern commentators of creating this problem because of his radical distinction between the mind and the body,[60] but although this may have aggravated it, the medieval debates about the role of forms and their relation to external objects show that its roots lie elsewhere. The Scholastics confronted the same kind of difficulties in another form by their double commitment to the Aristotelian doctrine of the primacy of senses on the one hand, and to the thesis that the intellect lacks material organs on the other.[61] How can a form received first in the sense organ also be received in the immaterial intellect?[62]

Aquinas's position on the question of the origin of the intelligible species is, as on so many matters, a compromise between Augustinian Platonism and Aristotelian naturalism. The intellect is said to possess the species potentially by participation, and although they are ultimately traceable to a purely intelligible first cause, namely God, they "are said to proceed from that principle through the medium of sensible, material things." Material things are *actually* sensible but not actually intelligible. The possible intellect is brought from potentiality to actuality by a being that is actual, namely, the agent intellect, which Aquinas takes to belong to the soul (ST, Ia. 84, 5).[63]

At least two kinds of representations are involved in this account: the sense images and the intelligible species abstracted from these images. The solution suggested by Aquinas to the question of what constitutes in fact the (direct) object of knowledge or understanding is the same for the intelligible species as for the sensible species or images. The latter, as he says, are *not what is sensed,* they are rather *that by which* sensation takes place. The intelligible species, similarly, are not the objects understood, but *that by which* the intellect understands.[64] It is not the stone that is present in the soul but its form, from which it follows that the soul, by means of the species, knows things that are outside the soul. It is not the abstracted species, but that of which it is a likeness, that is known or understood. However, the species can, secondarily, be that which is understood, if the intellect reflects on itself and by that reflection understands both its own understanding and the species by which it understands. What is understood first (directly), therefore, is the thing of which a particular species is a likeness, with the species being secondary objects of understanding (ST Ia. 85, 2). The intelligible species has a twofold role: it is on the one hand *that by which* the intellect knows the external object, and which, as such, is not itself an object of knowledge, and it is, on the other hand, through reflection, a secondary object of understanding.[65]

The species posited by Aquinas to explain how things are presented to the soul were interpreted literally by many of his followers as imagelike entities representing through likeness with the thing represented. This was the unquestioned assumption of the influential theory of multiplication of the species elaborated by Roger Bacon (ca. 1220–1292) and his followers (the "perspectivists") in explaining vision, which became the standard explanation of sense perception in the thirteenth and fourteenth centuries.[66]

The theory of sense perception that Descartes opposes can be seen as one variant of the Baconian theory, which was subject to criticism already by late medieval philosophers. Though Bacon does not understand the propagation of species literally as a (mechanical) transmission of impressions, but rather as a process of successive actualizations of the potentials preexisting in various media, it was interpreted by some as a mechanical transmission of images or likenesses.[67] Because the species—or as they were also called, "likenesses," "images," also "virtues," "phantasms," "forms," or "intentions," which can be "produced both by substance and by accident, spiritual and corporeal"— were taken to be impressed, through the action of the object, on the passive senses, and through abstraction on the intellect, and also because they were understood as exact likenesses of the things causing them, they were thought to be able to make their object present, that is, to *re*present it to the mind.[68]

Among the earliest critics of the species theory were Durandus of St. Pourçain and Petrus Olivi (Franciscan theologians) who preceded Ockham in rejecting the species from their account of cognition.[69] Petrus Olivi's main argument against the Baconian theory is that it is the last species in the chain of multiplication, and not the object causing it, which is directly perceived. The argument is basically the same as the one raised against the so called veil-of-ideas theory, with which Descartes has been charged, although, according to recent critics, its most typical early defender is Locke.[70]

Henri of Ghent and Duns Scotus agreed that species are neither corporeal, nor spiritual entities, nor are they substantial forms of any kind. They took them instead to have a diminished form of being *(esse diminutum)*. Their discussions concerning the intelligible species are of particular interest. While both seemed to have accepted the theory of the multiplication of species in the explanation of sense perception, both had difficulties with the assumption that the process of multiplication continues into the immaterial intellect. Henry rejected the whole assumption of intelligible species as superfluous.[71] Scotus, for his part, introduces his notion of intuitive cognition as a direct, non-mediated apprehension of a particular existent present to the senses or the intellect.[72]

Although Ockham starts out as an adherent of a Scotist view, which accords *esse cognitum* or *esse objectivum* to nonexistent objects of thought (including universals), he later abandoned the assumption of separate objectively existing, intentional objects. Among the criticisms raised against it was that it compromised direct realism, and that the positing of such entities is redundant. Ockham seems in the end to have accepted some version of an adverbial theory, according to which acts of thought are, for instance, "acts-of-thinking-of-a-golden-mountain and are directed to their real objects by their properties," not by an intentional object.[73] Ockham thus opts for the view that extramental singular things are the direct objects of apprehensions (which are either intuitive or abstractive) and can depend either on the senses or the intellect. Instead of species, Ockham posits "habits" that are caused by intellectual intuitive apprehensions of singulars and that somehow remain in the intellect, enabling the intellect to renew at will the abstractive apprehensions in the absence of the object.[74]

The terminology contrasting "formal" versus "objective" aspects of concepts is undoubtedly taken over by Descartes from Suárez, who reported the difficulties debated by his predecessors concerning representation and its objects and presented his own solution to it.[75] With the distinctions and the terminology adopted from the Scholastics, Descartes inherits many of the problems discussed by his predecessors. We need a much more detailed knowledge of their views of representation to determine precisely what Descartes contributes to the debate, and notably, whether he had any original solutions to the difficulties encountered by earlier accounts or merely repeated the old difficulties in a new form. At best, the account of representation Descartes gives is incomplete—at worst, it is inconsistent. It all depends on how its gaps are filled out.

Like his predecessors, Descartes posits a vehicle in the mind that "receives" the idea actually conceived, and he refers to it as the idea taken materially. The idea taken materially (the idea as "act") exists as a mode of mind and as such has actual or formal reality. The actual (formal) reality of the idea, hence, is the reality of an occurrent operation of an individual mind conceiving something—for instance, my present thinking of the sun, as distinguished from my earlier thought when doubting I would see it today. It is a process—it has duration—although it has no extension. When speaking of the idea in its formal reality, Descartes speaks of the particular mental operation by which a thing is thought of. In addition to its formal reality as an act, every idea has a content—the idea taken objectively—but taken objectively, the idea has no formal reality in itself. It has a mind-independent structure—which is that of the thing it represents: the objective reality or form by virtue of which the thing thought of can be cognized, whether or not instantiated in actual reality. Mind or thinking provides the subject, the stuff or what Descartes in his correspondence with Hobbes characterizes as "metaphysical matter"—that is being informed or modified by the idea actually entertained, which is just the thing thought of in its objective (possible) being, without its formal (actual) being. There is one formal thing—the idea as a mode or act of mind—considered under two different aspects: that of its actuality, and that of its content.

It is important, as noted above, not to confuse the *formal reality of the idea,* which applies only to the idea as an act or operation, with the *idea taken formally,* which applies to the mind-independent form. The latter has no actual (formal) reality independent of its particular instantiation; it is a form or nature, a possible thing that may or may not exist actually. Thoughts come and go in a continuous flow, and so do the particulars that are thought of, but this does not affect their nature—their objective reality (thinkability or possibility)—which remains what it is whether or not actually conceived.

Descartes's distinguishing two aspects of ideas in terms of different modes of reality may be seen as an attempt to account for mental representation without positing representational entities over and above the mental act itself. No intermediate entities are posited, because the reality pertaining to the idea as form—the objective reality—is not the reality of actually existing beings.[76] Because the domain of intelligibility or possibility requires no other foundation than God's will, ideas as forms (possible beings) require no external causes other than the act by which God posited them and the minds that can think them.[77]

While Descartes also uses "idea" both for the mental act and its object, covering ideas in both their aspects, Malebranche deliberately departs from Descartes's usage in taking "the word 'idea' . . . to signify uniquely the objective reality." As Steven Nadler interprets him, Malebranche thinks ideas *are* objective realities,[78] stressing hereby their complete independence from the mind. To stress their independence from the human mind, Malebranche goes as far as to place ideas in God's mind. Malebranche thereby avoids the ambiguity of

Descartes's use of "idea" in the general sense: objective reality is the reality of ideas in God's mind. Malebranche may be more consistent in his use of objective reality, but confronts other difficulties through the idealism he commits himself to.

Had Descartes been more consistent in his use of terms, we might have been spared some unnecessary controversy. Had he, for instance, spoken throughout of the reality that ideas *display (exhibeat)* instead of, as he occasionally does, the reality that they have or possess, the attribution of a copy or veil-of-ideas theory of representation to Descartes might have been avoided. Talking of ideas (instead of things) as having objective reality, however, comes naturally to Descartes because of the general use he makes of the term "idea" to cover both the act of thinking and its content and because he thinks of the act and the object as inseparable. It is this broad use of the term "idea" Malebranche protests against when reserving the term only for the objects of thought. When being more careful, Descartes too, as we have seen, reserves the term "idea"—its proper sense—for the latter. But he need not, like Malebranche, put them in God's mind to stress their independence of the human mind. For Descartes, ideas, in the strict sense of the word, are mind-independent because they are created by God, but beyond that, as mere possibles, they have no actuality and hence require no ontological foundation, nor do they need to be located anywhere. A particular thought act depends on the individual mind of which it is a modification, but its content is mind-independent and cannot be reduced to a mental mode. Talking of the objective reality of ideas when referring to the mental act is as improper as saying of ideas, in the strict sense, that they are "in" the mind. Neither expression should be taken literally.

Steven Nadler complains that there is little agreement, "both in the seventeenth century and today, on just what makes an idea 'representative'" and that, although the notion of "representation" is central to Descartes, Arnauld, Malebranche, and others, they tell us "next to nothing" what they mean by this term.[79] The only clarification we get is negative—accounts of how ideas do not represent, for instance, by presenting likenesses or images of things. Does this mean that representation by way of ideas is inexplicable and that according to seventeenth-century Cartesians, it does not stand in need of any explanation?[80] Nadler's suggestion certainly applies to Arnauld, who echoing what

Descartes says about the term "thought," insists that the word "idea" is so clear that it cannot be explained because there are none that are more simple or clearer.[81] Descartes takes "thought" to refer to a simple nature that cannot be explained because it is irreducible. We know what thought is when we understand the meaning of the term.

Addressing the complaint of those contemporary philosophers who object that Descartes, "having failed to describe representation in intelligible terms, . . . postulated a magical mental realm that does not have to be described intelligibly," Alan Donagan has argued that Descartes never tried to explain representation, but just reminded us of this familiar phenomenon "that it occurs, and that it is irreducible."[82]

Donagan is surely right in that representation for Descartes was irreducible, if irreducibility is taken to mean not reducible to physical phenomena or explainable in terms of physical laws. But it does not follow that Descartes took it to stand in need of no account or did not try to provide one. The next chapter considers some of the problems Descartes's account of representation in terms of objective reality runs into when including what he takes to be confused and obscure thoughts like sensory perceptions with the clear and distinct ideas of the intellect under the general heading of (representational) ideas.

5

Sensory Perceptions, Beliefs, and Material Falsity

1. Impressions, Ideas, and Representations in the Early Work

To what extent is Descartes's theory of ideas as developed in the Third Meditation consistent with the account of sense perception developed much earlier in the *World* and the *Optics?* Is the later view of ideas consistent with the explanation of sensory perception offered in the scientific treatises? Does the distinction between act and object apply also to sensations, and are sensory ideas representational in the same sense as clear and distinct ideas in the strict sense of the term? If not, how do they represent, and what cognitive value does Descartes attribute to sensations?[1]

To answer these questions, let me begin with a brief look at the account of sense perception first sketched out in the *Rules* (before or around 1628) and more fully developed in the *Optics* (published in 1637). It is largely a generalization of Descartes's mechanistic theory of optics to the physiology of perception. Because of the metaphor of vision it involves, this account has been seen as a form of representative theory of sensory perception, but it has also, at the other extreme, been taken as a form of direct empirical realism.[2] The direct empirical realism imputed to Descartes is the view that cerebral impressions are the only direct objects of perception, whereas the version of representationalism to which it is contrasted holds that nothing but (immaterial) ideas can be directly perceived.[3] Considering some of the grounds for such classifications is useful in trying to understand the view Descartes may be seen as advocating. Both interpretations are misleading and rest on the questionable assumption that ideas constitute for Descartes the immediate objects of perception.[4]

In giving his first account of our cognitive powers in the *Rules*, Descartes, as we saw in Chapter 1, section 4, uses the language of traditional faculty psychology. He retains the usual classification of faculties based on different functions, but substitutes for the Scholastic theory a strictly mechanistic account of the workings of the external and internal senses. Knowledge is reserved for the intellect alone, which can be helped or hindered by the imagination, the senses, and memory (AT X 395, 398, CSM I 30, 32). Since memory—at least the memory called corporeal—turns out to be essentially the same as imagination, there are only two "modes of knowing" ("faculties") besides pure understanding to be scrutinized.[5] Descartes already insists that truth or falsity in the strict sense can be in the intellect alone, although they often "originate from the other two modes of knowing," the senses and the imagination (AT X 396, CSM I 30).

Descartes's theory, so far, is vague and sketchy and does not say much about the intellect or truth and falsity. But in Rule Twelve a new account of the physiology of sense perception is proposed, which is a generalization to all the senses of his mechanistic version of Kepler's optical theory, and which is more fully developed in the *World* and the *Optics*.[6] He uses the Aristotelian example of the wax and the seal, not as an analogy, but as a concrete illustration of the mechanical impression of figures and shapes in the sense organs and in the part of the brain where the so-called common sense and imagination are located. The corporeal modifications of the brain are called now "figures," now "ideas," now "pictures" or "images" (AT X 413–417, CSM I 40–42), but are always taken to be geometrical patterns traced on the surface of some part of the brain corresponding to the common sense and imagination. It is also assumed that the differences between qualities perceivable by the senses can be explained by differences only in the shapes of the figures impressed in the corporeal imagination. It should be noted that this is presented as a useful and economical supposition, not as a true theory (AT X 413, CSM I 41).

Some commentators have taken this early account to involve a direct epistemological realism on the ground that since ideas are patterns of corporeal movements in the brain, the mind has direct cognitive awareness of some physical objects, namely, of the corporeal patterns or ideas that constitute the immediate objects of perception.[7] This reading is supported by the assumption that Descartes had not yet worked out his reductive conception of matter as mere extension and was therefore not in a position to claim, as he did later, that the essence of matter can be known through the intellect alone, by mental inspection. Instead, he held that the intellect depends on its close association with the corporeal imagination for conceiving material things,[8] and took his mechanistic theory of perception to provide both an epistemological and ontological foundation for the new mathematical method.[9]

This mistaken supposition originates mainly in the account given in Rule Twelve of the "corporeal" imagination.[10] What strikes me about this account, however, is that while Descartes takes "idea" to be a (physical) *representation* of the thing presented to the senses, it is the external thing represented, not the idea itself, that is the proper object of perception. For he explains how the perception of external things can be facilitated by forming "certain abbreviated representations," which can then be displayed to the senses in place of the things themselves (AT X 417, CSM I 43). What is perceived is the external thing "displayed to the senses"—first directly, and then, when it is no longer present in itself, by means of some schematic (geometrical) representation. The latter can be presented to the senses in the absence of the thing represented, and its traces are easier to retain in memory than those of the thing itself. In both cases the perception of the external object seems to be occasioned by an unnoticed "idea" (or "representation") impressed on the corporeal imagination (the brain) and caused by the action of the object on the senses.

Descartes gives detailed instructions (in Rules Fourteen and following) for how extended things should be represented in the imagination by means of schematic figures, in order to be more distinctly conceived by the intellect.[11] The schematic figures are, of course, essential to Descartes's mathematico-physical method, and the hypothesis that they could be systematically correlated with the extended objects they represent via patterns impressed in the brain certainly contributes to Descartes's great confidence in that method. But there is no need to assume that Descartes held the brain patterns to be objects of direct perception, nor does anything he says indicate that his new method was grounded in that kind of empirical realism.[12] This assumption, moreover, takes no account of the difference between the physical conditions for the functioning of the imagination and the senses on the one hand, and the exercise those faculties as powers of the immaterial mind on the other.

It is true that Descartes departs from his later usage of the term "idea," where it is restricted to purely mental representations, in applying it to the figures or schematic representations impressed in the corporeal imagination in the brain. But this does not justify the assumption that brain patterns are directly perceived by the mind, unless it is *also* assumed that ideas are the direct objects of mental acts and that nothing other than ideas can be directly perceived. This latter assumption, however, is questionable.

In Rule Twelve, the effects of external bodies on the corporeal imagination and the nerves are said to be sufficient to explain all the movements of animals as well as the movements in humans that are carried out without reason. Since humans are also endowed with reason, however, the changes in the corporeal imagination are accompanied by "awareness." This is awareness not of movements in the brain, but of sensible (phenomenal) qualities occasioned by those movements and by the external things taken to cause them.[13]

Not only the real distinction between the mind and the body but also the fundamental unity of mind and its cognitive capacities are clearly granted in Rule Twelve:

> [T]he power through which we know things in the strict sense is purely spiritual, and is no less distinct from the whole body than blood is distinct from bone, or the hand from the eye. It is one single power, whether it receives figures from the "common" sense at the same time as does the corporeal imagination, or applies itself to those which are preserved in the memory, or forms new ones . . . In all these functions the cognitive power is sometimes passive, sometimes active . . . It is one and the same power, when applying itself along with the imagination to the "common" sense, it is said to see, touch, etc.; when addressing itself to the imagination alone, insofar as the latter is invested with various figures, it is said to remember; when applying itself to the imagination in order to form new figures, it is said to imagine or conceive; and

lastly, when it acts on its own, it is said to understand . . . According to its different functions, then, *the same power is called either pure intellect, or imagination, or memory, or sense-perception.* (AT X 416, CSM I 42–43; my emphasis)

It should be noted that it is the intellect alone, a purely spiritual power, that imagines and has sensations, insofar as these are more than mechanical movements, that is, are accompanied by awareness. The intellect is said to "*receive* figures from the common sense at the same time as does the corporeal imagination" when sensing. When it remembers, imagines, or conceives, it is said to apply itself to the figures in the (corporeal) imagination or common sense.

Because the intellect is said to apply itself to corporeal (cerebral) pictures, it has been concluded that the latter must constitute the direct or immediate objects of awareness.[14] But one should be very careful not to take those expressions too literally. Again using the wax analogy, Descartes compares the intellect, when it is passive, to the wax, and when it is active to the seal, because like the wax it receives ideas from the "common" sense, and like the seal it can impress or transmit "ideas" (figures) to the corporeal imagination and the nerves. But we are warned that the wax–seal example, this time, is to be taken "merely as an analogy, for nothing quite like this power is found in the corporeal things" (AT X 415, CSM I 42), and not literally, as it is when applied to the impression of figures via the senses in the brain. As noted above, the latter are themselves representations of a kind; they are figures representing the external things causing them. But the intellect, when "applying itself" to those figures, does not perceive them as geometrical figures representing external things. What the intellect directly perceives are the things causing those figures, namely, the external objects and their qualities. They, *not* the cerebral traces they cause by acting on the sense organs, are what the intellect knows, remembers, senses, or imagines.[15] Here, as later, the cerebral impressions function more like signs making us think of the things they signify than as images portraying their model because of some pictorial or structural likeness. That the visual analogy involved in the talk about the mind directing itself to or considering "images" in the brain is not to be taken literally is confirmed by Descartes's using the analogy later, where the term "idea" is reserved for the *mental* representing and its application to brain events is rejected as improper.[16]

I do not wish to deny that Descartes takes intellectual intuition to consist in a kind of direct contact between the mind and its object (the so-called simple natures) and that, following an influential tradition, he describes intuitive knowledge as a direct seeing (or mental vision) of the objects attended to and of the necessary connections between them.[17] But direct mental intuition can be, for Descartes, only of intellectual (intelligible) objects—of what is clearly and distinctly perceived, not of what is perceived by the senses—at least not before the purported object of sensory perception has been critically examined by the intellect.

The simple natures are defined (in Rules Eight and Twelve) as simple with regard not to their existence but to our intellect—to what can be clearly and distinctly understood without being analyzed into further elements—and thus are what in the order of knowledge are most accessible to the understanding (AT X 399; AT X 418). They are also taken to be real constituents of existing (actual) things, but they are not given to the senses as such—they are not objects of sensory perception. As we saw (Chapter 1, section 5), Descartes divides the simple natures into purely intellectual, purely material, or common to both (AT X 399; AT X 419). Those that are purely material (as shape, extension, motion, and so on) are known to exist only in bodies (AT X 419, CSM I 45). But it does not follow that they can be conceived or perceived only through sense perception or imagination. For though Descartes holds that they *can* be most easily conceived with the aid of corporeal images,[18] he does not claim that they *cannot* be known at all without the aid of corporeal representations. On the contrary, as simple natures, they are taken to be self-evident (AT X 420), and as such they surely can be known without assistance from the imagination or the senses.[19]

Knowledge in the sense of *Scientia*, here as later, is restricted to what is perceived by the intellect alone, that is, to what can be the object of direct intuition or deduced from what is directly intuited, namely, the simple natures (AT X 423–424). It is a matter of sensory experience how contingent, composite things appear and affect our senses, but knowledge of their true properties and constituents (the simple natures) is a matter of intuition and judgment, which depend on the intellect and require a critical analysis of what exactly is given in experience: "[T]he intellect can never be deceived by any experience, provided that when the object is presented to it, it intuits it in a fashion exactly corresponding to the way it possesses the object, either in itself or in the imagination" (AT X 423, CSM I 47).[20]

To intuit in a fashion "exactly corresponding" to what is possessed in the imagination is, so I understand it, to abstain from judgment about what is not directly given in the imagination—for instance, about what, in external bodies, the brain, or the organs, may cause the mind to imagine what it presently imagines. We must not judge that what is pictured in the imagination "faithfully represents the objects of the senses, or that *the senses take on the true shapes of things,* or in short that external things are just as they appear to be." The only thing the wise can judge with confidence is that "whatever comes to him from the imagination is really depicted in it"—in other words, that *something* is depicted in the corporeal imagination as a result of a stimulation of the corporeal organs. He will never assert that what passes from the external world via the senses to the imagination "passes, complete and unaltered, *unless he knows this through some other reasons*" (AT X 423, CSM I 47; my emphasis).

The sensory act thus cannot by itself give us certainty of the veridicality of its content. We must have other grounds from the intellect itself for making true and certain judgments about the nature of things causing our sensations.[21] Thus, far from providing an epistemological justification of the reliability of the senses or the corporeal imagination, Descartes's physiological theory (itself the product of some form of Descartes's "marvelous" method) shows how very little can in fact be known through sense perception alone. Indeed, his physiological theory undermines any claims to direct and *certain* knowledge of material things based primarily on the senses.[22]

The physiology of perception developed in Descartes's later scientific writings does provide an empirical account of perception, which shows that sensory ideas are representational without involving any resemblances and which also explains their occurrence in terms of mathematical physics. It has been argued that the "*generalized* concept of representation" that is central to this account, and which covers various forms of representation other than that of pictorial resemblance, was introduced in the *World* and the *Optics*.[23] This concept is at work, notably, in the physiological explanation of color ideas in the *Meteors,* which shows that although these ideas bear no resemblance to the things causing them, there are systematic "interconnections among them that represent real relations in nature."[24]

But I want to claim that this generalized notion of representation is not something Descartes introduced in the *World* after having first defended some form of direct empirical realism. The very same notion can be found already in Rule Twelve, where it is suggested that the infinite diversity of figures suffices to express all the differences between sensible things (things perceived by the senses), and that we can conceive any such differences (for instance, between two colors) as a difference in geometrical configuration (AT X 413, CSM I 41).

One could invoke against my reading the recurrent use in the *Treatise on Man* of "idea" or "form" for the figures traced by the animal spirits on the pineal gland, together with the claim that these ideas are what the rational soul *considers immediately* in imagining or sensing an object (AT XI 176, CSM I 106). This has been taken to suggest a direct realism,[25] but I think it merely shows that Descartes's terminology was not very clear and he had not yet fully worked out his philosophy of mind.[26] That Descartes took the figures or ideas that the mind is here said to consider immediately not to be direct objects of perception, but rather causes or occasions for sense perceptions, is clear from the preceding paragraph, where the same figures are treated as signs giving occasion not only to perceptions of sensory qualities but to feelings and passions as well.[27]

That Descartes calls these cerebral impressions "ideas" may be just a careless concession to the theory he opposes, according to which resemblances of things are literally transmitted from the sense organs to the brain, where they are contemplated by the mind.[28] It is this very assumption and the visual metaphor it involves that his physiological theory of sense perception is supposed to replace. According to Schuster's reading of Rule Twelve, the *vis cognoscens* constitutes as it were "a spiritual pair of eyes within the brain, there to attend to patterns delivered upon the corporeal screen of the brain loci,"[29] but, as we have seen (Chapter 4, section 2), it is this metaphor that Descartes explicitly rejects in the passage from the *Optics* quoted above.

The generalized concept of representation Descartes adopts does not commit him to the kind of disastrous representative theory of sense perception that drives a wedge between the knower and the known so often imputed to him, nor does it involve an indirect representational realism of the kind ascribed to Locke. Descartes's theory of sense perception undercuts the Scholastic ontology of forms and species, and its assumption that sense perceptions are resemblances of external things representing their real features in some unproblematic way. But it preserves a causal—or quasi-causal—link between the things acting on the senses and the ideas representing them, though the ideas are acts through which the external things are represented, and are not themselves objects of representation. One form of the representative theory attributed to Descartes holds that ideas are the direct objects of perception, but in the absence of any ontological link between mental ideas and physical matter, the mind finds itself entrapped with its ideas without direct cognitive access to physical things—it knows them only through perceiving their duplicates. A modified version of this theory, attributed to Locke and described as "representational realism," holds that some sensory ideas (those of primary qualities) are faithful reproductions of features of extended things, while those of secondary qualities do not represent anything.[30] On this account some sensory ideas resemble the features they represent and are caused by, while others, caused by the same primary qualities, do not resemble them and hence can have no representative content at all.

The attribution of this kind of theory to Descartes is quite unjustified because he does not distinguish, in the way Locke does, between primary and secondary qualities: *no* sense perceptions (including spatial perceptions), for Descartes, represent by way of likeness, and the so-called primary qualities (which correspond to the simple natures of Rule Twelve) are not perceived by the senses at all but by the intellect.[31] Moreover, while Descartes holds that the sensations caused by the action of physical things on the sense organs make us aware of their presence,[32] he does not hold that the ideas themselves are separate objects of perception, as required by the representationalist reading. On that reading, ideas are "reified"—they are construed as representative entities separated from the mental act, constituting, as it were, a third kind of thing intervening between the knower and the known. Neither in the case of his theory of ideas in general nor in his

account of sense perception did Descartes ever hold an "object theory" of ideas.[33]

2. "Idea" in the Later Work: The Problematic Intentionality of Sensations

Descartes reserves the term "idea" in his mature work for what "in-
forms" *the mind* when it is "directed to" or affected by certain traces in
the brain (as contrasted with the images depicted by those traces *in the
brain*).[34] That same metaphor of the mind directing itself toward some
part of the brain, which in the context of the early writings has been
taken as evidence for direct empirical realism, occurs here in what is
usually seen as a clearly representationalist framework, where a literal
reading of the metaphor makes no sense. The cerebral images are not
actually perceived at all, but "ordained by nature" to give the soul
sense perceptions of various kinds. This natural institution theory
seems to be the only answer Descartes can give to the question of how
particular brain traces are connected with ideas.[35] The mind, therefore, cannot be directed to cerebral images. Nor is it directed to the
idea understood as a separate mental entity, because Cartesian ideas
are not entities separate from the act conceiving them and intervening
between the mind and the thing represented—they are not what is
represented, but that by which external things are represented. Act
and object are inseparable in that they always occur together (AT VII
8, CSM II 7):[36] there are no objectless ideas. But the object of our cognitive (representative) acts are, at least in the case of clear and distinct
ideas, mind-independent external things themselves in their objective
reality.[37]

Descartes divides ideas, when considered objectively as representations, into three categories with respect to their origin: they are either innate (dispositions), or adventitious (sense perceptions), or
composed by us (factitious) (AT VII 37–38, CSM II 26). Sense perceptions are adventitious because they seem to come from outside: their
occurrence does not depend on the activity of the mind itself.

If ideas are representational acts, they are necessarily about something: what they are about—their object—distinguishes them from
other acts of the same kind. I may be unable to give a distinct account
of the object of my perception in having a sensation of cold, but I can

at least distinguish between, say, cold and heat, and what makes the difference is a corresponding difference in their objects, or what I take to be their objects.

But is this to say that sensations are ideas like those listed above as examples of ideas taken objectively, ideas of God, of the sky, or of a chimera? What about sensations of pain or pleasure, feelings of uneasiness, moods, melodies, and so on; do they always have an object individuating them? In short, are sensations really ideas in the strict sense of the word? The question is pressing because only ideas in the strict sense are representations of external, mind-independent things. If sensations do not have a representational content or object, what role do they play in our knowledge of reality?

The model for representation that Descartes uses in defining ideas in the strict sense is pictorial representation: ideas are said to be, *as it were*, images of things. I have tried to show that, if taken literally, this metaphor is highly misleading. Unlike images, ideas do not represent by pictorial likeness, and they are not entities interposed between the perceiver and the model. Yet ideas are like images in being actual presentations of the things they represent in their objective reality, which I have argued means that they present their objects as possible things (things of which existence can be predicated without contradiction) to the mind.[38] But what things are presented to the mind by the confused and more or less obscure sensory and emotional states?

Unlike some recent commentators, I take representation to be a general feature of all ideas: they all represent or are about something even when, as with sensory ideas, there is no telling what thing they are about. Sensory ideas do not lack objective reality but rather are so obscure that their objective reality cannot always be distinguished from their material or formal reality as mental acts.[39] But however obscure and confused they may be, they are still ideas in Descartes's restricted sense of the term.

Claiming otherwise is to say either that sensory ideas do not represent at all or that if they represent, they do so in some different sense of representation.[40] A distinction between different kinds of representation, however, would create more problems than it solves. It would leave us with two sets of representative ideas—those having and those lacking objective reality—in which case the representative character of the former would remain unexplained. It would also leave us with two notions of falsity and the task of explaining the relation between them. What Descartes calls "material falsity," I contend, is not due to a lack of objective reality. But how then is it to be understood?

3. Judgment, Truth, and Falsity in Sensory Perception

In order to discuss the perplexing notion of material falsity introduced by Descartes in the Third Meditation, we must look at his account of judgment and error. It is one of his professed doctrines that ideas, when considered in themselves, without being referred to anything else, cannot be false. Falsity occurs in judgments, and a judgment depends on an independent act of the will: there can be no falsity, properly speaking, in ideas as such.[41] Material falsity, however, seems to be an exception to this rule: it is described as another kind of falsity, intrinsic to some adventitious ideas, notably those of sensory qualities like heat and cold, of which there is no telling whether they are true or false (AT VII 44, CSM II 30). Is Descartes confusing idea with judgment or, worse, is this to be seen as another instance of inconsistency in his theory of ideas?

The brief account in the Third Meditation is very unsatisfactory, yet I think it is possible to make perfectly good sense of the view, once all the things Descartes says on this obscure topic are put together. I take materially false ideas to be complex ideas involving unnoticed, and hence uncontrolled, mistaken beliefs, which render their representative contents misleading.[42] That they easily mislead in this way has to do with their inherent lack of distinctness as ideas of sense. But because they can represent, the way of representing exemplified by clear and distinct ideas of the intellect cannot be an exclusive paradigm of representation.

Truth or falsity applies only to ideas in the strict sense as representations, but when considered in themselves—that is, not referred to anything else—they are true, not false (AT VII 37, CSM II 25–26). Merely having an idea, of a goat or a chimera, or feeling pain or desiring something cannot involve falsity. Falsity comes with judgment, which involves an act of volition affirming or denying the object represented by the idea. The most common mistake consists in judging, without sufficient evidence, that "the ideas which are in me resemble, or conform to, things located outside me" (AT VII 37, CSM II 26).

The difficulty here does not arise because ideas constitute a veil between the thinker and the external world: external things are the direct objects of thought even when they are not actually present, provided they are clearly and distinctly perceived. (See Chapter 4.) The difficulty is twofold. It consists, first, in ascertaining which ideas are clear and distinct enough to present things in their true nature, and second, in determining whether what is clearly and distinctly conceived is also actually present here and now. It is, in short, a problem of distinguishing between ideas that present things completely and adequately and ideas that are too confused to give us knowledge of the true nature and existence of things.[43] Confused ideas of sense, however, cannot just be discarded on account of being confused, because they have an important cognitive function, namely, informing us of the presence of external things and of the various ways in which they affect us.

We are concerned here only with ideas in the strict or primary sense, that is, ideas taken objectively. That is a mixed lot, ranging from sensory images to concepts and propositions. In the Third Meditation, they are classified as innate, adventitious, and factitious, and the examples discussed by Descartes span everything from ideas of particular things like a man, the sky, or a goat to concepts or notions like "thing," "truth," or "thought." The latter appear to be innate ideas, while the former, like sensory impressions (seeing the sun, feeling the fire), seem to be adventitious. Ideas of sirens, hippogriffs, and the like seem to be factitious—of my own invention (AT VII 37–38, CSM II 25–26).

An idea need not be verbal or discursive, but most ideas can be expressed by a term or a proposition. It is not how they are expressed (by terms or propositions) that marks off, say, ideas belonging to the imagination from ideas of the pure intellect; it is the manner of conceiving them. The former are conceived with, the latter without, an image.[44] Ideas in Descartes's primary sense range from the innate ideas I have called subpropositional thoughts, to self-evident "common" notions, which are propositional, to "adventitious" ideas, like obscure feelings and sensations and less obscure visual images of sensory objects, which are all nonpropositional. Are they all, when considered in themselves, *qua* modes of thought, true, giving no "material for error"? Descartes's answer is accompanied by a reservation: "[I]f I considered just the ideas themselves simply as modes of my thought, without referring them to anything else, they could *scarcely* give me any material for error" (AT VII 37, CSM II 26). We are warned that there are exceptions, namely, instances of materially false ideas.

Descartes's account of judgment is, as Margaret Wilson puts it, "fraught with difficulties and confusions."[45] There are a number of reasons for this, but they do not include, as Wilson thinks, confusion between falsity and error. Truth and falsity, for Descartes, apply to ideas taken objectively no matter what kind of ideas are involved. As ordinarily understood, however, truth value is attributed only to propositions, while nonpropositional ideas or mental representations are taken not to be bearers of truth value. Truth or error can come in only when I affirm or deny, say, the adequacy of the idea as a representation of the external object it is taken to represent. But a proposition is either true or false independently of any affirmations or denials. It might appear here that Descartes confounds falsity and error. One may entertain in one's mind a proposition that is false without being in error, as long as one merely considers it, without taking it to be true. So what Descartes should have said, Wilson observes, is "that ideas 'perceived by the understanding' may be (true or) false, but error arises not in the 'perception,' but in the affirmation."[46]

Like his late medieval predecessors, Descartes does, however, distinguish between merely entertaining an idea and assenting to or dissenting from it.[47] Assent and dissent were commonly considered functions of the intellect. Thus, in the presence of a clearly and distinctly perceived notion, assent is produced by the intellect automatically. Assent of the intellect can also be caused by the will in cases of nonevident notions, when, for instance, proposition is perceived as merely probable. But unlike most of his Scholastic predecessors, Descartes holds that affirmation and denial are always functions of the will, not of the intellect. He also seems to hold, in his most radical declarations, that the will is unrestrained or unconditioned in its capacity to assent or dissent.[48]

This is perhaps the most original and controversial aspect of Descartes's theory of judgment. The intellect is always passive, and its acts are restricted to the passive reception of ideas, whereas affirming and denying are seen as acts of the will. Ideas—whether simple or propositional, sensory or intellectual—all belong to the class of passions of the soul, which Descartes contrasts with the class of actions, the latter comprising acts of the will and the active use of the imagination.[49] As passions, ideas normally present themselves to the mind without its having any active part in how they are compounded. This accounts for why Descartes thinks that predicative notions and propositional concepts can be entertained without being false—they are passive ideas as long as they are merely considered or conceived as presented to the intellect. Only by assenting to them as true or rejecting them as false, which requires an act of the will, do they become true or false judgments. Not only does conceiving come before judging, ideas can be operated on by the imagination without any judgment made on their truth or falsity.[50]

This aspect of Descartes's theory of judgment is one his followers have found most difficult to accept. Spinoza, for instance, argues that will and intellect are inseparable in the context of belief or judgment. The affirmation of the will always involves an idea, say of a triangle, and the idea of the triangle involves the affirmation that its three angles are equal to two right angles. The idea of a triangle cannot be conceived without this affirmation, which belongs to its essence. Thus Spinoza thinks that he has proved that the will and the intellect are one and the same—that an idea involves affirmation as soon as it is conceived.[51]

Spinoza denies that we have a power of freely affirming or denying what we perceive. He grants that the will extends more widely than the intellect, if by intellect is meant only what can be understood by clear and distinct ideas; but the will, he argues, does not extend more widely than the faculty of conceiving or perceiving. There can be no volitions without perceptions, though there can be volitions without clear and distinct perceptions. Suspending one's judgment is not an act of the will, according to Spinoza. When we say that someone suspends his judgment, we are saying only that he sees that he does not have an adequate perception of the thing perceived. Suspension of judgment does not, for Spinoza, involve the will, but consists in the recognition of an inadequate or imperfect perception.[52]

According to contemporary views, a belief or judgment consists of a propositional content plus a propositional attitude. To judge something is to entertain a proposition plus have an epistemic attitude to it: taking it to be true or false, or doubtful, or likely, or whatever. The same distinction can be found in Descartes's account of judgment, though he thinks that this attitude is voluntarily chosen. Spinoza not only denies the last claim, but he does not allow for any distinction between propositions and propositional attitudes. Ideas or propositions come to the mind as judgments, that is, as affirmations or denials.[53]

In spite of his distinction between will and perception, that is, between act and content, and his explicit claim that assent or denial to a content *can* be freely chosen, Descartes would not disagree with Spinoza that ideas or propositions normally come to the mind as judgments, and that they are, as such, either true or false. But unlike Spinoza, Descartes does not hold that thinking or entertaining an idea is the *same* as explicitly affirming that it (or its propositional counterpart) is true.

Take my sensory idea of the sun: the sun, as I see it, is not much bigger than a melon. This idea, if spelled out in a proposition about the size of the sun, would clearly be false. Merely seeing the sun, or thinking of the propositional counterpart of the sun as given in visual perception, does not, however, entail any error: it is true that the sun, as I see or imagine it, does not appear bigger than a melon. Error arises only when I affirm what I do not clearly perceive, for instance, that this sensory idea presents the sun in its true nature, and hence that the sun in the heavens has the size it appears to have. Only the latter is a judgment in the proper sense of the word, whose truth value depends on the truth value of the propositional content it affirms.

Consider, again, a difference between merely entertaining a proposition and affirming it to be true that is central to Frege and also recognized by medieval logicians.[54] Having a thought is one thing, affirming it to be true is another. Descartes's predecessors commonly assumed that insofar as assent is assent to a proposition, it depends on the intellect. The notion apprehended causes assent if it is true, for a rational mind assents, naturally, to true, evident propositions, and the will comes into play only when the notion apprehended is not evidently apprehended or intuited—when there is some doubt about its truth. This is also assumed by Descartes: clear and distinct ideas are true, something he promotes into a rule of truth and norm of rationality.[55] Yet, because assent is ultimately a function of the will (as opposed to caused by the normal functioning of the intellect), it can not only be withheld in doubtful cases but it is also freely given (or withheld) even in the case of clear and distinct perception.[56]

If Descartes takes assent to be dependent in the end on the will that directs our attention and thereby renders us responsible in a special way for our judgments, he does not hold that all judgments are explicitly formed or always require a deliberate act of will. Sensory ideas, for instance, are said to appear to us as "adventitious" ideas, or as "foreign to me and coming from the outside" (AT VII 37–38; AT IX 29, CSM II 26). This means that they come with some (unnoticed) judgment concerning their origin, by which they are, automatically as it were, referred to an external cause. Such judgments, according to the analysis in the Sixth Replies of the processes underlying sense perception, belong to the third grade of sense, although they depend on the intellect (AT VII 437, CSM II 295). These judgments are generally unnoticed and hence not deliberately made, but are occasioned by movements of the sensory organs and the (second grade) sensations by which these movements affect us (AT VII 436–437, CSM II 294). They are implicit in the sensory perceptions themselves; and that is why they are referred to the senses, although they depend on the intellect. This is precisely what renders sensory perceptions particularly suspect and accounts, I contend, for their "material falsity." Descartes thus seems to allow for unnoticed judgments—judgments that are accepted without self-conscious assertion, and where the assent is caused in some other way, without deliberate reflection on the truth value of its content. The assent is caused, yet to the extent that the will could have acted to withhold assent, there is a sense in which it depends here too on the will.

In discussing judgments, Descartes is concerned primarily with existential judgments and hence with ideas of actually or possibly existing things *(res),* not with conceptual or eternal truths, which have no existence outside the mind. We know that the latter are true as soon as we conceive them clearly and distinctly, because to so conceive them is to see that their denial involves contradiction (AT VIII-1 22–23, CSM I 208–209). There is no question whether the proposition "The whole is greater than its parts" is true, because anyone who understands its terms sees that it is and assents to it without hesitation.

Ideas of real things, on the contrary, represent particular things that may or may not exist in the actual world.[57] The judgments that are problematic are not about the natures or essences of things, but about their actual existence. It is one thing to conceive a particular thing, say, this piece of wax with its changing appearances, another to affirm its existence with the sensory qualities it is perceived as having (being yellow, tasting of honey, smelling of clover, feeling hard, having this thickness and this size, and so on). To the extent that the piece of wax can be clearly and distinctly conceived (as this piece of extended, flexible matter capable of changing in determinable ways under determinate circumstances), it is a *res,* that is, a real or possible thing existing independently of my sensations of it. One can think of it with this particular size, shape, and movement whether or not one affirms that it exists as thought of (AT VII 30–32, CSM II 20–21). In this sense all clear and distinct ideas are true in themselves: they are true when taken exactly for what they are—namely, as presentations of real things in the above sense of possible things. A true idea of a particular thing is an idea that has or presents the same degree of being or reality objectively that the thing of which it is an idea would have formally, if it existed in actual reality.

Although Descartes does not seem to think of ideas primarily as propositions, it is reasonable to suppose that they all have, at least when they are clearly and distinctly conceivable, some propositional counterpart. Whatever the idea represents clearly and distinctly can be described with a proposition that, as such, is either true or false. Even so, one can consider or entertain a proposition without affirming or denying it, and likewise, one can consider a nonpropositional idea, the propositional counterpart of which would be false, without affirming or positing the existence of its object.[58]

A further element of Descartes's theory to be considered is the distinction made in the *Rules* between simple and complex ideas. The former, which are also called simple natures, do not have propositional counterparts, yet they are described as evident in themselves. Is this to say that they have some kind of prepropositional truth? Their simplicity is epistemic: they are simple and indivisible in the sense that they are grasped in a simple undivided act of intuition or mental "seeing." As such they are self-evident and "never contain any falsity" (AT X 420, CSM I 45). Considering the examples Descartes gives of such "simple natures"—for instance, doubt, knowledge, ignorance, volition, which are classified as "purely intellectual," or shape, extension, and motion, which are classified as "purely material," or those that are "common," like existence, unity, and duration (AT X 419, CSM I 44–45)—it would be more natural to say that they are the units or elements out of which complex ideas (propositions) are formed, but that they do not, in themselves, have any truth value. But Descartes insists that they are true, without any falsity, in themselves.[59] Falsity originates from the combination of elements the nature of which is not conceived with sufficient clarity and distinctness. This holds for sensory perceptions as well. Our knowledge of composite, contingent natures is said to depend either on experience or on our imagination. By experience Descartes means "whatever we perceive by means of the senses, whatever we learn from others, and in general whatever reaches our intellect either from external sources or from its own reflexive self-contemplation" (AT X 422, CSM I 46–47). The intellect, according to this passage, can never be deceived by any experience, provided that it is intuited exactly as presented to it, that is, without passing any judgment about the true nature of what is thus represented through the senses. We can go wrong only when "we ourselves compose in some way the objects of our beliefs" (AT X 423, CSM I 47).[60]

4. Material Falsity

The difficulty caused by Descartes's notion of materially false ideas is first taken up by Arnauld. As noted before, Arnauld does not find any problem with the idea of objective reality and the necessity of positing a cause of ideas taken objectively. What he worries about is the apparent inconsistency created by the introduction of the notion of "material falsity" in the explanation of the errors caused by sensory ideas. The very examples given by Descartes to illustrate this notion, like that of the idea of cold for instance, which is said to represent a pure nonbeing as a real being, seem to create more confusion than clarity (AT VII 206–207).[61]

Thus, in examining various ideas representing corporeal things with respect to their differing degrees of objective reality, Descartes notices that his ideas of sensory qualities (the list includes light and colors, sounds, smells, tastes, heat and cold and the other tactile qualities) are so confused and obscure that

> I do not even know whether they are true or false, that is, whether the ideas I have of them are ideas of things or of non-things. For although, as I have noted before, falsity in the strict sense, or formal falsity, can occur only in judgements, there is another kind of falsity, material fal-

sity, which occurs in ideas, *when they represent non-things as things*. For example, the ideas which I have of heat and cold contain so little clarity and distinctness that they do not enable me to tell whether cold is merely the absence of heat or vice versa, or whether both of them are real qualities, or neither is. And since there can be no ideas which are not as it were of things, if it is true that cold is nothing but the absence of heat, the idea which represents it to me as something real and positive deserves to be called false; and the same goes for other ideas of this kind. (AT VII 44, CSM II 30; my emphasis)

Material falsity hence is connected with obscurity and confusion: the idea of God, for instance, cannot be materially false because it is "utterly clear and distinct and contains in itself more objective reality than any other idea." It is, indeed "the truest and most clear and distinct of all my ideas" (AT VII 46, CSM 31–32).

Objective reality comes in degrees, as we have seen, and so does certainty, but truth does not come in degrees. Arnauld points out the inconsistency in speaking of truth and falsity of ideas when falsity (and truth) in the strict sense can occur only in judgments. If the idea of cold is a positive idea, it represents something real; if, on the other hand, it is just an absence (of heat), then it cannot exist objectively, that is, there can be no idea having objective being of what formally is an absence of being, or nonbeing.[62] The example of cold is, however, a bit misleading, for Descartes does not take cold to be absence of heat.

Arnauld's general point against Descartes is, however, well taken. Descartes confuses judgment with an idea: the idea of cold is false because it is not the idea of cold, that is, the *judgment* that it is the idea of cold is false, but the idea within you is "completely true" (AT VII 297, CSM II 145).

Descartes, in answering, first stresses that ideas taken materially, as mere operations of the intellect, can have no reference to the truth or falsity of their objects. Arnauld's objection turns on taking ideas not materially but in the *formal* sense *(formaliter)*. To the perplexity of the reader, ideas taken in the formal sense here turn out to be ideas taken objectively: "Since ideas are forms of a kind, and are not composed of any matter, when we think of them as representing something we are taking them not *materially* but *formally*" (AT VII 231, CSM II 163). Descartes's remark that he had found the word "materially" used this way in the first Scholastic author he came across (in Suárez's *Metaphysical Disputations*) is not very helpful. If material falsity applies to ideas, as Descartes says, in the "formal sense," and the idea taken formally here is the idea taken objectively, it is not easy to see how he could avoid inconsistency.[63] For he claims *both* that *no* ideas can involve falsity when considered solely in themselves (AT VII 37, CSM II 26), *and* that among the ideas taken objectively some are false in themselves, that is, "materially false."

An idea is materially false if it "can provide subject-matter for error." To provide subject matter for error is the same as to provide subject matter for (give occasion to) false *judgments* (AT VII 233, CSM II 163). Now any idea that is not sufficiently clear and distinct can in principle provide subject matter for false judgments, and be in this sense materially false: some give greater, some lesser scope for error, although those that "give the judgement little or no scope for error do not seem to deserve to be called materially false as much as those that give great scope for error," as sensory ideas do.[64] But if it is only a matter of degree, of more or less confusion, one does indeed wonder with Arnauld whether Descartes is not after all confusing a judgment with an idea, particularly since his answer seems to concede the point: ideas are materially false insofar as they give occasion to false judgments, which is to say that they are not false in themselves.

But Descartes's claim that ideas do not give material for error when considered in themselves, without referring them to something else, comes (as we noted) with a qualification, which needs to be considered.[65] This permits Descartes to admit exceptions, to be found among the confused ideas of sensory qualities. Such ideas are confused partly because they are commonly taken to represent real qualities of external things, which according to Cartesian science they cannot do for the simple reason that external things have no such properties (AT VII 43, CSM II 29–30). It is, however (as the answer to Arnauld makes clear), not merely a question of whether what they are taken to represent *is* real, but a question of how they *appear* to us, how they are immediately perceived (AT VII 234, ll. 18–24, CSM II 164). What renders them problematic is that, because of their obscurity and confusion, it is impossible to judge whether what they represent is some real entity that exists (or can exist) formally outside the senses.[66]

Material falsity, hence, is ascribed to sensory ideas on account of their obscurity and confusion. An idea is obscure when it is not clear in the sense of being fully present to the mind (like an object of vision in fog or at great distance), and it is confused, as opposed to being distinct, when it is not possible to spell out analytically what the idea contains objectively and how its object is to be delimited from other things. The most confused sensory ideas—emotions or feelings (like thirst or pain)—can be very clear, in the sense of being manifest, and yet be at the same time irremediably confused (*Principles* I, art. 45–46 (AT VIII-2 21–22, CSM I 207–208)). Not only are they subject to constant change (compare the wax analysis) and cannot, therefore, be present to the mind for a very long time, but their connection to the things causing them (external bodies and their movements) is unintelligible.[67] They are radically different from the clear and distinct ideas of the intellect, which are transparent to anyone who bothers to examine them with sufficient care, for the content of sensory ideas remains opaque no matter how much we try to analyze or specify it.[68]

Yet there are contexts in which these opaque sensory perceptions can be both clear and distinct, namely, when they are considered as such in the strict sense of sensations or feelings. Moreover, in spite of their inherent lack of distinctness, which makes them useless as means of discerning the true nature of the things causing them, they have an important pragmatic function: not only do they function as natural signs indicating the presence and action of external things on the senses, but they enable us also to discriminate those things that are of importance to the mind–body union on which they depend. They are pragmatically reliable even when they contribute little or nothing to our knowledge of the true nature of corporeal things. Thirst indicates the need of water or refreshments, tiredness that it is time for rest, and so on.

> For the proper purpose of the sensory perceptions given me by nature is simply to inform the mind *(ad menti significandum)* of what is beneficial or harmful for the composite of which the mind is a part; and to this extent they are sufficiently clear and distinct. But I misuse them by treating them as reliable rules for immediate judgements about the essential nature of the bodies outside us, about which they give nothing but very obscure and confused indications. (AT VII 83, ll. 15–23, CSM II 58)

Now if sensory ideas can be used as (mostly) reliable signs instituted by nature for pragmatic (biological) purposes, they can hardly be inherently *false*. Obscurity and confusion are hence not for Descartes (as they may be for Spinoza) the same as falsity. The opacity of sensations may be irremediable and yet sensations may be true in themselves, as argued in the passage analyzing grades of certainty of sensory perception in the Sixth Replies (AT VII 438). Here again, falsity is said to require judgment, an act of the intellect that belongs to the third grade of sensory perception. But this is not *sensation* in the very restricted sense relevant here, which belongs to the second grade.[69] There is no falsity in sensations *stricto sensu,* at the second grade of sensory response (AT VII 438, CSM II 296). This latter category comprises all the "immediate effects produced in the mind" by the motion of the particles of the bodily organ to which it is united. The list includes the very same perceptions (pain, pleasure, thirst, colors, heat, cold, and the like) that in the Third Meditation are discussed as instances of materially false ideas.

This suggests that Descartes may not, after all, regard sensations as an exception to his view that all ideas, when viewed solely in themselves, are true, which is suggested also in the *Principles* I, art. 65 and 70 (AT VIII-1 32, 34).

The only sense I can make of this is to conclude that material falsity pertains not to simple sensations in the strict sense as such, but rather to unanalyzed, confused, and complex sensory ideas, whose components turn out to be, on closer scrutiny, incompatible. Material falsity, I contend, occurs only in the ideas described as belonging to the third grade of sensory perception, which involves unnoticed or unconscious judgments. (Compare Chapter 3, section 5; this chapter note 41.) Sensations of sound, color, and the like are true in themselves, whereas our spontaneous *takings* of sounds, colors, sensations of heat or cold (not to speak of pain, thirst, and similar feelings) as real mind-independent things constitutes materially false ideas. Such ideas are complex and carelessly compounded ideas that present nonthings as things—that is, present things that cannot possibly exist. They combine modes of mind with modes of extension that cannot co-exist in corporeal things, as when locating the sensed heat in the burning wood, the pain in the foot, the sound that I hear in the ringing bell, and so on.[70] The sensory perceptions, through which things acting on our senses are represented, are compounds consisting of inherently confused sensations (representing how our bodies and minds are affected) and unnoticed, spontaneous, mostly false judgments about the things affecting us, to which they are spontaneously referred.

Descartes does not say very much about how the unnoticed judgments that are associated by habit or nature with sensory ideas come about, and what he says is not, as Margaret Wilson has shown, too helpful.[71] What is clear, however, is that sensations are not primarily perceived as such. That is, they do not present themselves as discrete impressions or "sense data," but come to the mind in connection with other ideas, against a background of judgments in terms of which they are instinctively or habitually interpreted. I see a bent stick in water, not light or patches of color, shapes, and so on, and the various visual sensations that compose my idea of the stick are not given as such but are identified only after reflection on the nature of the purported object of perception; they are, we could say, the outcome of a phenomenological reduction or analysis. What are perceived are primarily external things with their characteristic appearances.

If the sensations involved in ordinary perceptual ideas are thus not primarily given as sensations of various kinds, they can, like the unnoticed judgments of the third grade of sensory perception, be sorted out by the attentive mind for critical inspection. This, indeed, is what the Cartesian method prescribes, and it is only by such a method that real and true—that is, clear and distinct—ideas can be distinguished from materially false and confused ones. The extent to which sensory perceptions can be trusted depends on the judgments connected with them. What makes us go wrong are not the sensations themselves, but the unnoticed judgments in terms of which they are spontaneously and habitually interpreted. By reflecting on and critically analyzing our sensory experiences, we are able to sort out what is directly perceived by the senses (the ways things import to and affect us) from the spontaneous judgments associated with them (about the ways things are). An essential part of Descartes's method consists, precisely, in rendering the unnoticed and mostly precipitated judgments involved in sensory perception explicit and thereby subject to critical evaluation.[72]

The sensory idea of the bent stick in water is a case of a confused, compound idea that is materially false insofar as it is spontaneously taken to present the stick in its true nature. We could say (with Alan

Gewirth) that material falsity belongs to compound ideas whose interpretive content of which goes beyond their direct content: ideas to which we have, without noticing it, added something we do not immediately perceive.[73]

If this is granted, material falsity differs from formal falsity not because judgments are not involved, but because they are implicit and unnoticed, and therefore difficult to disentangle from the actual sensations themselves, thus giving us material for error.[74] Material falsity arises from, but is not the same as, the obscurity and confusion of an idea. To be materially false, a confused idea must involve in addition implicit, unnoticed false judgments about what it contains or, confusedly, presents to the mind. Because of the opaque character of sensory ideas, *any* judgment about their content other than that it is caused by something external is liable to be false or misleading (*Principles* I, art. 70 (AT VIII-1 34, CSM I 218)).

It is interesting to note that Arnauld himself, some twenty years after the exchange with Descartes, analyzes false ideas as complex ideas involving unnoticed judgments. As Jean-Claude Pariente has shown, Arnauld in his *Logique* (1662) comes to accept the Cartesian theory of ideas, which he had difficulty understanding and accepting in commenting on the *Meditations* in 1640. In objecting to Descartes, Arnauld (like Spinoza) took the correspondence between the idea and its *ideatum* in a strong sense, as complete agreement between the two.[75] But it is clear, as Descartes's answer to Arnauld brings out, that he does not take the correspondence between the idea and its *ideatum* as a complete resemblance (adequacy) nor as holding in the same degree for all ideas. The confusion of a sensory idea hence consists not in (as Arnauld wrongly assumed) the confusing one idea with another, but in the difficulty of discriminating what objective reality it presents, which makes us liable to precipitated implicit judgments about its nature and status.

The talk of implicit judgment may seem problematic in a Cartesian context: if judgment involves voluntary assent or denial, one wonders how there could be unnoticed judgments at all. Yet there clearly is unnoticed, spontaneous assent or denial involved in those ideas Descartes characterizes as materially false.[76] Assent depends on the will, and hence is voluntary—yet it is not consciously willed. This means that assent, and hence judgment, can occur at different levels of consciousness: it certainly is not always deliberate but can be produced by fortuitous association, or impulse, or in some other ways, and once it has been so produced it is enforced by habit. Although Descartes, like the Stoics, seems to think that assent is always subject to voluntary control if it is attended to, he does not think that it is always the object of attention. Normally we pay very little attention to how we think, or on what grounds we believe what we do. So even if there were no act of thought without some act of willed assent, and even if the latter depended only on the will itself, so that it could be deliberately undone or endorsed, most thoughts and judgments occur spontaneously by natural causes and unreflected impulses. We are, as it were, programmed by natural institution, acquired habits, and training (in learning language) to respond to different perceptual situations by different judgments, as when accepting without reflection that the stick immersed in water is bent, that the pain is in my foot, or that it is good for me to drink whenever I feel thirsty.

This does not commit Descartes to the view that sensations are nonrepresentational and hence without any cognitive value, which is obviously something he rejects. Sensations function as signs, and as such indicate something that we need to be aware of and cannot figure out in any other way: the actual presence of external things, their nature and the changes they undergo, how they relate to each other, and, most important, how they affect us and our bodies. It does commit him, however, to the view that the objective reality of sensations is problematic—although no more problematic than the reality they represent, namely, the ways immaterial minds intermingle with and are affected by extended bodies. Sensations and other thoughts caused by the body represent whatever they represent by virtue of a contingent quasi-causal connection instituted by nature, but they have no determinate, distinctly conceivable content that could be analyzed in terms of purely mental or purely material modes—the only ones that we have a distinct grasp of. Whatever meaning sensations evoke to the mind interpreting them, it is associated or assigned to them by natural institution or by habit. The framework within which they function as signs is the union of the mind and the body as instituted by nature and they have no meaning outside the context of that union whose preservation and welfare they serve. Because of their relation to the union and its ends, they cannot reveal the things causing them in their true, independent nature.[77]

But if this is granted, and if, as I have argued, the clear and distinct ideas of the intellect present things in their true nature, then the attribution of the veil-of-ideas theory to Descartes is not supported by his view of sense perception either. Sensory ideas can form a veil of ignorance when they are misused or, when materially false ideas, mixed up with precipitated, false beliefs, are affirmed as true judgments.[78] But when taken for what they are, as informing us of how things affect us and how they matter to us and our lives (including our science), even the most confused sensations need not be construed as forming a veil hindering us from seeing the true nature of the things causing them. Since their function is not to give us insight into the metaphysical nature and structure of the world around us, but merely to inform us of our place in it and to "help us get around," the ontological mistakes that the uncritical perceptual beliefs generate can, on the contrary, be of great pragmatic and hence also scientific utility.[79]

6

Passions and
Embodied Intentionality

[I]t is nevertheless very difficult to understand that a soul, as you
have described it, after having the habit of reasoning so well, can
lose it all on account of some vapors, and that, although it can
subsist without the body and has nothing in common with it,
it is yet so ruled by it.
—Princess Elisabeth to Descartes

The emotions or passions belong to that third category of thought or
experience that can be referred neither to the soul nor to the body
alone, because its instances depend on the "close and intimate union
between the mind and body," and, unlike other thoughts, "do not consist in thought alone" (AT VIII-1 23, CMS I 209). More than any other
thoughts, the emotions express and testify to our embodied condition.
Not only do they constitute the main evidence for the close union between the mind and the body, their principal function is to serve and
preserve this union.

It was Princess Elisabeth who inspired Descartes to write his treatise
on *The Passions of the Soul.* She may have been the first (perhaps the
only) of Descartes's correspondents and contemporaries to take his
doctrine of the mind–body union seriously. She took him seriously
enough to present him with questions that he took to be entirely appropriate, and which, ultimately, he was unable to answer satisfacto-
rily.[1] She also seems to have granted him in the end the fact of the
union in spite of its philosophical difficulties, since she accepted it as
the proper framework for understanding human psychology and the
passions in particular.

Like Elisabeth, I take Descartes's teachings on the mind–body union
seriously, and I thus take it that Descartes never accepted the radical
Platonic "substance" dualism his main philosophical efforts to prove a

real distinction between the mind and the body would seem to imply. He remained fundamentally Aristotelian in his conception of human nature, maintaining that the nature of a human being consists in a real and substantial union, the body constituting an organic whole informed by a rational soul or mind. This means that the *human* mind is essentially *embodied,* and not an immaterial spirit that finds itself accidentally lodged in the body, like a pilot in his ship.[2] That it is really united to the body means that it is, "as it were, intermingled *(quasi permixtum)* with it" (AT VII 81, CSM II 56)—a view that clearly threatens his dualism. It also raises problems for the view of the mind as an independent agent controlling and mastering the passions of the body, which is presupposed in his moral therapy.

This is to admit that Descartes's philosophical anthropology does not seem, in the end, very consistent with the clear-cut mind–body dualism one would expect him to defend. Descartes never completed his project of writing on man; whether for lack of time or because of the difficulties, given his starting points of such a project, we will never know. The main constituents of his anthropology—the mechanist physiology, the view of reason as an autonomous power of judgment, and the theory of the passions as body-dependent thoughts—were worked out independently of each other and in different contexts.[3] The theory of passions, for example, is a subject in which Descartes took an interest only late in life, and mainly as a consequence of questions raised by his correspondents. On the other hand, his view of reason as an autonomous power, and the radical conception of the freedom of the human will on which it is based, were central to his epistemology and philosophy. Yet, until the correspondence with Elisabeth, Descartes focused on reason mainly as an instrument of knowledge. Elisabeth brings him to reflect more seriously on its practical, moral, and therapeutic uses.[4] The last two chapters examine how his conception of reason and his theory of passions come together and whether they form parts of a coherent, although incomplete, doctrine. Their leading concern is to see how Descartes's account of reason and will and their relation to emotions differs from traditional rationalist and "cognitivist" accounts. To what extent can he sustain the idea of reason as an independent governing principle, while according such great importance in our lives to body-dependent thoughts such as feelings and emotions?

1. The Context and Novelty of Descartes's Approach to the Passions

If Descartes does not address the question of the interplay between the passions and reason until Elisabeth brings it to his attention, he does not answer it until *Les Passions de l'âme*. A first draft of the theory he develops there is sketched in a letter to Elisabeth of October 6, 1645. The letter starts by discussing a question Descartes says he has sometimes been pondering: whether it is "better to be cheerful and content, imagining the goods one possesses to be greater and more valuable than they are, and ignoring or not stopping to consider those one lacks, than to have more consideration and knowledge, so as to know the just value of both, and thus become more sad" (AT IV 305, CMSK 268; my translation). The answer summarizes the main themes of Descartes's scattered views on ethics, and reveals where he sides but also where he parts from the Stoics. The supreme good—the good in itself—consists in the exercise of virtue, not in joy.[5] He distinguishes the exercise of virtue, which consists in "the possession of all those goods whose acquisition depends on our free will *(libre arbitre)*," from "the satisfaction of mind which results from that acquisition" (AT IV 305; CSMK 268). His conception of virtue as the right use of reason, where the emphasis is on the intention to use it as well as one can (AT XI 445–447, CSM I 384), differs in interesting ways from that of the Stoics, who would settle for nothing less than actual knowledge of the true good.[6] Yet he follows the Stoics, against Augustine and the Church Fathers, in declaring that the highest good is attainable by the power of human reason alone, without the assistance of faith, revelation, or divine grace, and he also shares their concern with securing independence through self-reliance.[7] At the same time he emphasizes, with the Augustinians, the role of the will and its priority in relation to the intellect.[8]

This leaves him in two minds about how to answer the question he put in the letter to Elisabeth. For joys that do not depend on our own actions (our free acts of thought) are based on luck and do not belong to the good acquired through the exercise of virtue—that is, through the right use of reason and will. Not only do they depend on circumstances out of our control, but when their true nature is revealed, joys that are badly founded bring regrets and inward bitterness. He writes: "It is a greater perfection to know the truth than to be ignorant of it, even when it is to our disadvantage," and it is therefore preferable to have less joy and more knowledge. However, he hastens to add, if there is a choice between considerations that are equally true but differ in the amount of joy they bring, prudence itself advises us to prefer those that give us more satisfaction. One should use one's skills above all to consider things "from the point of view which makes them seem most to our advantage, provided that this does not involve self-deception" (AT IV 306, CSMK 268). But we also read in the *Passions* that since in the contingencies of life "we cannot avoid the risk of being mistaken, it is always much better for us to incline towards the passions which tend to the good than . . . towards those which relate to the evil, even if it were only to avoid it; and *even a false joy is often more valuable than a sadness whose cause is true*" (AT XI 435, CSM I 378; my emphasis).

If Descartes seems ambivalent here,[9] he is not necessarily inconsistent, because the point of view adopted in this last passage is that of the mind, and not that of the mind–body union, which prevails in the letter. Considered merely as a state of the mind, a false joy is more worth having for the pleasure it gives than a true sorrow (art. 141 (AT XI 434, CSM I 378)). If only soul were involved, joy and love would always be better than hate and sorrow. However, this kind of hedonism is not the basis for Cartesian ethics as it concerns action and hence the mind–body union, for there "sadness is in some way primary and more necessary than joy, and hatred more necessary than love; for it is more important to reject things which are harmful and potentially destructive than to acquire those which add some perfection which we can subsist without" (art. 137 (AT XI 430, CSM I 376)).

Descartes also points out in the letter to Elisabeth that the pleasure of the soul in which happiness *(béatitude)* consists is not directly dependent on joy, nor does it presuppose bodily well-being. For we enjoy tragedies all the more the sadder they make us, as we can also enjoy the strains of bodily exercise (like hunting and tennis):

The cause of the contentment that the soul gets from these exercises, consists in that they make it notice the strength, or skill, or some other perfection of the body to which it is united; whereas the contentment it receives from weeping at some pitiable or tragic episode in the theatre derives mainly from its impression of performing a virtuous action in having compassion of the afflicted; and in general the soul takes pleasure in feeling moved by the passions *(elle se plaît à sentir émouvoir en soi les passions)*, no matter what their nature, provided that it remains in control of them. (AT IV 309, CSMK 270; my translation)[10]

The secondary or (as Descartes calls them in the *Passions*) interior emotions are here invoked not only as a means of detaching ourselves from miseries caused by events beyond our control, but are also seen as independent sources of positive enjoyment. This latter point is generalized to all the passions, including those that depend directly on the body: it is possible, Descartes thinks, to find enjoyment in them all! (See also art. 147–148 (AT XI 440–442, CSM I 381–382.)) Here he clearly parts company with the Stoics, yet he finds the means to achieve the control required to make passions endurable and even enjoyable in a psychological theory that has some striking similarities to the Stoic theory. Adapted to Descartes's dualism and mechanistic physiology, the psychological model developed by the early Stoics seems to offer a particularly apt framework for his new approach to the mastery of the passions. It is, I want to suggest, his belief, shared with the Stoics, about the unity of the mind, combined with the mechanistic physiology he develops in the *Traité de l'Homme*, that explains Descartes's optimism concerning the power of reason not only to oppose but to regulate the passions in the pursuit of virtue. However, finding the Stoic conception of virtue too austere and suitable only for melancholics (AT IV 276, CSMK 261), Descartes sees the passions not as the main obstacle to virtue, but as essential means to achieve it and to enjoy it.

That emotions have a positive role was commonplace in traditional criticisms of Stoicism both by Aristotelians and Thomists, as well as by Augustine and his followers. What is new and interesting in Descartes's theory is the way his uncompromising adherence to a monistic psychology, where passions are defined as thoughts and hence as states of the mind itself, is combined with a causal analysis of passions, which makes them dependent on the body and also accords them a natural function in the framework of the mind–body union.[11]

When turning in the letter just quoted to examine "these passions in more detail so as to be able to define them," Descartes starts out by referring to an earlier (lost) draft of a treatise on animal physiology (that Elisabeth has read) and summarizing the main points of the theory of perception there outlined. He explains how through the action of external objects on the sensory organs, impressions are formed in the brain and how the brain "is also acted on by the soul which has some power to change cerebral impressions just as those impressions in their turn have the power to arouse thoughts which do not depend on the will."[12] All thoughts aroused in the soul by the cerebral impressions but without the "concurrence of the will and therefore without any action of the soul" are called "passions" in a general sense, although in a stricter sense "the term is restricted to thoughts which are caused by some extraordinary agitation of the spirits, . . . whose effects are felt in the soul itself" (AT IV 310, CSMK 270). Passions in this stricter sense are emotions, and they thus form a subset of a larger class of thoughts, which are caused by various kinds of movements in the body, and include external and internal sensory perceptions and feelings. The passions in this wider sense are contrasted to thoughts that are caused by the will and depend on the mind itself, and which are called its actions, and they also differ from the latter on account of their obscurity and confusion. But the active thoughts caused by the will, too, can make an impression in the brain, at least when the imagination is involved, and so can cause that particular agitation of the spirits characteristic of the passions in the strict sense.

This distinction between actions and passions is fundamental for the theory developed in *Passions of the Soul.* Its opening paragraph declares that "the defects of the sciences we have from the ancients are nowhere more apparent than in their writings on the passions," and since their teachings on this subject are "so slight and mostly so implausible," there can be no hope of finding the truth "except by departing from the paths they have followed" and writing "just as if I was considering a topic that no one had dealt with before me" (AT XI 327–328, CSM I 328). The self-confidence here expressed is not untypical, but it has rarely been more out of place than in this context, for the next sentence reads: "In the first place, I note that whatever takes place or occurs is generally called by philosophers a 'passion' with regard to the subject to which it happens, and an 'action' with regard to that which makes it happen" (AT XI 328, CSM I 328). This distinction is commonplace in the writings of the "ancients" on the subject;[13] moreover, the study of the passions was a booming field, and the literature on the subject in the late sixteenth and early seventeenth centuries was abundant.[14] Descartes may nonetheless have been justified, at least to some extent, in feeling that he was onto something new because of the systematic way he applies this distinction in the context of his mind–body dualism and physiology. He is, after all, among the first to have outlined a systematic mechanistic theory of the workings of the human body, and his intention "was to explain the passions only as a natural philosopher, and not as a rhetorician or even as a moral philosopher" (AT XI 326, CSM I 327). This, moreover, is not the only point on which Descartes can claim originality in his treatment of the passions, since he also develops an original account of the intentionality of emotions, which is worth a closer examination.

2. Passions as a Subclass of Thoughts

Passions, in the sense of emotions, are a subclass of thoughts in Descartes's wide sense of that word, which covers everything that happens within us in such a way that we are aware of it (AT VIII-1 7, CSM I 195).[15] Thoughts are complex phenomena, involving both acts of awareness and objects or contents. They are representational or intentional acts. Although it is disputed whether for Descartes all the various phenomena he calls "thoughts" actually are intentional, my view is that even sensations instantiate some form of prereflective intentionality, in advising the mind of the presence and changes in external bodies acting on the senses.[16] If having an object is essential to phenomena that are intentional, emotions surely meet these conditions. Cartesian emotions, however, are not reducible to propositional thoughts, since they are, in a sense to be explained, bodily and mental states. More than any other thoughts, they are "embodied" in that they never occur without their characteristic facial and behavioral expressions.[17] They instantiate, I will argue, a special kind of embodied intentionality.

The fact that Descartes gives so much space in his *Passions* to the description of the bodily states causing and accompanying the emotions has led commentators to classify his view among physiological or sensation theories.[18] That is wrong: Cartesian emotions, although expressed in bodily states and behavior, remain essentially cognitive. They are not, *qua* bodily, mere expressions of "brute" or "blind" nature, but also complex patterns of acquired and learned reactions, carrying meanings and functions of their own.[19] Contemporary cognitivists who identify emotions with cognitive or intentional states, taking the latter to be propositional attitudes, ignore the insight that Descartes's redefinition of "mind" and "thought" expresses, namely, that states of mind come in more than one kind and need not be propositional beliefs or desires in order to qualify as thoughts. Thoughts that are clear and distinct have to be propositional, but most of our thoughts are not clear and distinct. Thoughts can be more or less clear and more or less distinct, and the obscure and confused thoughts come in a whole variety, ranging from false beliefs to feelings, sensations, and moods that, even if they cannot be expressed in propositional form, are nonetheless thoughts—that is, intentional phenomena having a meaning or an object. Those who overlook Descartes's distinction between thoughts that are clear and distinct and thoughts that are obscure and confused might be tempted (following the Stoics) to construe the latter simply as false beliefs. Obscurity and confusion are, however, not merely a question of intellectual error: confusion is not the same as false belief. False beliefs are often part of the passions, but they do not constitute them in the way the Stoics take them to.

3. Actions and Passions

The distinction between action and passion, crucial to Descartes's project of mastering the passions, is introduced in the very first article of *Passions of the Soul,* where Descartes contrasts his own pioneering approach with that of the ancients, whose treatment of the subject he has found so insignificant and implausible. Yet he starts out by making one of the most ancient of philosophical distinctions the basis of his new theory.

> Whatever takes place or occurs is generally called by philosophers a "passion" with regard to the subject to which it happens and an "action" with regard to that which makes it happen. Thus, although an agent and patient are often quite different, an action and passion must always be a single thing *(une même chose)* which has these two names on account of the two different subjects to which it may be related. (AT XI 327, CSM I 328)

I will deal shortly with the philosophical problem created by this distinction for Descartes's substance dualism, but let us first look at how he uses the distinction.

The modes or thoughts of the human mind are actions or passions depending on whether the mind itself or some external agent causes them. In a very general sense, all perceptions that are not caused by the mind itself are passions. We read in article 17:

> Those I call its actions are all our volitions, because we experience that
> they proceed directly from our soul, and seem to depend on it alone.
> Whereas, on the contrary, one can generally call its passions all kinds of
> perceptions or cognitions to be found within us, because it is often not
> our soul that makes them such that they are, and the soul always re-
> ceives them *from things that are represented by them.* (AT XI 342, CSM I
> 335; my emphasis)

The term "passion" is used here in a wide sense to cover all thoughts that are *received from things that are represented by them,* whether intellectual (God, soul, angels, mathematical proofs, and so on) or corporeal. This suggests, first, that all passions are representational, and, second, that there is a sense in which even the pure volitions or acts of the soul can be called passions, since actions and passions are not really distinct but the same things considered from the point of view of the subjects to which they are related.[20] Thus when I will something, for instance, when I want to understand an argument, or go out fishing, or break up an engagement, my wish is an action to the extent it depends only on my mind. Yet it is at the same time a passion insofar as I perceive it:

> For it is certain that we cannot will anything without thereby perceiving
> that we are willing it. And although willing something is an action with
> respect to our soul, the perception of such willing may be said to be a
> passion in the soul. But because this perception is really one and the
> same thing as the volition, and names are always determined by what-
> ever is most noble, we do not normally call it a "passion," but solely an
> "action." (AT XI 343, CSM I 336)

Volitions, since they are actions and depend only on the mind, are said to be *nobler* than other thoughts that are merely received in the mind. This characterization reveals Descartes's commitment to the traditional hierarchy of perfections, according to which activity is superior to passivity and the soul as a self-mover is considered more perfect than things governed by external causes.[21] This distinction between what depends on the mind's own activity and what depends on the action of external causes—in particular on the body to which the mind is united—is of crucial importance to the Cartesian project of mastering the passions, but it also introduces major problems. For one thing, it is not always clear how actions are distinguished phenomenologically from passions. As I will argue, passions, which are mental states caused and maintained by actions in the body, are first (mistakenly) perceived as the mind's own actions because they so strongly incline the soul to some volition. If actions are perceived as passions and passions present themselves as inclinations of the will, how are we, who cause or suffer them, to tell them apart? This is a problem not only at the phenomenological level, but also for Descartes's ontology because passions in the strict sense of the word both depend causally on motions in the body and are identified with those motions (art. 2 (AT XI 328, CSM I 328)). The problem is how a passion in the mind can be considered as one with the actions in the body causing it.

Let us note, first, that the distinction between actions and passions is not absolute, but depends on the subject to which it is related, that is, on its antecedent cause. It therefore cuts across the distinction between form (soul) and matter (body) in various ways. Some actions of the soul are passions in the body, while some actions in the body are passions in the soul, even though matter is active only in a secondary sense. In corporeal things, as Descartes explains to Regius, "all actions and passions consist only in local motion," which is called "an 'action' when the motion considered is in the body that imparts the motion, and a 'passion' when it is considered in the body that is moved" (AT III 454, CSMK 199). There is only one primary, efficient cause in the physical universe, and it is God, who in creating passive and inert matter set it in motion and who also sustains that movement through his continuous creation.[22] The mind is passive in relation to God, and it is also passive in contemplating ideas not made by the mind itself but received from an external source, whether sensible or intelligible. Its activity, however, is not restricted to intellectual acts. It is not only in conceiving or reasoning about purely intelligible things that the mind is active, for imagination and memory, which require bodily organs, can be active too. I can willingly imagine or conceive corporeal things (geometrical figures, a machine of highly intricate design, for instance, or the picnic that was cancelled because of the rain), as well as recall them to my memory.[23]

This does not help us understand how what is an action in one thing can be a passion in another, when the things involved are really distinct substances in the strong Cartesian sense of being mutually incompatible. If passions are thoughts, they are modes of the mind, while the actions causing them are motions and hence modes of the body. How can cause and effect be a single thing, and how can particular modes of the mind be identical with particular modes of the body?[24]

Paul Hoffman finds this same doctrine of identity of action and passion in Aristotle, who illustrates it by the example of teaching and learning, which are one and the same actuality *(energeia)* referred to different subjects—to the teacher as an action and to the student as a passion. The teacher brings about acquisition of knowledge in the student, who acquires it. Although teaching is not the same as learning, they are different ways of looking at the same actuality. Hoffman, who worries about the location of the actuality considered, concludes that it is in the student, because the student undergoes the alteration in learning, as the sensory soul in Aristotle's theory of perception is altered in receiving the form from the agent acting on the senses.[25] But in Descartes's theory of passions, the action definitely is in the body, so in saying that action and passion are one thing, Descartes commits himself to the startling claim that there are modes that are straddling, that is, at once modes of the mind and of the body, claiming furthermore that "a mode can be a mode both of thinking and extension."[26]

But consider another Aristotelian example—that of the action of the knife in cutting and the passion of being cut in the object cut. Cutting and being cut are one and the same actuality and are only conceptually separable. There is no point in asking about the location: the cutting is done by the knife and being cut takes place in the object, but neither can be actual without the other, and they occur at once, in the same location. Action and passion are two aspects or ways of conceiving one and the same actuality; we do not need a third category beyond the subject acting and the object acted on to conceive it as one actuality. Nor do we need any qualities straddling the knife and the object cut.[27]

The same point applies also to the mind and the body as constituents of the mind–body union. Admittedly, it is not clear how to conceive the action or the agent—here neural motions in the brain—as the same thing as the passion felt in the soul. But this is nothing over and above the general difficulty we have in conceiving, clearly and distinctly, the mind–body unity that Descartes thinks is inconceivable either in terms of thought or extension, and yet is clearly experienced.

This may seem too quick a response to Hoffman's difficulty, but it does take it very seriously. The point is that we do not gain anything by taking the mind–body union, as Hoffman does, to be a third kind of substance, to which emotions can be attributed as a third kind of mode straddling the two recognized by Descartes as objects of knowledge.[28] For Descartes, the only main attributes for our knowledge of things are extension and thought, to which all properties distinctly conceived have to be referred (*Principles* I, art. 48–53). For the rest, "we also experience within ourselves *(in nobis experimur)* certain other things which must not be referred either to the mind alone or to the body alone" and which are said to arise "from the close and intimate union between mind and body" (AT VIII-1 23, CSM I 209). What is clearly experienced, however, is not distinctly known precisely because it cannot be fully accounted for in terms of either extension or thought. It is a consequence of Descartes's dualism that we cannot have a clear and distinct knowledge of the modes of the compositum: its affections can be known only in being actually experienced. This experience of the composite and its affections, although cognitive, is not on a par with the knowledge we have of the two substances composing it, when considered apart from each other. It is better, therefore, to refer to it as "experience" to distinguish it from the clear and distinct cognition that constitutes certain knowledge. Such experience might involve beliefs, but they would be neither very clear nor distinct, and hence would not be well grounded.

As a consequence of their ambiguous status as affections both of mind and body—of the mind as embodied—thoughts of this kind cannot be known in any other way than as experienced, they cannot be objects of adequate knowledge. They can be known only to the extent they are referred either to the mind or to the body alone, which means they can be known only to a point. Describing bodily motions and neural states will never give me the full story of what a sensation or an emotion is. Nor will analyzing states of the mind ever give me a full account of emotional states. There is no way of picking out thoughts of this kind without their concomitant bodily changes and the neural motions causing them, nor can those motions be identified as causes of particular emotions without the emotional reactions with their typical physiognomic and behavioral expressions. For the action-passion identity is a token-token and not a type-type identity,[29] which means there is no way to connect these two descriptions to make the story complete, because there is no general way of relating the two kinds of state. The psychosomatic and social history of each individual will determine what kind of emotional response external things will elicit from her, and these individual histories cannot be caught in terms of any general, exactly statable, psychophysical laws.

Descartes's dualism is, in Davidsonian terms, an "anomalous dualism." The impossibility of establishing nomic connections between physical and mental states is a consequence of Descartes's radical distinction between the mind and body, which renders their descriptions incompatible and their causal interaction unintelligible. We know by experience that nature has joined certain bodily movements with certain thoughts, but we cannot give a full explanatory account of the connection.[30] Hence the mind–body union as a third primary notion and the appeal to "the institution of nature" (see section 9). The latter tells us that certain bodily motions are, by nature or habit, associated with certain states of the mind, but it does not explain the association: that they coincide is a brute fact of experience.

I conclude, therefore, that only at the level of our lived experience can we speak of actions and passions as two sides of the same actuality—as different aspects of what is experientially given as one single phenomenon. This notion of the identity of (bodily) actions and (mental) passions together with his mechanistic account of the former provides the ground for Descartes's confidence in being on to something radically new in his account of the passions.[31] Because the passions are states of the mind that are caused by the body and not by the mind itself, the conflict between reason and passions is not, as in the Platonic tradition, a conflict within the soul between its higher, rational parts and its lower, irrational parts. It is, instead, a conflict between the mind and the body or, more precisely, between thoughts depending on the mind and thoughts depending on the body (AT XI 364,

CSM I 345–346), the key to the mastery of passion being the knowledge of their causes. This is why Descartes feels justified in saying that he treats the subject from an entirely new point of view, namely, that of the physicist or philosopher of nature.[32] He is confident that the knowledge of the laws of nature, and in particular of the functioning of the human body, will help us master and control the passions that depend on the movements of the body. On this account, the passions are not irrational—not opposed to reason; they are consequences of the mind–body union—more precisely, of the natural order instituted by God, and as such they have a function and a value of their own, which may or may not be in full accord with reason.

4. The Functions Attributed to the Body

All the functions of the living body that Descartes thinks can be explained mechanically are attributed to the body. They comprise the principles of life and movement, which his predecessors attributed to the vegetative and the animal or sensitive soul respectively, but that Descartes sees no problem in explaining mechanistically. The principle of movement in the body is, for Descartes, heat in the heart, which accounts for the circulation of blood. All the organic and physiological functions of living bodies can be explained through heat—a mechanical phenomenon—and other movements in the body.[33] Although Descartes's account of the anatomy and functions of the body draws on previous physiological literature (and notably the Galenic tradition), it is truly innovative in purporting to use rigorously mechanistic principles.[34] His aim is to show that all the functions of the body, not only reflexive but also other movements, that would seem to involve some conscious activity, awareness, or control can be mechanistically explained (art. 13 (AT XI 339, CSM I 334; my emphasis)).[35] He observes:

> [T]he machinery of our body is so composed that all the changes occurring in the movement of the spirits may cause them to open in some pores in the brain more than in others . . . Thus every movement we make without any contribution from our will—as often happens when we breathe, walk, eat, and, indeed, when we perform any action that is common to us and the animals—depends only on the structure of our limbs and the course that the spirits, excited by the heat in the heart,

follow by nature in the brain, nerves and muscles, in the same way as
the movement of a clock is produced through the mere strength of its
spring and the configuration of its wheels. (AT XI 341–342, CSM I 335)

References to clockwork—the artifact that impressed the seventeenth
century as the paradigm of a machine—abound in Descartes and his
followers, playing for seventeenth-century metaphysicians the role that
the computer analogy plays for contemporaries. Descartes uses many
metaphors (a statue of earth, a pneumatic organ, a hydraulic machine), but the underlying idea is that the living organism works like a
clock, that is, like a mechanical automaton that once it is wound up
continues to move according to the laws of motion as long as its essential components are functioning.[36] Unlike his (materialist) followers,
however, he does not think that the model of the clock is applicable to
the functioning of the mind; it functions instead as a kind of water-
shed separating bodily functions that can be explained mechanically
from those of the mind, which cannot, because they depend on its own
acts.

As many commentators have noted, Descartes did not succeed in
carrying through a thoroughly mechanistic program in physiology.
Not only does his notion of mechanism, because of the machine analogy it relies on, presuppose a finality that escapes a mechanistic account, so does the notion of function he uses. This finality is taken for
granted and not explained, and it presupposes a *Deus ex machina*,
whose aims human science cannot penetrate.[37] The purposes and order instituted by the supreme artificer are often indirectly referred to
(in the Sixth Meditation and in the *Passions*) in terms of "nature," and
to what "nature"—our nature as mind–body composites—teaches us
(AT VII 80–90, CSM II 56–62). I will henceforth refer to them loosely
as the "institution of nature."

5. The Functions of the Soul and Perceptions Referred to the Soul in Particular

Having dealt with the functions "belonging solely to the body," Descartes turns to those of the soul, to which there is nothing more to attribute "except our thoughts" (*Passions* I, art. 17 (AT XI 342, CSM I
335)). Those thoughts (perceptions) that do not depend on the soul's

own actions "come to the soul by means of the nerves, and they differ from one another in that we refer some of them to external objects which strike our senses, others to our body or some of its parts, and others lastly to our soul" (art. 22 (AT XI 345, CSM I 336–337)).

What does Descartes mean here by "refer to" *(rapporter à)*? The idea seems to be that these thoughts are perceived *as* proceeding from either external objects, from internal states of the body, or from the mind itself. Thus there are three different kinds of body-dependent thoughts: (i) sense perceptions received through the nerves and the stimulation of the external senses, which are referred to the external things causing them: light to the light source, heat to the fire, and sound to the bell that is ringing (art. 23); (ii) sensations received through the internal senses, which we refer to our body or some part of it, like hunger, thirst, sensation as of cold or warmth (art. 24); and (iii) perceptions that are received through the senses but that *are referred to the soul alone.* They are said to be "those whose effects are felt as in the soul itself" and whose proximate cause, to which they could be referred, is commonly unknown (art. 25–27). Emotions, joy, anger, and the like belong to this last class.

In referring the heat to the fire or the sound to the bell, for instance, I take the phenomenon of heat or sound to be in the external things causing them, and I take the feeling of hunger to be in the stomach, or that of pain in my injured limb. But what about the third kind of perceptions received by means of the external or internal senses? Why are they referred to the soul and what does that mean?

It is tempting to interpret "refer to" here as some kind of spontaneous (though normally incorrect) judging,[38] though the judgments could not be formed through conscious assent or denial, and we are not aroused to passions by our judgments. I prefer understanding "perceptions" here as something more like what Aristotle and the Stoics would call "appearances," and look at the classification proposed as one among appearances on the basis of their apparent sources—that is, on the basis of what *appears* to the perceiver to be their actual causes. If appearances here involve beliefs or judgments, they are implicit and unnoticed. In referring heat to the fire, I (prereflectively) take the heat to be in the fire. In referring an emotion to the soul, I take it as a state internal to the soul itself, although in fact it has its cause and origin in the body. That is, it is presented—appears to me—as a state of my soul. Having thus distinguished the passions in the strict sense of the word from the other two kinds of body-dependent thoughts, Descartes offers his "general" definition of the passions: "The perceptions, or sensations *(sentiments)* or emotions of the soul which we refer particularly to it, and which are caused, maintained and strengthened by some movements of the spirits" (art. 27 (AT XI 349, CSM I 338–339)). He explains that he calls the passions "perceptions" (in contrast to "actions"), but not in the sense of distinct knowledge because the close union of the soul and the body renders them obscure and confused, so that "those who are the most agitated by their passions are those who know them least." In calling them feelings *(sentiments)* Descartes emphasizes that they are received in the same way as the objects of the internal or external senses are known (AT XI 349–350), presumably, in the same confused manner. Finally they are even better called emotions, because they "agitate and upset" the mind more than any other thoughts (art. 28 (AT XI 350, CSM I 339)).

It is not easy to fit these characterizations together. Let us consider in particular the first, which contrasts them with thoughts classified as actions or volitions. Recall that volitions in the primary sense are actions of the soul, which are experienced as thoughts "coming directly from" and also as "seeming to depend only" on the soul (AT XI 342, CSM I 335). What difference is there between being "experienced as coming from" and "seeming to depend only on" the soul on the one hand, and "being referred to" the soul on the other? Presumably the difference is that we are, in the first case, aware of causing them ourselves, and hence in full control of them, whereas they are, in the latter case, not directly in our control. Like the sensations, which come without our consent (AT VII 75, CSM II 52), the emotions come unbidden and present themselves to us as inclining our will whether we want it or not. They are caused by movements in the body but are referred to the soul, like the sensations that also depend on movements in our body but are referred to some external thing taken to cause them.

Now consider this in the light of article 19, where Descartes stresses that "the perception is really one and the same thing as the volition" and that although, with regard to the soul, it is an action to will something, it is also a passion to notice *(apercevoir)* that volition (AT XI 343, CSM I 336). What exactly are we supposed to think of it? The only reason Descartes seems to give for nonetheless calling these perceptions or passions actions is that "names are always determined by what is the most noble" (AT XI 343, CSM I 336). What we have on the one hand is actions (of the mind) perceived as passions (of the mind), and on the other hand passions (of the mind) that are actions in the body but that, since we perceive no proximate (bodily) cause to which we could relate them (that is, since we do not *perceive* them as actions in the body), are referred to the soul itself, which, as I understand it, means that we perceive them as if they were its own actions. *As if,* for they are in fact actions only when related to the body. They appear to us as our own actions, which they are not.

Phenomenologically the passions are distinguished from other sensations by the fact that they are referred particularly to the soul, which I take to mean that they are experienced or felt as if in the soul itself. But they also differ causally (art. 29) from other body-dependent perceptions by the particular neural motions in the brain that not only cause, but also maintain and strengthen them. Through these movements (of which we are not directly aware) they differ from the volitions, which "also can be called emotions of the soul that are referred to it, but which are caused by the soul itself" (AT XI 349, CSM I 338–339). Only the latter, which are also felt in the soul itself, are caused by the soul, by its own rational judgments. Descartes calls them "intellectual" or sometimes also "interior" emotions,[39] and they are as a rule more constant and stable than those caused and maintained by particular neural motions.

No thoughts "agitate or upset" the soul *(l'agitent ou l'ébranlent)* as much as the passions (art. 28 (AT XI 350, CSM I 339)). This again is due to those very particular neural motions that constitute their "ultimate and most proximate" cause. These movements, in fact, have a double function: they cause, maintain, and strengthen the passions, and they prepare the muscles of the body for the appropriate behavioral reactions:

> For it must be observed that the principal effect of all the human passions is that they move and dispose the soul to will *(vouloir)* the things for which they prepare the body. Thus the feeling of fear moves *(incite)* the soul to will to flee, that of courage to will to fight, and similarly with others. (art. 40 (AT XI 359, CSM I 343))

The very same motions of the animal spirits in the brain, which arouse and maintain in the mind the feeling of fear, dispose the members of the body to flee the danger, just as those motions that arouse courage prepare the body to fight. The function of the passions is always to move the soul to will whatever behavioral reaction or action they prepare the body for.[40] The cerebral motions that dispose the body to take action are felt in the soul as a passion, that is, as a strong inclination of the will to perform that action.

Descartes calls these particular motions of the animal spirits the "ultimate and proximate" cause of the passions because they constitute the last link in the causal chain that triggers the passions—its first link being always a perception of an object—for instance, the sight of an approaching beast that is taken to be threatening. How the object is perceived, as frightful or not, depends not on its real properties but on how the motions in the brain caused by the perception affect me— that is, on what representations they bring to my mind. This again depends in part on nature and in part on my earlier experiences and beliefs. The same motions that are ultimate with respect to the object perceived are proximate in relation to the soul that they affect: they are what immediately and directly affect the soul, occasioning whatever thoughts or emotions have been associated with them.[41]

6. The Psycho-Physiology of Passions

Let me try to illustrate this account of how passions are aroused in the soul and expressed in the body by contrasting it with the so-called James–Lange theory, which it has been seen as anticipating. Take the passion of fear, which as we saw accompanies certain neurophysiological changes that prepare the body to flee. On Descartes's account it is not because the soul first perceives a threatening danger that the passion of fear arises; the passion arises because the body is first prepared for flight. The passion of fear is the perception of some turmoil and inclination of the soul caused directly (through the pineal gland) by specific neurophysiological changes in the body.[42] It is hence not because of any prior belief that the approaching rottweiler, let's call him Fido, is dangerous that I become frightened; rather my fear is aroused directly by certain physiological changes that the visual and other impressions of the approaching beast *automatically*, without the intermediary of any beliefs, cause in my brain. The feeling of fear then alerts me, as it were, to a presumed danger; it is not a consequence of it, as common sense would have it (art. 35–36 (AT XI 355–357, CSM I 342)).

The physiological changes occurring during an emotional state are normally thought of as caused by the emotion and not the other way around. The order of explanation, according to William James, is inverted:

> Common sense says, we lose our fortune, are sorry and weep; we meet a bear, are frightened and run; we are insulted by a rival, are angry and strike. The hypothesis here to be defended says that this order of sequence is incorrect, that the one mental state is not immediately induced by the other, that the bodily manifestations must first be interposed between, and that the more rational statement is that we feel sorry because we cry, angry because we strike, afraid because we tremble, and not that we cry, strike or tremble, because we are sorry, angry or fearful, as the case may be. Without the bodily states following on the perception, the latter would be purely cognitive in form, pale, colourless, destitute of emotional warmth. We might then see the bear, and judge it best to run, receive the insult and deem it right to strike, but we could not actually *feel* afraid or angry.[43]

Not only does James invert the order of explanation in claiming that the bodily changes characteristic of emotions "follow directly on the PERCEPTION of the exciting fact," he seems to *identify* the emotion with the experience of these same bodily changes, in writing that "our feeling of the same changes as they occur IS the emotion."[44]

But Descartes does not go this far. He does not reduce the emotions to simple feelings or brute sensations of some internal bodily changes, nor are they identified with brain states, or described as perceptions of such states.[45] On the other hand, they are not reducible to purely mental states either; they are, as we saw, referred to the soul itself—that is, they are taken to be states of the mind itself—but this does not exhaust their content since they also involve perceptions of the object triggering them and, once the passion has been aroused, some representations or implicit beliefs about its usefulness for the mind–body union (art. 52 (AT XI 372, CSM I 349)). These evaluative beliefs are, as we saw, not formed through reflective judgment; they are representations expressed in characteristic behavioral reactions, which are occasioned directly by the neurological changes the beliefs are (by nature or habit) associated with. Nature has instituted certain movements in the brain to affect the mind with a sensation of pain "as if in the foot" (AT VII 87, CSM II 60) and other movements to affect it with passions that are perceptions of things as if fearful or loveable or as mattering to us in some other way. The passions are crucial for the preservation and well-being of the mind–body union, and they achieve this because of their double effect of inclining the mind to will what they prepare the body to pursue (art. 137–139 (AT XI 430–431, CSM I 176–177)). Their first and main cause is always a cognitive act, namely, a perception of some object (person or situation) that matters for us and that they represent as unusual, good or bad, as worth of loving, hating, rejoicing about, desiring, fearing, or the like.

Descartes's classification of the particular passions is based on differences in the ways their objects are perceived and affect our bodies and in the ways these affections are reflected in the mind. None of this, to repeat, is a matter of forming explicit judgments about their objects, but of how, because of the way they affect our bodies, their objects are represented by the mind, before any conscious deliberation about their value occurs. The immediate somatic effects of the perceptual act—which cause, maintain, and strengthen the passion—are as inseparable from it as the side of a coin from the coin or as the cutting from the being cut.

7. Representing and Referring Passions to the Soul

This should help clarify the reading of the definition of passions as being "referred to the soul" (art. 27) suggested above. The passions are directly caused, maintained, and strengthened by movements in the body, but since we do not perceive the movements that constitute their proximate cause, they appear to be caused by the mind itself. As we saw, however, emotions caused by the mind itself are volitions, so that in referring them to the mind, we take them to be our own volitions—just as in feeling pain in the foot we spontaneously take the pain to exist in the foot we refer it to. That is, we perceive passions as inclinations of our own will because we are unaware of their last and proximate cause, of those cerebral motions that are direct effects (by mechanical associations established through habit or nature) of some perception. All it takes to change an inclination of will to actual willing is an act of assent, which can be caused without noticing.

If this is right, this notion of referring is but another application of the one introduced in the Third Meditation, where the term *rapporter à,* which is the French rendering of Descartes's Latin *referare* used in his account of representation (AT VII 37, l. 14; cf. AT IX 29). "Idea" or "perception," in Descartes's wide use of these terms, covers, as we have seen (Chapter 4, section 1), *both* the act of thinking *and* its content, the thing represented. Thoughts belonging to this wider category are said to have "various additional forms" (L. *alias quasdam praeterea formas*):

> [T]hus when I will, or am afraid, or affirm, or deny, there is always a particular thing which I take as the object of my thought, *but my thought includes something more* than the likeness of that thing. Some thoughts in this category are called volitions or emotions, while others are called judgements. (AT VII 37, CSM II 26; my emphasis)

Qua thoughts, volitions and emotions always have objects, but they have other forms as well. As ideas in the strict sense of the term, they are individuated through the object represented, but as ideas in the wider sense, they are also individuated through their formal or actual reality as various kinds of acts of mind. In being afraid of Fido, my fearing Fido is a different thought from my seeing Fido showing his teeth, hearing Fido barking at me, or feeling his teeth closing around my hand.

But Descartes's account also distinguishes between the object of the actual thought and its cause, and this is where the notion of "referring to" occurs in the Third Meditation. Not only is there always some particular thing that is the object of my thought, but my actually thinking of that object thus and so and the mode in which I think of it have causes, and the object to which they are referred and their causes need not coincide in Descartes's account of body-dependent perceptions.[46] I can fear Fido without seeing or hearing him, indeed, without him being around at all: just thinking of meeting that big beast is enough to unnerve me and make my limbs shake. Generally the actual causes of adventitious ideas bear no resemblance to the ideas they cause or, more properly, give occasion to the mind to entertain. Seeing Fido is normally caused by Fido's action on my sense of sight, and what I see—the color of his fur, his size, shape, teeth, and so on—I refer to Fido, taking my sensations to be qualities of the dog in front of me. The emotion of fear (my strong inclination to run and seek protection and the accompanying belief that Fido is dangerous and should be avoided) caused by those impressions of the dog, on the other hand, are referred or related to my mind itself.

There are not two different senses of representation here—one explicable in terms of objective reality (applicable to external objects) and the other in terms of causal reference (applicable to body-dependent thoughts).[47] My fear is not an object of representation; I do not represent it, I feel it, and in feeling fear, I represent its object as threatening or dangerous. Fear as an emotion is a mode of representing or thinking of a thing. Even emotions that do not have particular objects, moods for instance, are modes of thinking about things in general.

In the context of the *Meditations,* referring is not an alternative way of representing but part and parcel of the representational act, that is, it is one of the "various additional forms" ideas can take as formally real acts of thinking, namely, volitions or emotions, and affirmations or denials (that is, judgments). Sensations too clearly belong on this list. Referring an idea to its apparent cause takes different forms depending on the mode of representing considered, on whether the thought is a volition, sensation, emotion, or judgment. It is in referring the content of my thought, which in itself is without falsity, to a presumed particular cause that falsity and error arise (AT VII 37–38).[48] I can be mistaken about the danger Fido represents or about having pain in my foot, but not about actually fearing Fido or feeling pain as in my foot. Or think of the attraction Descartes confesses having felt for cross-eyed persons, just because he was in love as a child with a cross-eyed girl. The inclination to love somebody with that particular look and to think of her as loveable, that is, to think that joining oneself willingly to her is good, is one thing, but to accept the latter judgment as true is another, for only the latter is liable to falsity.[49]

I take the analysis of perceptions and their classification on the basis of their (apparent) causes in *The Passions of the Soul* to be continuous with the discussion of adventitious ideas in the *Meditations* III and VI. Insofar as representing something in the mode of sensation or emotion involves a spontaneous attribution of a cause to that thought, sensations and emotions are, like judgments, complex thoughts, and as such they can be false (materially false) and misleading. They differ from judgments only to the extent that they do not involve deliberate assent or denial. They cause spontaneous beliefs about things, which if we are not on our guard readily turn into false judgments. Emotions, likewise, turn from inclining the will to volitions proper, if we are not attentive enough to withhold from assenting to their inclinations. Emotions are in this respect even worse than sensations, because in addition to presenting us with uncritical, habitual, or spontaneous beliefs about objects perceived and their value, they are, in being referred to the soul itself, taken as expressing our own (rational) evaluations and inclinations to act. Because of the particular movements in the body (art. 27 (AT XI 349, CSM I 338–339)) that make the body disposed to act, while at the same time inclining the soul to assent to the beliefs they call forth and to the actions they prepare for, the impulse to assent is so strong that unless immediately withheld, it will automatically ensue.

A common mistake is to think that, for Descartes, the passions, as representations referred to the mind itself but caused by cerebral motions, would represent those motions.[50] But that surely cannot be, since we do not perceive those motions at all. To be angry is not to represent one's blood as boiling or represent some neural agitation in the brain. What is represented in anger is some wrong unjustly inflicted on one, the person or circumstances taken to be the cause of it, and a strong inclination to retaliate, which is felt as a tension in the limbs or the whole body, ready to attack, as it were. Another mistake is to think that the passions represent the state of mind itself, that they are self-referential. Both readings substitute the causes of the emotion for its object or content.

That passions are referred to the mind itself means, as I understand it, that the mind or subject having the passion sees herself not as passive but as an agent, for she appears to herself as the active agent of the particular inclination of the will that she experiences. That is, the passions present us with the illusion of being the autonomous agents of our spontaneous evaluations and actions—an illusion that is not dissipated until one becomes aware of their true nature and origin, in finding oneself overcome by them, unable to control or alter them. Passions present themselves as inclinations of our will, as if they were grounded in our own evaluative judgments about their objects and hence as having rational grounds. In fact they are directly triggered by neural motions, but because we do not perceive those motions, we mistakenly refer the passions to our mind, taking them to be express evaluations of our rational mind itself and hence to be grounded on good reasons. Instead they are, to use Spinoza's characterization, like conclusions without premises.[51] In fearing Fido, in feeling my heart beat and my body prepared to seek protection, I find myself representing Fido as a dangerous beast, thinking that running away is the right action to take. This seems like a rational sequence of thoughts—one I refer to the soul and take to be the outcome of my own deliberation. In fact it is not, for I have no "evidence" that Fido is dangerous other than the impressions and confused beliefs occasioned by the physiological effects the perception of rottweilers happen to produce in my body. For all I really know, Fido could be the most faithful, gentle companion, come to protect, not to attack me.[52]

8. The Function and Classification of Passions

To support this reading, we need to look more closely at Descartes's analysis of particular passions. So far we have been concerned mainly with the difference between passions and other body-dependent perceptions, and for this purpose the consideration of their last and proximate (bodily) cause has been sufficient. But in order to classify the various passions in the strict sense it is necessary to consider also their first or primary causes. Those who describe Descartes's theory of emotions as merely physiological overlook their first causes. For, as mentioned above, the physiological states constituting their last and proximate cause are normally themselves caused by the perception of some external object, and not just any object, but some object that *is perceived as* important in some way. Passions differ from each other through the different ways their objects incline the will. In fact, the particular inclinations of the will (to pursue or avoid the things represented as their objects) that the perceptions of these objects cause constitute the passions or emotions as a specific kind of mental state.

> I observe moreover that the objects that move our senses do not excite different passions in us on account of all the differences in them, but only because of the different ways in which they may harm or benefit

us, or in general have importance for us; and that the function of all the passions consist solely in this, that they *dispose our soul to will* the things which nature deems useful for us, *and to persist in this volition;* and how moreover the same agitation of the spirits which normally causes the passions *disposes the body to make movements which help us to attain these things.* (art. 52 (AT XI 371, CSM I 349); my emphasis. See also articles 137–147)

Passions are felt, intensely, as volitions to pursue or avoid their objects. Yet they are not, as we have seen, volitions in Descartes's technical sense—they are not actions of the mind itself—because they depend on neural motions that are not under direct voluntary control. Unlike intellectual emotions caused by the mind, by its rational evaluative judgments, the passions do not depend on prior judgments about the value or importance of their objects. The inclinations of the will that the perception of the objects trigger occur prior to any evaluation or judgment that it is useful, harmful, good or bad, and the latter are reactions to, not causes of, our emotional states.

This is why passions are *both* mental *and* physiological states. They always have these two sides: they consist, on the level of the body, in specific motions of the animal spirits, disposing the body to some behavioral reaction, and, on the mental level, in the effect these motions and dispositions have on the mind, in causing the will to consent to the action-impulses they prepare the body for. To fulfill this latter function they have to be representational in a distinctive way: it is not enough that they have objects; their objects have to be represented as important—as *mattering* in one way or another. But, again, this does not mean first judged as mattering in one way or another, prior to inclining the will. On the contrary, it is by inclining the will that they are perceived as important or mattering to us. Different objects excite different passions "only because of the various ways in which they may harm or benefit us, or in general have importance for us" (art. 52). In making us aware of our needs and our relations to others, the passions help us adjust to our physical and social environment, and this is their primary function. They embody a kind of instinctive, natural knowledge about what is beneficial or harmful or important in some other way. They are useful as long as they "strengthen and prolong thoughts in the soul which it is good for the soul to have and which otherwise might easily be erased from it." But they can also cause a lot of harm "in their strengthening and preserving these thoughts more than is needed, or in their strengthening and preserving others on which it is not good to dwell" (AT XI 383, CSM I 354).[53]

So the first cause of a passion is always some perception (thought) or other that has to be processed through the imagination in order to move the animal spirits in the special ways required for a particular state of passion to arise.[54] Since people's inclinations disposing them to passions differ, the same perceptions or judgments have very different effects on different people, as Descartes explains when giving his first account of passions to Elisabeth. For instance, after hearing the announcement of some imminent danger threatening their town, each of its inhabitants will make a judgment about the evil this might cause them, but although such a judgment "is an action of their soul and not a passion," and although the same judgment may be found in many, all are not equally affected by it. How they will be affected depends on their habits and inclinations and on the kind of representations that the announcement is likely to evoke in them. The latter are, indeed, crucial, for, as Descartes explains: "Before their soul will receive the emotion, in which alone the passion consists, it has to make this judgement, or else *at least it has to conceive the danger without judging, and imprint its image in the brain* (which is done through another act called imagination)" (October 6, 1645 (AT IV 312, CSMK 217); my emphasis).

It is not necessary to make a judgment about the imminent danger in order to react emotionally to it, for imagining it is sufficient, at least for those who are easily moved this way. It is also necessary because only by imagining the danger will the spirits in the brain move in the special ways characteristic of the passions, affecting the heart muscles and the circulation of the blood so that "the whole body becomes pale, cold and trembling, and the fresh spirits returning from the heart to the brain are agitated in such a way that they can serve to form no other images there than those which excite in the soul the passion of fear, *all of which happens so quickly one after another that it seems like one single operation*" (AT IV 313, CSMK 271–272; my emphasis).

Descartes notes that our thoughts usually depend on more than one cause, but that they are called after "their main cause or the one with which we are mainly concerned." This is why people often confuse sensations or feelings like pain with a passion like sadness, or pleasurable sensations with joy. They also sometimes confuse the inclinations or habits disposing one to passions with passions proper, which are, however, "easy to distinguish" (!) since the latter consist in emotions of the soul preceded by a judgment or at least some evaluative conception of the object of the passion.

This may suggest two different, though connected, accounts of the genesis of the passions. The first would be in line with the cognitive account favored by the Stoics: the mind is disposed, by inclination or habit, to a certain kind of emotional reaction in response to an appearance, which becomes a passion when it is endorsed by assent of reason, which turns it into a (false) judgment: I love because I judge that the object of my love is indeed worthy of love, or I fear the danger to which I am alerted because I judge that it is indeed life threatening, or the like. The second is more in line with the account in the *Passions of the Soul*.[55] Here no judgment is required: it is enough to conceive or imagine the object of passion in a certain way without making any judgments concerning it. The power of imagination, which requires bodily organs, plays a crucial role here, and although Descartes describes it as an action of the mind, he does not do so on account of the mind's activity. What count are the patterns or traces produced through imagining in the brain, for it is only when the "image" or conception is somehow "imprinted" in the brain that the chain of neurophysiological reactions characteristic of passions gets started (AT III 312, CSMK 271). Here it is not the judgment that a person is good that arouses the passion of love, but on the contrary, the passion of love makes her appear good and worthy of the love the perception of her inspires.[56]

A true evaluative judgment does not, on the other hand, by itself cause any emotional reaction. Although Descartes stresses the activity of the soul not only in making judgments, but also in imagining, and thereby in determining the courses of the spirits, such acts are at best indirectly controlled by the will. What Descartes says about the mechanisms of the passions indicates that our power to control our imagination is fairly limited. It follows from his "natural institution" principle that most of the thoughts and representations that cause our passions and emotional responses are elicited automatically by association and the movements of the spirits, and they will prevail as long as the latter remain effective.

Consider some examples of Cartesian passions. The first emotion that Descartes lists in the second part of his treatise, surprisingly, is a purely cognitive emotion, wonder *(admiration)*. It is atypical as a passion in not being accompanied by the usual movements around the heart ("not having the good or the bad, but merely the knowledge of the object one admires, for object" (art. 71 (AT XI 381, CSMK 353)), but is nevertheless classified as a passion because of its immediate causes and effects. It is described as "a sudden surprise of the soul which brings it to consider with attention the objects that seem to it unusual and extraordinary" (art. 70 (AT XI 380, CSMK 353)). Its first cause is an object or situation encountered for the first time, which is represented to the soul by the movements in the brain as unusual. Descartes does not explain how movements in the brain can represent some object "as unusual and worthy of consideration" (art. 70 (AT XI 380, CSM I 353)). The cerebral impressions somehow cause the mind to take the object or situation perceived as "worthy of consideration." More precisely, an inclination to consider the object in that particular way is automatically triggered in the mind by the pattern of movements in the brain, an inclination that can be described as a kind of conditioned response or reflexive reaction. The brain impression is not, of course, itself an object of awareness, but an unconscious physical cause that makes us attentive to the object or situation that caused it in two ways: by keeping our sensory organs alert to the stimulation and by inclining us to consider if the object causing it is worthy of closer examination. It thus fulfills the double function of a passion: it inclines the mind to will and thereby to assent to the behavioral response for which it prepares the body.

Admiration or wonder disposes us to acquire knowledge and is useful mainly in that, by mobilizing our attention, it makes us learn and retain in our memory things that were unknown to us (art. 75). Excessive wonder (astonishment or blind curiosity) is harmful: wondering, for instance, at things of little or no consideration may entirely prevent or pervert the use of reason (art. 76–78) and we should, therefore, use reflection and that particular attention that our "will can always impose on our understanding *when we judge* that the thing presenting itself to us is worth it" (art. 75). The distinction between unreflective evaluative beliefs ("representations") and judgments formed after critical reflection through voluntary assent is here explicitly made. This, of course, is the whole point of knowing the causes of the passions: to determine whether a particular emotional response is appropriate or, on the contrary, is excessive and harmful, and hence whether it is rational to assent to it. Descartes seems confident that the mind always has this power of giving or withholding assent, and hence of endorsing or rejecting the representations and evaluations presented to it, and that it thereby also has the power, at least indirectly, to control excessive and harmful passions.

Among the other five passions listed by Descartes as simple and primary ("all the others are composed of some of these six, or else they are species of them") are love, hatred, desire, joy, and sadness (art. 69 (AT XI 380, CSM I 353)). Love is defined as "an emotion caused by the movements of the spirits, which disposes the soul to join itself willingly to objects that appear to be agreeable to it," while hatred impels it "to want to be separated from objects which present themselves to it as harmful." In emphasizing that these emotions are caused by the spirits, Descartes wants to distinguish emotions "which are passions and depend on the body" from those rational "judgements that also bring the soul to join itself willingly with things it deems good, and separate itself from those it deems bad" as well as from the "intellectual" emotions produced by these judgments (art. 79). The emotion of love consists in an inclination of the will to join itself to (or consider as united to) what appears to the soul as good. It is a bit mysterious what joining oneself willingly (de volonté) to something involves. It is not a desire, which always relates to the future, but "the assent (consentement) by which one considers oneself henceforth as joined to what one loves, in such a manner that one imagines a whole of which one considers oneself as only one part, and the object loved the other" (AT XI 387, CSM I 356).[57]

The emotion of desire on the other hand is defined as "an agitation of the soul caused by the spirits, which disposes the soul to wish, in the future, for the things it represents to itself as agreeable" (art. 86). It differs from love and joy in having no opposite: aversion, which is usually opposed to it as the avoidance of evil to the search of good, is not a different movement from desire but, as it were, its other side.[58] Joy is defined as "a pleasant emotion which the soul has when it enjoys a good which impressions in the brain represent to it as its own." And sadness finally "is an unpleasant listlessness which affects the soul when it suffers discomfort from an evil or deficiency which impressions in the brain represent to it as its own" (art. 91–92). Note that the cerebral patterns are the vehicles of the representations involved here, which is why the talk of implicit judgments seems particularly inadequate. The representations are those that strongly incline the mind to assent to them, and which, if assent is not withheld but given by impulse, are turned into judgments that are likely to be false.

All the other emotions are varieties or combinations of the above, and they all come in two kinds: those that are aroused directly through physiological disturbances and those generated by rational judgments alone.

The first kind are passions proper and are always prompted by movements in the brain, which are said to *represent* things to the soul. This, as I have stressed, is not to say that the cerebral movements or patterns are themselves perceived as representing anything, but rather that they evoke, by natural institution or habit, representations in the mind. They thus function, like sensations, as a kind of (unconscious) signs of a natural language that the mind spontaneously interprets. Descartes compares the relation between passions and cerebral movements to the relation between the meanings of spoken words and the sounds which constitute the utterances: in hearing them, we think of their meanings and not of the sounds we hear.[59]

The second kind of emotions are purely intellectual, which depend only on rational evaluative judgments that the mind makes independently of any cerebral movements affecting it. Unlike the first kind of emotions, where things are evaluated through representations that come unbidden to the soul, without any action on its part, in this latter kind reason evaluates the object to be good or bad. Thus when Descartes says that "joy results from the belief *(opinion)* that we possess some good, and sadness from the belief that we have some evil or deficiency," these beliefs can be of two different kinds, depending on whether they are formed directly by the soul's own activity or prompted by cerebral movements.[60]

The distinction between intellectual emotions and body-dependent emotions is based on their genesis, how they are caused. Because intellectual emotions are generated by the mind itself, they contain nothing that is confused or obscure; they could also occur in a disembodied mind, an angel, for instance. Love, as a purely rational or intellectual emotion, would consist "simply in the fact that when our soul perceives some present or absent good, which *it judges fitting for itself, it joins itself to it willingly, that is, it considers itself and the good in question as forming two parts of a single whole*" (AT IV 601, CSMK 306; my emphasis). Other rational considerations about the value of an object or its relation to us create corresponding inclinations of our will: the intellectual emotions of joy, love, sadness, hate, and so on are constituted by these movements of the will, "in so far as they are rational thoughts, and not passions, and could exist in our soul even if it had no body." Love for knowledge and the sadness in lacking it are good examples of intellectual emotions, which typically contain nothing obscure, nothing of which the soul could not have perfect knowledge, "provided it reflected on its own thoughts" (letter to Chanut, February 1, 1647 (AT IV 601–602, CSMK 306)).

It is unlikely, however, that any embodied mind would ever experience an intellectual emotion in its purity: "But while our soul is joined to the body, this rational love is commonly accompanied by the other kind of love, which can be called sensual or sensuous, and which . . . is nothing but a confused thought, aroused in the soul by some motions of the nerves, which makes it disposed to this other more clear and distinct thought in which rational love consists" (AT IV 602, CSMK 306). The body-dependent passion of love, which in itself is obscure and confused, disposes the mind to entertain the "more clear and distinct thought," that is, the judgment that its object is so fitting that it immediately wants to join itself to it. Note again that the passion proper consists not in this judgment, but in the will's disposition to entertain and endorse it, which is produced by bodily movements. The passion of love is "nothing but a confused thought, aroused in the soul by some motion of nerves, which makes it disposed to have the other, clearer, thought which constitutes rational love" (AT V 603, CSMK 306–307).

The same holds for other rational emotions. Because no thoughts ever come singly to a Cartesian mind, and because the institution of nature has joined each thought to some bodily movement, all intellectual emotions are immediately followed by cerebral movements, which, according to mechanical laws, cause other thoughts and emotions. Thus the intellectual love for the purest of objects, whether God or rational knowledge, normally comes with all the obscure feelings and sentiments that were connected with that emotion during our first experience of love. The exceptions are those emotions Descartes calls "interior" and that are secondary—the enjoyment of shedding tears or feeling sorry, for instance, or of meeting the strains of physical challenge—and presuppose a primary passion caused through neural movements of the body.[61]

9. The Institution of Nature as the Key to the Mastery of Passions

The principle underlying this account—"the institution of nature"—works through natural and habitual association. It is of the greatest importance for Descartes's moral therapy and is restated many times in his correspondence and *The Passions of the Soul.*[62] It is illustrated by common experience, for instance, of how the taste of some disgusting medicine that one has been forced to take during illness remains forever associated with the same feeling of disgust, while, conversely, the very thought of medicine tends to evoke that feeling. Descartes also gives an unusual and more interesting example: the emotion of love is forever associated with the physiological changes occurring in our body when our soul, having been joined to the body in the mother's womb, for the first time experienced it.

> For it seems to me that . . . its first passions must have occurred when at some time the blood or some other (nutritive) juice entering the heart, was more suitable than usual for maintaining its heat, which is the principle of life, which caused the soul to join itself willingly to that juice, that is, to love it, and at the same time the spirits flowed from the brain to the muscles capable of pressing or agitating the parts of the body from which the juice had come to the heart, so as to make them send more of it . . . That is why these same movements of the spirits have ever since accompanied the passion of love. (art. 107 (AT XI 407–408, CSM I 365–365))

As Descartes notes in the letter to Chanut quoted above, the feeling caused by the physiological changes accompanying a passion (for instance, the feeling of heat around the heart characteristic of love) and the thought by which one considers oneself as willingly united to the object one loves are different thoughts, so that the former can occur without the latter—that is, one can feel as if one were in love without being inclined to love any particular object. Likewise, we may know that some object is very much worth being united to and yet, even while joining ourselves willingly to it, experience no passion, because our body is not in the right disposition. In most cases, however, the two kinds of love come together: "[F]or the two are linked in such a way that when the soul judges an object to be worthy of it, this immediately makes the heart disposed to the motions which excite the passion of love; and when the heart is similarly disposed by other causes, that makes the soul imagine lovable qualities in objects in which, at another time, it would see nothing but faults" (AT IV 603, CSMK 307).

That certain motions in the heart should in this way be connected to certain thoughts "which they in no way resemble" is explained, again, by the "soul's natural capacity of union with a body," which gives it the possibility of "associating each of its thoughts with some motions or other dispositions of this body in such a way that when these same dispositions recur in the body they induce the same thoughts in the mind, and conversely" (ibid.). All this is compared to how in learning a language "we connect the letters to the pronunciation of certain words, which are material things, with their meanings, so that when we later hear the same words, we conceive the same things, and when we conceive the same things, we remember the same words" (AT IV 604, CSMK 307). Descartes also observes that the bodily dispositions that accompanied our first thoughts are undoubtedly more closely connected to them than later ones, which accounts, for example, for the connection of love with that special feeling of heat around the heart. He explains to Chanut that the soul is likely to have felt joy at its first moment of union with the body "because it is not credible that the soul was put into the body at a time when the body was not in a good condition, and a good condition of the body naturally gives us joy." Joy is immediately followed by love for the suitable nutrition that accounts for its good condition, but may turn into sadness if food is lacking or hatred if it receives unsuitable food. These are our first four passions, and the only ones "we had before our birth." Descartes thinks they were "then only sensations or confused thoughts, because the soul was then so attached to matter that it could yet not do anything else except receive various impressions from it." It is only after some years that it begins to have other joys and loves, and "whatever intellectual element its joys or loves involve" is "accompanied by the first sensations which it had of them" and also by "the motions and natural functions which then occurred in the body" (AT IV 605–606, CSMK 308). This means that even the obscure sensations experienced before birth already contain, confusedly, something "intellectual" (joy being the thought of possessing some good, and love the thought of willingly joining oneself to something appearing as good).

It is, Descartes writes, only the fear of boring his correspondent that keeps him from showing "in detail how all the other bodily conditions which at the beginning of our life occurred with these four passions still accompany them." At the same time, he recognizes that "it is because of these confused sensations of our childhood, which remain joined with the rational thoughts by which we love what we judge worthy of love, that the nature of love is difficult for us to understand. And . . . many other passions, such as joy, sadness, desire, fear and hope, etc. mingle in various ways with love and thus prevent us from discovering exactly what constitutes it" (AT IV 606, CSMK 308).

The institution of nature explains why certain kinds of movements in the body are joined to certain kinds of thoughts. Particular circumstances and habits explain the individual variations between the associations of movements and thoughts in different persons, like the aversion experienced by some when feeling the smell of roses, or the fear of cats, or similar things, because of impressions that remain imprinted in the brain throughout a person's life, although the incident first causing it has long been forgotten (art. 136 (AT XI 428–429, CSM I 375–376)).[63] Although nature or accident has joined certain movements in the pineal gland to certain thoughts, we may join them to others to obtain emotions we find more useful or desirable, indirectly, by training ourselves.[64]

The function of the passions varies, as we have seen, with the point of view from which they are considered.

> [A]ccording to the institution of nature, they are all related to the body, and have been given to the soul only in so far as it is joined to the body; so that their natural function is to dispose the soul to consent and contribute to actions which may serve to preserve the body or render it in some way more perfect. (art. 137 (AT XI 430, CSM I 376))

What serves the body to which the soul is united is good for the soul, but the soul has to be, as it were, reminded of it, since it does not attend to the needs of the body all the time. It has joys and pleasures of its own, and might, for instance, be lost in wonder and joy over the discovery of a new mathematical proof if the feelings of hunger did not remind it of dinnertime.

Although the passions are good and natural in themselves, they can cause harm if we were to follow them blindly as animals without reason do. They are harmful in particular because they tend to present goods or evils as greater than they really are: "As we also see that the animals are often deceived by the appearances (by lures), and that to avoid small evils they throw themselves into greater ones. That is why we must use experience and reason in order to distinguish good from evil and know their true value, so as not to take the one for the other or bring ourselves to anything excessively" (art. 138 (AT XI 138, CSM I 377)). Moreover, looked at from the point of view of the soul, the function of the passions is different than seen from the point of view of the body. Since the body is less important from its point of view, the passions should be considered mainly insofar as they belong to the soul.[65]

The aim of the mastery of passions for Descartes is not, as in the Stoic therapy of passions, to train oneself to resist or eliminate them altogether, but to resist only those that are false, and this is mainly a matter of sorting out well-grounded inclinations of the will from ungrounded ones. But the means by which such inclinations can be opposed are the same for Descartes as for the Stoics, because both hold that the mind (or reason), through its free capacity of assent, has the power to refrain from assenting to and acting on excessive and misleading passions.

A judgment proper requires a perception of the intellect and an act of assent or denial that Descartes attributes to the will. A proposition can be entertained by the intellect without being assented to or denied, and there is no judgment proper unless it is also deliberately accepted or denied. The representations that are part of the passions characteristically present themselves to the mind without a deliberate, conscious act of assent on its part. Instead of being formed through the mind's own reflective activity, the representations inclining our will in passions are, as I have argued, evoked mechanically, by the movements of the animal spirits to which they have been joined through "natural institution" and by association.[66] In this they resemble the appearances of the Stoics, which come with the first motions of passions and only when assented to by the rational mind turn into passions (false beliefs).

This should not obscure the differences between the Cartesian and the Stoic theory. Cartesian passions are complex psycho-physiological states, which are expressed in mental and bodily dispositions—the inclinations of the will in the passion expresses corresponding dispositions to act in the body, and they have important, positive functions of their own. It may be tempting, in the framework of Descartes's mind–body dualism, to treat them either as states of the mind or as physical states, but such reductive readings neglect the fact that they are states of the mind–body union, and that their mental and physical causes and effects are not merely concomitant but interdependent. Any account that isolates or gives priority to what goes on at either level is therefore bound to distort the Cartesian theory,[67] which takes passions in the mind to be the same thing as actions in the body in a way we can clearly experience but not understand distinctly. The capacity to control the passions, for Descartes as for the Stoics, depends on the mind—its rational volitions.

10. Reason versus Passions

The right use of reason, Descartes tells Elisabeth, "consists only in examining and considering without passion the value of all the perfections, of the body as well as of the mind." He also says that all the passions are enjoyable, and even that they can be all the more useful the more they are excessive, once they are subjected to reason (letter to Elisabeth, September 1, 1645 (AT IV 286–287, CSMK 265)).

But passions do not seem to be excessive while being subjected to reason, as Elisabeth is quick to point out, expressing skepticism about the greater utility of excessive passions (letter to Descartes, October 28, 1645 (AT IV 322)). Moreover, if the function of passions is to make us aware of the utility and harmfulness of external things for the mind–body union, how could it be possible to examine the perfections of the body or of the mind *without* passion?

Emotions, as we have seen, consist in inclinations of the will, and the stronger the emotion, the more it inclines the will: excessive passions incline the will excessively. A passion can be an excessive inclination, for instance, to assent to a representation of some minor good as greater than it is or some evil as good and desirable. A passion can also be an excessive inclination to act on false beliefs. What can reason do in such circumstances? The soul, according to Descartes, acts through its volitions: "simply by willing something it brings about that the little gland to which it is closely joined moves in the manner required to produce the effect corresponding to this volition" (art. 41 (AT XI 359–360, CSM I 343)).[68] But can one will things one is not inclined or disposed to will?

Reason certainly cannot change the inclinations of the will, although it can, thanks to the power to do otherwise, refrain from assenting to them. For the human soul has absolute power only over its own actions:

> [T]he will is by its nature so free that it can never be constrained. Of the first two kinds of thought I have distinguished in the soul—the first its actions, i.e., its volitions, and the second its passions, taking this word in its most general sense to include every kind of perception—*the former are absolutely within its power* and can be changed only indirectly by the body, whereas the latter are absolutely dependent on the actions which produce them, and *can be changed by the soul only indirectly*, except when it is itself their cause. (art. 41 (AT XI 359–360, CSM I 343))

The power it has over its passions is thus, at best, indirect:

> Our passions, too, cannot be directly aroused or suppressed by the action of our will, but only indirectly through the representation of things which are usually joined with passions we wish to have and opposed to the passions we wish to reject. (art. 45 (AT XI 362, CSM I 345))

All this follows from the principle that "[e]ach volition is naturally joined to some movement of the gland" and may be joined to others only through effort and rehabituation (art. 44). Excessive passions are useful only to the extent that they are good. Descartes agrees with Elisabeth "that the remedies against excessive passions are difficult to practice," and he also admits that they "are insufficient to prevent bodily disorders; but they may suffice to prevent the soul from being troubled by them and losing its free judgement," adding that no desires that are for the good, for instance, for the necessities of life, can be too excessive—only bad desires and passions need controlling (letter to Elisabeth, May 1646 (AT IV 411, CSMK 287)). There are different kinds of excess, and all are not to be avoided: for instance, excess of courage is temerity only when it goes beyond the limits of reason; but while it remains within them, it can have still another excess, which consists simply in the absence of irresolution and fear (letter to Elisabeth, November 3, 1645 (AT IV 331–332, CSMK 276))

No matter how good our judgment or how industrious we are in manipulating our passions, it does not seem possible ever to gain full control over violent passions. Because of disturbance resulting from the specific movements in the blood and the animal spirits causing and accompanying the passions

> they remain present to our mind in the same way as the objects of senses are present to it as long as they are acting upon our sense organs. The soul can prevent itself from hearing a slight noise or feeling a slight pain by attending very closely to some other thing, but it cannot in the same way prevent itself from hearing thunder or feeling a fire that burns the hand. Likewise it can easily overcome the lesser passions, but not the stronger or more violent ones, except after the disturbance of the blood and the spirits has been calmed. The most the will can do while this disturbance is at its full strength is not to yield to its effects and to inhibit many of the movements to which it disposes the body. For example, if anger causes the hand to strike a blow, the will can ordinarily restrain it; if fear moves the legs to flee, the will can stop them; and similarly in other cases. (art. 46 (AT XI 364, CSM I 345))

We can always refrain from acting, or so Descartes claims, but the only thing we can control directly are our thoughts or judgments, and only to the extent that they depend on our mind itself.

But this raises the question whether it is the will or the intellect that ultimately is in control. The question may seem inappropriate, for doesn't reason presuppose both powers? In article 47 Descartes stresses, once again, the unity of the soul:

> For there is within us but one soul, and this soul has in it no diversity of parts: it is at once sensitive and rational too, and all its appetites are volitions. It is an error to identify the different functions of the soul with persons who play different, usually mutually opposed roles—an error which arises simply from our failure to distinguish properly the functions of the soul from those of the body. (AT XI 365, CSM I 346)

There is no conflict between parts of the soul or between faculties having different roles. There may be conflict between movements of the will caused by the body and those caused by the mind, however, and that seems to be an internal conflict after all. Descartes continues to use the ancient metaphors of conflict, powers, strength, and weapons. Anger lifts my hand to strike a blow, but my will can stop its movement. The strength or weakness of my soul is measured by whether and how such conflicts are settled: "the strongest souls belong to those in whom the will by nature can most easily conquer the passions and stop the bodily movements which accompany them" (AT XI 367, CSM I 347).

It is not merely a matter of stopping those movements, however, but of stopping them in the right way, by using the soul's own weapons. The passions can be changed or hindered by other passions—but that does not count as mastering them. The right way to stop them is by "firm and determinate judgements bearing upon the knowledge of good and evil, which the soul has resolved to follow in guiding its conduct" (AT XI 367, CSM I 347). If such judgments are themselves based on some passion and happen to be false, they can still serve as proper weapons as long as they are firm and determinate, that is, as long as they are consistently used against opposing passions. The difference between a resolution that proceeds from a false opinion and one based on knowledge is that only by following the latter can one be assured of never having to regret one's action.

The attainment of such security is a dominant theme of Descartes's occasional moral reflections, where the lack of indecision, irresolution, and uncertainty that the right use of reason is supposed to bring about is placed among the highest of goods that depend only on ourselves.[69] It takes long and repeated meditations to get used to what reason tells us—namely, that only thoughts are entirely in our power—because our natural appetites and habits induce us to believe that we can control the whole world: "We have so frequently experienced since childhood that by crying or commanding we could make our nurses obey us and get what we want, that we have gradually convinced ourselves that the world was made only for us and that everything was our due" (AT II 37, CSMK 98).[70] But the only thing we can control absolutely are our thoughts, and the power to do so is within the reach of every person in possession of her reason (AT IV 307, CSMK 269). "There is no soul so weak that it cannot, if well directed, acquire an absolute power over its passions" (art. 50 (AT XI 368, CSM I 348)).

Anyone who has read Descartes's account of the passions with care is bound to wonder at this optimism. It is not difficult to agree that "we are able, with a little effort, to change the movements of the brain in animals devoid of reason," but is it evident "that we can do so still more effectively in men"? Even if we could, why think that changing their brain movements would make them better directed? Can a soul that is "weak" by nature be well directed? The last sentence of article 50 is ambiguous: It is evident, we there read, that "even those who have the weakest souls could acquire absolute mastery over all their passions if one [we?] employed sufficient ingenuity in training and guiding them" (AT XI 370, CSM I 348).

It almost sounds as if Descartes thinks that there are after all some external things that arc (absolutely?) in our power, namely, the thoughts of other people. This, however, goes against his own teaching, the purpose of which is to show that people can, at best, train themselves to master their own thoughts.[71] On this, the last paragraphs of the *Passions* sound less optimistic. Descartes there admits that the remedies he has recommended for excessive passions depend on such extraordinary forethought and diligence (involving among other things the correction of one's natural faults by separating within oneself the movements of blood from the thoughts to which they are usually joined) that "there are few people who have sufficiently prepared themselves in this way for all the contingencies of life," and that "no amount of human wisdom is capable of counteracting these movements when we are not adequately prepared to do so" (AT XI 486, CSM I 403).[72]

Descartes still ventures to put forward a general remedy applicable, he says, to all excesses of passions. Whenever one notices a certain agitation in one's blood, one should take this as a signal that whatever presents itself to one's imagination is likely to mislead "the soul and make the reasons for pursuing the object of its passion appear much stronger than they are and the reasons for not pursuing this object much weaker." One should, therefore, refrain from making any immediate judgment about them and instead work on distracting oneself by other thoughts until time and rest calm down the disturbances in our blood. When no delay is possible, one should apply oneself to consider and follow reasons opposed to those that the passions seem to dictate, hoping thus to avoid too great mistakes.

Notice the behaviorist motif: the disturbances of the blood are what inform us of the great confusion in the mind. And so it is, because a mind in a state of passion is not able to tell its rational thoughts and voluntary inclinations from its passive or pathological inclinations; for there is only one soul, which is both rational and sensitive, and all its appetites are its volitions. Since the only thing that distinguishes passions from pure volitions are their causes, and since the causes of passions are not available for direct mental inspection, we are, as everyone knows from personal experience, at pains to see what reason dictates. It is not from inspecting our own thoughts that we are going to sort out which reasons do and which do not stand up to a critical intellect.

In addition, since "many people do not know what they believe, since believing something and knowing that one believes it are different acts of thinking, and the one often occurs without the other," one must, to find out what people, including oneself, actually believe, attend to their (and one's own) actions, rather than to what they say (or pretend to themselves).[73]

While philosophical self-reflection may be the best means we have for getting clear about our thoughts, it is of little avail when our passions most upset us.[74] The wise man, it might seem, had better walk around with a thermometer on his chest to check his temperature before making any important decisions or choices. I doubt that would be of much help, however, and conclude for my part that, here as elsewhere, we may have to rely on what each of us takes to be the best of our inclinations and judgments and follow them wherever they take us, leaving it to others to judge to what extent they can be seen as rational. This would be to follow Descartes's own example when he confesses to Elisabeth: "I even also dare believe that interior joy has some secret force to render fortune more favorable," something he holds not out of sheer superstition, but on the basis of "an infinity of experiences, and with that the authority of Socrates." Socrates may have gone too far in remaining in his home every time his genius counseled him not to go out. "But, regarding the important actions of life, when we meet with circumstances so doubtful that prudence cannot teach us what we ought to do, it seems to me one has great reason to follow the advice of one's genius, and that it is useful to have a strong persuasion that the things we undertake without repugnance, and with the liberty that ordinarily accompanies joy, will not fail to succeed well for us" (letter to Elisabeth, November 1646 (AT IV 529, CSMK 296–297)). I take this to mean that we have, according to Descartes, strong reasons for following our confused inclinations and emotions in those numerous circumstances of our lives where the light of reason fails to give us guidance.

The Cartesian account of the passions and their mastery leaves us with many questions, some of which are discussed in more detail in the next chapter, which looks more closely at the conflicts of the soul and the power Descartes ascribes to will and reason in the control and mastery of passions, as well as at some antecedents of Descartes's views.

7

Free Will
and Virtue

This chapter examines Descartes's conception of the will and the role
he attributes to reason and will in the exercise of the highest virtue,
which is also a remedy against excessive passions. He calls that virtue
"generosity," and it is defined in the *Passions of the Soul* as having two
components: first, the knowledge that nothing is truly in one's possession except the free will, and that there is nothing one ought to be
praised or blamed for except using it well or badly; and second, a firm
and constant resolution of using it well, "that is, never to lack the will
to undertake and carry out whatever one judges to be best" (art. 153
(AT XI 445–446, CSM I 384)). It is at once a virtue—the highest virtue—and a passion, the object of which is the soul's own action, and
serves as a "general remedy for all the disorders of passion" (AT XI
454, CSM I 388). It brings together his transformed conception of reason with a new and problematic conception of the will. The locus
of the power that Descartes thinks we have over our volitions is the
free assent by which the mind becomes, as it were, a self-mover with respect to present perceptions, representations, or inclinations: nothing
over or beyond the mind itself determines whether to accept or reject
them. There is controversy over how Descartes's most radical pronouncements on this freedom, which he calls freedom of choice (also
occasionally free will), should be interpreted. While many take them
as evidence that he espouses a classic libertarianism, others have tried
to ignore them or explain them away to make Descartes's view of the
will consistent with a compatibilism more in line with rationalist requirements. Although I take seriously those controversial pronounce-

ments and the extreme voluntarism they imply, I do not see them as committing Descartes to irrationalism or indeterminism.

Recent scholarship has drawn attention to the new ways of thinking about the will and choice developed by medieval philosophers opposing the Thomist interpretation of the Aristotelian model of action, which they perceived as too intellectualistic and also too determinist to leave room for the choice of ends they thought rational agency and moral responsibility required. I contend this debate between voluntarism and intellectualism forms the general context for the philosophical problems to which Descartes's notion of free choice of the will purports to be an answer and that, if it is intelligible, it is so only in the light of the kind of ethical determinism that the "voluntarists" rejected: that the good as perceived by the intellect necessarily inclines the will to pursue it. A central aim of this chapter is to substantiate that claim by considering some ancient and medieval antecedents of the Cartesian notions of will and agency.

1. From Conflicts of Soul to Conflicts of Will

Descartes claims in article 41 of the *Passions* that "the will is so free by nature that it can never be constrained" and that thoughts which are actions proper are "absolutely in its power and can only indirectly be changed by the body." The passions, on the other hand, in the most general sense of the term, are said to be "absolutely" dependent on the actions producing them, so that the soul can change them only indirectly. "And the activity of the soul consists entirely in the fact that simply by willing something it makes the little gland to which it is closely joined move in the manner which is required to produce the effect corresponding to this volition" (AT XI 359–360, CSM I 343). For instance, the volition to recall something moves the pineal gland to direct "the spirits towards different regions of the brain until they come upon the one containing traces left by the object we want to remember," producing thereby the special movement in the gland that (by the institution of nature) "represents the same object to the soul, and makes it recognize it as the one it wanted to remember" (AT XI 360, CSM I 344). The soul thus commands in the same way through its will both its own acts of attention and the movements of the body (AT XI 361, CSM I 344).

All thoughts in the soul are correlated to some movement in the gland, and as soon as an act of volition is formed, the corresponding movement occurs, a correlation that is natural, though it can be changed by "effort or habit." However, the will is not the only agent moving the gland, since it also moves according to actions in the body, which do not depend on the will. The mere volition to think of, imagine, attend to, or remember something does not always produce the movement in the gland required to produce it. For one thing, the volition is never a volition to move the gland, but to think of something or to move one's limbs in a certain way, and the connection of thoughts with movements of the gland and the rest of the body depends on nature, conditioning, or habituation (AT XI 362, CSM I 344–345). In the case of passions, where the power of the will is at best indirect, the movements of the gland they cause are usually vivacious and persistent, since their function is not only to cause but also to maintain and strengthen the particular inclinations of the will in which the passions consist. Therefore they remain in force as long as those movements continue, which prevents the soul from having full control over its passions, and the best it can do during such disturbance is not to give in and to refrain from the movements (or actions) they make the body disposed to (AT XI 363–364, CSM I 345).

How does Descartes think this can be accomplished? In the previous chapter some doubts were raised concerning the extent of the power of the soul. Aren't there impulses to move or act so strong that no reasoning can stop or counteract them? We often find ourselves overcome by fear, jealousy, anger, or sexual desires so violent that the ensuing actions appear quite compulsory. It seems unlikely that we can be taught always to repress or hide the spontaneous expressions of our secret passions. There is no soul so weak, we read in article 50 of the *Passions*, that it cannot, if well directed, acquire an absolute power over its passions. But to counteract a strong passion, it seems, one needs more than mere right reason and judgment: judgment, by itself, does not affect the course of the spirits in the brain. Can one will anything one is not actually disposed to will—can one change actual dispositions and inclinations without a prior disposition against them?

In giving his own account of conflicts of the soul—traditionally construed as conflicts between on the one hand appetites of the lower parts of the soul (the "irascible" and the "concupiscible") and on the other hand reason—Descartes advances several problematic claims. First he declares that the conflicts that supposedly occur between the sensitive soul (the appetites) and the rational soul (the will) consist simply in mutually opposed movements produced in the gland (by means of the animal spirits and the body) and by the soul (by means of its will). Second he identifies the rational with the sensitive and appetitive soul, and declares that all appetites of the soul are volitions! What were traditionally considered to be appetites of the lower parts of the soul, depending on the body, Descartes considers to be appetites of the higher, rational part of the soul, which he calls "volition":

> For there is within us but one soul, and this soul has no diversity of parts: it is at once sensitive and rational too, and *all its appetites are volitions*. The mistake that has been made in having it play different characters that are usually opposed to each other arises from a failure to distinguish properly its functions from those of the body; to which alone we should attribute everything that can be noticed in us that is contrary to our reason. (AT XI 364–365, CSM I 346; my emphasis and translation)

Two explanations seem to be at work here. On the one hand, conflicts of soul are construed as conflicts between a rational mind and a body mechanically moved by its own nature and external stimuli. On the other hand, they are internalized to the will itself, which finds itself torn between volitions occasioned by the body inclining it in one direction and volitions caused by the mind or reason inclining it in opposed directions. But how can appetites caused by the body be counted as volitions, given that the term "volition" is reserved for actions of the mind over which the mind is supposed to have absolute control?[1] We have already seen a sense in which all thoughts, including actions, are passions in a wide sense of the word; we now find that there is a wide sense in which even bodily appetites and, a fortiori, all the passions are *volitions*.

This is bound to cause confusion. Volitions are traditionally connected with the (rational) soul in its active, dynamic aspect; they are the inclinations moving the soul when it is active. When restricted to the rational activity of the soul, volitions are motions caused within and by the soul itself—let us call them "self-caused" volitions. When extended to all the motions of the embodied Cartesian soul, volitions are of two kinds: either self-caused or caused externally by the body. Perhaps Descartes thinks both can be called volitions of sorts, because they are immediately experienced as motions or inclinations of one and the same soul. But how then can the rational mind distinguish the volitions that are caused by the body from those of which it is itself the cause? *Qua* movements of the pineal gland they differ through their causes, the first being initiated by the mind itself and the second by movements in the bodily organs. On the phenomenological level, *qua* volitions, they are similar in that both incline the soul toward some end or activity. Yet we are supposed to be able to discriminate between them by an awareness of having or not having full control over them— of whether we are or not their cause. Descartes seems to waver between the old conception of an independent mind or reason with a nature and appetites of its own, which is detached enough from the body and its sensual appetites to be able to tell the latter apart from its own purely rational inclinations, and a very different conception ensuing from his mind–body union where an undivided soul is united to the whole body, and it is far from clear how these different conceptions can be reconciled. His view of the will and the therapy of passions presupposes the former, while his account of the passions themselves is based on the latter.

Plato argues for the division of the soul precisely to avoid the difficulty of attributing opposed simultaneous actions to one and the same agent,[2] while the Stoics oppose the division in order to avoid positing forces within the soul capable of acting against reason: construing the passions as false beliefs, that is, states of the rational soul, gives the latter a power over them that it cannot have within the framework of the tripartite soul. Descartes seems to follow the Stoics here, and he ends up with what appears to be contrary simultaneous volitions in the same soul, a difficulty he tries to avoid, like the Stoics, by distributing them over time. The conflicts, typically, are between the movements of the gland caused by the body that "have an influence on the will" and the volition to oppose them, for example: "between the force with which the spirits push the gland so as to cause the soul to desire something, and the force with which the soul, by its volition to avoid this thing, pushes the gland in a contrary direction" (AT XI 365, CSM I 346). Because the will has no direct power over the passions, it has to make an effort to consider successively several different things, some of which may change the course of the spirits for a moment, and some of which may fail to do so, thereby failing to change the motions in the nerves, blood, and heart that maintain the motions causing the passion, all of which makes "the soul feel itself impelled almost at the same time to desire and not to desire one and the same thing; and that is why one has imagined two conflicting powers within it" (AT XI 365–366, CSM I 346).

There is a genuine conflict, however, in that "the same cause that produces a certain passion in the soul often also produces certain movements in the body," in spite of and without contribution of the will, as when fear moves our legs to run, but which the soul, if it has the will to be courageous, may try to stop (ibid.). These conflicts are described as a struggle between mechanical forces acting in opposed directions, although the mechanical analogy cannot apply to the action of the immaterial soul on the body. Mastering the passions is described in terms of the strength displayed by the will in these struggles *(combats)*:

> It is by success in these conflicts that each person can recognize the strength or weakness of his soul. For undoubtedly the strongest souls belong to those in whom the will by nature can most easily conquer the passions and stop the bodily movements which accompany them. But there are those who never put their strength to test, because they never make their will fight using its own weapons, but only with those which some passions supply it with to resist some others. What I call its proper weapons are firm and determinate judgements regarding the knowledge of good and evil, which the soul has resolved to follow in guiding its conduct. (AT XI 366–367, CSM I 347)

The "strongest" souls are those whose judgments are based on true knowledge of good and evil. Then come those who have strength and resolution enough to follow determinate judgments to guide their actions, but whose judgments are false because based on present or past passions "by which the will has previously allowed itself to be conquered or seduced" but to which it still clings even when the passion is gone (art. 40 (AT XI 368, CSM I 347)). The weakest souls cannot determine themselves to follow any judgments at all but let themselves be constantly carried away by their present passions, which incline the will to different sides, "using it *(l'employant)* to battle against itself."

The passion of fear, for instance, can represent death as the greatest of evils to be avoided at any price, while ambition "represents the dishonor of flight as an evil worse than death." The two passions incline the will in contrary directions, opposing it against itself, rendering "the soul enslaved and miserable" (art. 48 (AT XI 367, CSM I 347)). Descartes thinks that such misery can be avoided with the help of firm and determinate judgments: the strength of the soul consists in the firmness of its evaluative judgments, which truth can provide. Rational volitions are nothing but true judgments of value, and the greater the knowledge of the good, the stronger and steadier the resolution of the will in its pursuit.[3] None of this is very original, and one may wonder about Descartes's entitlement, given his own conception of our cognitive and conative faculties, to fall back on such traditional conceptions.

2. The Elements and Antecedents of Descartes's Moral Psychology

Let us take a brief look at two classic models of explanation of mind and action that are good to keep in mind when trying to understand and assess Descartes's account of conflicts of soul. The first is the Aristotelian psychological model of a tripartite soul, based on Plato's division of the soul into a rational, irascible, and concupiscible (or sensitive) part, to which Descartes explicitly opposes his own view of the mind as one and undivided.[4] Their admission of two at least potentially conflicting forces within the soul is precisely what is denied in the second model with which I am concerned here, the monistic model of the Stoics that offers some striking similarities with the Cartesian account of the structure and workings of the human mind.[5] In his evaluation of passions and their functions Descartes is much closer to the Aristotelian model, but in his conception of the mechanics of mental operations, not least in his analysis of passions, he is much closer to Stoic views.[6]

According to the Aristotelian model, passions originate in the lower, nonrational parts of the soul that the Scholastics call concupiscible *(epithumetikon)* and irascible *(thumos).* They are not in themselves irrational: the latter, for instance, can understand and listen to reason, and to that extent can also help reason to subject the former, which, although it lacks the capacity to reason, is rational enough to obey reason's commands. Desires and passions are in themselves important motive forces: they tie the human mind to the world of contingent things in which it is not only embodied but which is a condition for its actualization as a human mind, and which therefore naturally matters to it. If they become, as they often can, excessive, they can—at least in principle—be moderated without having to be eradicated or extinguished. The conflicts between reason and passions, in this model, are conceived basically as conflicts between the ruling part, reason, which through habituation and education can make the lower parts its allies, and when required, fight their irrational impulses. The true self is composed of the three parts together, and it is rational when the three parts are in harmony and the rational part in control of the others— that is, when the latter are obedient to reason.

The model represents a form of psychological dualism in dividing the soul into one higher, rational, and governing power, and another reason-obeying but in itself nonrational part whose functioning involves the bodily senses and other organs. Each of the parts of the soul is taken to come with cognitive and conative components of its own, and the mastery of passions assumes that the appetite of reason, the highest part, has a natural authority to which the lower parts will, in the well-ordered and well-trained soul, naturally subordinate their own lower appetites. This model, where the regulation of the passions rests on strong presuppositions of a natural harmony between the appetites of three parts, had many problems discussed throughout antiquity. It was particularly problematic in the context of Christian doctrines emphasizing the corruption of human nature and the weakness of human reason.

I will not dwell on this dualistic model that, as we saw, Descartes explicitly rejects. He does not accept any distinction of parts *in* the soul—the soul for him, as for the Stoics, is one and undivided. Since he thinks he can explain all the specific functions attributed to the so-called lower parts of the soul mechanistically, the postulation of parts or kinds of soul to explain the movements and vital functions of animals is superfluous. What remains are the cognitive functions, which animals lack and are attributed to humans only, and which Descartes, like the Stoics, see as functions of reason or thinking. Also like the Stoics, Descartes opposes the idea of conflicts between rational and irrational forces or desires within the soul itself.[7] He sees them as the effect of contrary forces acting on the pineal gland, some caused by the course of the animal spirits in the body and others directly through its own actions (AT XI 364–365).

For Descartes, any will or volition that conflicts with rational volitions based on true judgments is the effect of bodily motions, not of some irrational forces within the human soul itself. He does not, however, deny the appearance of conflicts or even battles in the soul; on the contrary, he describes them with the help of military and mechanical metaphors as conflicts of opposed forces, which can be compared in terms of their strength. But those are mere literary devices, which abound in Seneca and his followers too. The essential point is that these conflicts should not be seen as involving contrary forces originating from and dividing the soul from within as it were. The psychological dualism of the Aristotelian model is replaced by Descartes's mind–body dualism, which gives the Stoic idea of controlling the passions a new basis: insofar as they are caused by bodily motions construed mechanistically, they can be controlled—at least in principle—indirectly through their causes.

Let us look briefly at the Stoic account of passions and rational agency. The Stoics identify the soul or the true self of a human being with reason.[8] They distinguish between actions and passions of the soul and connect the former with knowledge and voluntary assent, which are treated as the locus of moral responsibility and the vehicle through which reason can oppose and eventually eradicate the passions. The passions *(pathe)* that Chrysippus describes as false opinions or judgments *(doxa)* are complex and violent emotional states that would be considered a subclass of emotions or passions in other classifications. They are, first of all, moral judgments, involving assent to a false evaluative proposition (one containing a moral predicate), and they express, moreover, a strong impulse striving for what the proposition suggests. All appearances do not move us in the same way, that is, they do not all trigger the same kind of sudden, unexpected impulses. Those—the so-called *hormetic* impressions—that once assented to become passions in the Stoic sense of the word are more violent than others. The passions *(pathe)* are contrasted to the calm and steady emotions—*eupatheia*—characteristic of the Stoic sage, which are purely rational motions based on true knowledge. For passions are violent impulses to act that are always founded on false opinions, yet they too are rational in that they have been assented to by the rational agent, who, because the assent given is in his own power, bears full responsibility for acting on the impulses assented to. In Chrysippus's view, passions are in the agent's control because they are judgments formed by assenting to a proposition that is, explicitly or implicitly, embedded in a hormetic appearance, and that, as soon as it is endorsed, is translated into action. It is up to the agent to give or withhold her assent to the initial appearance, and thereby to the impulse and action it moves her to.[9]

In the early Stoic theory basic passions are divided in two different pairs: desire *(epithumia)* and fear *(phobos)* on the one hand, and pleasure *(hedone)* and pain or distress *(lupe)* on the other. The first pair, desire and fear, consist in judgments about some external good that it is either worth pursuing or avoiding. The second pair consists of subordinate passions, pleasure and pain, which are judgments about our own emotional reactions to the first, to the effect that it is good or bad to react in a certain way.[10] As long as a passion remains in force, it is possible neither to oppose nor to regulate it. The first task, therefore, of the therapy supposed to cure us from our passions is to work on the pleasure or pain they give us and on the (false) opinion about the propriety of so reacting that these involve. The main task, however, is to correct the false opinions about the good or bad that constitute the primary passions and to acquire knowledge about which things are in fact worth pursuing or avoiding. Most things that are judged by mortals good or bad are, from the Stoic point of view, indifferent: they have no value in themselves, and whatever value we attribute to them is therefore incorrect. This is why the Stoic therapy is not a matter of moderating passions, but of eradicating them: it is not a matter of coming to see that things are not so bad or good as we in our hasty judgments take them to be, but that the things we spontaneously praise or shun are neither good nor bad in themselves. From the moral point of view—that of eternity, which alone matters to the rational agent—they are supremely indifferent.

One of the many problems in this theory has to do with the affective responses involved in passions, which do not seem to be rational or to involve assent. They are called first motions or preliminary passions *(propatheia)*, and their role and nature are controversial.[11] Although these first motions are described as involuntary physiological reactions they resemble the passions proper in that they move the soul to fear or desire what presents itself to it. Seneca mentions them in analyzing the genesis of anger and gives us the following account, in which four different phases are distinguished. The process starts with (1) an initial appearance or impression, say, of injustice, to which the mind responds, first with (2) an involuntary agitation that can be no more controlled than the urge to yawn when someone else yawns, or to blink when something is flicked at the eye, followed by (3) assent to the impression of having been unjustly wronged, which is voluntary, and (4) an uncontrollable impulse to take revenge (anger) that outleaps reason and carries it away.[12] This analysis recognizes as part of the process emotive reactions that are involuntary but do not constitute emotions as such since they are mere "bodily agitations," but which grow into passions as soon as the impressions causing them are assented to. Seneca thinks that they can be controlled by reason because an impulse that has been "generated by decision, can be eliminated by decision."[13]

For Seneca, as for the early Stoics, assent depends on reason alone. In spite of the fact that the mind—reason—is already moved by an involuntary agitation caused directly by the appearance, reason can still react to the appearance, approving or rejecting the false beliefs about the propriety of so reacting (finding it pleasant, painful, deserved, or undeserved) that present itself to it. So the uncontrollable impulse in which the passions consist can be prevented by reason, and this is the sense in which they are rational and hence voluntary states, for which the agent bears full responsibility. Even though the passions are *not* the product of deliberate decision, they always presuppose an implicit assent that the agent could have chosen to withhold.[14]

Descartes also seems to work with a notion of spontaneous or habitual assent, which, through reflection, can be made the object of explicit, voluntary deliberation and decision. Since it is not the only element common to Descartes's and the Stoic accounts, one may wonder why no detailed comparison between them has been undertaken. Many of Descartes's views seem to reflect his knowledge of Stoic and neo-Stoic views, whose influence can be seen in so many works of moral philosophy in the sixteenth and seventeenth centuries,[15] and the advice he offers Elisabeth is imbued with Stoic rhetoric and moral philosophy. The power ascribed to reason by the Stoics and by Descartes raises the question of the extent to which passions can be viewed as conscious, intentional phenomena amenable to rational control through right judgment. Since the most explicit treatment of these questions can be found in Seneca, Seneca's views are particularly interesting from the point of view of Cartesian scholarship.[16] The dilemma they both confront is the choice between a view of passions as depending on irrational forces that reason cannot control, and a view of them as states that, though perverted, are states of reason itself and therefore within its power. Both have to deal with how reason can oppose "irrational" inclinations that it cannot help finding itself moved by; both show the same concern for responsibility and its internal, psychological conditions, in particular, for the role of assent in endorsing the false opinion that turns a preexisting desire into action.

Michael Frede sees the Platonic and Aristotelian view of affections and desire as located in the lower parts of the soul, and the Stoic view that they are false beliefs arising from voluntary judgments, as two different responses to the Socratic view of virtue as knowledge and the paradoxes it involves. In treating the emotions as *pathe* in the sense of pathological affections or diseases of reason itself and in claiming that they can be cured by knowing the true value of things, the Stoics basically defend what they took to be the Socratic position.[17] Descartes picks up elements from the Platonic-Aristotelian as well as from the Stoic views. He distinguishes, as we have seen, between the point of view of the mind–body union and that of reason in evaluating things, and thinks that both can be subordinated to a common goal, which is that of the whole mind–body union. What is good for the body cannot be indifferent from the point of view of Cartesian reason, which has endorsed its end as its own and therefore finds it rational to pursue it as long as it serves the preservation and well-being of the whole union and through that reason itself. It cannot therefore be a question for Descartes, as it is for the Stoics, to categorically oppose or reject the passions that depend on the body, but instead to weigh them against the inclinations of reason, giving each their due. For Descartes as for Socrates, virtue consists in knowledge of the good that is one's own, but he follows the Aristotelians in thinking that virtue is not exclusively cognitive, since it *also* consists in the disposition of the will to follow reason, and it is, moreover, both a habit and a passion. (See AT XI 445–454 and 481; and the discussion below in section 9.)

3. Voluntary Agency, Assent, and Will

The Stoic theory of agency has been taken to exemplify what contemporary discussions refer to as a "two-parameter analysis of action" (the so-called belief–desire model), which makes its earliest appearance in the Aristotelian practical syllogism. The main factors involved are, first, a desire or "pro-attitude" and, second, a belief or a cognitive component (a propositional attitude). Animals are moved to action by desire, but, in order to move the animal, the desire must be activated by some belief that the conditions for its fulfilment are present. Aristotle uses the practical syllogism as an explanatory model, which shows how the two factors (desires and beliefs) interact in causing an action and explains what goes wrong in the case of weakness of the will.[18] Its premises state the necessary and sufficient conditions for the action, which cannot fail to occur once they are fulfilled. The central idea in this model is that the information provided by the relevant cognitive capacities (*aisthesis* or *phantasia* or *dianoia,* depending on which part of the soul provides it), "activates or triggers the desire which is ready and awaiting among the animal's dispositions. The proximate cause of the action, then, is neither the desiderative state nor the information, but the activated desire which results from the combination of these two explanatory factors."[19] The term used by Aristotle *(horme)* to describe the impulsion to move, in *De Motu Animalium* and elsewhere, recurs in the Stoic description of animal action, and like the Stoics, Aristotle stresses the central role of *phantasia* in activating the desire. Although the practical syllogism does not use, in a systematic way, the ideas of "assent" and "commands to oneself," which are central to the Stoic analysis of human action, Aristotle comes close to doing so: the decisive report provided by *phantasia* about the environment can, Inwood argues, be seen as "a forerunner of assent in the Stoic theory."[20]

Inwood's comparison of the Aristotelian and Stoic accounts of action purports to show how logical and linguistic concepts (like syllogisms, verbs of saying or deciding, commands, and so on), which are prominent in the Stoic account, are already used, though unsystematically, by Aristotle in discussing the causes of action. It was "left to the Stoics to realize fully that the goal and point of one's actions could be verbally formulated and become a conscious intention."[21] So if the movements of brute animals depend on merely two factors, presentation and impulse, human action for the Stoics is the outcome of the interplay of four powers: presentation *(phantasia)*, assent *(sunkatathesis)*, impulse *(horme)*, and reason *(logos)*.[22] Assent depends on reason, which operates through assent: the capacity to form linguistic or propositional thoughts, together with the power reason has to assent or withhold assent, are, as it were, the agents of rationality. Reason is in charge because it possesses this power to assent without which the hormetic impulse cannot be activated. Hence the monism: whatever impulse I act on is rational in that it moves me only because I have assented to it; sense perceptions and passions too are rational thoughts to the extent that they are propositional and involve assent.[23] It is only because we need not assent to every incoming appearance or impression that, as rational agents, we can discriminate between them, and thus also "choose" the impulses by which we let ourselves be carried away. Julia Annas argues that what we assent to are statements as to what ought to be done or brought about, hence assent, in perception as in action, is "the point at which things are 'up to' the agent."[24] While we cannot help receiving the appearances that come to us, and hence the impulses they trigger, we can help assenting to the statements concerning what to do or bring about that come with those impulses.[25] There is a sense in which the only thing we can ever be said "to *do* is assent; the rest is up to nature," for it is the only thing for which we can be held responsible. This does not mean, however, that assents are actions, because they do not presuppose an impulse of their own: assent is not caused by yet another impulse or appearance.[26]

The crucial question, of course, is under what conditions assent can be withheld and what it consists in, whether it is to be viewed as a mere mechanism, as a kind of mental action, or as the forming of an intention or commitment to act. To withhold assent is to suspend one's judgment. It is only in the case of clear and distinct *true* impressions or propositions (the so-called *kataleptic* presentations) that assent is automatically—and necessarily—caused by the impressions themselves.[27] Is this to say that there is no necessity to assent in other cases, that assent is up to us merely because in the absence of evident impressions nothing forces us to accept a given appearance, or judgment about the good or bad at hand? Some causes are perfect, others imperfect, or auxiliary. Those that are "up to us" (assent) seem to be of the latter kind. Through this power of assent, the moral agent has some control over the chain of causes determining action.[28] She can at least react to appearances at hand by discriminating *(diakrinein)* and judging them, assenting to them or rejecting those that are not evident. Her impulses and actions are invariably caused by her assent to a hormetic impulse, and she is responsible for them only to the extent that it was in her power not to assent. Her responsibility is the same whether or not the assent is explicit, whenever she could have refused to assent. I am responsible for my actions, even when I am not aware of how or why I assented to them. As Inwood writes, it is "automatically true that if someone acted he also assented. And implicit assent is all that the Stoics thought they needed to hold a man responsible for his actions."[29] The point seems to be that it is always possible to make explicit the reason for action (that is, the proposition concerning what to do), and this, in fact, is what moral reflection and responsibility are all about.[30]

The Stoics were not concerned with freedom as much as with voluntary action—action whose principle is within the agent and not in external forces—and they located this internal principle in the power of assent. At some point, the followers and critics of the Stoics came to connect assent with the idea of freedom, which later was seen as the essence of the will.[31] There is a lot of controversy whether a "modern" notion of will and choice can be found in the writings of the ancients at all, and if not, where and how it originated. I will not enter into that discussion[32] except to note some developments that are relevant for the late medieval views on will and free choice anteceding Descartes's notion of free will.

The first thing to note is that the ancient philosophers, Stoics as well as Aristotelians, recognized that reason is not a merely passive receptor of ideas, nor a mere instrumental inference-maker, but also and essentially a source of activity (motion). According to this "classic" notion of reason, which prevailed throughout the Middle Ages and early modern times, reason has its own intrinsic inclinations and preferences by which it is moved. Aristotle, following Plato's division in the *Republic* (IX, 580c–e), distinguishes three kinds of inclinations or appetites, corresponding to each of the parts of the soul. The lowest is moved by sensual appetite *(epithumia),* the second by anger (or temerity, *thumos),* and the highest by rational desire *(boulesis).* Although *boulesis* is a form of desire *(orexis)* or appetite, it is, according to Aristotle, located in the reasoning part of the soul. (See *Magna Moralia* 1187b36–7, and *Topics*

126a13.) It is the rational desire for the highest good that sets the general end of our actions, and voluntary action is the result of choice or decision *(prohairesis)* of the best manner to achieve the goal that we desire. It is "up to us" *(eph'hemin)* and depends on our own desire and deliberation whether we choose to do or not to do an action (NE 1139a31-b6).[33]

Cicero translates *boulesis* as *voluntas,* which became a standard rendering of this term. The translation is, as Kahn observes, misleading to the extent that it implies that Aristotle's *boulesis* is the only form of voluntary inclination, whereas for Aristotle, an action can be voluntary *(hekousion)* if it results from passion or appetite, without any intervention of the rational will.[34] What later developments tie together as different acts of one single power, called *voluntas,* are various more or less loosely connected concepts in Aristotle's analysis of intentional action: the voluntary *(hekousion),* what is "up to us" or in our power *(eph'hemin),* rational desire *(boulesis),* and decision or choice of the means through deliberation *(prohairesis)* to achieve the end set by the (prevailing) desire. The main agent of this change, according to Kahn, was Aquinas, who not only attributes all of the aforementioned to the will, but who accords to the will a place next to the intellect as "the two intrinsic operations of the soul as such, both of them capable of being performed without a bodily organ."[35] Aquinas's concept of the will, however, remains fundamentally intellectualistic: the will is a thoroughly rational power, which is invariably moved by the greater good perceived by the intellect. The knowledge of the truly good and of the means to attain it necessarily triggers assent, so that if there is a choice with respect to the end—a power to withhold assent—it works only in lack of full knowledge.

This picture is explicitly endorsed by Descartes in some contexts, and can be seen as his "default" view: rational agents naturally desire the good and opt for it when its attainment is within the reach of reasonable means. There are other contexts, however (as will be seen in section 8), where the will is dissociated from reason or intellect. Descartes seems to think it is possible, deliberately and with full knowledge, to refuse to assent to or pursue a clearly and distinctly perceived good—if for no other reason than wanting to demonstrate one's power to oppose reason (AT IV 173, CSMK 245). The will is free to pursue things opposed to the good recognized by the intellect, and can thus set up goals of its own against those clearly and distinctly perceived by the intellect, without this being a case of weakness of will in the Aristotelian sense.[36] The power of assent—this unmoved mover that the Stoics think can oppose the most haunting appearances and violent surges (if it does it quickly enough) by merely refusing to accept them as true—has here freed itself from all ties to reason and hence to classical rationality. Does Descartes then commit himself to an absurd and irrational doctrine? Or is he laying the ground for a new conception of rationality, that of an autonomous agent who can set her own ends and commit herself to the laws of reason and morality unconditionally because she is not determined to do so out of natural necessity? Before discussing these questions, let us look again at what Descartes says about reason, and examine more thoroughly his view of the will.

4. Reason as the Power of Judging Well

We encountered already in the early *Rules* the metaphor of reason as a natural light that it is our duty as serious truth-seekers to develop, "not with a view of solving this or that Scholastic problem," but so that our intellect should show our will *"what decision it ought to make in each of life's contingencies"* (AT X 361, CSM I 10; my emphasis). If the intellect, here, is the light showing what ought to be done, it takes the will to make the actual decision to do or pursue it. The aim in seeking knowledge "should be to direct the mind with a view to forming true and sound judgements about whatever comes before it" (AT X 360).[37] Judgments and beliefs are taken to be a matter of voluntary decision, and the forming of *true* judgments as a matter of learning to discern what is true and of making, on the basis of clear and distinct perceptions, the right inferences.[38]

In this metaphor, truths are there to be discovered, and the intellect is seen as a natural capacity for detecting them. There is some ambiguity as to who is using this light of the intellect—who is directing the mind that Descartes understands to be one and undivided, whose sole activity consists in willing, that is, in accepting or rejecting, pursuing or avoiding what is presented to it as true or false. If we can speak of the intellect as a truth-detecting device or mechanism, its use is not mechanical, since it takes a decision involving the will on where and how to apply it. While Descartes often speaks of intuition and pure inferences as acts of the intellect, as operations performed by the mind, he speaks as often of our using the intellect or reason as human agents in making judgments. He switches from one to the other in the same sentence, as in writing: "the deduction or pure inference of one thing from another can never be performed wrongly by an intellect which is in the least degree rational, *though one may fail to make the inference if one does not see it*" (AT X 365, CSM I 12; my emphasis). Intuition is defined as "the conception of a clear and attentive mind," while deduction "is not something a man *(homo)* can perform wrongly" (AT X 368, CSM I 14).

Whatever expression he uses, it is clear Descartes is concerned from the start with reason as a faculty of a human mind that, as embodied, always finds itself situated in some real-life context. He thinks of reason as a natural light or capacity present in all human beings, to be used in all contingencies of life. Not only are the simple things that form the starting point of true and certain deductions such that everyone can see or intuit them,[39] but the deductions themselves are understood as a series of simple intuitions, where one proceeds from one self-evident notion or proposition to another that is clearly seen to follow from it, and which anyone who cares to attend to it can see as following.

Also in the *Discourse* a rational person is described as one whose reasoning as well as actions are guided by reason, that is, by a well-directed and well-applied faculty of judgment. Not only is reason taken to be somehow in our voluntary control, but it is also assumed that it should direct us in all circumstances of life. Does it follow that good (true) judgment is all we need for acting well? Descartes seems to endorse this view in the *Discourse* Part III:

> For since our will tends to pursue or avoid only what our intellect represents as good or bad, we need only to judge well in order to act well, and to judge as well as we can in order to do our best—that is to say, in order to acquire all the virtues and in general all the other goods we can acquire. (AT VI 28, CSM I 125)

In answer to Mersenne, who raises the specter of Pelagianism, Descartes quotes the "common doctrine of the School" that "the will does not tend towards evil except in so far as it is represented to it by the intellect under some aspect of goodness" and the saying based on it, "whoever sins does so in ignorance" *(omnis peccans est ignorans),* and continues:

> so that if the intellect never represented anything to the will as good without its actually being so, the will could never go wrong in its choice. But the intellect often represents different things to the will at the same time; and that is why they say "I see and praise the better, but I follow the worse" which applies only to weak minds. (AT I 366, CSMK 56)

If Descartes here endorses the "ethical determinism" favored in the rationalist tradition, he does not consistently adhere to it, in fact he cannot given his own distinctions and arguments and, in particular, given his view of the will. The will, being an active power, operates independently of the passive intellect, which means it is not restrained by what the intellect presents to it. The mind can will (or accept) what it does not understand and what may be false, and it can also, paradoxically, reject what it understands to be true or good. This view, to be discussed later, is explicitly stated only in his later correspondence.

Descartes's fullest account of the will is given in the Fourth Meditation where he introduces his doctrine of judgment in the context of his theodicy, to free the omnipotent and veracious God who warrants our clear and distinct ideas from responsibility for our errors. He notes that his errors depend "on the faculty of knowledge which is in me, and on the faculty of willing or freedom of choice *(a facultate eligendi, sive ab arbitrii libertate);* that is, they depend on both the intellect and the will simultaneously" (AT VII 56, CSM II 39). Whereas the intellect, which passively perceives ideas "on which judgements can be made" and which can contain no error as such, is restricted and finite, Descartes says he "cannot complain (!) that the will *(voluntatem)* or freedom of choice which I received from God is not sufficiently extensive or perfect" since he knows by experience that it is "not restricted in any way." He writes:

> It is only the will, or freedom of choice, which I experience within me to be so great that the idea of any greater faculty is beyond my grasp; so much so that it is above all in virtue of the will that I understand myself to bear in some way the image and likeness of God. For although God's will is incomparably greater than mine, both in virtue of the knowledge

and power that accompany it and make it more firm and efficacious, and also in virtue of its object, in that it ranges over a greater number of items, nevertheless it does not seem any greater than mine when considered formally and strictly in itself *(in se formaliter et praecise spectata)*. This is because the will simply consists in our ability to do or not do something (that is, to affirm or deny, to pursue or avoid); or rather, it consists simply in the fact that when the intellect puts something forward for affirmation or denial or for pursuit or avoidance, our inclinations are such that we do not feel we are determined by any external force. (AT VII 57, CSM II 39–40)

Descartes then goes on to explain that the freedom to choose in the sense described at the end of the quoted passage does not require the ability to go both ways *(in utrumque parte ferri posse)*, that is, the ability to do or not to do something. On the contrary:

[T]he more I incline in one direction—either because I clearly understand that reasons of truth and goodness point that way, or because of a divinely produced disposition of my inmost thoughts—the freer is my choice. Neither divine grace nor natural knowledge ever diminishes freedom; on the contrary, they increase and strengthen it. But the indifference I feel when there is no reason pushing me in one direction rather than another is the lowest grade of freedom; it is evidence not of any perfection of freedom, but rather of a defect in knowledge or a kind of negation. (AT VII 58, CSM II 40)

What Descartes says here—in particular in the last two quotations—does not seem consistent. Is he claiming that the ability to do or choose otherwise is part of the essence of the will? What weight then should be given to the qualification introduced above by the "or rather" *(vel potius)*, which reduces it to an ability to follow the inclination to the good. It would be a mistake, I think, to read Descartes as claiming that the freedom of spontaneity that he describes as the highest degree of freedom *excludes* the ability to do otherwise, because the latter is mentioned as the very essence of will in itself, which is infinite or unrestricted and by which we are images of God.[40] Not only is it infinite, it is one and indivisible so that "its nature rules out the possibility of anything being taken away from it" (AT VII 60, CSM II 42), and hence it does not come in degrees, as the liberty of spontaneity does. This seems to rule out any interpretation according to which the two-way power is not essential to the will. All Descartes says is that it is not required that the will be indifferent in the sense of being equally inclined in two opposite ways, and it is such indifference that is characterized as the "lowest grade of freedom" (AT VII 58, CSM II 40). That kind of indifference is the evidence not of any perfection of freedom, but rather of a defect of knowledge, for he explains: "[I]f I always saw clearly what was true and good, I should never have to deliberate about the right judgement or choice; in that case, although I should be wholly free, it would be impossible for me ever to be in a state of indifference" (AT VII 58, CSM II 40). Freedom in this sense is exemplified by his inability to refrain from judging as true something that he realized very evidently—for instance, that it follows that he exists from the very fact that he raises the question whether anything exists:

> I could not but judge that something which I understood so clearly was true; but this was not because I was compelled so to judge by any external force, but because a great light in the intellect was followed by a great inclination in the will, and thus the spontaneity and freedom of my belief was all the greater in proportion to my lack of indifference. (AT VII 58, CSM II 41)

The text is certainly not very clear, as it first claims that the will consists simply in the ability to do or not to do something, and then explicates this as a power to follow a strong inclination, which would reduce it to freedom in the traditional sense of being able to follow one's natural inclination as opposed to being compelled by external causes or circumstances. Why would Descartes mention the power to do or not to do—that is, the power to do otherwise—in telling us what the will taken strictly consists in, if all it really consists in is the ability to follow spontaneously the decrees of the intellect? As it turns out, Descartes, when pressed by Mesland, comes to recognize another kind of indifference, which does not consist in mere lack of knowledge but in a real positive power to do or not to do something, which we have even when determined by the good or the true. He also recognizes "indifference of the will" as self-evidently known through experience, in replying to Gassendi's objections to his account of error in the Fourth Meditation, and does not hesitate there to equate it with freedom (AT VII 377,

CSM II 259). The distinction between two kinds of indifference goes some way toward clarifying the problem, but it certainly does not solve it. The question remains whether there are two kinds of will (and freedom), and if so, how they are related and what the freedom do to otherwise consists in.

5. Descartes's Notion of a Free Will

Consider some of Descartes's statements concerning the will that defenders of compatibilism (or necessitarianism) have found most problematic. The earliest one is a remark in his unpublished notes (1619–1620?) where free choice is listed as the first of three marvels made by God (the other two are things out of nothing and God in man) (AT X 218). Among the latest is article 31 of the first part of the *Principles of Philosophy*, published twenty-four years later:

> [I]t is a supreme perfection in man that he acts voluntarily *(per voluntatem)*, that is freely; this makes him in a special way the author of his actions and deserving praise for what he does. We do not praise automatons for accurately producing all the movements they were designed to perform, because the productions of these movements occur necessarily. It is the craftsman *(artifex)* who is praised for constructing such carefully-made devices; for in constructing them he acted not out of necessity but freely. By the same principle, when we embrace the truth, our doing so voluntarily is much more to our credit than would be the case if we could not not embrace it. *(Magis profecto nobis tribuendum est, quia voluntarie id agimus, quam si non possemus non amplecti.)* (AT VIII-1 18–19, CSM I 205)

We have already seen how Descartes declares, in *Passions of the Soul*, that our volitions depend entirely on the actions of the soul that produce them, and that "the will is by its nature so free that it can never be constrained" (AT XI 395–360). But the most explicit statement of a radical power of choice is found in a later letter to Mesland in 1645, where Descartes stresses that freedom involves "indifference" not only in the sense of characterizing "the will when it is not impelled one way rather than another by any perception of truth or goodness," which represent the lowest degree of freedom, but also in the sense of a positive faculty of determining oneself to one or the other of two contraries *(positiva facultas se determinandi ad utrumlibet e duobus contrariis)*, that is to say, to pursue or avoid, to affirm or deny. I do not deny that the will has this positive faculty. Indeed, I think it has it not only with respect to those actions to which it is not pushed by any evident reasons on one side or the other, but also with respect to all other actions, so that when a very evident reason moves us in one direction, although morally speaking we can hardly move in the contrary direction, absolutely speaking we can. *For it is always open to us to hold back from pursuing a clearly known good, or from admitting a clearly perceived truth, provided we consider it a good thing to demonstrate our freedom by so doing.* (AT IV 173, CSMK 245; my italics)

In these quotes, Descartes understands freedom of the will to involve three tenets. (1) It is the highest of human perfections and the sole basis for moral praise or blame. (2) It consists in a positive two-way power—that is, a capacity to determine oneself to one or the other of two contraries, which presupposes that nothing beyond the will itself determines which of the two will be pursued. (3) It is a matter of evident and indubitable inner experience that we have a will that is undetermined in its capacity of choice.[41]

In defending these three tenets Descartes endorses a form of voluntarism, more particularly, of ethical voluntarism in the sense used by Bonnie Kent and Vernon Bourke. In examining the emergence of this doctrine in medieval discussions of will and reason, Kent distinguishes three senses of voluntarism. The earliest is psychological voluntarism, which she sees as originating with the first Franciscan masters in Paris, which "signifies little more than a general emphasis on the affective and volitional aspects of human nature." The second, which arises among Bonaventure's successors, Kent (following Vernon Bourke) calls "ethical voluntarism." It "signifies a strong emphasis on the active character of the will, the claim that the will is free to act against reason's dictates, and the conviction that moral responsibility depends on this conception of the will's freedom." The third kind of voluntarism signifies "a strong emphasis on God's freedom (or 'absolute power') to will anything not involving a contradiction" and began, she suggests, with Duns Scotus or William of Ockham;[42] we could call it "theological voluntarism."

Descartes not only defends both of the latter, radical forms of voluntarism, but also seems to go beyond them in that Descartes's God can will things that involve contradiction (in a sense of "can" that remains beyond our grasp). This latter doctrine is relevant here, since it is only through our will that we bear a similitude to God, and our will is said to be, like God's, unrestrained by any limits.[43] If Descartes goes beyond his predecessors in ascribing a power to God to create *ex nihilo* the eternal truths, he also goes beyond them in extending to the true the two-way power they think we have with respect to the good: we are free not only to pursue or avoid the good but also to affirm or deny a truth clearly and distinctly perceived. Thus he can claim that it is much more to our credit when, in embracing the truth, "we do so voluntarily than would be the case if we could not not embrace it" (AT VIII-1 18–19). "Voluntarily" means freely and presupposes a power to do otherwise that is in some sense undetermined. Descartes's God, to the great dismay of Leibniz, makes the true and the good, without any prior reason or necessity, as a king creates the laws of his kingdom. The human mind finds the true and the good imprinted on it, like the subjects of a kingdom have its laws imprinted on their hearts.[44] It has no more power to change them than the subjects have with respect to the laws decreed by their king, but it nevertheless retains, as they do, the freedom to subject itself to or to oppose the laws.

The first question to be faced is whether Descartes had a consistent conception of what freedom of the will consists in. His thinking on this topic, as on many others, evolves, and it is not very clear whether the changes are merely a matter of clarification or rather an abandonment of one position in favor of another.[45] His first view, which seems to conflict with the voluntarism suggested by the quoted passages above, is defended in the texts considered in the previous section, and in particular in the Fourth Meditation, where the highest kind of freedom seems to coincide not with any indeterminacy but with an experience of necessity and determination. Descartes does not hesitate to underwrite, in correspondence, the dictum: *"ex magna luce in intellectu sequitur magna propensio in voluntate,"* and his gloss on it is that "if we see very clearly that a thing is good for us, it is very difficult—and, on my view, impossible, as long as one continues in the same thought—to stop the course of our desire" (AT IV 116, CSMK 233–234). In this same letter, however, he tries to persuade his correspondent, who is a

Jesuit, of his total agreement with his position, which appears much more radical. For he concludes: "And so, since you regard freedom not simply as indifference but rather as a real and positive power to determine oneself, the difference between us is merely one of names—for I agree the will has such a power."[46]

Is Descartes inconsistent or is he, as many scholars argue, a compatibilist who wants to avoid offending his voluntarist correspondents?[47] How can he claim both that the will is determined by the good clearly perceived and yet has a "real and positive power to determine itself" independently of the perceptions of the intellect? Some recent scholars ignore his most radical pronouncements and others attempt to explain them away, in an effort to make Descartes's view consistent and continuous with Aquinas's intellectualism, which is more in line with contemporary accounts of action. Before taking a stand on that issue, I must consider whether pronouncements like the above amount to a coherent view—whether any sense can be made of them.

Much depends on how one describes the phenomenon of the will and what experiences its freedom is supposed to refer to. Harry G. Frankfurt expresses the dilemma in asking: "What are we talking about when we talk about 'the freedom of the will.' Neither in common speech nor in the special vocabulary of philosophers does the term 'free will' have an unequivocal standard use." It is unclear what function the notion is supposed to serve in our thinking about ourselves, or what possibility of experience it is supposed to grasp. Neither the idea of freedom nor that of will have any precise sense. It is no wonder, he concludes, "that the discussions of the freedom of the will tend to be murky and inconclusive."[48]

This does not hinder people from talking about it and even from feeling confident about what to say. Rogers Albritton, for instance, claims to know that his will is free, though he does not know what that means. Albritton quotes the line from article 41 of the *Passions of the Soul* cited above, and adds the following, from a dinner conversation reported by Burman: "Let everyone just go down deep into himself and find out whether or not he has a perfect and absolute will, and whether he can conceive of anything which surpasses him in freedom of the will. I'm sure that everyone will find that it is as I say" (April 16, 1648 (AT V 159, CSMK 342)). While Albritton is inclined to agree with these words attributed to Descartes, Frankfurt testifies that all that happens to him when he tries to look deep down into himself is that he tends to become a bit disoriented. He would rather talk about "volitional necessity" than freedom here, for what strikes him about the will are our common experiences of its constraints and limits—our inability to perform acts of willing other than the ones we actually have.[49] Our will in general, according to Frankfurt, is characterized by what Descartes thinks holds for our passions, namely, that they are not in our direct control but incline our will whether we want it or not—indeed, they are externally induced, involuntary volitions. The fact that we cannot will to love anyone we do not love (or cease at will to love someone not worthy of our love) shows that our will is, to a large extent, subject to our passions, which are caused by contingent and disorderly movements in the body. Add to this the experience of necessity Descartes himself appeals to in confronting his inability to doubt what he clearly and distinctly understands, all of which contributes to the difficulty of understanding his notion of a free will.

6. From Free Decision to Free Will: Medieval Debates about Agency

If we are hard put today to explain what having a free will could mean, we may get some help in understanding what Descartes is up to by turning to the medieval context in which freedom of the will first became the issue to which Descartes's pronouncements on will and freedom may be seen as a response. For that kind of talk of the freedom of the will originated in a specific historical context and hardly makes much sense apart from the theoretical framework of mental powers and faculties within which the will's freedom was first posited. It takes its inspiration from a tradition opposing itself to what was perceived as an overly intellectualistic account of human agency—one which according to its critics did not leave room for certain intuitions about free choice that they took to be crucial to moral responsibility. If I can do no more than roughly gesture at it here, I hope at least to show that if Descartes's belief in a free will is, as Spinoza observed, a matter of dreaming with one's eyes open,[50] there were many to share that dream. For them, those who claimed the opposite—namely, that the will is necessitated—seemed to act with their eyes closed, more like sleepwalkers than responsible agents. Even a brief look at its ancestry supports my contention that the determinism, to which the Cartesian theory presents itself as a challenge, is neither that of physical laws nor divine preordination, but a version of ethical determinism, which sees the will as necessarily determined by the good, more particularly, by the knowledge of the good to be pursued, a view that Descartes himself endorsed at an earlier stage.[51] In emphasizing the priority of will over intellect in his account of free agency, Descartes sides with those in the voluntarist tradition who saw Aquinas's version of the Aristotelian doctrine—or a certain interpretation of it—as conflicting with faith and threatening Christian morality.

The controversy initially was not about freedom of the will but rather free decision or choice—*liberum arbitrium*. Freedom, in Augustine and his followers, is predicated on *arbitrium*, decision or choice. The notion of will, *voluntas*—Cicero's translation of Aristotle's term for rational appetite—had to be invented, since there is no room for it in the Aristotelian tripartite soul, each part of which comes with an appetite or desire of its own.[52] Charles Kahn thinks that although Augustine's notion of the will marks the beginning of a philosophical articulation of this idea, it was not accomplished until Aquinas's "synthesis of Augustinian will with Aristotelian philosophy of mind."[53] René Gauthier, on the other hand, claims that there is no such thing as an Augustinian conception of the will, because "of all the traits of the 'will' in Augustine, there is not a single one that is not found earlier in the Stoics."[54]

If one takes free choice to be essential to the will, Augustine (and the Stoics before him) do seem to have an important part in developing that notion. Augustine famously argues in his so-called Free Will Defense that God, who is good, cannot possibly do evil, but that since evil exists, and since God is just, God can punish those who do evil. To the question concerning the cause of doing evil, he answers, "Everyone who does evil is the cause of his own evildoing," and he argues not only that sin is voluntary ("we do evil by free decision"), but that the will is uncaused or the cause of its own willings.[55]

A leading thread in the medieval discussion concerning the relation of reason and will in decisionmaking is the question of what powers moral agents have to be granted in order to be held responsible for their actions.[56] Aristotle and his followers agree that only voluntary actions—actions performed in the absence of external compulsion—can be moral actions. But voluntary, for Augustine and his followers (most of whom, as Bonnie Kent points out, think of themselves as good Aristotelians too), cannot be merely a matter of natural appetites or tendencies. If it were, there is really nothing that the agent, who comes to the world with a given set of appetites and natural tendencies, is responsible for. Further conditions are required, and one of them seems to be freedom of decision with respect to the end pursued: a decision or choice between good and evil. Such choice presupposes absence of any internal compulsion: whatever natural inclination the will has, whatever end it naturally pursues, it must also have the power to resist or reject it.[57]

Augustine, Bonaventure, and their voluntarist followers have little to offer by way of explaining this power of free choice. It is noteworthy that they all appeal to a common, evident, and undeniable experience of freedom, and they take the freedom they experience to involve a power of choice between opposites. The fullest account is given by Duns Scotus, but for the Subtle Doctor to make the required distinctions, a systematic faculty-psychology had to be worked out, and that we owe to Aquinas. Once Aquinas had spelled out his version of the Aristotelian theory in full detail, its deterministic features became a source of worry for the philosophers and theologians in Paris who were already concerned with necessitarianism in the teachings of the philosophers on more than one account.[58] Among the claims about the will that the Thomists defended but that the voluntarists had difficulties with is the Aristotelian idea that the will, by its nature, tends to the good or, as Aquinas says (quoting for this purpose Augustine), "all seek happiness with one will," which he takes to mean that there is one thing that the will wills necessarily, namely, happiness.[59]

Aquinas, in discussing the topic of the will, does not ask whether it is free, but how voluntariness relates to necessity. He distinguishes between different kinds of necessity, based on Aristotle's four types of causes. It turns out that the first type, relating to formal and material causes, which are internal and pertain to the nature of the thing, are necessary, and that their necessity is absolute. Aquinas accepts this as a natural limitation of human freedom. In fact, he does not see it as a limitation, but as a necessity that is compatible with voluntariness. This is what voluntary means: the willingness to achieve one's natural end or goal, the perfection of one's nature. When Aquinas speaks of freedom, he relates it to choice or decision, which is about means to the end. We are free to choose the means to achieve our end, but we are not free to deliberate about the end itself.[60]

This is one of the points that the voluntarists fought: the end, whether the good or happiness, is not once and for all determined: there is room for deliberation not only about the means, but also genuine choice as to the ultimate end to be pursued. Freedom of the will, in this context, seems to acquire the precise meaning of freedom with respect to the end pursued.[61]

7. Toward a Non-naturalistic Account of Moral Agency

Some critics of Aquinas, in challenging the above-mentioned thesis of the will's being necessarily determined by the pursuit of the good or happiness, seem to commit themselves to the psychologically problematic claim that anyone could will unhappiness or misery. Scotus, in discussing this, points out that it is true that the will naturally tends to happiness, and in most cases seeks happiness, both in general and particular, but he argues that it does not follow that it also wills happiness necessarily. He bases his argument on some assumptions and distinctions worth detailed discussion and scrutiny, but which can be only briefly mentioned here.[62]

Scotus accepts the Aristotelian idea of the highest kind of human desire as a rational desire toward the perfection of the intellect, assimilating it to the claim of Augustine and Anselm that happiness is what all human beings desire. But this natural desire or appetite for perfection, he argues, does not exhaust the nature of the will. He adopts Anselm's distinction between two affections of the will, which he calls affection for happiness and affection for justice. These are two aspects of the highest kind of desire or appetite in the Aristotelian scheme, two sides of the rational appetite *(boulesis)* or will. But they are importantly dissimilar. The affection (or inclination) to "happiness" is natural, which means that it is necessary: the will cannot will *(velle)* misery, it cannot not will *(nolle)* happiness. But this holds true for the rational will in only one of its aspects: the "nobler" aspect of the will, the affection for justice, is not determined by this kind of natural necessity—it is not properly a natural appetite at all. The inclination to justice is as basic in the will as the inclination to happiness, but it is not oriented toward the realization of one's natural potential—toward what is good for me by virtue of my nature. The will for justice transcends nature and the natural will: it can go beyond what my nature dictates. My (rational) nature dictates that I seek my own good *(bonum sibi)*—happiness—but the will for justice (which is the basis for my moral nature) tends to the good in itself *(bonum in se),* to what is intrinsically good, not good for any other aim.[63]

Scotus also distinguishes between the tendency toward an end and the actualization of this tendency. The former is passive, the latter active. "Natural will" can mean both the natural tendency, which is passive, and the power to elicit an act according to this natural tendency, which is active. This latter power, even as a part of the natural will, is free: it is not, like natural tendencies are, determined by the end. Will, properly, denotes the latter and not the former, for "the natural will is really not will at all, nor is natural volition true volition, for the term 'natural' effectively cancels or negates the sense both of 'will' and 'volition.'"[64]

Contrast this to the more traditional picture, where the will is called free whenever it elicits an act in conformity with its natural inclination, which is always aimed at its own advantage, at the realization of its own natural potential. This corresponds to what Hume calls "freedom of spontaneity," as opposed to the "freedom of indifference" he rejects.[65] According to Anthony Kenny, Descartes never departed from the view that freedom in the proper sense of the word consists in this kind of freedom of spontaneity, freedom to act in accordance with one's rational nature, following the clear and distinct perceptions of one's intellect.[66] Duns Scotus, however, would not call this freedom, in the proper sense of the word, nor, as I read him, would Descartes, unless such freedom also presupposes the power to do otherwise (which Hume with most rationalists would deny). Scotus writes: "The will is called free, however, in so far as it lies in its power to elicit an act opposed to this inclination, *for it possesses the power to elicit or not elicit an act in conformity with this inclination."*[67]

It is by virtue of this active power that the will is a free master of its own acts, a power Scotus elsewhere calls a "two-way power," and which yields his answer to the question how the will could be free with respect to its natural tendency to seek happiness. Even when the rational will elicits actions in accord with the affection for happiness (for the advantageous), those acts are free because the will could have not elicited them: it could have *not* acted to elicit them. It is true that the will as natural appetite necessarily and perpetually seeks happiness and always seeks it in the highest degree. But if this were all there is to the will, there could be no freedom, for the will would always tend to and be activated by the object that the intellect sees to be the greater of particular goods available. Scotus argues against Aquinas that the will does not will happiness generally or particularly by necessity, but that it wills contingently whatever it wills. So even if it is true that the will in most cases seeks happiness when the intellect has no doubt that happiness consists in this particular thing, it does not seek to attain it out of necessity. The inclination by which it always tends to happiness is passive and necessary, and does not move the will unless it is actualized. The actual, elicited inclination to happiness is not necessary, for it depends on another, active tendency, which is free. The will always remains free with respect to its power not to elicit an act. Scotus writes:

> I grant that in most cases it will have an act of volition, but it does not necessarily have any act. Hence, when it is shown happiness, it can refrain from acting at all. In regard to any object, then, the will is able not to will or nill it, and can suspend itself from eliciting any act in particular with regard to this or that *(unde quodlibet obiectum potest voluntas velle nec nolle et a quolibet actu in particulari potest se suspendere circa hoc vel illud)*. And this is something anyone can experience in himself when one proffers some good. Even if it is presented as something to be considered and willed, one can turn away from it and not elicit any act in its regard.[68]

Nota bene: "turn away from it." This is an active power: it is not a matter of weakness, of being distracted, or forgetting, but of acting—determining oneself—not to elicit an act of will at all, and hence refrain from willing what one is naturally inclined to will, by not eliciting any act of will. It does not have to be because of a failure of memory or attention that the righteous turns his thoughts away from the right kind of subject, the contemplation, for instance, of the Holy Trinity, for he may freely determine himself not to do that and to think instead of something else, in full awareness that this is not conducive to true happiness.[69] He neglects his duty by choice, and when he does do it, he also does it freely, not because his will is determined by the perceptions of his intellect. Having made his decision, his will may be determined, but the decision was free at the instant he made it, because he could, at that instant, have refrained from making it.

Duns Scotus, like his predecessors, takes it that this freedom is a fact of experience, but he goes beyond them in trying to explain it. Because of its power to elicit or not to elicit its own acts, the will, Scotus argues, is the only rational potency in the proper sense of the word: the only power that can determine itself with respect to opposites. Scotus calls it "superabundant sufficiency," and sometimes also "a positive indeterminacy."[70]

John Boler has argued that if Aquinas's account of the will and voluntary action is meant to be continuous with a general account of appetitive behavior throughout nature, Scotus's moral psychology can be seen as an attempt to show that the will escapes the limitations of natural appetite and it cannot, given its complex structure, be explained in the same terms. Because of its two affections and its active power to elicit contrary acts, the will can only in part be accounted for in terms of the teleological scheme of natural tendencies and goals. This is not a matter of adding another higher inclination or appetite (for justice) to the Aristotelian scheme of natural powers, but to recognize that the Aristotelian scheme does not apply to the will in its entirety.[71] Natural appetites are subject to natural causes, but the rational will is not, because justice—the good that is sought for its own sake *(bonum in se)*—is not an efficient or final cause: it is *not* sought in the pursuit of some natural good or end. To seek justice is a matter not of natural (for example, psychological) motivation but of moral obligation that transcends the order of natural causes, and hence it cannot be explained in terms of those causes, whether efficient or final. The moral order is separated from the natural order of things—it belongs not to the realm of natural causes at all but to the "logical space of reasons."[72] This idea that reasons belong to a normative order not reducible to the order of causes finds an early expression in the voluntarist conception of a will that is undetermined in its power of choice—a power that Scotus spells out as the ability of the will to elicit or not elicit its acts independently of its natural tendencies and inclinations. Let us now see what light this can shed on the Cartesian doctrine of the will.

8. Interpreting Descartes's Voluntarism

Spinoza does not spare his irony when commenting on the freedom of the will that Descartes claims gives us not only an absolute power over our thoughts but also an indirect power, through their effects on the pineal gland, of controlling and directing the movements of the body. For Spinoza the belief in a free will shows nothing but one's ignorance of the true causes of one's actions. Leibniz for his part is quick in pointing out that Descartes's theory is based on a mistake in Descartes's formulation of the laws of motion.[73]

Translated into the framework of mechanical causation in a deterministic universe, the assumption of undetermined agency is undoubtedly problematic. Descartes just waved his hand when Elisabeth and Gassendi confronted him with the question of how the immaterial mind can act on the mechanically moved extended body (and be affected by its movements), given that bodily motions can be changed only by mechanical impact. The relation of free agency to natural or metaphysical determinism is an issue he does not address at all, except in the theological context of God's foreknowledge.[74] I have said nothing of these problems here, but have focused instead on the context in which the issue of free will first originated, which is the only context where free choice of the will can make much sense, and in relation to which Descartes's controversial pronouncements on the free will are best understood. Even if Spinoza and Leibniz were justified in their criticisms of his account (or lack of account) of the mechanisms through which the will is supposed to act on the body, to the extent that they deny the power of choice, they do not do justice to the controversies and intuitions about moral agency his conception of the will responds to.

Descartes, it would be fair to say, did not think much about moral agency. Nevertheless, he was sensitive enough to the issue that when challenged to spell out his view, he does not hesitate to use the very terms and notions introduced by Duns Scotus in defense of a strong form of ethical voluntarism. It is striking that when talking of the second kind of indifference, which he says he always accepted, he refers to it as a *positive faculty of determining itself,* and that in talking (in the *Principles*) of the freedom that constitutes the ground for merit, he describes it as a power to embrace or not embrace the truth in the presence of clearly perceived reasons. Given all the statements in which Descartes adheres to the "common" Thomistic doctrine of the School,[75] this may seem just an accident. But it is not, for from his earliest writings, he emphasizes the "wonder" of freedom, and throughout his epistemological writings he stresses the voluntary character of assent and the responsibility involved in giving it to the perceptions of the intellect.[76]

One may ask, of course, whether, given his mind–body dualism, Descartes needed to posit a two-way power of the will. For isn't the freedom he needs implicit in his dualism? Doesn't the human mind, while united to the body, preserve its independent rational nature, and is anything else required for it to be free from determination by the causal laws governing the bodily movements? The soul has its own rational nature, by virtue of which it transcends the laws of physical nature, which means that Descartes provides the framework for a nonnaturalistic account of human action without having to appeal to yet another kind of indeterminism, beyond the already problematic assumption of an immaterial mind operating independently of the laws of mechanical causation.

But it does not take much reflection to see that this would be unsatisfactory. Given its own rational nature, and given its union with the body that obeys its own laws, the Cartesian mind seems threatened by a double determinism.[77] Finding the standards of truth and goodness, and hence an objective hierarchy of values, fixed for it, it would be determined not only to assent to what the intellect clearly and distinctly perceives as true, but also to pursue what it perceives as the good. It would have no choice with respect to its end, and would be, when working properly and without impediments, a kind of rational automaton. The power to follow clear and distinct perceptions would not be the highest kind of freedom, it would also be the only kind of freedom, for whenever the mind is less than fully determined by clear and distinct ideas, it is prey to determination by natural causes through the mechanical movements of the pineal gland, ready to pursue whatever objects represented by its cognitive powers incline it most strongly at the time.[78]

I want to suggest it is the awareness of this problem that led Descartes to opt for a more radical position. He seems in fact to go even further than Scotus or his followers in asserting—against what I have called his own default position—that it is possible, even in the presence of evident reasons, to hold back from admitting a clearly perceived truth. (See the passage from the second Mesland letter quoted in section 5.) Descartes seems to treat truth and falsity on a par with the ends and values moral agents can, according to the voluntarist view, deliberate about, and reasoning itself (right reason) becomes a matter of moral choice and commitment. In his view, we have more merit in embracing the truth when we do it freely than we would if we were unable to resist it.

Is Descartes then serious in claiming that we are free not to embrace the truth even when perceiving it clearly and distinctly? Why would it not be enough for us to be free not to assent to less than fully clear and distinct perceptions? Does he really need to postulate such an ability to hold us responsible for error?

I side with those who think this is precisely his claim, even if the textual evidence remains, in the end, inconclusive. It is difficult, in particular, to reconcile the two letters to Mesland (1644 and 1645) with one another. Kenny, however, saw no problem in reconciling what Descartes says in the Mesland letter quoted above with other statements in which he clearly adheres to what Kenny calls his "regular doctrine," which is the common, Thomistic doctrine. Descartes himself states that doctrine as follows in the earlier letter to Mesland (May 2, 1644), which is worth quoting at more length:

> I agree with you when you say that we can suspend our judgement; but I tried to explain in what manner this can be done. For it seems to me certain that *ex magna luce in intellectu sequitur magna propensio in voluntate,* so that if we see very clearly that a thing is good for us, it is very difficult—and, on my view, impossible, as long as one continues in the same thought—to stop the course of our desire. But the nature of the soul is such that it hardly attends more than a moment to a single thing; hence, as soon as our attention turns from the reasons which show us that the thing is good for us, and we merely keep in our memory the thought that it appeared desirable to us, we can represent to our mind some other reason to make us doubt it, and so suspend our judgement, and perhaps even form a contrary judgement.[79]

Kenny thinks these two letters to Mesland are "perfectly compatible," thus opposing Ferdinand Alquié, who sees the second letter as constituting a clear break with the position defended in the first letter. Kenny argues that when Descartes says in the letter of 1645 "that it is always open to us to hold back from pursuing a clearly known good, or from admitting a clearly perceived truth, he need not mean that we can do it at the very moment of perceiving the good and the true. Rather, we must distract our attention, as he said in the 1644 letter." It is enough, for instance, "to dwell on the thought that it would be a good thing to demonstrate our free will by perversity."[80] The 1645 letter would confirm this in suggesting a reason for diverting one's attention: dwelling on the idea that to demonstrate one's freedom by not assenting to the true clearly and distinctly perceived would be a good thing renders the perception of the truth itself confused and obscure. It is because demonstrating one's freedom is now perceived as a greater good—is more clearly perceived than the truth—that it is possible to refrain from assenting. What Descartes talks about, therefore, is not a genuine power to refuse assent, but a distraction from the idea necessarily causing the assent.

This reading may seem persuasive if it is assumed that the Aristotelian-Thomistic model of free choice is the only rational way to think of will and voluntary action. Recent historical work has shown, however, that this model was heavily criticized already in late medieval times by thinkers who, although influenced by Augustine and Anselm, thought of themselves as good Aristotelians—as more true to Aristotle, in fact, than Aquinas himself.[81] They challenged the traditional Aristotelian model in a number of ways, which Calvin Normore summarizes as follows. To the Aristotelian thesis (1) that "everything that moves is moved by another," its critics oppose the thesis that "the will is a self-mover." Against the claim (2) that deliberation or choice is merely about means, not about ends, they take deliberation to be possible also about ends. To the idea (3) that everything pursued is pursued under the aspect of good, they oppose the idea that the will has no necessary orientation to the good.[82]

In light of this alternative way of thinking about will and choice, which at the end of the thirteenth century and for a long time after was the prevailing model, Descartes's apparently inconsistent pronouncements can be reconciled in another way than the one suggested by Kenny. Between the Scylla of tragic existentialism that Kenny sees Alquié as committing Descartes to (tragic because he thinks that the only positive use that can be made of this radical freedom is turning away from being and the good)[83] and the Charybdis of the compatibilism that Kenny ascribes to him, a third way of understanding his position suggests itself. It consists in interpreting the account of will Descartes gives in the Fourth Meditation and later in light of Scotus's distinction between a natural, passive inclination to the good or happiness and an active power to elicit or not elicit it. Like Scotus, Descartes thinks that because God so created it, the human will is naturally and necessarily inclined to the true and the good (also created by God), an inclination that is greater the more clearly and distinctly its objects are perceived. But this inclination is not all there is to the will, since it consists essentially in a power to do or not to do, to elicit or not elicit, its own acts. The positive power of determining itself, to which Descartes refers, is just this active power to elicit or not elicit (actualize) a prior inclination of the will,[84] and this is all he needs to defend his view that we ourselves bear full responsibility for how we direct our thoughts and hence for pursuing or not pursuing the true and the good.

A natural objection to make here on behalf of Kenny's reading is that "holding back from pursuing a clearly known good" or from "admitting a clearly seen truth" happens for a reason, and that the reason for which it is done is still what, at the moment, is perceived as a greater good (that of demonstrating one's freedom). But this misses the point that the "goods" in such case are not commensurable. Demonstrating one's freedom by rejecting the true good is not another good on the objective, rational scale of perfection. So if it is preferred over any good on that scale, it is not preferred for its greater goodness; choosing it is rejecting the scale and the good itself as a standard of value. From the point of view of reason or intellect there are no other standards. So it is not that the intellect gets momentarily confused: the idea of demonstrating one's freedom by not opting for the greater good presupposes that the latter is clearly and distinctly perceived at the very moment one so decides—otherwise there would be no freedom to demonstrate, there would just be confusion or distraction.

The choice here is not made under any prior aspect of good, even though Descartes's formulation in the 1645 letter may suggest it is, when he writes that we consider demonstrating our freedom a good thing. The act of willing, by which one chooses to deny the good or the true to demonstrate one's freedom, is posited as a good only in being elicited: it is not willed because of its goodness, but is good only to the extent it is actually willed. The act of will by which the true good is rejected is prior to the evaluation of the act, and even when it has been chosen (preferred), it is and remains evil on the objective scale of perfection.

It is unlikely that a sane person would make such a choice, in particular if the "good" to be rejected were a truth clearly and distinctly seen, and it is also "morally impossible"—that is, not conceivable for a moral, rational agent. Yet it is conceivable absolutely and is a real possibility, and only because of this possibility can the will determine itself to assent to the true or pursue the good clearly perceived freely, by its own decision. Only because she is free to pursue or not pursue the good can an agent make the pursuit of the true and the good (on the objective scale of perfection) truly her own end. Without this freedom, she can be determined by the true and the good, but not because of her own will and commitment. To explain not assenting by turning away one's attention merely postpones the problem. For now an account needs to be given of how the attention gets distracted in the first place. To be distracted, in the presence of clear and distinct perceptions, assent must already have been withheld.[85] The idea of the will as a self-mover is the idea of a will acting without prior reason.

The notion of a free will involving a power of opposites undetermined with respect to the end is one expression of the idea that the will of a moral agent operates on a different level than the natural will, and that moral acts cannot be reduced to natural causes, efficient or final causes. The moral good is an end that necessitates not by natural necessity, but by rational commitment and the obligation that creates. The inclination to pursue it is part of our moral nature, and so is the power to elicit or not elicit this inclination. The same holds for the inclination to the true, which is part of the nature of our reason itself, and here too it is up to us whether to elicit such inclinations or not. We cannot be moral beings and not pursue the good, and we cannot be rational and not accept the true. But having the power to control the inclinations of our will leaves room for choice between good and evil, between rationality and irrationality, and it is only to the extent we can make that choice and freely commit ourselves to the true or the good that we can pursue them as autonomous agents.

There need not be tragedy in such choice, because opting for not assenting to the true clearly and distinctly perceived does not (as it would on Alquié's reading) mean willing falsity any more than the Scotian agent in not eliciting its inclination to happiness can be said to will unhappiness (or nill happiness). Having the option, even for a moment, to withhold assent to clear and distinct perceptions is all that is required for moral agency and for making continued adherence to those perceptions a ground for desert. Again, it may not be morally possible to deny a truth clearly perceived—that is, while remaining committed to pursuing the true and the good—yet it is, absolutely speaking, possible. We are free, at any moment, to forsake that pursuit. It is not astonishing that Descartes does not raise this possibility in the *Meditations,* the aim of which is certain knowledge, and which presupposes a prior commitment to the truth. We have more reason to wonder why he mentions the two-way power at all in that connection; the only explanation I can think of is that he already holds the view of the will as a self-mover, which has the ability to pursue or not pursue any object it is presented with.

9. Generosity: The Passion of Virtue

The idea of the will as a self-mover implies that the will can move without natural causes, whether final causes pertaining to its nature as rational will or mechanical causes acting on the body to which it is united and whose appetites are also its volitions. The will as self-mover can move for reasons, but it is free to move also without reason, and hence, in so moving, to determine itself what reasons it acts for. The highest virtue consists precisely in the will's moving itself within the strict limits of right reason. This is the core of Cartesian ethics and therapy of passions, and it is the topic of this last section.

But first let us consider once more Descartes's doctrine of judgment and will in the context of the *Meditations* where it is developed. Having proved, to his satisfaction, the existence of God, on which "every single moment of my entire existence depends," Descartes recognizes that "it is impossible that he should ever deceive me" (AT VII 53, CSM II 37), and hence faces the peculiar problem of having to explain the causes of his errors. He finds that he is "something intermediate between God and nothingness": his nature is such "that in so far as I was created by a supreme being, there is nothing in me to enable me to go wrong or lead me astray; but in so far as I participate in nothingness or non-being . . . it is no wonder that I make mistakes." Error, according to a line of argument familiar to Platonists and Augustinians, is a defect and not something real that depends on God. God surely has not endowed him with a faculty of judgment such that he could go wrong while using it correctly. Yet experience shows him to be "prone to countless errors," which shows that the faculty of judgment he has received from God is not infinite (AT VII 54, CSM II 38).[86] On closer inspection, it turns out that error depends on the concurrence of two causes, each faultless in itself: the intellect, which is finite, and the will, which is infinite in its power of choice. The will is not to blame because it "is extremely ample and also perfect of its kind," nor is the intellect or the power of understanding. Even if the latter is finite, whatever is within its reach is perfectly understood, so the intellect too is perfect within its limits. The cause of his errors, Descartes concludes, lies in the fact that "the scope of the will is wider than that of the intellect; but instead of restricting it within the same limits, I extend it to matters which I do not understand" (AT VII 58, CSM II 40).

For Gassendi (as for Spinoza) this doctrine makes little sense.[87] The scope of the intellect, Gassendi objects, cannot be narrower than that of the will, "since the will never aims at anything which the intellect has not already perceived" (AT VII 314, CSM II 218). Rather, it is even wider, for the apprehension of the intellect always precedes the pursuit or avoidance of something by the will. Moreover, things that are only poorly understood are neither judged nor pursued because they leave the will indifferent. The will cannot extend to things that escape the intellect, and it always follows the perceptions of the intellect. If it goes wrong, it is not the will but the imperfect perceptions of the intellect that are at fault. If we cannot guard against error since we always go for what at the time seems the more likely, we can guard against "persisting in error," and if we want to use our judgment correctly we should "not so much restrain our will as apply our intellect to develop a clearer awareness, which the judgement will always then follow" (AT VII 317, CSM II 220).

This may sound like philosophical common sense (if there is such a thing), but not to Descartes. We should not, if we are to use our reason well, assent to anything that we do not know for certain is true (what is clearly and distinctly perceived), and the fact that we do assent to many such things shows that the will is involved. If I were, for example, to judge (with Gassendi) that the mind is a rarefied body, I would assent to what I do *not* clearly and distinctly understand (that the mind, which is thinking, is the same thing as a body, which is extended), and hence extend my will to what escapes my intellect. Similarly, if you judge that an apple, which unknown to you has been poisoned, is good and nutritious on account of its looks, smell, and taste, you extend your will beyond the limits of your intellect: you so believe because you will to believe it, not because you know it. "You simply want to believe it, because you have believed it before and do not want to change your view" (AT VII 376–377, CSM II 259).

We would not survive for many days if we tried to use our will as Descartes thinks we should: never assenting to what we do not sufficiently understand. But luckily our assent—by institution of nature—is not in our full control: without even noticing it, we assent to (and act on) habitual and spontaneous judgments we could not even begin to inspect. Did Descartes really think they could always be controlled? He does not accept Gassendi's proposal that will and intellect are of equal scope: "So, while I do admit that there is nothing we will of which we do not understand something in some manner *(de quo non aliquid aliquo modo intelligamus)*, I deny that our understanding and willing are of equal scope. For any given object we can will many things about it and yet be very few of which we have knowledge" *(possumus enim de eadem rem velle permulta, et perpauca tantum cognoscere)* (AT VII 377, CSM II 259). Descartes goes on to explain that in making a false judgment, we do not use our will in a bad way, but the object of our will happens to be other than we thought it was. Thus, when I am taken in by the enticing smell of the poisoned apple and think it would be good for me to eat, the object of my will—the healthiness of the apple—just is not there. There is nothing wrong in my will itself, but I direct it to something that does not exist (some quality of apples, for instance, which is not instantiated in the apple I want to eat). Similarly, there is nothing wrong with my intellect, but I judge that it is more extensive than it is, for instance, that it perceives something healthy where there is no such thing.

Descartes defends freedom of indifference against Gassendi's denial by appeal to plain experience. In fact, he claims that Gassendi (who denies having such experience) presupposes it in recognizing that we can avoid persisting in error; for how could we fail to persist "unless the will had the freedom to direct itself without the determination of the intellect, towards one side or the other" (AT VII 378, CSM II 260)? This is not, however, a fair argument for the kind of indifference Descartes wants to defend. The indifference Gassendi's view presupposes belongs to what Descartes regards as the lowest degree of freedom, where the will is *less* than sufficiently determined by the perceptions of the intellect, and that is not the radical indifference Gassendi is denying.

Descartes, however, has his own experience of freedom of indifference from having carried his methodic doubt to its extreme limits in questioning reason itself in the Second Meditation, and this may well underlie his conviction that we have absolute power over our thoughts, which enables us to withhold assent even in the case of evident perceptions. But our thoughts are the only thing that are thus directly in our power, so we are responsible only for the ways we conduct our thoughts. This holds not only for theoretical knowledge, where strict obedience to the truth rule is required (AT VI 18–19, CSM I 129; cf. AT VII 35, CSM II 24), but also for action, where the third maxim of Descartes's "provisional" morality recommends one should always try to master oneself rather than fortune and change one's desires rather than the order of the world. This can be achieved by becoming accustomed "to believing that nothing lies within our power except our thoughts, so that after doing our best in dealing with matters external to us, whatever we fail to achieve is absolutely impossible so far as we are concerned."[88] Since it is through the desires they produce that passions govern our behavior (AT XI 436, CSM I 379),[89] it is our desires "we should take particular care to control; and here lies the chief utility of morality" (AT XI 436, CSM I 379). Desire is good if it conforms to true knowledge and bad when based on error, of which the most common is the failure to distinguish adequately the things that depend wholly on us from those we cannot in any way control. The things that depend on us are those that depend on our free will, and we can never desire them with too much ardor, for virtue consists precisely in "doing the good things that depend on us." Error is not a matter of desiring too much but of desiring too little (AT XI 436, CSM I 379), which happens because we pursue many other less useful and mostly vain desires, from which only two general remedies can free us.

The first is a frequent reflection on Providence or fate—the immutable necessity with which things have been determined to happen from all eternity (AT XI 438, CSM I 380). We can desire only what we consider in some way possible. How do we determine what is possible?

> [W]e must recognize that everything is guided by divine Providence, whose eternal decree is infallible and immutable to such an extent that, *except for matters it has determined to be dependent on our free will,* we must consider everything that affects us to occur of necessity . . . so that it would be wrong for us to desire things to happen in any other way. But most of our desires extend to matters which *do not depend wholly on us or wholly on others,* and we must therefore take care to pick out just what depends only on us, so as to limit our desire to that alone. (AT XI 439, CSM I 380; my emphasis)[90]

If we consider all external goods as equally beyond our power, we will not regret lacking goods we seem entitled to "when we are deprived of them *through no fault of our own*"—that is, having done the best we can to get them. If we do not succeed, we need feel no regrets and can follow the ancient philosophers in making a virtue out of necessity, by, for instance, not desiring to be healthy when ill or free when imprisoned "any more than we *now* desire to have bodies of a material indestructible as diamond or wings to fly like the birds" (AT VI 26, CSM I 124; my emphasis).

But who would not desire to be healthy when sick or free when imprisoned, no matter how unlikely the possibility of the fulfillment of such desire would be? And did Descartes, by saying we do not *now* desire to have indestructible bodies or wings, anticipate the time when all parts of our bodies are replaceable so that indestructible bodies could become common objects of human desire?

Descartes can be seen as combining two apparently conflicting ideals: the Stoic ideal of individual submission to fate through freedom from vain and immoderate desires, and a technological ideal of changing the world (rendering ourselves, as it were, the masters of the universe). The former forbids us to desire the latter, which, however, Cartesian reason urges us to attempt. For it requires we always do the best we can in dealing with external matters, acquiring all the knowledge of which we are capable, and through knowledge all the other "true goods" within our reach (AT VI 28, CSM I 125), including any technological and medical innovations that "would facilitate our enjoyment of . . . all the goods" we find on Earth.[91]

Descartes thinks that generosity, the second of the two general remedies against vain and immoderate desires, which is also a general remedy against all the passions as well as the highest virtue, offers a means of balancing the two ideals. It puts a lot of weight on our intentions, and thus helps to absolve us from regrets when things we cannot control interfere with our plans. But more important, it works as a moderator, and hinders us from undertaking anything the consequences of which we have insufficient knowledge and that we may have to regret. As a virtue of self-mastery through self-knowledge, generosity could be seen as a modern variant of the ancient virtue of temperance *(Sophrosune)* discussed by Plato in *Charmides*. But the aspiration for moral perfection through self-knowledge does not seem to marry too well with the more exalted idea of absolute control over our thoughts and, through them, over our actions, and seems in conflict with that for great achievements which are also expected of the generous, like using science to change the world.[92]

Generosity is both a passion and a virtue, a passion for virtue, which means that it is a self-sustaining virtue: it sustains and enforces itself in being exercised. Descartes defines virtues as "habits of the soul which dispose it to certain thoughts, so that they are different from these thoughts but can produce them, and in turn be produced by them." The same thoughts can be produced by the soul itself, "but it often happens that some movement of the spirits strengthen them, and that in this case they are both actions of virtue and passions of the soul" (AT XI 453, CSM I 387–388).

Descartes calls what he takes to be the highest virtue *générosité*, but it has little to do with generosity in our contemporary sense of the word. It is related to what the Scholastics, following Aristotle, called magnanimity *(Magnanimitas)*, and like the latter it seems so dependent on good birth that one could easily think that souls are unequal in this respect. Yet Descartes does not doubt that a good education corrects the defects of birth (AT XI 453–454, CSM I 388). It is the virtue of justified self-esteem, that is, "it causes a person's self-esteem to be as great as it may legitimately be," and it has a cognitive and a conative component. For it consists partly in the knowledge that nothing is truly one's own but the free disposition of one's volitions and that the use one makes of this freedom is the only thing for which a person deserves praise or blame. It consists in part also in feeling "a firm and constant resolution to use it well—that is, never to lack the will to undertake and carry out whatever one judges to be best." Having a good will in this sense—being committed to do always the best one can—is to "pursue virtue in a perfect manner" (AT XI 446, CSM I 384).

The object of the knowledge of which this virtue consists is my power of free choice and the use I make of it, and the corresponding passion is the firm resolution to use that power well. Descartes insists that "the exercise of our free choice *(libre arbitre)* and the power we have over our volitions" is the only thing for which we deserve praise or blame: "For we can reasonably be praised or blamed only for actions that depend of this free choice, and it makes us in some way like God in making us masters of ourselves, provided we do not lose the rights it gives us through cowardice *(lâcheté)*" (AT XI 445, CSM I 438).[93] God-like, again, yet human: we have a divine-like power that we are prone to lose as soon as we cease to work on keeping it. This is a familiar idea for philosophers, though Descartes insists, more heavily perhaps than any of his predecessors, on the likeness we bear to God, while he locates this likeness in a power that we as humans are most likely to misuse.[94]

I have translated *lâcheté* literally as cowardice in the above quote, where CMS uses "timidity" and Voss, with hesitation, "laziness."[95] Neither translation captures the weight of the burden that the freedom Descartes invokes places on us. It is a moral obligation to use that freedom, which is a hard thing to do and requires constant attention and commitment to one's duty as a responsible human agent. Relaxing just for a while, and fooling oneself that one understands and knows what to do when one has not searched enough, is not unnatural, yet it is cowardly, given the power one has been endowed with to refrain from giving in to present inclinations too early, before full clarity has been reached, or to know there is nothing further to be done to reach it. When deciding what to do one must follow one's best judgment, even while fully aware that it may not be the right thing to do.

The recognition of our fallibility and of the frailty of the power that alone constitutes a legitimate ground for praise or blame is an essential part of this virtue. True generosity never comes without humility (or tolerance, or readiness to forgive), for humility consists in recognizing one's past errors and one's liability to future errors and, thereby, in the awareness of one's finitude and limits. Since everyone has the same power to use her free choice well or badly, and it depends only on oneself, there is nothing one can take pride in or brag about that others are not able to possess as much or more of, for nothing else depends wholly on oneself.[96] Generosity thus protects us both from vicious humility and false pride or vanity *(orgueil)* and serves as a general cure against all other passions as well.

How, then, can the virtue-passion of generosity be acquired and how is it supposed to work in the regulation of other passions (art. 156 (AT XI 447–448, CSM I 385))? It has, as we saw, a cognitive component consisting in the knowledge *that* we have a power of free choice and the knowledge of *how* we use it, and a conative or volitional component consisting in the constant will to use it as best we know how, and also in the feeling using it well produces in us. It is on account of the latter that it is classified as a passion. An essential element of a passion is the bodily movements causing and accompanying it. Although the movements of generosity and humility, which are virtues, are less apparent, they also have their characteristic bodily causes and effects. There is, Descartes says, no reason to suppose that the movement of the spirits that serves to strengthen badly founded passions like false pride or vicious humility could not serve to strengthen a passion that is well founded as well. False pride, like generosity, consists in the good opinion we have of ourselves, but it differs from generosity in that it has no reasonable basis, while it is justified in the case of the generous person's self-esteem. The movements accompanying the two kinds of self-esteem are the same (as, I presume, are the outward posture and gestures).[97] The movements of generosity are composed of those of wonder (of which self-esteem is a species), of joy, and of love ("self-love as much as love for the cause of self-esteem"), passions that make it up. The movements causing wonder are of two kinds: the first are caused by a sudden surprise and hence are vigorous from the start, while the second continue in a uniform way. Those of generosity are characteristically of the latter kind: they are "firm, constant and always very similar to each other." However, their object and first causes ("the power to make use of our free choice, which causes us to value ourselves, and the infirmities of the subject who has this power, which cause us not to esteem ourselves too highly") are so "marvelous" that each time we think of them they are a source of new wonder (AT XI 452–453, CSM I 387). Thus all the bodily movements accompanying the passions out of which generosity is composed contribute to causing, reinforcing, and sustaining the passion that disposes the soul to the good will in which the corresponding virtue consists. What starts out as a deliberately willed commitment grows into a firm and steady disposition or habit. The more vigorous and the steadier the motions sustaining it, the less likely it is to be overthrown by less well grounded passions, and in this sense it can fulfill the role of their moderator and master. It gets additional support, presumably, from the pleasure it gives, as other interior, self-generated emotions do. Descartes wants to persuade us that if one lives so "that his conscience cannot reproach him for ever failing to do something he judges to be the best (which is what I here call 'pursuing virtue'), he will receive from this a satisfaction which has such a power to make him happy that the most violent assaults from the passions will never have sufficient power to disturb the tranquillity of his soul" (AT XI 441, CSM I 382).

Earlier some doubts were raised concerning the power Descartes attributes to reason in the battle against the passions. It now appears that Cartesian reason can get support from the passions themselves in its endeavor to master them—support, moreover, from a passion that is also a virtue depending only on ourselves, and this may go some ways toward answering those doubts. Reason is not an independent operator acting as it were from above on the passions of the body; it is embodied in the passionate will and, because of the corporeal movements sustaining the will, in the body itself. Many other questions remain unanswered—some of them particular to the Cartesian theory, others shared with virtue theories in general. Among the latter is the question of how one would instill in oneself a passion for virtue if that is not where one's will—or reason—is already directed. Among the former is what an agent is doing with her freedom of choice if she were to refuse to follow the light of her intellect (and so demonstrate her freedom), unless one is prepared to accept the perplexing conclusion that this lengthy discussion suggests, namely, nothing. For the deliberate rejection of clear and distinct perceptions cannot in the end be described as doing something, since it does not fit the description of (rational) agency or action as usually understood.

It is worth dwelling on why this is so perplexing. Doing nothing in this context cannot be for Descartes just a matter of omission, of not using a capacity, for withholding an act in the presence of a strong inclination is, for him, one way of exercising this capacity. Thus, in the famous second letter to Mesland quoted in section 5, we read that freedom is exercised at two stages: in the acts of the will before they are elicited, and after they are elicited (!). *Before* an act is elicited, freedom of the will entails indifference in the second, strong sense of power to do otherwise, but not in the first sense of indifference, where the reasons for and against are equal. Once the act of will is elicited, freedom involves no indifference in either sense of the word: the more reasons there are to determine us, the freer we are.

> For a greater freedom consists either in a greater facility in determining oneself or in a greater use of *the positive power which we have of following the worse although we see the better.* If we follow the course which appears to have more reasons in its favour *(in quo plures rationes boni apparent),* we determine ourselves more easily; but if we follow the opposite, we make more use of that positive power; and thus can always act more freely in those cases where we see much more good than evil than in those cases which are called *aidiaphora* or indifferent. (AT IV 174, CMS 245)

Our supreme perfection essentially involves a power to freely determine ourselves in the pursuit of the true and the good, which entails that we are also free not to be determined by the true and the good. This is described as a positive power, of which we need more in deliberately misusing or not using it, than when using it properly. Once the will has determined itself to the good, it takes less effort to follow it than it takes to oppose it.

Being able to do nothing can be taken in two ways. The doings we are talking of here are, primarily, acts of will: assenting to or denying a proposition, pursuing or avoiding whatever course of action presents itself as the right thing to do. In that context being able not to do anything means having the ability to refrain from eliciting any of the acts to which we are most inclined at the moment. We have that ability in all circumstances, whether we exercise it well or badly, or by cowardice neglect to exercise it at all. For any act of will, there is the possibility at the time of its actualization not to will. Whatever in fact we will, we are responsible for it because we could have not willed. We could have not assented to the thought that entailed the thought that caused the commotion which led to the action we now regret.

The idea comes from the Stoics, and it looms large—in different forms—in Augustine's writings on the will, as in those of his medieval and Scholastic followers who were uncomfortable with the Thomistic solution. But I do not know if anyone before Descartes took seriously the idea that the ability not to assent could actually be exercised over and against perfectly clear and distinct perceptions. It is not clear what exercising it in such cases (refusing assent to evident perceptions) really means, and this brings us to the second sense of doing nothing, which may be of some help here.

Doing nothing can mean doing something that turns out not to be anything—not to be anything one thought one was doing. This sense was touched on above, and it belongs to the Platonic strand of Augustinianism in Descartes's doctrine. Assenting to a perception that seemed clear enough (like Gassendi's idea of the soul as a rarefied body) but was nothing but confused is merely an illusion of doing something, and so is pursuing something thought to be good but that turns out to be of little worth or even harmful, like going for the poisoned apple. In such cases, the power not to act turns into not-doing-anything in the second sense—it is literally a turning to nothing: willing what is not. This may be unintelligible, but no more nor less than the much discussed case of the Fallen Angel or of Original Sin, which were often "explained" in terms of wanting to be God, wanting one's will to be like God's, unbound by any commands, putting up one's will against God's command, or if one prefers, against the laws of rationality. What can be said of the Cartesian God—that in him willing and seeing and making are one and the same—is not true of humans. Willing to be like God, humans find themselves willing nothing, because their will, unlike God's, does not make things (or truth). They are under the illusion of willing something, an illusion of exercising an ability they do not have, comparable, perhaps, to that of persons who think they are moving an amputated limb.

A last question to ponder is how it happened that one of the conditions for voluntary, and hence free, action came itself to be described as an action, something of which "voluntary" or "free" can be predicated and, moreover, of which unconditioned freedom is seen as an essential attribute. How did decision (*prohairesis*), which Aristotle saw as the cause of action, and one of its elements, assent, come to be considered as actions themselves, and the will or reason as agents, when they were originally introduced to explain voluntary action and rational agency? Does this internalization of choice and rational agency serve any elucidatory purposes or is it just a way of repeating in mentalistic terms the point that our volitions and commitments are in an important sense our own and that our moral actions depend on us in a way natural events explainable by causal or teleological schemes do not?

If it does not bring much new light on the phenomena of action and agency, studying the philosophical discussions of their conditions does tell us how, at different times, they have been conceived. The history of those discussions remains to be written. The question of how the relations between intellect and will have been seen is worth exploring more fully also for what it tells us about philosophical ideals and illusions. A most interesting theme to explore would be the various aspects in which humans have been taken to resemble God. For Aristotle the important likeness is in our capacity to use our theoretical understanding, and to think like God about unchanging truths with the independence *(autarcheia)* and joy such thinking gives (NE X). For Descartes, it lies in the will and the share we have in the infinitude of God's will. But since our intellect does not work as God's and is of limited extent, our will is the only thing we share with him, and hence the joys that come from using our will in a God-like manner do not come unmixed. It is a greater struggle for a Cartesian mind to be God-like than it is for an Aristotelian mind, and it does not come without anxiety because it is not evident what ends it should be used for. It is not an accident that the peace of mind and clear conscience brought by a good will have a higher priority than any other goods on Descartes's list of our blessings.

Notes

Preface

1. Gilbert Ryle, *The Concept of Mind* (London: Hutchinson, 1948), p. 8.

Introduction

1. For a defense of this view, see Richard Rorty, "The Historiography of Philosophy: Four Genres," in Richard Rorty, J. B. Schneewind, and Quentin Skinner, eds., *Philosophy in History* (Cambridge: Cambridge University Press, 1984), pp. 49–76.
2. Letter to Mersenne, April 15, 1630 (AT I 137, CSMK 21).
3. Richard H. Popkin, *The History of Scepticism from Erasmus to Spinoza* (Berkeley: University of California Press, 1979, 1984), p. 174.
4. Stephen Gaukroger, *Descartes: An Intellectual Biography* (Oxford: Clarendon Press, 1995), pp. 11–12.
5. Martial Guéroult, *Descartes selon l'ordre des raisons* (Paris: Montaigne, 1952); Margaret D. Wilson, *Descartes* (London: Routledge and Kegan Paul, 1978).
6. Margaret D. Wilson, "History of Philosophy in Philosophy Today; and the Case of Sensible Qualities," *Philosophy in Review*, PR Centennial issue (January 1992): 191–243, 208.
7. Wilson may not have defended this view, but her statement suggests she sees no problems with it. See "History of Philosophy in Philosophy Today." In my view, progress in philosophical problem solving cannot be assessed, in hindsight, independently of the assumptions concerning goals and standards of present-day philosophical pursuits implicitly or expressly adhered to by a commentator. The exclusive application of those standards in determining what is relevant for understanding a

historical text, or for assessing what counts as a solution to a given problem, will be unavoidably whiggish. Second, although reading our present-day concerns into problems discussed by "the great dead" may be rewarding for some purposes, for example, in helping us articulate our own views better, it is not likely to further very much our understanding of *their* problems and concerns.

8. An illuminating illustration of this point is given by Peter Hylton in his discussion of Russell's concern with the nature of a proposition. See Peter Hylton, "The Nature of a Proposition and the Revolt against Idealism," in Rorty, Schneewind, and Skinner, eds., pp. 375–397.

9. Compare Robert M. Adams, who while stressing the importance of philosophical argument and critique for "historical understanding in philosophy," defends the historical approach adopted in his study of Leibniz along similar lines. He also points out: "Progress in philosophy is more likely to consist in understanding possible alternatives than arriving at settled conclusions. And we are familiar enough with the familiar; part of what the great dead philosophers offer us is alternatives to our usual ways of thinking.—Part of what we are doing in studying the history of philosophy, moreover, is placing our own philosophizing in its largest context in a conversation that has been going on for many hundred years. Just as we are understanding better what we are doing in any discussion if we accurately remember and understand how it has gone, so we are likely to understand our philosophizing better if our conception of its longer historical context is accurate." Robert M. Adams, *Leibniz: Determinist, Theist, Idealist* (Oxford: Oxford University Press, 1994), pp. 5–6.

10. Étienne Gilson's work, from the publication of the two parts of his doctoral thesis *La liberté chez Descartes et la théologie*, and *Index scolastico-cartésien* (both at F. Alcan in Paris, 1913) to his *Études sur le rôle de la pensée mediévale dans la formation du système cartésien* (Paris: J. Vrin, 1952), has been of great importance, as has the work of his students, e.g., Henri Gouhier, *La pensée religieuse de Descartes* (Paris: J. Vrin, 1924), *La pensée métaphysique de Descartes* (Paris: J. Vrin, 1962), and *Cartésianisme and augustinisme au XVIIᵉ siècle* (Paris: J. Vrin, 1978). For a recent study on Descartes's debt to Augustine and Neo-Platonism, see Stephen Menn, *Descartes and Augustine* (Cambridge: Cambridge University Press, 1998). The first lengthier study on Descartes's immediate Scholastic background is Jorge Secada, *Cartesian Metaphysics: The Late Scholastic Origins of Modern Philosophy* (Cambridge: Cambridge University Press, 2000).

11. With the exception of studies comparing Descartes's doctrines directly

with Augustine's. See the literature cited in note 10. Gilson's work on Cartesian philosophy and its antecedents is colored by his commitment to Thomism. The ideological distortions of the pictures drawn of dissenters from orthodox interpretations of Aquinas in many studies of medieval philosophy, and their impact on our understanding of the late medieval philosophers, are discussed by Bonnie Kent, *Virtues of the Will: The Transformation of Ethics in the Late Thirteenth Century* (Washington, D.C.: Catholic University of America Press, 1995), chap. 1.

1. From Methodology of Science to Philosophy of Mind

1. The important distinction in Descartes's cognitive vocabulary between two senses of knowledge as *cognitio* and as *Scientia* has been traced recently by John Carriero, who locates Descartes's use of *Scientia* in the Aristotelian tradition as a Latin translation of Aristotle's *episteme*. We can have cognition in the sense of a system of justified, doubt-proof beliefs without having *Scientia*, but we cannot, according to Carriero's illuminating reading of the Cartesian circle, have *Scientia* without knowledge in the sense of *cognitio* of God. *Scientia* involves more than proof or justification: it involves an understanding of the position of the epistemic subject itself as a knower in the general order of things, and this understanding requires cognition of God who created us and our cognitive abilities. John Carriero, "Cognitio, Scientia, and the Cartesian Circle," manuscript, pp. 11–16; see also Myles Burnyeat, "Aristotle on Understanding Knowledge," in Enrica Berti, ed., *Aristotle on Science: Proceedings of the 8th Symposium Aristotelicum* (Padua: Editrice Antenore, 1981), pp. 97–139.

2. This terminology, which is from Wilfrid Sellars, is a bit misleading, since Descartes never pretended his mechanistic picture of the physical world, like Sellars's "Scientific Image," was a true or exhaustive picture of the ontological furnishings of the world. The Cartesian world, early as late, contains minds, thoughts, and human beings composed of mind and body, which would belong to Sellars's "Manifest Image" only. I use the contrast to help myself to the idea of an unabridgeable gulf between the two, which was the long-term consequence of the introduction of a new mathematical and hypothetical mechanistic science of nature.

3. The reading here offered owes much to the work of Ferdinand Alquié, who more than anyone has drawn attention to the intellectual history and evolution of Descartes's thinking, but it differs from his in seeing a greater continuity between the views on mind outlined in Descartes's

early methodological writings and those that developed when he worked out his metaphysics. See Descartes, *Oeuvres Philosophiques,* 3 vols., ed. Ferdinand Alquié (Paris: Editions Garnier Frères, 1963–1973), vol. 1, p. 20, and vol. 2, p. 2; cf. also F. Alquié, *La découverte métaphysique de l'homme chez Descartes* (Paris: Presses Universitaires de France, 1950).

4. On the alleged circumstances of his encounter with Beeckman, see AT X 46–51, and AT X 162–163. He is so eager to express his gratitude that he declares in his letter to Beeckman, April 23, 1619: "If, by accident, something comes out from me which would not be despisable, you would be entitled to consider it fully yours" (AT X 163).

5. See Descartes's letters to Beeckman from the fall of 1630 (AT II 154–167), which do not give a flattering picture of their author.

6. Beeckman's journal reports that Descartes, whom he describes as very well versed with Jesuits and other learned scholars, had told him that he had never encountered anyone who applied (joined) mathematics to physics as well as he. Beeckman refers, in the same place, to himself and Descartes as "Physico-mathematici paucissime" (AT X 52). For recent accounts of the development of Descartes's scientific interests and of his relationship with Beeckman, see Daniel Garber, *Descartes' Metaphysical Physics* (Chicago: University of Chicago Press, 1992), pp. 9–11; Stephen Gaukroger, *Descartes: An Intellectual Biography* (Oxford: Clarendon Press, 1995), chap. 3.

7. To Beeckman, March 26, 1619 (AT X 157–158, CSMK 3). The translations of the quotations given are in general those of CSM and CSMK. Occasionally I have substituted some terms or formulations with what I believe to be more accurate ones. Whenever the translation departs from CSM without mentioning any other translators they are my own.

Descartes refers again a month later to the discoveries he prided himself on earlier (and all of which were not all that well founded) and to other genuine inventions with the compass, on which he will not give just partial reports but on which he plans to write some day a whole work, one that in his own opinion will be new "and not entirely despisable" *(novum nec contemnendum)* (AT X 163, CSMK 4). This indicates that Descartes already had some idea of a more general geometrical method in mind at this early stage. See Alquié, ed., *Oeuvres,* vol. 1, p. 42 n. 2. Gaukroger gives a nice account of how Descartes's work on proportional compasses led him to think about the theoretical foundations of their workings in the form of an algebraic theory, and to connect his own mathematical inventions to the idea of a *mathesis universalis,* which clearly preoccupied him at this time. Gaukroger, *Descartes,* pp. 92–103.

8. The first continuous text we possess is the unpublished and incomplete *Rules*, which is likely to have been composed in 1628 (some think between 1626 and 1628), though parts of it may well have been sketched out already in 1619. About the composition and dating of the text, see Jean-Paul Weber, *La constitution du texte des Regulae* (Paris: Société d'édition d'enseignement supérieur, 1964); Daniel Garber, *Descartes' Metaphysical Physics* (Chicago: University of Chicago Press, 1992), pp. 13–16, 313 n. 42 and references there given; J. A. Schuster, "Descartes' *Mathesis Universalis:* 1619–28," in Stephen Gaukroger, ed., *Descartes: Philosophy, Mathematics and Physics* (Brighton: Harvester Press, 1980); Gaukroger, *Descartes,* chap. 5.

9. According to Baillet between 1620 and 1623, see the texts quoted in AT X 191–203.

10. See Garber, *Descartes' Metaphysical Physics,* pp. 15–16 and the references given at p. 313 nn. 53–54.

11. Ibid., p. 15. Descartes himself refers in a correspondence to the favorable impression he made on his audience composed of the scientific elite in Paris, and of which Villebressieu, to whom the letter is addressed, was part. (The passage quoted is from a fragment that has been included in a letter probably from the summer of 1631, although the dating is somewhat unclear and the meeting referred to took place in 1628.) He claims to have convinced everybody, on that occasion, that "my principles are more certain *(mieux établis),* more true and more natural than any of those that are currently received among the learned," demonstrating thereby the fruitfulness and superiority of his "fine rule or natural Method" (AT I 213, CSMK 32). For his mathematical and scientific work during this period, see the excellent account given by Garber, *Descartes' Metaphysical Physics,* chap. 1.

12. AT X 214, ll. 10–11, CSM I 2; AT X 215, ll. 5–7, CSM I 3. In another remark "soul" *(anima)* and "mind" *(mens)* are used interchangeably: "I use the term vices for diseases of the soul *(morbos animi),* which are not so easy to recognize as diseases of the body. This is because we have frequently experienced sound health of the body, but never of the mind *(mentis)*" (AT X 215, CSM I 3).

13. See Descartes's correspondence with Beeckman, January–April 1619 (AT X 151–166), and September–October 1630 (AT II 154–167).

14. On Beeckman's interest and work in music, see Gaukroger, *Descartes,* pp. 74–80 and the references there given. Neither Beeckman nor Descartes were interested in compositional theory; their interest in music was mainly scientific and philosophical. Beeckman's own contribution was in acoustics and harmonic theory. In addition to a corpuscular the-

ory of sound, he was, according to Gaukroger (p. 74), "the first to offer a geometric proof of the inverse proportionality between string length and frequency." See also the introduction of Frédéric de Buzon in his bilingual edition and translation of René Descartes, *Abrégé de Musique— Compendium Musicae* (Paris: Presses Universitaires de France, 1987). As de Buzon notes, Descartes's theory differs from Beeckman's as well as from those of the influential mathematical Renaissance musical treatises of Zarlino (whose theory of harmony he basically reproduces but in a unified and much simplified summary) and Salinas in a number of ways. The most notable difference between Descartes's and Beeckman's physico-mathematical theory of music is Descartes's greater emphasis on the psychological and esthetic effects of musical sound, effects that he does not think are reducible, as Beeckman seems to have believed, to the physics of sound. De Buzon, *Abrégé de Musique*, pp. 6–7, 14–15. Gaukroger notes that Descartes, who mostly follows Zarlino, goes beyond him in one interesting respect having to do with the representation of the mathematical ratios in terms of line lengths instead of number, and in insisting that the proportional relation between the object (the sound) and the sense (of the listener) must be arithmetic instead of geometric because the former is simpler and hence easier (less strenuous) for the sense to perceive (AT X 91); Gaukroger, *Descartes*, pp. 75–76. Another noteworthy difference between Descartes's theory and Renaissance theories pointed out by de Buzon is the absence of any interest in linking musical harmonies to celestial ones. Descartes thinks of music neither as a reproduction of a cosmic order nor as a formal game but as an art of producing pleasurable effects on the mind by way of the senses. The emphasis in Descartes's theory is therefore on the properties of sound as they affect the human mind. These properties are not exhausted by quantifiable relations of pitch and rhythms or duration. Descartes also refers on the first page of his treatise to such nonquantifiable features as the "likeness" or conformity between the human voice and the mind *(spiritus)* to account for the fact that the human voice is of all sounds the one we enjoy the most. He also notes that because of the "sympathy and antipathy of passions" it is more enjoyable when it comes from a friend than from an enemy (AT X 90, ll. 1–4); de Buzon, *Abrégé de Musique*, p. 9 and ff. See also Tuomo Aho, "Descartes's Musical Treatise," in T. Aho and M. Yrjönsuuri, eds., *Norms and Modes of Thinking in Descartes. Acta Philosophica Fennica* 64 (1999): 233–248.

15. But see the interesting and pioneering commentary by Jean-Luc Marion, *Sur l'ontologie grise de Descartes. Science cartésienne et savoir Aristotelicien dans les Regulae* (Paris: J. Vrin, 1975); and recently Jorge Secada,

Cartesian Metaphysics: The Late Scholastic Origins of Modern Philosophy (Cambridge: Cambridge University Press, 2000).

16. Many important and interesting questions concerning the nature of the method itself and the relation between logic and Descartes's logic of discovery, which are central for the understanding of the *Rules,* are only briefly touched on, and mainly in the notes, because they do not belong to the main concerns of this book.

17. The first part of the *Rules* presumably date from 1619. The commentary to the first rule stresses, in an often-quoted passage: "For all the sciences are nothing but human wisdom, which always remains one and the same *(humana sapientia, quae semper una et eadem manet),* however different the subjects to which it is applied" (AT X 360, CSM I 9). The interpretation of this text poses numerous problems. It is clearly unfinished, the manuscript has disappeared, and we do not know with certainty when it was written. It is generally taken to have been composed around 1628, but to judge from the extant text, it seems based on, and perhaps also includes, earlier notes and drafts (cf. note 8). Yet it is of central importance because it is the only systematic exposition of the method to which Descartes attached so much importance. The fact that he never finished it poses many questions that cannot be pursued here. For different interpretations, see Garber, *Descartes' Metaphysical Physics,* chap. 2 and the references there given. See also Gaukroger, *Descartes,* chap. 4.

18. Baillet writes: "Un autre ouvrage latin, que M. Descartes avoit poussé assez loin, et dont il nous reste un ample fragment, est . . . Studium Bonae Mentis. Ce sont des considérations sur le désir que nous avons de scavoir, sur les sciences, sur les dispositions de l'esprit pour apprendre, sur l'ordre qu'on doit garder pour acquérir la sagesse, c'est à dire la science avec la vertu, en joignant les fonctions de la volonté avec celles de l'entendement." He also tells us that Descartes's aim here was to break new ground, but that he pretended to work only for himself and a friend to whom he addressed his treatise, referring to him as Museus, and who according to some was Beeckman (AT X 191). Later, in the *Discourse,* Descartes writes: "And it was always my most earnest desire to learn to distinguish the true from the false in order to see clearly into my own actions and proceed with confidence in this life" (AT VI 10, CSM I 115).

19. Rules Thirteen to Twenty-one deal with the application of the method in mathematics in which Descartes saw a paradigm of the method he was developing (AT X 442, CSM I 58–59). The *Rules* were planned to include three parts of twelve rules each. The first twelve rules explain the

central idea of the method and the ideal of science that it serves. They are, as hinted in Rule Twelve, meant to apply to what Descartes calls "simple propositions," which, as will be seen, comprise simple and basic self-evident notions and ideas of any kind. They also give us a picture of the epistemology and cognitive psychology on which the methodological project is based. The second set of twelve rules would explain the application of the method to mathematical subjects, that is, to numbers and figures. According to hints given by Descartes, the third set of twelve rules he had planned to write were meant to explain how to apply the method to the physical sciences. Descartes never wrote it. But it is clear that he thought the practice of the method on mathematical problems, which he describes as problems which although abstract are "perfectly understood," was most useful as a preparation for tackling those that he describes as "imperfectly understood" (AT X 428–429, CSM I 50–51).

It is a matter of dispute among commentators whether Descartes envisaged the reduction of the kind of problems dealt with in physical sciences, which are "imperfectly understood," to "perfectly" understood ones. By the latter he seems to mean well-defined problems where what is sought is a unique function of what is given, and which can be expressed in the form of equations. Did Descartes think, at this point or later, that all problems could be reduced to problems of the former kind? If he ever thought so, the fact that he never got around to writing the third part indicates that he gave up that idea. But it is not clear that he envisaged such a reduction—indeed, one is hard put to detect the use of a mathematical method in Descartes's physics. The nature of the method Descartes was searching for is discussed in Gaukroger, *Descartes,* chap. 4. For a clarifying discussion of the relation between Descartes's general scientific program (and programmatic statements at various times) and his actual practice as a scientist, see Desmond Clarke, *Descartes' Philosophy of Science* (Manchester: Manchester University Press, 1982).

20. AT VI 2, compare Rule One quoted above (AT X 360).
21. The original text has "induction" in the place of "deduction," but that seems to be a misprint. In the previous rule Descartes mentions experience and deduction as our only two ways to knowledge (AT X 365). Here, where he explicitly deals with the only two ways to certain knowledge, experience is replaced with intuition. Is this to say that intuition is considered as a kind of (mental) experience? Descartes clearly is not very particular about his terminology at this stage. Compare also Rule Seven (AT X 383). For Descartes's many uses of the terms *experientia*

and *experio,* see Clarke, *Descartes' Philosophy of Science,* chap. 2. As Clarke shows, the understanding of any evidence, including sensory, requires intuition for Descartes. Desmond Clarke, "Descartes's Use of 'Demonstration' and 'Deduction,'" *Modern Schoolman* 54 (1977): 33–44, reprinted in G. J. D. Moyal, ed., *Descartes: Critical Assessments,* 4 vols. (London: Routledge, 1991), vol. 1, p. 244. As I understand it (for instance, Rule Twelve), any experience has to be ascertained through intuition: only what is directly intuited, whether the object of intuition be sensible or purely intelligible, can be evidently and certainly known.

22. See, e.g., Étienne Gilson, *Introduction à l'étude de Saint Augustin* (Paris: Librairie philosophique J. Vrin, 1969), chap. 5 and the texts of Augustinus there quoted, esp. pp. 108–109.
23. The same point is stressed in Rule Twelve.
24. Stephen Gaukroger deserves credit for stressing the role of intuition and the novelty of Descartes's view of deductive reasoning in terms of intuitive grasps of relations between intuitively seen truths. But his psychologistic account of intuition and of the kind of conviction it carries seem problematic to me, and his arguments for connecting the Cartesian notion of intuition and the criteria of evidence to the rhetorical tradition also seem a bit far-fetched. See Stephen Gaukroger, *Cartesian Logic: An Essay on Descartes's Conception of Inference* (Oxford: Clarendon Press, 1989), pp. 118–124; Gaukroger, *Descartes,* chap. 4. A more natural point of comparison, I argue, can be found closer at hand, in the late medieval discussions of the role of intuition in evident cognition.
25. See Duns Scotus, *Quodlibetal Questions. Q.* 6, in John Duns Scotus, *Opera Omnia* (Paris: Vivès, 1981), vol. 25, pp. 243–244; William Ockham, *Ord.* I, Prologue, q.1, a.1, OTH I, pp. 36–37; cf. 27, q.3, OTH IV, p. 242. See also Douglas C. Langston, "Scotus's Doctrine of Intuitive Cognition," *Synthese* 96 (1993): 3–24; Marilyn McCord Adams, *William Ockham* (Indiana: University of Notre Dame Press, 1987), vol. 1, pp. 502 and ff.
26. For discussions on the difference between these notions and the judgments they produce, see, e.g., William Ockham, *Ord.* I, Prologue, q.1, a.1, OTH I, pp. 36–37; cf. 27, q.3, OTH IV, p. 242; Adams, *William Ockham,* vol. 1, pp. 502–506. For a discussion of some of the differences between Descartes's and his predecessors' use of intuition, see my "Intuition, Assent and Necessity: The Question of Descartes's Psychologism," in Aho and Yrjönsuuri, eds., *Norms and Modes of Thinking in Descartes,* pp. 99–124.
27. That Descartes was familiar with the distinction between the operations of simple apprehension on one hand and those of judgment and rea-

soning appears also from his Reply to the Second Objections (AT VII 139). Among the problems discussed in this tradition, which are not very different from the epistemological issues that Descartes's early account of cognition raises, but which he came to address later, are questions concerning the role of the intellect and the will in judgment, the nature and mechanisms of assent, the degrees of evidence, and the conditions of perfect intuition and evident assent. For a clarifying and instructive overview of Scholastic precedents of modern views of acts and objects of judgment, see the first two chapters of Gabriel Nuchelmans, *Judgment and Proposition: From Descartes to Kant* (Amsterdam: North-Holland Publishing, 1982). For a tentative comparison of Descartes's view on intuition to that of Ockham, see Lilli Alanen and Mikko Yrjönsuuri, "Intuition, jugement et évidence chez Ockham et Descartes," in Joël Biard and Roshdi Rashed, eds., *Descartes et le Moyen Age* (Paris: Librairie philosophique J. Vrin, 1997).

28. They were discussed by Duns Scotus, Ockham, Buridan, and their followers. For an account of the discussions among Ockham's successors, see Alexander Broadie, *Notion and Object: Aspects of Late Medieval Epistemology* (Oxford: Clarendon Press, 1989).

29. That Descartes had this tradition in mind is suggested also by Jean-Luc Marion, who shows that Duns Scotus's and Ockham's notion of intuitive cognition can be found also in Suarez (Marion traces it to the connection made by Aristotle between the intellect *(nous)* and the senses *(aisthesis)* in *Éthique à Nicomaque*). For textual references see René Descartes, *Règles utiles et claires pour la direction de l'esprit en la Recherche de la vérité*, trans. and annot. Jean-Luc Marion (The Hague: Martinus Nijhoff, 1977), pp. 120 ff. For Aristotle's distinction between *nous* and *episteme* or demonstrative knowledge, see *Analytica Posteriora* 100b 5–17; see also the discussion in *Nicomachean Ethics* bk. 6, 1139b–1143b, in *The Complete Works of Aristotle*, vol. 2, rev. Oxford trans., ed. J. Barnes (Princeton: Princeton University Press, 1984).

30. I return to some of these problems in Chapter 5.

31. For different interpretations of this rule and more generally of the method Descartes is taken to expound in the *Rules,* see Garber, *Descartes' Metaphysical Physics;* Schuster, "Descartes' *Mathesis Universalis*"; Emily Grosholz, *Cartesian Method and the Problem of Reduction* (Oxford: Oxford University Press, 1991); Marion, *Sur l'ontologie grise de Descartes.* One of the difficulties here is that Rule Four itself seems to be composed of fragments from different periods. What is noteworthy in the passage quoted in the text is that Descartes does not, as is often assumed, contrast ordinary mathematics to some more general mathe-

matical discipline *(mathesis universalis)*, but opposes the disciplines that treat of numbers and figures to a more fundamental one of which numbers and figures are not at all parts, but merely "garments." I take this to show that he must have had in mind something even more general and abstract than algebra or any other discipline operating with figures and numbers. The latter are illustrations, they make this more fundamental and general abstract "science" or "method" accessible, with the help of figures and numbers, to the human mind. Similar points are made, for example, in Rule Fourteen (AT X 438, and AT X 452). See the notes of Alquié, ed., *Oeuvres,* vol. 1, p. 98 n. 1, but see also the work of Schuster cited above.

32. There is little agreement on the dating of the different parts of this commentary—at least one part seems to have been written much earlier than the rest, probably before or after Descartes's exalted dream, and seems connected to his 1619 vision of a marvelous science. See Schuster, "Descartes' *Mathesis Universalis*," pp. 45–55; Weber, *La constitution du texte des Regulae.*

33. Both involve the application of the method to nonmathematical topics and are thus, presumably, offered as illustrations of a generalized use of the method. But since it is neither very clear what exactly the method they are supposed to illustrate consists in, nor what, if anything, the two examples could have in common, it is not easy to tell what they show about it. See, e.g., the discussions in Schuster, "Descartes' *Mathesis Universalis*"; Garber, *Descartes' Metaphysical Physics,* chap. 2.

34. See Schuster, "Descartes' *Mathesis Universalis*."

35. I understand the passage as in the translation by CSM, not as by J. Brunschsvicg; see Alquié, ed., *Oeuvres,* vol. 1, p. 135. Presumably, "what follows" means the next set of twelve rules.

36. That there is an obvious inconsistency between the method Descartes preaches in his programmatic writings and the practices he follows as a scientist is often pointed out, and scholars have been hard put to detect or trace his own application of the rules he recommends in the accounts he gives of his scientific discoveries and theories. See Clarke, *Descartes' Philosophy of Science;* Garber, *Descartes' Metaphysical Physics.*

37. What Descartes thought prudent to reveal and to hide on different occasions varied. Compare Garber, *Descartes' Metaphysical Physics,* p. 46.

38. He adds that he is going to explain this last action (of the understanding alone) "in its proper place." The reference is unclear. As to the workings of what is here called *ingenium,* it is described in the subsequent rules, in particular Rule Fourteen to Rule Sixteen. For a detailed discussion of the cognitive role attributed by Descartes at this stage

to the imagination and its representations, see Gaukroger, *Descartes*, chaps. 4–5.

39. *"Quod sponte obvium est"* AT X 411 (translated by CMS as "what presents itself to us spontaneously" CSM I 39).

40. "As we have already said, there can be no falsity in the mere intuition of things, be they simple or composed, nor are they, in this sense, called questions, but they acquire that name as soon as we decide *(deliberamus)* to make a determinate judgment about them" (AT X 432, CSM I 53).

    Frege distinguishes among grasping a thought or proposition, acknowledging it as true in an act of judgment, and asserting it in a sentence. See "Logical Investigations," in Gottlob Frege, *Collected Papers on Mathematics, Logic, and Philosophy,* ed. Brian McGuinness (London: Basil Blackwell, 1984), pp. 355–356. A thought is merely grasped in a question; its truth is expressly acknowledged or recognized to be true only in the assertoric sentence: "We express acknowledgement of truth in the form of an assertoric sentence" (p. 356). The mental acknowledgment of its truth is, for Frege, judging—the expression of the judgments is its assertion in a spoken or written sentence. Frege adds in a note that "it seems to me that thought and judgment have not hitherto been adequately distinguished. Perhaps language is misleading. For we have no particular bit of assertoric sentences which correspond to assertion; that something is being asserted is implicit rather in the assertoric form" (p. 356 n. 1). They were, however, distinguished and amply discussed by medieval logicians, and the distinction is reflected in Descartes's own account of judgment. The comparison of Descartes with his medieval predecessors or with Frege is problematic to the extent that it is not always clear that Descartes's objects of intuition qualify as bearers of truth value in the ordinary sense. For the simple notions, as we have seen, include a variety of things, and it is not clear that they always are propositional. They can be concepts as well as what Descartes later on refers to as "eternal" truths (the so-called common motions or axioms) or whatever, in a given epistemological context, can be an object of perfect intuition. For a fuller discussion, see Chapter 5, section 4.

41. For Descartes's use of these terms see the *Principles of Philosophy* (AT VIII 1, ll. 27–30, CSM I 212–214).

42. "Atque perspicuum est, intuitum mentis, tum ad illas omnes extendit, tum ad necessarias illarum inter se connexiones cognoscendas, tum denique ad reliqua omnia quae intellectu praecise, vel in se ipsi, vel in phantasia esse experitur" (AT X 425, CSM I 48).

43. "Omnem humana scientiam in hoc uno consistere, ut distincte videamus, quomodo naturae istae simplices ad compositionem aliarum rerum simul concurrant" (AT X 427, CSM I 49).

44. For interesting discussions of these questions see, e.g., Gaukroger, *Cartesian Logic*, chap. 1; Gaukroger, *Descartes,* pp. 112–113; Grosholz, *Cartesian Method and the Problem of Reduction,* pp. 8 ff.; Calvin Normore, "The Necessity in Deduction: Cartesian Inference and Its Medieval Background," *Synthese* 96 (1993): 437–454; Ian Hacking, "Proof and Eternal Truths: Descartes and Leibniz," *Proceedings of the British Academy* 59 (1973): 1–16.

45. Schuster, at one extreme, takes the earliest statements on the method as programmatic bravado more than grounded in actual practice, quoted by Garber in *Descartes' Metaphysical Physics,* p. 318 n. 5. See also Schuster, "Whatever Should We Do with Cartesian Method? Reclaiming Descartes for the History of Science," in Stephen Voss, ed., *Essays on the Philosophy and Science of René Descartes* (New York: Oxford University Press, 1993). Garber for his part is mainly interested in understanding "how the method of the *Rules* and the *Discourse* does and does not apply outside mathematics, to Descartes's larger program in metaphysics and natural philosophy," and does therefore not deal "in any detail" with "the connection between Descartes's method and his mathematics" (*Descartes' Mathematical Physics,* p. 318 n. 5). Garber takes the example of the anaclastic line in Rule Eight as showing how the method was supposed to apply to physics, and he also takes it to represent Descartes's "considered view on the method" (ibid., p. 320 n. 6; pp. 35–36).

46. It is not far-fetched to suppose that Descartes may have realized that there is no one common method applicable to all sciences, beyond, perhaps, the very general heuristic prescriptions presented in the four rules of the *Discourse on the Method,* and which, presumably, represent the core of the recommendations developed in the first twelve rules.

47. As suggested by Grosholz, *Cartesian Method and the Problem of Reduction,* p. 8. But see Clarke, *Descartes' Philosophy of Science.*

48. Descartes's opposition to syllogistic logic should not be seen as an opposition to formal reasoning. His algebra, as Petri Mäenpää argues, represents a new formalism developed in response to the failures of Clavius and others who worked on formalizing mathematics with help of Aristotelian syllogisms. Not only does Descartes's algebraic language represent the first proper and still actually used mathematical formalism, he also introduced a system of rules reducing a system of equations successively to simpler ones that is "essentially formal: it warrants the reduction of a system of equations of a certain form to another" by spelling out the form in terms of degrees of equation, its variables, and parameters. By reading Descartes's methodological descriptions of the *Geometry* and the *Rules* in light of his actual mathematical practice, Mäenpää shows that they can be seen as forming a coherent whole that consti-

tutes a genuine logic of discovery "in the sense of a deductive method of finding solutions to problems." The set of loosely connected informal heuristic rules constitute merely an epistemological description of the method itself, which is presented in the mathematical work as "the deductive mathematical system of algebraic analysis." Anticipating later developments in mathematical logic (Frege and Russell), Descartes relegates the formal rules from the epistemological to the mathematical level. Petri Mäenpää, "Descartes and the Logic of Discovery," paper presented at the workshop "Descartes: Mind, Method and Modalities," University of Helsinki, September 1966, unpublished manuscript, p. 13.

49. The role of the imagination in making the abstract algebra applicable to real problems of extended bodies is explained by Schuster, "Descartes *Mathesis Universalis*," and by Gaukroger, *Descartes,* chap. 5. I cannot agree however, for reasons developed in Chapter 5, on the epistemological role they attribute to the pictures drawn in the imagination.

50. To Mersenne, February 27, 1637, AT I 350.

51. I do side with those who, unlike Alquié, take the doubt of the *Discourse* to have basically the same intent and the same extension as it has in the *Meditations,* even if it is more developed and forceful in the latter text. See the notes in Alquié, ed., *Oeuvres,* vol. 1, pp. 602–604. I discuss Descartes's use of skeptical arguments in my "Cartesian Doubt and Skepticism," in J. Sihvola, ed., *Ancient Scepticism and the Sceptical Tradition. Acta Philosophica Fennica* 66 (2000): 255–270.

52. Apart from the letters of Descartes to Mersenne, April 15, May 6, and May 27, 1630 (AT I 144–145, 150–153), where it is first expounded, it is presupposed at several points in the argument of the *Meditations* (AT VII 62), for instance, and explicitly addressed in the Replies, first to Gassendi's objection (AT VII 380), in the Sixth Replies (AT VII 432, 435–436), and in the later correspondence to Mesland (AT IV 119). I have discussed this doctrine elsewhere, Lilli Alanen, "Descartes, Omnipotence and Kinds of Modality," in P. H. Hare, ed., *Doing Philosophy Historically* (Amherst, N.Y: Prometheus Books, 1988), pp. 182–196, revised and expanded version in "Descartes, Conceivability and Logical Modality," in Tamara Horowitz and Gerald Massey, eds., *The Role of Thought Experiments in Science and Philosophy* (Savage, Mass.: Rowman and Littlefield Publishers, 1991), pp. 65–84.

53. In spite of ingenious attempts, like that of Stephen Menn, to prove that it really is and was taken by Descartes to be an Augustinian doctrine, I remain persuaded, with Henri Gouhier, Jean-Luc Marion, and others that it constitutes a radical break with traditional Scholastic and Augus-

tinian conceptions of God, and I contend moreover that it also breaks, in significant ways, with traditional views of rationality. This is also how Leibniz understood it (cf. note 54). See Stephen Menn, *Descartes and Augustine* (Cambridge: Cambridge University Press, 1998), chap. 8, sec. A.

54. For Leibniz's own position, which he sees as the traditional Thomist one, and for his criticism of the doctrine that he attributes to some "Scotists" and to Descartes, see, e.g., G. W. Leibniz, *Essais de Théodicée*, 184, in *Die Philosophischen Schriften von G. W. Leibniz*, ed. C. I. Gerhardt (Berlin: Weidmann, 1875–1890), vol. 6, pp. 226, 614.

55. "Again, there is no need to ask how God could have brought it about from eternity that it was not true that twice four make eight, and so on, for I admit this is unintelligible to us. Yet on the other hand I understand, quite correctly, that there cannot be any class of entity *(in ullo genere entis esse posse)* that does not depend on God; I also understand that it would have been easy for God to ordain certain things such that we human beings cannot understand *(ut a nobis hominibus non intelligatur)* that they could be otherwise than they are. And therefore it would be unreasonable *(a ratione alienum)*, just because there is something which we do not understand and do not see why we should understand it, to doubt what we correctly do understand. Therefore we should not suppose that the eternal truths 'depend on the human intellect or on other existing things'; they depend on God alone, who, as the supreme legislator, has ordained them for eternity" (AT VII 436, CSM II 294).

56. I argue for this reading in the essays referred to in note 52.

57. It is noteworthy that although Descartes never changes his position or even wavers on this controversial doctrine, and presupposes it throughout his work, he never bothers to develop any explicit defense of it in his published writings. Having worked it out and propounded it in his letters to Mersenne, he addresses it explicitly only in passing, and when challenged, as in responding to the Fifth and Sixth Objections (AT VII 380, 435–436).

58. See Gaukroger, *Descartes*, p. 144.

59. See Descartes's correspondence in AT I 13–279 about his work and changes of project during his first years of retreat in the Netherlands, and in particular the letters to Mersenne from April 15, 1630, and November 25, 1630.

60. Gaukroger, *Descartes*, pp. 210–217.

61. That the interests that motivated the latter were purely scientific at this time appears from a letter to Mersenne at the end of 1632 (AT I 263).

62. He gives the reason for delaying the publication of this work in his letter to Mersenne at the end of November 1633 (AT I 270).

63. On Descartes's scientific work and contributions, see Gaston Milhaud, *Descartes Savant* (Paris: F. Alcan, 1921), and more recently Garber, *Descartes' Metaphysical Physics,* and Gaukroger, *Descartes.* As it unfolds, Descartes's account of nature, as many commentators have observed, increasingly takes the form of a philosophical *roman de la nature* than that of rigorous scientific treatment based on mathematical proof and inductive empirical evidence that a reader of his early methodological writings might expect. It also includes numerous assumptions taken over from the Scholastics physics that it is supposed to replace. See Alquié's introductions and notes to Alquié, ed., *Oeuvres,* vol. 1, and Descartes's letters to Mersenne between November 1633 and April 1634 (AT I 271–272, 281–282, 285–286).

64. For the first hypothesis, see Richard Popkin's influential *History of Skepticism from Erasmus to Spinoza* (Berkeley: University of California Press, 1979), chap. 9, esp. pp. 172–175. A recent example supporting the second explanation can be found in Gaukroger, *Descartes,* pp. 11–12.

65. See Hiram Caton, *The Origins of Subjectivity: An Essay on Descartes* (New Haven: Yale University Press, 1973).

66. I have discussed Descartes's arguments for dualism at some length in Lilli Alanen, *Studies in Cartesian Epistemology and Philosophy of Mind. Acta Philosophica Fennica* 33 (1982), and in "Descartes's Argument for Dualism and Different Kinds of Distinction," in S. Knuuttila and J. Hintikka, eds., *The Logic of Being* (Dordrecht: Reidel Publishing, 1986), pp. 223–348.

2. The Mind as Embodied

1. The first mention of the small "treatise" he was working on at this time occurs in a letter of July 18, 1629, to Father Gibieuf (AT I 17, CSMK 5). That Descartes would have done nothing else than reflect on questions of metaphysics is hard to believe: his correspondence shows him occupied also with intense scientific work. See the last section of Chapter 1 and the references there given.

2. AT VII 17, CSM II 12. The full title is *Renati* DES-CARTES MEDITATIONES DE PRIMA PHILOSOPHIA, *in qua Dei existentia et animae immortalitas demonstratur,* and it was published first in Paris in 1641, accompanied by the Objections and Replies. The second edition appeared in Amsterdam in 1642 with a slightly changed and longer title, in which, notably the subtitle is changed to *in quibus Dei existentia, et animae humanae a corpore*

distinctio, demonstratur (AT VII xix–xx). Instead of proving the soul's immortality, the proof establishes the "distinction of the human mind from the human body." The French translation that appeared in Paris 1647 bears the title LES MEDITATIONS METAPHYSIQUES DE RENÉ DES CARTES TOUCHANT LA PREMIÈRE PHILOSOPHIE, *dans lesquelles l'existence de dieu, et la distinction réelle entre l'ame et le corps de l'homme, sont demonstrées* (AT IX x).

3. Most recently by, for example, Marleen Rozemond, *Descartes's Dualism* (Cambridge, Mass.: Harvard University Press, 1998); and Joseph Almog, *What Am I? Descartes and the Mind–Body Problem* (Oxford: Oxford University Press, 2002), whose readings represent two almost diametrically opposed views of what Descartes's real distinction amounts to. See note 10.

4. Gilbert Ryle, *The Concept of Mind* (London: Hutchinson, 1975 (1949)), pp. 115–116.

5. Descartes's use of Aristotelian terms and formulas in accounting for the mind–body union is well known and amply documented in the works of French scholars. For discussions and different interpretations of the view that this terminology, borrowed from a philosophy he rejects, covers, see Étienne Gilson, "Commentary to Descartes," *Discours de la méthode* (Paris: J. Vrin, 1967 (1925)), pp. 431 ff.; Gilson, *Étude sur le rôle de la pensée médiévale dans la formation du système cartesien* (Paris: J. Vrin, 1975 (1930)), chap. 3; O. Hamelin, *Le système de Descartes* (Paris: Alcan, 1911); M. Guéroult, *Descartes selon l'ordre des raisons* (Paris: Aubier Montaigne, 1953), vol. 2; H. Gouhier, *La pensée métaphysique de Descartes* (Paris: J. Vrin, 1962), chap. 12 and following. For recent discussions, which examine Descartes's mind–body union in light of its Scholastic background, see Paul Hoffman, "The Unity of Descartes's Man," *Philosophical Review* 95 (1986): 342–349; Rozemond, *Descartes's Dualism.*

6. For a nuanced and lucid discussion of some of the differences between Descartes's account of human consciousness and the views attributed to him in Peter Strawson's *Individuals* (London: Methuen, 1949) (or to the "Cartesian strawman," as Annette Baier calls the defender of the views that Strawson attacks and to which he opposes his own account of persons), see A. Baier, "Cartesian Persons," reprinted in her *Postures of the Mind* (Minneapolis: University of Minnesota Press, 1985). See also, e.g., Robert C. Richardsson, "The 'Scandal' of Cartesian Interactionism," *Mind* 91 (1982): 20–37; Alan Donagan, "The Worst Excess of Cartesian Dualism," in A. Donagan, A. N. Perovich, and M. V. Wedin, eds., *Human Nature and Natural Knowledge* (Dordrecht: Reidel Publishing, 1986); Marjorie Grene, *Descartes* (Minneapolis: University of Minnesota

Press, 1985). But see also Margaret Wilson, who seems to follow Ryle and Strawson in interpreting Descartes's view of man as a strict and "robust" dualism and in insisting on the incoherence of this view. Although Wilson notes the exaggerations of Ryle's charges against Cartesian dualism and even thinks Strawson's arguments against Descartes can be challenged, she still considers their criticism fundamentally to the point. Interestingly, Wilson is aware that Descartes might have responded to the charges they raise by talking of the mind–body union as a third thing, but does not discuss this possibility. Wilson feels, incorrectly I believe, that Descartes "should have stuck to his guns," that is, presumably, to the two-subject dualism to which Wilson thinks he is committed. Margaret Wilson, *Descartes* (London: Routledge and Kegan Paul, 1978), pp. 206–220; M. Wilson, "Cartesian Dualism," in Michael Hooker, ed., *Descartes: Critical and Interpretive Essays* (Baltimore: Johns Hopkins University Press, 1978), pp. 197–211.

7. For a recent argument that he did not and indeed could not defend the mind–body union, see Stephen Voss, "Descartes: The End of Anthropology," in J. Cottingham, ed., *Reason, Will and Sensation: Studies in Descartes's Metaphysics* (Oxford: Clarendon Press, 1994).

8. It surfaces in Rule Twelve, and is more fully developed in the incomplete *Treatise on Man (De l'homme)* (AT XI 119–202) planned as an appendix to the unpublished *World (Le monde)*, which was written in 1629–1633.

9. In particular Discourse One (AT VI 81–93) and Discourse Four to Discourse Six (AT VI 109–147).

10. For a thorough and lucid recent discussion of this argument as well as of the problem the notion of a substantial union poses for Descartes, see Rozemond, *Descartes's Dualism*. I have discussed Descartes's use of the notion of a "real distinction" and defended his argument as proving a merely modal conclusion in my essay "On Descartes's Argument for Dualism and the Distinction between Different Kinds of Beings," in S. Knuuttila and J. Hintikka, eds., *The Logic of Being: Historical Studies* (Dordrecht: Reidel Publishing, 1986). The trouble with this line of argument is that it is not clear, in the end, whether the real distinction thus understood can be upheld. There are good reasons to question that the separability of mind and body is a real possibility, and some have recently been discussed by Joseph Almog, who bites the bullet and concludes that Descartes did not really hold that view at all. Descartes is not, as he puts it, an "existential separatist" but an "integrative dualist," and in the latter view the very conceivability of a particular mind presupposes the existence of the body of the particular person, although it allows for a separability of (formal) generic nature or "whatness" of

mind and body. See Almog, *What Am I?* chaps. 1 and 3. For my own part, I remain struck by the lack of symmetry between the two main attributes on which Descartes's proof turns, that of the mind, which is clearly and distinctly known only through the Cogito, which does not give much beyond the immediate certainty of its existence, qua thinking, and that of the body qua extended, whose nature and general properties we know and can prove a great deal more about than is the case with the mind, but whose existence we cannot ascertain without the help of God as a warrant of clear and distinct ideas. This means that I am skeptical as to the force of the Cartesian "real distinction": the dualism Descartes proves is not a substance dualism of which one could make sense using ordinary philosophical ways of understanding the terms "attribute" and "substance." Some reasons for this skepticism are given in my "Descartes on the Essence of Mind and the Real Distinction between Mind and Body," in L. Alanen, *Studies in Cartesian Epistemology and Philosophy of Mind. Acta Philosophica Fennica* 33 (1982).

11. Descartes's third primitive notion has been interpreted recently along such lines by, for instance, Janet Broughton and Ruth Mattern, "Reinterpreting Descartes on the Notion of the Union of Mind and Body," *Journal of the History of Philosophy* 16 (1978): 23–32; and Tad M. Schmalz, "Descartes and Malebranche on Mind and Mind-Body Union," *Philosophical Review* 101 (1992): 281–325. But compare Hoffman, "The Unity of Descartes's Man," at 339–369, and Hoffman, "Cartesian Composites," *Journal of the History of Philosophy* 37:2 (April 1999): 251–270. I turn to this question in section 6 of this chapter.

12. See sections 2, 5, and 6 of this chapter and the texts there cited.

13. What follows below is largely a revised version of my paper "Descartes's Dualism and the Philosophy of Mind," *Revue de Métaphysique et de Morale* 3 (1989): 391–413.

14. Ryle, *The Concept of Mind*, pp. 19–24.

15. Ibid., p. 154.

16. "A mind's reports of its own affairs have a certainty superior to the best that is possessed by its reports of matters in the physical world" (ibid., pp. 14, 154).

17. See, for instance, Anthony Kenny, "Cartesian Privacy," in A. Kenny, *The Anatomy of the Soul* (Oxford: Basil Blackwell, 1973), pp. 113 ff.

18. See *De l'homme* (AT IX 119 ff., CSM I 99 ff.); *Passions of the Soul* (AT XI 351 passim, CSM I 339 ff.); *Discourse on the Method* (AT VI 46–56, CSM I 133–139); *Optics* (AT VI 109 ff., CSM I 164 ff.); *Principles* IV (AT VIII-1 315 ff., CSM I 279 ff.); and "La description du corps humain" (AT XI 223–290, CSM I 314–324).

19. To Arnauld, July 29, 1648 (AT V 222, CSMK 358; emphasis mine). Cf.

also letter to Elisabeth, May 21, 1643 (AT III 664, CSMK 218). What this experience shows us and the sense in which it counts as self-evident is discussed extensively below, sections 3–8.

20. See, e.g., AT VII 228, CSM II 160; letter to Regius, January 1642 (AT III 493–503, CSMK 206–209); *Principles* IV, par. 189 (AT VIII-1 315, CSM I 280); *Passions* I, art. 30 (AT XI 351, CSM I 339). Compare Geneviève Rodis-Lewis, "Le domaine propre de l'homme chez les Cartésiens," *Journal of the History of Philosophy* 2 (1964): 157–188; and G. Rodis-Lewis, *L'oeuvre de Descartes* (Paris: Vrin, 1971), vol. 1, pp. 351–365. See also, in addition to the literature quoted in note 5, Jean-Marie Beyssade, "La classification cartésienne des passions," *Revue Internationale de Philosophie* 136 (1983): 278–287. The similarities between the Cartesian and the Aristotelian view of man are ignored by those antidualists who like to contrast what they consider a true "Aristotelian view" of man to the "Platonistic-Cartesian" view that Descartes allegedly held and that, insofar as it seems easier to accommodate to a materialist or functionalist theory of man, is also considered more respectable than the latter. See, e.g., Anthony Flew, *A Rational Animal* (Oxford: Clarendon Press, 1978), pp. 197, 207. See also Norman Malcolm, *Problems of Mind: Descartes to Wittgenstein* (New York: Harper Torchbooks, 1971), pp. 5 ff.; David M. Armstrong and Norman Malcolm, *Consciousness and Causality* (Oxford: Basil Blackwell, 1984).

21. AT III 660–661, 684, and AT IX 213. Compare Spinoza, who asks how a philosopher who would "affirm nothing which he did not clearly and distinctly perceive, and who so often had taken to task the scholastics for wishing to explain obscurities through occult qualities, could maintain a hypothesis, besides which occult qualities are commonplace. What does he understand, I ask, by the union of the mind and the body. What clear and distinct conception has he got of thought in most intimate union with a certain particle of extended matter?" *Ethica* Part V, preface. Spinoza seems to be echoing Descartes's own remarks on substantial forms in the letter to Regius, January 1642 (AT III 506, CSMK 208), quoted below in section 3.

22. Letter to Elisabeth, May 21, 1643 (AT III 665, CSMK 218). See also AT III 692–694, CSMK 227; AT V 222, CSMK 356.

23. AT III 693, CSMK 227. The real "scandal" of Cartesian mind–body dualism, I take it, is this problem of the conceivability of the union, and not, as shown also by Richardsson in "The 'Scandal' of Cartesian Interactionism," that of the interaction between the mind and the body. See section 7 below, esp. note 67. Compare Guéroult, *Descartes selon l'ordre des raisons,* vol. 2, chap. 17, sections 4–7. Guéroult thinks that Descartes,

while considering the union fundamentally unintelligible, does offer a partial explanation of it in terms of the finality of the union. This explanation, as Guéroult admits, is at best partial and limited, and poses problems of its own. Gouhier, on the contrary, argues that the real problem for Descartes is not to conceive the mind-body union, which is an immediate given of experience, but to conceive the real distinction between mind and body. Gouhier, *La pensée métaphysique de Descartes,* chap. 12. However, having produced, as he thinks, a conclusive proof of a real distinction between mind and body, Descartes certainly could not just fall back on the Scholastic doctrine of their substantial union and its finality as a solution to the problem of his critics. I find Gouhier's suggestion that Descartes would not have seen their difficulty at all quite implausible. Ibid., pp. 326–328, 364. On the contrary, as the quote referred to above testifies, Descartes admits that conceiving the mind and the body as distinct and at the same time as really united (one thing) is a logical impossibility.

24. To Elisabeth, May 21, 1643 (AT III 665, CSMK 218).

25. To Mersenne, April 26, 1643 (AT III 648–649, CSMK 216); see also letter to Elisabeth, May 21, 1643 (AT III 667, CSMK 219); letter to Arnauld, July 29, 1648 (AT V 222–223, CSMK 357–358); and the Sixth Replies (AT VII 441–442, CSM II 297–298). Cf. Gilson, *Étude sur le rôle de la pensée médiévale dans la formation du système cartesien,* Part 2, chaps. 1, 7.

26. Cf. Beyssade, "La classification Cartésienne des passions," p. 284. See also Gouhier, *La pensée métaphysique de Descartes,* p. 354. On the difference between the notions of "real quality" and "substantial forms" and their different explanatory roles, see Rozemond, *Descartes's Dualism.*

27. Descartes's only psychological treatise, *The Passions of the Soul* is, as has often been pointed out, a treatise in the physiology of emotions, and Descartes is conscious of treating the subject from an entirely new point of view, as a "physicist." See the prefatory letter of August 14, 1649, to the *Passions* (AT XI 326, CSM I 327); see also Chapter 7.

28. This picture, incidentally, has more in common with the program Hume and the empiricists tried to carry out: to develop a science of the mind based on introspection and aiming at the discovery of the general laws governing human thought and behavior by methods analogous to those used by Newton in discovering the celestial mechanics. See, e.g., David Hume, *Treatise on Human Nature,* ed. L. A. Selby-Bigge, rev. P. H. Nidditch (Oxford: Oxford University Press, 1978).

29. Ryle, *The Concept of Mind,* pp. 14–15.

30. Ibid., pp. 154–155. Compare Wilson, *Descartes,* p. 150.

31. Descartes writes: "[C]onsider that every night we have a thousand

thoughts, and even while awake we have a thousand thoughts in the course of an hour of which no trace remain in our memory, and which seem no more useful than thoughts we may have had before we were born." To Gibieuf, January 19, 1642 (AT III 478–479, CSMK 203).

32. On the differences and "asymmetry" between Descartes's notions of the mind and the body, see Wilson, *Descartes*, pp. 92–99; Alanen, *Studies in Cartesian Epistemology and Philosophy of Mind*, pp. 52–53, 64, 86 ff.

33. *Principles* I, par. 9 (AT VIII-1 7, CSM I 195). Compare AT VII 160, CSM II 113 and AT VII 176, CSM II 124. In Descartes's general use of these terms, "soul" *(anima)*, "mind" *(mens)*, and "thought" *(cogitatio)* are synonyms (AT I 36, AT VII 174, CSM II 123, AT II 36). For a more detailed discussion of Descartes's notion of thought and consciousness, see Chapter 3.

34. For a defense of this reading, see Alanen, *Studies in Cartesian Epistemology and Philosophy of Mind*, pp. 25–44.

35. For this characterization, see Wilson, *Descartes*, p. 151.

36. Systematically, once the hypothesis of the Deceiver has been overthrown and the rule of evidence established, all general principles and truths meeting Descartes's criterion of being clearly and distinctly perceived are on the same level and known with equal certainty (the nature and the existence of bodies included). See AT VII 78, CSM II 54; AT VIII-1 328, CSM I 290.

37. AT VII 335, CSM II 232; AT IX 205; AT VII 219, CSM II 154–155. Insofar as the knowledge of the nature of the mind is concerned, nothing much has in fact been said, and Gassendi seems quite right in characterizing the mind or self Descartes has discovered as "an unknown somewhat" (AT VII 275, CSM II 192). See Alanen, *Studies in Cartesian Epistemology and Philosophy of Mind*, pp. 30, 52–53, 60.

38. AT VII 80–81, CSM II 55–56. See also *Principles* II, par. 2 (AT VIII-1 41, CSM I 224); letter to Gibieuf, January 19, 1642 (AT III 479, CSMK 203); letter to Regius, January 1642 (AT III 493, CSMK 206). See also the discussions in, e.g., Guéroult, *Descartes selon l'ordre des raisons*, vol. 2, chaps. 15 ff.; Gouhier, *La pensée métaphysique de Descartes*, Richardsson, "The 'Scandal' of Cartesian Interactionism," pp. 32 ff.

39. A human being considered in himself is an *ens per se* and not *per accidens*, Descartes writes, "because the union which joins a human body and soul to each other is not accidental to a human being, but essential, since a human being without it is not a human being." To Regius, January 1642 (AT III 508, CSMK 209).

40. See also AT IX 176–177; AT VIII-1 22, 41, 315–317, CSM I 208, 223–224, 280–281.

41. To Regius, January 1642 (AT III 493, CSMK 206); letter to More, August 1649 (AT V 402, CSMK 380).

42. AT VII 81, CSM II 56; AT VII 87–88, CSM II 60–61; AT XI 430, CSM I 376. Cf. also *Principles* IV, pars. 189, 197 (AT VIII-1 315, 322, CSM I 279, 285). Cf. the discussion in Guéroult, *Descartes selon l'ordre des raisons,* vol. 2, chap. 15; cf. also Chapter 5.

43. The *Principles* was published in Latin in 1644. A letter to Huygens, January 31, 1642, announces the project of publishing soon a *Summa Philosophiae,* and in April 1643, he tells Colvius that he is working on its third part. See Descartes, *Oeuvres Philosophiques,* 3 vols., ed. Ferdinand Alquié (Paris: Editions Garnier Frères, 1963–1973), vol. 3, p. 83.

44. As suggested, for instance, by Schmalz, "Descartes and Malebranche," p. 286.

45. For references, see the discussion in ibid., pp. 284–289; Rozemond, *Descartes's Dualism,* chap. 5, section 5.5.

46. Such a doctrine would create more problems than it solves. How, for instance, would thoughts like sensations, if they were not modes of thought, relate to "pure" thoughts and other modes of the thinking substance? I here side with John Cottingham, who while justly noting the importance of Descartes's "trialistic" scheme in his account of human psychology, also stresses that Descartes never wavered about his fundamental dualism and never suggested that a third ontological category would be involved here. John Cottingham, *Descartes* (Oxford: Basil Blackwell, 1986), pp. 130–131; J. Cottingham, "Cartesian Trialism," *Mind* 95 (1985): 218–230.

47. Descartes opposes the Scholastic solution to the problem of the hylomorphic union that consists in treating the mind and body as incomplete substances in themselves; for Descartes they can be considered as incomplete only in relation to the human being that they together compose. See the letter to Regius already quoted and Descartes's answer to the Fourth Objections (made by Arnauld), where he explains how the soul can be both distinct from the body and really united to it and part of the nature of the whole composite that it forms with the body, by comparing it to the arm and the nature of the whole man to whom it belongs: "Now someone who says that a man's arm is a substance that is really distinct from the rest of his body does not thereby deny that the arm belongs to the nature of the whole man. And saying that the arm belongs to the nature of the whole man does not give rise to the suspicion that it cannot subsist in its own right. In the same way, I do not think I proved too little in saying that the mind is substantially united to the whole body, since that substantial union does not prevent our hav-

ing a clear and distinct concept of the mind on its own, as a complete thing" (AT VII 228, CSM II 160). It is complete in the special sense that we can know that it exists without knowing anything else. See also the letter to Gibieuf (AT III 474–478, CSMK 201–203). It is not complete in the sense of a fully self-subsistent Aristotelian substance, for instance, a man or a dog. For while the hand can be cut off and still remain a substance, it does not instantiate a natural form of an *ens per se* without the nature of the animal to which it belongs.

48. But compare the discussions referred to below in note 65.

49. Compare the enumeration of things that can be known with absolute or metaphysical certainty given in the *Principles* IV, art. 206, which includes mathematical demonstrations, the knowledge that material things exist, and "all evident reasonings about material things" (AT VIII-1 328–329, CSM I 290–291).

50. *"Qui quidem etiam clare percipi possunt, si accurate caveamus, ne quid amplius de iis judicemus, quam id praecise, quod in perceptione nostra continetur, et cujus intime conscii sumus"* (*Principles* I, par. 66 (AT VIII-1 32, CSM I 216)). See also *Principles* I, par. 46 (AT VIII-1 22, CSM I 208) and par. 68 (AT VIII-1 34, CSM I 218).

51. Gouhier, *La pensée métaphysique de Descartes,* pp. 342, 340 n. 58; compare Hamelin, *Le système de Descartes,* p. 279.

52. See the discussion in Gilson, *Étude sur le rôle de la pensée médiévale,* p. 249. I return to this question in Chapter 5 in discussing clearness and distinctness.

53. Compare *Principles* II, par. 3 (AT VIII-1 41, CSM I 223–224).

54. *"Qui quidem etiam clare percipi possunt, si accurate caveamus, ne quid amplius de iis judicemus, quam id praecise, quod in perceptione nostra continetur, et cujus intime conscii sumus"* (*Principles* I, par. 66 (AT VIII-1 32, CSM I 216)). See also *Principles* I, art. 68 (AT VIII-1 34, CSM I 208, 218). The French translation has *connaissance claire et distincte,* where the Latin has "clearly perceived": I suspect it was Descartes's view that these things can only be clearly perceived but not distinctly. AT IX-2 55. Cf. AT VII 81–82, CSM II 56–57; AT VIII-1 41, CSM I 223–224.

55. *New Essays on Human Understanding* (hereafter NE) II, xxix, par. 4, pp. 255 ff., par. 8, p. 258. I have used C. I. Gerhardt, ed., *Die Philosophischen Schriften von Gottfried Wilhelm Leibniz* (Hildesheim: Georg Olms, 1960), vol. 5; and G. W. Leibniz, *New Essays on Human Understanding,* ed. and trans. P. Remnant and J. Bennett (Cambridge: Cambridge University Press, 1981). Page references are to the latter, English edition, which follows the edition by A. Robinet and H. Schepers of *Nouveaux essais,* published 1962 by the Akademie-Verlag of Berlin. For a helpful

discussion, see Robert Brandom, "Leibniz and Degrees of Perception," *Journal of the History of Philosophy* 19 (1981): 454.

56. NE II, xxix, par. 4, p. 255. Similarly, we can be said to know clearly and without any doubt if a poem or work of art is good or not, because "there is a *je ne sais quoi*" that we find pleasing or shocking, without being able to explain, exactly, what it is. But an assayer who can distinguish true gold from an imitation by certain proofs or marks that constitute the definition of gold has not only a clear but also a distinct knowledge of gold; his idea of gold is both clear and distinct. See "Meditation on Knowledge, Truth, and Ideas," in Leibniz, *Philosophical Papers and Letters,* ed. and trans. L. E. Loemker (Dordrecht: Reidel Publishing, 1969), pp. 291–295; Brandom, "Leibniz and Degrees of Perception," p. 454.

57. AT VII 82, CSM II 56–57; AT VIII-1 41, CSM I 224.

58. On the contrary, that clearness does not entail transparency is clear from many of Descartes's remarks about the passions. Thus, for instance, the persons who are most agitated by their passions are not the ones who can be said to know them best. See Chapter 6.

59. For the view that the confusion of sensory perceptions is conceptual, see Norman Malcolm, *Thought and Knowledge* (Ithaca: Cornell University Press, 1977), p. 48. See also the discussion in Guéroult, vol. 2, pp. 134–139, 191 ff., and the references there given. I discuss Malcolm's suggestion in Chapter 3.

60. It is of the most confused and unintelligible thoughts or states of mind, namely the passions, that all good and evil in life depends, "so that persons whom the passions can move most deeply are capable of enjoying the sweetest pleasures of this life." AT XI 488, CSM I 404; see also AT XI 441–442, CSM I 381–382. Concerning the confusion characterizing emotional states and its causes, see Descartes's correspondence, in particular the letters to Chanut, February 1, 1647 (AT IV 600–617, CSMK 305–313), and June 6, 1647 (AT V 52, CSM I 320). On the part played by the body and the emotional states caused by the body in our mental and moral life, see François Azouvi, "Le rôle du corps chez Descartes," *Revue de Métaphysique et de Morale* (1978): 1–23.

61. Rozemond, *Descartes's Dualism,* p. 173.

62. Armstrong and Malcolm, *Consciousness and Causality,* pp. 100–101.

63. See the letter to Chanut, February 1, 1647 (AT IV 604, CSMK 307), and *Passions* I, art. 41 (AT XI 360, CSM I 343), where it is assumed that every thought leaves some cerebral trace and is also joined, by nature and habit, to some movements in the brain and where the power of the soul to control and master the passions is made to depend on this fact. A dif-

ferent reading is defended by Wilson, who stresses the differences between Descartes's own "robust" and antiquated dualism and some modern versions of Cartesian dualism in this respect. Descartes, according to Wilson, not only denied the identity of mental and bodily states but also excluded any correlation between those mental states Descartes calls purely intellectual acts and capacities and any physical, cerebral states. The exercise of pure understanding, for instance thinking of God or of the mind in itself, is, she claims, "carried on independently of all physical processes; any physiological study will necessarily be irrelevant to it." Wilson, *Descartes*, p. 181, and Wilson, "Cartesian Dualism," pp. 197–211. She, undoubtedly, is right in insisting that the scientific account of the brain and the physiological correlates would be considered by Descartes completely irrelevant to the understanding of the acts and states of the mind *qua* mental acts and states. But I think Wilson exaggerates the contrast between what she calls historical and "contemporary" Cartesian dualism, and the evidence that Descartes held that the acts of the pure intellect, in the mind's present embodied states, actually could occur without any physiological correlates, is inconclusive. Cf. Alanen, *Studies in Cartesian Epistemology and Philosophy of Mind*, pp. 16–17.

64. Norman Malcolm, "Descartes' Proof That He Is Essentially a Non-Material Thing," in Malcolm, *Thought and Knowledge*, pp. 54–84. Compare Alanen, "On Descartes's Argument for Dualism," pp. 232–236.

65. See the Fourth Objections and Descartes's reply quoted above in note 47. See also Gouhier, *La pensée métaphysique de Descartes*, pp. 323 ff.

66. See Daisie Radner, "Descartes' Notion of the Union of Mind and Body," *Journal of the History of Philosophy* 19 (1971): 159–170; Janet Broughton and Ruth Mattern, "Reinterpreting Descartes on the Notion of the Union of Mind and Body." But see also Daniel Garber, who argues that Descartes's third primitive notion constitutes a philosophically respectable solution to the problem of interaction, but that it is nevertheless unsatisfactory as an answer to Elisabeth's question because it is in fact applied by Descartes to all forms, also physical causality, and is hence not specific to the domain of the mind–body union. See Garber, "Understanding Interaction: What Descartes Should Have Told Elisabeth," *Southern Journal of Philosophy* 21 (1983): 15–32.

67. Compare Gouhier, *La pensée métaphysique de Descartes*, pp. 326 ff.; Richardsson, "The 'Scandal' of Cartesian Interactionism," and Donagan, "The Worst Excess of Cartesian Dualism," p. 316; and above in note 23.

68. Gouhier, *La pensée métaphysique de Descartes*, pp. 351–354; Radner, "Descartes' Notion of the Union of Mind and Body."

69. In Gouhier's words: "une science positive des rapports de l'âme et du corps." Cf. Gouhier, *La pensée métaphysique de Descartes,* p. 344.
70. Donald Davidson, "Mental Events," in D. Davidson, *Essays on Actions and Events* (Oxford: Clarendon Press, 1980), p. 213.
71. Beyssade, "La classification cartésienne des passions."
72. Compare Guéroult, who thinks that what we can have in this domain is, at best, a substitute for science. See the Sixth Meditation and Guéroult's comments to it in *Descartes selon l'ordre des raisons,* vol. 2, chap. 20.
73. Maurice Merleau-Ponty, *L'Union de l'âme et du corps chez Malebranche, Biran et Bergson,* ed. Jean Deprun (Paris: Librairie philosophique J. Vrin, 1978), p. 15.
74. See, for instance, the reservations expressed by Descartes concerning the possibility to clearly know and detail passions and emotional states in his letters to Chanut, February 1, 1647 (AT IV 605–606, CSMK 308), and June 1647 (AT V 57, CSMK 322). Compare also the correspondence with Elisabeth.
75. "It is the ordinary course of life and conversation, and abstention from meditation and from the study of things which exercise the imagination, that teaches us how to conceive the union of the soul and the body" (letter to Elisabeth, June 28, 1643 (AT II 692, CSMK 227)).
76. AT II 694, CSMK 228. Cf. the letter to Arnauld, July 29, 1648, quoted above in section 2.
77. Compare note 23.
78. Aristotle, *Nicomachean Ethics* bk. 1, 1094b, in *The Complete Works of Aristotle,* vol. 2, rev. Oxford trans., ed. Jonathan Barnes (Princeton: Princeton University Press, 1984).
79. To quote Norman Malcolm: "[O]ur attributions of attitudes, emotions, feelings to people only make sense in relation to their interests, concerns, engagements, family ties, work, health, rivalries—and make no sense at all as attributions to disembodied minds, or to brains or machines." Armstrong and Malcolm, *Consciousness and Causality,* p. 101.
80. Quoted in ibid.
81. Cottingham, *Descartes,* pp. 131–132.

3. Thought, Consciousness, and Language

1. *"Cogitationis nomine intelligo illa omnia, quae nobis consciis in nobis fiunt, quatenus eorum in nobis conscientia est: Atque ita non modo intelligere, velle, imaginari, sed etiam sentire, idem est hic quod cogitare"* (*Principles* I, par. 9 (AT VIII-1 7, CSM I 195)). Cottingham renders the Latin *conscius* as "being aware of" and *conscientia* as "awareness." The French text uses *"apercevoir immediatement"* (AT IX-2 28). In the definitions given at the end of the

Second Replies, the stress is on the immediacy of the awareness: "I use this term to include everything that is within us in such a way that we are immediately aware of it. Thus all the operations of the will, the intellect and the senses are thoughts. I say 'immediately' so as to exclude the consequences of thoughts; a voluntary movement, for example, originates in a thought but is not itself a thought" (AT VII 160, CSM II 113). In the Third Replies the acts of thoughts are contrasted to those of the body as falling under the "common concept of thought, or perception or consciousness" *(qui omnes sub ratione communi cogitationis, sive perceptionis, sive conscientiae, conveniunt)* (AT VII 176, CSM II 124).

2. Descartes held himself the first to assert that the soul or the mind consists only in thought or the faculty of thinking, and this, I believe, is one of the few cases where his claims to originality are fully justified. See AT VIII-1 2, 347. Compare David Hamlyn, *Metaphysics* (Cambridge: Cambridge University Press, 1984), pp. 163, 167.

3. Robert McRae notes that there are three main senses of "idea" to be found among Descartes's successors, all of which can be traced to Descartes's writings: idea as an *object*, idea as an *act*, and idea as a *disposition*. The first is the one used by Malebranche, Locke, and Berkeley, the second by Spinoza and Arnauld, and the third by Leibniz, according to McRae. See R. McRae, " 'Idea' as a Philosophical Term in the Seventeenth Century," *Journal of the History of Ideas* 26 (1965): 176–190, 176. Compare Chapter 4.

4. They presuppose some stimulation of the sensory organs and, in the last instance, some agitation of the animal spirits in the brain. See Rule XII (AT X 416, CSM I 42); *Optics* (AT VI 130).

5. Many French scholars take this to be the case. Some understand Descartes to mean by thought what we in the twentieth century would call consciousness. Anscombe and Geach, for instance, tend to give "consciousness" as a general translation of Descartes's *cogitatio*. Descartes does use *"cogitatio," "perceptio,"* and *"conscientia"* as interchangeable in the Third Replies (AT VII 176, CSM II 124).

6. To Hyperaspistes, August 1641 (AT III 423, CSMK 189); letter to Gibieuf, January 19, 1642 (AT III 478–479, CSMK 203).

7. See Chapter 6, section 9 and references there given.

8. To avoid any associations to the contemporary talk of consciousness or qualia as a specific mental phenomenon, I will henceforth use the term "awareness" and "being aware of" instead of "consciousness" and "being conscious of" whenever possible.

9. See *Discourse on the Method* Part VI; the letters to More (AT V 278, CSMK 366; AT V 345, CSMK 374).

10. To More, February 5, 1649 (AT V 278, CSMK 366); letter to More, April 15, 1649 (AT V 344, CSMK 374).

11. See *Discourse* (AT VI 56–57, CSM I 140); letter to Newcastle, November 23, 1646 (AT IV 573–574, CSMK 302–303).

12. Many of Descartes's predecessors, notably Augustine and Ockham, certainly took this for granted.

13. For instance, Norman Malcolm, "Thoughtless Brutes" (1972) in N. Malcolm, *Thought and Knowledge* (Ithaca: Cornell University Press, 1977), p. 47; Zeno Vendler, "Descartes on Sensation," *Canadian Journal of Philosophy* 1 (1971): 1–14.

14. According to Zeno Vendler, Descartes was right in denying that animals do not have thoughts in the sense of propositional thought, but he need not have denied them all mental life. Although mental states like sensations, feelings, imaginations, pains, moods, melodies, and so forth do not have such content and do not, therefore, qualify as thoughts in a proper sense of the word, they still are felt or experienced and are, as such, attributable also to speechless creatures. Consciousness in this wider sense is not a property restricted to language users—it is common to all kinds of animals. Z. Vendler, *Res Cogitans* (Ithaca: Cornell University Press, 1972), p. 155; see also Vendler, "Descartes on Sensation."

15. He continues: "Such speech is the only certain sign of thought hidden in a body. All human beings use it, however stupid and insane they may be, even though they may have no tongue or organs of voice; but no animals do. Consequently this can be taken as a real specific difference between humans and animals" (letter to More, February 5, 1649 (AT V 278, CSMK 366)). See also the letter to More, quoted in note 17.

16. See AT VI 57, CSM I 140; and the letter to Newcastle, November 23, 1646 (AT IV 573, CSMK 302–303).

17. A couple of months later he writes to the same correspondent: "But I hope to publish this summer a small treatise on passions, in which it will be seen how I think that even in us all the motions of our limbs which accompany our passions are caused not by the soul but simply by the machinery of the body. The wagging of a dog's tail is only a movement accompanying a passion, and so is to be sharply distinguished, in my view, from speech, which alone shows the thought hidden in the body" (AT V 344, CSMK 374). Animals, differently from human children who have the same nature as adult persons, "never develop to a point where any certain sign of thought can be detected in them" (AT V 345, CSMK 374).

18. AT V 277, CSMK 365–366. Cf. *Discourse* Part V (AT VI 56, CSM I 141).

19. As he defines it, thought, in the contemporary sense of the word, covers

at least three related concepts. The first "is more or less equivalent to the philosophical idea of a proposition." The second covers the mental "frame": acts or states to which a propositional content is related, such as beliefs, hopes, decisions, desires, and so on. The third covers thoughts in the more general and vague sense of process of thinking about something or other, as in "to be engaged in or absorbed by thoughts." Vendler notes that these different senses are related, so that "the propositional sense of thought is presupposed in the understanding of the other two." Zeno Vendler, "Descartes on Sensation," pp. 1–14, 1–2. See also Vendler, *Res Cogitans.*

20. Instead of catching this distinction between the propositional and the nonpropositional, Descartes, Vendler complains, only sees a difference in degree between the clear and the confused. Vendler, *Res Cogitans,* p. 155. Compare Malcolm, *Thought and Knowledge,* p. 47.

21. To think, Malcolm claims, is broader than "to have thoughts," that is, to have "propositional thoughts." One can think, in an ordinary language sense of the word, without having "thoughts," without entertaining propositions. For examples, see Malcolm, *Thought and Knowledge,* p. 52.

22. Malcolm, *Thought and Knowledge,* pp. 47–48 and ff. Incidentally, this restricted notion of thought that, according to Malcolm and Vendler, sets apart humans from animals turns out to be a sense of thought that arguably can be applied to mechanical, automatic symbol processing. For reasons given below (section 4), however, it is highly unlikely that Descartes would have agreed that thinking in his sense of the word can be reduced to mechanical computation.

23. I will not, however, discuss Descartes's reductionist scientific program and its limitations here.

24. *Discourse* (AT VI 56–57, CSM I 140); letter to Newcastle, November 23, 1646 (AT IV 573, CSMK 302–303).

25. Compare the account given in the *Optics:* "[T]here is no need to suppose that something material passes from objects to our eyes to make us see colours and light, or even that there is something in the objects which resembles the ideas or sensations that we have of them. In just the same way, when a blind man feels bodies, nothing has to issue from the bodies and pass along his stick to his hand; and the resistance or movement of the bodies, which is the sole cause of the sensation he has of them, is nothing like the ideas he forms of them. By this means, your mind will be delivered from all those little images flitting through the air, called 'intentional forms', which so exercise the imagination of the philosophers" (AT VI 86, CSM I 153–154).

26. See the account given in *Le Monde* (AT XI 4). Compare AT VII 88; John

W. Yolton, *Perceptual Acquaintance from Descartes to Reid* (Minneapolis: University of Minnesota Press, 1984), p. 22. See also *Principles* IV, art. 189–198; Chapter 5, section 5.

27. Vendler, "Descartes on Sensation," p. 11.
28. Vendler, *Res Cogitans*, pp. 162 ff. What we have, according to Vendler, is first the mere experiencing or feeling of a "raw" sensation, something that can be had by animals as well as humans. As such, sensations, although they are felt, and hence more than mechanical movements, are not yet part of an individual consciousness. They are not objects of awareness, properly speaking, until some perceptual judgment like "I feel heat" or "I am tired" is formed.
29. Malcolm, *Thought and Knowledge*, pp. 45–46.
30. Ibid., pp. 48–49.
31. Compare the account of the complex ideas in Rule Twelve of the *Rules* (AT X 424–425), discussed in Chapter 1, section 5.
32. For a clarifying discussion of Descartes's positive account of sense perception analyzing his terminology and the different kinds of "projective" and "constructive" judgments occurring at the third level of perception, see Alison Simmons, "Descartes on the Cognitive Structure of Sensory Experience" (forthcoming, *Philosophy and Phenomenological Research*), and "Spatial Perception from a Cartesian Point of View" (unpublished manuscript).
33. See Gareth B. Matthews, "Consciousness and Life," *Philosophy* 52 (1977): 13–26, and the references there given. See also Chapter 6.
34. Noam Chomsky, *Cartesian Linguistics* (New York: Harper and Row, 1966), p. 4.
35. Ibid., p. 76 n. 4.
36. The thinking substance, as Chomsky interprets him, plays for Descartes the role of a creative principle alongside the mechanical principle accounting for bodily functions and motions. Ibid., p. 5.
37. Ibid., p. 78 n. 5, pp. 12 ff.
38. Ibid., pp. 31, 59.
39. John Haugeland, *Artifical Intelligence: The Very Idea* (Cambridge, Mass.: MIT Press, 1985), chap. 1.
40. See the enthusiastic account Descartes gives of his new method and its applications in the *Discourse* (AT VI 21, CSM I 121).
41. See Haugeland, *Artificial Intelligence*, p. 35. The rules involved, as Haugeland remarks in a footnote, need not be the same as the exact rules of logic or mathematics that apply only in the strictest contexts— for more ordinary thought or discourse " 'reasonableness' is more flexible, though perhaps still guided by rules" (ibid., p. 257 n. 16).

42. Ibid., p. 36.

43. I use "cognitivism" in the sense of Haugeland. See John Haugeland, "The Nature and Plausibility of Cognitivism," *Behavioral and Brain Sciences* 2 (1978): 218–260.

44. Vendler's definition of thought, discussed above at note 19, is typical. See also, e.g., Robert Cummins, *Meaning and Mental Representation* (Cambridge, Mass.: MIT Press, 1989), p. 19.

45. See John Haugeland, "The Nature and Plausibility of Cognitivism," reprinted in J. Haugeland, *Having Thought: Essays in the Metaphysics of Mind* (Cambridge, Mass.: Harvard University Press, 1998), pp. 36–40.

46. Thomas Hobbes, *Elements of Philosophy* (1656), *The English Works of Thomas Hobbes*, ed. Sir William Molesworth (London: John Bohn, 1839–1845), Part 1, chap. 5, pp. 29–30.

47. See Hilary Putnam, *Mind, Language and Reality: Philosophical Papers* (London: Cambridge University Press, 1975), vol. 2, chaps. 14–22.

48. An automaton, Descartes insists, would not deserve any praise or blame for its performances, since they depend on the state and disposition of its organs and on external stimuli, and, in the last instance, on its maker. See, e.g., AT VIII-1 18–19, CSM I 205; Chapter 7.

49. Cf. Alan Donagan, *Spinoza* (New York: Harvester Wheatsheaf, 1988), p. 40. The definition Donagan refers to is found in the Second Replies, stating that the term is used to "include everything that is within us in such a way that we are immediately conscious of it" (AT VII 160, CSM II 113).

50. Which is among the features referred to as essential for Cartesian thought, for instance, by Gilbert Ryle, *The Concept of Mind* (London: Hutchinson, 1975 (1949)), pp. 158–159; Matthews, "Consciousness and Life," pp. 13–26; and Margaret Wilson, *Descartes* (London: Routledge and Kegan Paul, 1978), p. 150.

51. For references and a more detailed discussion, see Chapter 2. See also, for instance, Daisie Radner and Michael Radner, *Animal Consciousness* (Buffalo, N.Y.: Prometheus Books, 1989).

52. Harry G. Frankfurt, *The Importance of What We Care About* (Cambridge: Cambridge University Press, 1988), p. 162 n. 5.

53. Ibid., p. 162.

54. Ibid.

55. Ibid.

56. See Donald Davidson, "Thought and Talk," reprinted in D. Davidson, *Inquiries into Truth and Interpretation* (Oxford: Clarendon Press, 1985), p. 158.

57. Ibid., p. 157.

58. See, for instance, the discussion by Alfred J. Ayer and Rush Rees,

"Could Language Be Invented by a Robinsoe Crusoe?" and Wilfrid Sellars, "Philosophy and the Scientific Conception of Man," reprinted in W. Sellars, *Science, Perception and Reality* (London: Routledge and Kegan Paul, 1963), p. 16.

59. One thinks of Augustine's *Soliloquies,* passages of which are construed as explicit dialogues between Augustine and Reason, or of his *Confessions,* which addresses God. See Augustine, *Confessions,* trans. H. Chadwick (Oxford: Oxford University Press, 1991).

60. Annette Baier has justly drawn attention to this in listing the awareness of a superior (perfect) thinker right after self-awareness as essential for thought ("Mind and Change of Mind") and she justly notes (in "Cartesian Persons") that Descartes, while downplaying the role of language for thought, emphasizes the importance of "that correctability by another which we post-Wittgensteinians find so essential to both speech and thought." Annette Baier, *Postures of the Mind* (Minneapolis: University of Minnesota Press, 1985), pp. 66, 78.

61. See *Principles* I, pars. 48 ff. (AT IX-2 23 ff., CSM I 208 ff.).

62. See the discussion in AT VII 44, CSM II 30; AT VII 232 ff., CSM II 162 ff.; Chapter 5, section 5.

63. Davidson, *Inquiries into Truth and Interpretation,* pp. 154–170, esp. p. 158.

64. To use the language employed in Rule Eight of the *Rules,* see Chapter 1, section 3.

65. See Chapter 1, section 8 and the references there given.

66. Descartes, however, differs from Kant in thinking that the authority of the norms of rationality is ultimately based on nothing other than that they are willed and ordained by God (AT VII 435, CSM II 293–294).

67. See, e.g., Augustine, *On the Free Choice of the Will (De libero arbitrio),* trans. T. Williams (Indianapolis: Hackett Publishing, 1993). Compare Chapter 1, section 3.

68. Articles 48–58 (AT VIII-1 22–23, CSM I 208–209). Later in the same text, the French translation adds: which "are nothing outside our thought" (AT IX 45). And the Sixth Replies stresses the point again: "Hence we should not suppose that the eternal truths 'depend on the human intellect or on other existent things'; they depend on God alone, who as the supreme legislator, has ordained them for eternity." They are efficiently caused by God in the way a king ordains a law, "although the law itself is not a thing that has physical existence, but is merely what they call a 'moral entity' *(ens morale)*" (AT VII 436, CSM II 294).

69. Wilfrid Sellars, "Fatalism and Determinism," in Keith Lehrer, ed., *Freedom and Determinism* (New York: Random House, 1966), p. 145.

70. Sellars, *Science, Perception and Reality,* p. 17.

71. Ibid., p. 6.
72. Ibid., p. 39.
73. This is not the place for interpreting Sellars, but I note, as an interesting question in passing: Can one be a conceptual thinker, according to Sellars, without being a person—or, in other words—would a being count as rational without being caught up in such a network of rights and duties? Or without seeing itself and being recognized as a member of some "we"? The question is interesting because it surely would exclude mechanical devices from such a community, and hence from the entitlement to count as conceptual thinkers, a possibility that many of Sellars's followers are keen to leave open.
74. Robert Brandom, *Making It Explicit* (Cambridge, Mass.: Harvard University Press, 1994), p. 5.
75. Ibid., p. 8.
76. Ibid., chap. 1.
77. Ibid., p. 10.
78. Ibid., p. 10. Naturalism here is not meant in the contemporary sense of physicalism.
79. The terminology contrasting regularity and "simple" regulism to regularism and authoritative norms is borrowed from Brandom, *Making It Explicit*.

4. Intentionality and the Representative Nature of Ideas

1. Thought and idea are sometimes used as synonyms. For instance, in the Latin edition of the *Discourse* we read *"de cogitatione, sive idea"* (AT IV 559). See also the letter to Clerselier, April 23, 1649 (AT V 354, CSMK 376). Descartes says to Hobbes that he uses "idea" to refer to what is established by reasoning (like the idea of "substance," which is inferred but not directly perceived) "as well as to anything else that is perceived in any manner whatsoever" (AT VII 185, CSM II 130). So idea can stand for concepts too, like that of God: "for by an 'idea' I mean whatever is the form of a given perception" (AT VII 188, CSM II 132).
2. CSM translates *subjectum*—the Latin for the Scholastic notion of matter or thing *(res)* of which a form is predicated or in which it inheres—as object, according to a modern usage. Descartes himself talks of objects of ideas in the definitions he gives in the Second Replies (AT VII 161). But he also defines substance there as the subject in which whatever attribute or property we perceive by a "real idea" immediately exists. See Definitions V–VII (AT VII 161, CSM II 114). The subject of thought here, however, is a real thing thought of.

3. Compare the letter to Mersenne: "[B]y the term 'idea' I mean in general everything which is in our mind when we conceive something, no matter how we conceive it . . . For we cannot express anything by our words, when we understand what we are saying, without its being certain *eo ipso* that we have in us the idea of the thing which is signified by that word." July 1641 (AT III 393, CSMK 185). What this "being in the mind" of an idea involves is discussed later.

4. To Mersenne, January 28, 1641 (AT III 295, CSMK 172).

5. See the discussion in Anthony Kenny, *Descartes* (New York: Random House, 1968), pp. 110–114.

6. Compare, on material falsity, Chapter 5, sections 4 and 5.

7. That Descartes thus can "make consistent (if highly metaphorical) sense of the wider definition of 'idea'" has not escaped Sellars, whose reading of Descartes's account of ideas is, to my mind, the most perspicuous offered by any contemporary philosopher or commentator. Wilfrid Sellars, "Berkeley and Descartes: Reflections on the Theory of Ideas," in Peter K. Machamer and Robert Turnbull, eds., *Studies in Perception* (Columbus: Ohio State University, 1978), pp. 259–311, 263. Descartes's account, justly so, is characterized by Sellars as a "proto-theory" consisting in "an extended system of metaphors" (ibid., p. 261).

8. Arnauld, who follows Descartes in identifying, generally, perception and idea, suggests a difference in emphasis between the two. A perception or idea is said to stand in two relations: "one to the soul which it modifies, the other to the thing perceived, in so far as it exists objectively in the soul. The word *perception* more directly indicates the first relation; the word *idea*, the latter." Quoted by Steven M. Nadler, *Arnauld and the Cartesian Philosophy of Ideas* (Princeton: Princeton University Press, 1989), p. 109. See also the subsequent discussion, ibid., pp. 128–129; Monte Cook, "Descartes's Alleged Representationalism," *History of Philosophy Quarterly* 4 (1987): 179–193, 187. For a clarifying account of Descartes's use of the term "idea," see Michael Ayers, "Ideas and Objective Being," in D. Garber and M. Ayers, eds., *The Cambridge History of Seventeenth Century Philosophy*, 2 vols. (Cambridge University Press, 1998), vol. 2, pp. 1063–1071, and the literature there referred to. See also Gary Hatfield, "The Cognitive Faculties" (ibid., chap. 28), on the Scholastic antecedents of Descartes's theory.

9. The distinction, in Searle's terminology, is between representative content and psychological mode, and it is reflected in his analysis of speech acts by that between propositional content and illocutionary force. See John Searle, *Intentionality* (Cambridge: Cambridge University Press, 1983).

10. See Edmund Husserl, *Ideas Pertaining to a Pure Phenomenology and to a Phenomenological Philosophy* (hereafter *Ideas*), trans. F. Kersten (The Hague: Martinus Nijhoff, 1982), vol. 2, par. 28, p. 54, and par. 33, p. 64.

11. "Each *cogito*, each conscious process, . . . *means something or other* and bears in itself, in this manner peculiar to the *meant*, its particular *cogitatum* . . . Conscious processes are also called *intentional;* but then the word intentionality signifies nothing else than this universal fundamental property of consciousness: to be consciousness *of* something; as a *cogito*, to bear within itself its *cogitatum*." Edmund Husserl, *Cartesian Meditations: An Introduction to Phenomenology,* trans. D. Cairns (The Hague: Martinus Nijhoff, 1973), p. 33. Compare *Ideas*, par. 35, p. 71.

12. *Ideas*, par. 38, p. 78.

13. Ibid., p. 79.

14. As Brentano notes, this same doctrine is also found in Thomas Aquinas's view that the object of thought is intentionally in the thinking subject. Franz Brentano, *Psychology from an Empirical Standpoint,* trans. D. B. Terrell (London: Routledge and Kegan Paul, 1973), vol. 1, bk. 2, chap. 1, p. 88.

15. Compare Nadler, *Arnauld and the Cartesian Philosophy of Ideas,* pp. 148 ff. and the references there given. Robert Pasnau notes that Aquinas uses the term *intentio* sometimes as the object of intellect's attention, and sometimes as a synonym of *verbus intellectus*. See R. Pasnau, *Theories of Cognition in the Later Middle Ages* (Cambridge: Cambridge University Press, 1997), pp. 134–137, and 259 and the references there given. Aquinas also speaks of the intentions of forms in accounting of sensory perception, and of the special intentions (of the usefulness or danger of things for the animal) apprehended by the *vis aestimative*, which are not sensory, and yet not, even when apprehended by the human soul, purely intellectual either. Thomas Aquinas, ST, I, Q. 78 a.3–a.4. A systematic study of the various uses of this term in later medieval theories needs to be made in order to trace the ancestry of the term "objective reality" that Descartes picks up. A very helpful overview of scholastic and humanist doctrines of the notions of *esse objective* and *conceptus objectivus* is given by Gabriel Nuchelmans, *Judgment and Proposition: From Descartes to Kant* (Amsterdam: North-Holland Publishing, 1982), chap. 1. For the views of some of the authors used at la Flèche, see Elizabeth J. Ashworth, "Petrus Fonseca on Objective Concepts and the Analogy of Being," in P. Easton, ed., *Logic and the Workings of the Mind: The Logic of Ideas and Faculty Psychology in Early Modern Philosophy* (forthcoming, North American Kant Society); and, by the same author, "Antonius Rubius on Objective Being and Analogy: One of the Routes from Early

Fourteenth-Century Discussions to Descartes's Third Meditation" (un-published manuscript). See also Roland Dalbiez, "Les sources scolas-tiques de la théorie cartésienne de l'être objectif à propos du 'Des-cartes' de M. Gilson," *Revue d'histoire de la philosophie* 3 (1929): 464–472, who traces Descartes's distinction between formal and objective con-cepts to Duns Scotus, as does Timothy J. Cronin, *Objective Being in Des-cartes and Suárez, Analecta Gregoriana* (Rome: Gregorian University Press, 1966), vol. 154, p. 206. See also Norman J. Wells, "Objective Being: Des-cartes and His Sources," *Modern Schoolman* 45 (1967): 49–61; and Wells, "Objective Reality of Ideas in Descartes, Caterus, and Suárez," *Journal of the History of Philosophy* 28 (1990): 33–61. See also below, section 7 and the literature there quoted.

16. See, e.g., Dagfinn Føllesdal, "Husserl's Notion of Noema," *Journal of Phi-losophy* 66 (1969): 680–687. For Husserl's view of intentionality and dif-ferent interpretations of Husserl's notion of content *(noema)*, see the in-troduction to the volume edited by Barry Smith and David Woodruff Smith, *The Cambridge Companion to Husserl* (Cambridge: Cambridge Uni-versity Press, 1995), pp. 14–27, and the literature there referred to.

17. *"Quaedam ex his [meas cogitationes] tanquam rerum imagines sunt, quibus solis proprie convenit ideae nomen: ut cum hominem, vel Chimaeram, vel Coelum, vel Angelum, vel Deum cogito. Alia vero alias quaesdam formas habent: ut, cum timeo, cum affirmo, cum nego, semper quidem aliquam rem ut subjectum meae cogitationes apprehendo, sed aliquid etiam amplius quam istius rei similitudinem cogitatione complectore; & ex his aliae voluntates, sive affectus, aliae autem judicia appellantur"* (AT VII 37, CSM II 27).

18. These metaphors constitute what Wilfrid Sellars calls "the extended sys-tem of metaphors that is Descartes' proto-theory of representation." Sellars, "Berkeley and Descartes," p. 261.

19. AT VI 38, CSM I 130; AT VII 37, CSM II 26. I return to the truth of ideas in the next chapter.

20. See Kenny, *Descartes,* pp. 96 ff., and Étienne Gilson's "Commentaire historique" to Descartes, *Discours de la méthode* (Paris: J. Vrin, 1967 (1925)), pp. 319–320.

21. According to Aquinas's version of this doctrine, when God knows things in thinking of His own essence as imitable by them, God knows them through ideas or archetypes that are purely intelligible. See Thomas Aquinas, ST, I, 15, 1 and 3, quoted by Gilson, "Commentaire historique"; and Étienne Gilson, *Index Scolastico-Cartésien* (1913) (Paris: J. Vrin, 1979), pp. 136–137.

22. But as Calvin Normore notes, something similar to the Cartesian use of the term "idea" for objects in the intellect (as distinguished from the

narrow Augustinian use of "idea" as exemplar in the divine mind) can be found already both in F. de Mayronne and Durandus of St. Pourcain, and, according to Normore, it also appears in Duns Scotus. Calvin Normore, "Meaning and Objective Being: Descartes and His Sources," in A. Oksenberg Rorty, ed., *Essays on Descartes's Meditations* (Berkeley: University of California Press, 1986), pp. 233–242, 232, and 235–236. See also the clarifying account in Nuchelmans, *Judgment and Proposition,* chap. 2, pp. 36–44.

23. *"Atque ita non solas imagines in phantasia depictas ideas voco; imo ipsas hic nullo modo voco ideas, quatenus sunt in phantasia corporea, hoc est in parte aliqua cerebri depictae, sed tantum quatenus mentem ipsam in illam cerebri partem conversam informant"* (AT VII 160). Compare letter to Regius 1641 (AT III 373, CSMK 183). It should be noted, however, that Descartes himself used "idea" for "figures" or traces in the corporeal phantasy in his early writings. Compare Chapter 5, section 2.

24. John Schuster, "Descartes's *Mathesis Universalis:* 1619–28," in S. Gaukroger, ed., *Descartes: Philosophy, Mathematics and Physics* (Brighton: Harvester Press, 1980), p. 60 and n. 90.

25. "The physical stimulus signifies the idea," as Yolton puts it. AT XI 4, CSM I 81. Compare Descartes, *Oeuvres Philosophiques,* 3. vols., ed. Ferdinand Alquié (Paris: Editions Garnier Frères, 1963–1973), vol. 1, p. 316 n. 2; and John W. Yolton, *Perceptual Acquaintance from Descartes to Reid* (Minneapolis: University of Minnesota Press, 1984), p. 22. Instead of perceiving the movements affecting it directly, the mind naturally interprets them—the interpretation, as I understand it, would consist in the mind's having ideas or sensations of a kind. Yolton describes Descartes's theory as a "reverse sign relation": ideas are not signs, they are the representing or interpreting of what the sign signifies. See ibid., pp. 26–27. Descartes tries "to assimilate physiological motions to natural signs, even though the signification relation in this case is not one of which we are aware." A semantic relation for Yolton is something between a causal relation and a purely occasionalist one. The notion of objective being, according to Yolton, marks the representative function of ideas and links it with the being of objects in the understanding. Ideas represent physical things by a natural relation in which physical motions are translated into cognitive functions (ibid., pp. 30–32). It is not clear why we should call it a *reverse* sign relation—could it not be, rather, a quasi-causal or semantic relation at a different level of consciousness?

26. Francisco Suárez, *De Mysterio Trinitatis* bk. 9, chap. 9, p. 5 (*Opera Omnia,* ed. D. M. André, 28 vols. (Paris, 1856–1878), 25:747), quoted by Normore, "Meaning and Objective Being," p. 235.

27. Normore, "Meaning and Objective Being," p. 236.
28. Ibid., pp. 225, 236.
29. Ibid., p. 237.
30. Ibid.
31. *"Quand on dit que nos idées et nos perceptions (car je prends cela pour la même chose) nous representent les choses que nous conçevons, et en sont les images, c'est dans tout autre sens, que lorsqu'on dit que les tableaux representent leurs originaux, et en sont les images, ou que les paroles prononcées ou écrites sont les images de nos pensées. Car, au regard des idées, cela veut dire que les choses que nous conçevons sont objectivement dans notre esprit et dans nostre pensée. Or cette manière d'estre objectivement dans l'esprit est si particulière à l'esprit et à la pensée, comme estant ce qui en fait particulièrement la nature, qu'en vain on chercheroit rien de semblable en tout ce qui n'est pas esprit et pensée"* (Antoine Arnauld, *Des vraies et des fausses idées* (1683) (Paris: Librairie Arthème Fayard, 1986), p. 45). Compare Nadler, *Arnauld and the Cartesian Philosophy of Ideas,* pp. 173–175.
32. Compare Alan Donagan, *Spinoza* (New York: Harvester Wheatsheaf, 1988), pp. 40–41, and note 42 below.
33. Normore, "Meaning and Objective Being," p. 238. A similar reading is developed in Nuchelmans, *Judgment and Proposition,* chap. 2, section 2.1.2.
34. For the emergence of this "modern" conceptualist view of modal notions, see Lilli Alanen and Simo Knuuttila, "The Foundations of Modality and Conceivability in Descartes and His Predecessors," in S. Knuuttila, ed., *Modern Modalities* (Dordrecht: Kluwer Academic Publishers, 1988), pp. 1–70.
35. See Chapter 1, section 8, and the literature there referred to.
36. The Latin translation of the *Discourse,* revised by Descartes and published in 1644, adds in a note: *"Nota hoc in loco et ubique in sequentibus, nomen Ideae generaliter sumi pro omni re cogitata, quatenus habet tantum esse quoddam objectivum in intellectu"* (AT VI 559).
37. See, e.g., Kenny, *Descartes,* p. 96.
38. It is noteworthy that the being or reality ascribed by Ockham to ideas is nothing over and above that of being thought of. It hence does not require any specific ontological category. See the text of Ockham quoted by Gilson, "Commentaire historique," p. 321.
39. Suárez, *Disputationes metaphysicae* II, 1, 1, quoted by Gilson, "Commentaire historique," p. 321; Gilson, *Index Scolastico-Cartesien,* par. 80, p. 49.
40. Gilson, "Commentaire historique," p. 321.
41. *"L'étonnement du P. Vatier nous montre que Descartes apportait quelque chose de nouveau en faisant du principe de causalité cet usage inconnu de la scolastique.*

Et, en effet, il n'y avait pas de problème spécial de la cause du contenu des idées dans la philosophie de l'École, parceque ce contenu, n'y étant pas considéré comme de l'être, ne requérait aucune cause propre. Ce désaccord fait le fond de toute une partie des objections de Caterus" (Gilson, "Commentaire historique," p. 322). Compare Alquié, ed., *Oeuvre,* vol. 2, p. 521 n. 1.

42. Indeed Arnauld seems to treat representation as one of those simple notions that are self-evident and cannot and need not be explained by any others. Arnauld, *Des vraies et des fausses idées,* pp. 44–46; see also note 81.

43. John F. Wippel, "The Reality of Non-Existing Possibles According to Thomas Aquinas, Henry of Ghent and Godfrey of Fontaines," *Review of Metaphysics* 33 (June 1981): 729–758, pp. 742 ff.

44. Ibid., p. 747.

45. On the alleged identity of Henry's and Duns Scotus's understanding of this intermediate kind of being, see Cronin, *Objective Being in Descartes and in Suárez,* who also notes the reappearance of this notion in Suárez and the similarity between Suárez's *conceptus objectivus* and Descartes's notion of objective reality.

46. Scotus writes: "[I]f it were supposed that I had been from eternity and that from eternity I had understood a rose, then from eternity I understood a rose according to its *esse essentiae* and according to *esse existentiae* and however it had no *esse* except [*esse*] *cognitum* . . . hence the terminus of understanding is *esse essentiae* or *esse existentiae*—and however that which is the object of the understanding has only *esse diminutum* in the understanding" (*Opera Omnia,* vol. 6, 469, par. 26), quoted by Normore, whose translation I here follow. Normore also notes that Scotus uses the term "idea" in the sense he attributes to Augustine, of the *esse cognitum* of a thing. Normore, "Meaning and Objective Being," p. 232.

47. What this causation involves is a matter of controversy. Normore takes Scotus's claim that what *can* be created is dependent on God to be an anticipation of Descartes's view. See Normore, "Meaning and Objective Being," pp. 232 ff. But see also the discussions in A. B. Wolter, "Ockham and the Textbooks: On the Origin of Possibility," *Franziskanische Studien* 32 (1950): 70–96; Wippel, "The Reality of Non-Existing Possibles," pp. 750–751. Simo Knuuttila takes Scotus to mean that God, in producing things in intelligible being, gives them "an ontological status, weaker than existence, as intentional correlates of divine thought," but that he does not hereby also create them *ex nihilo.* They have their possible being in and of themselves (logical possibility), independently of God. Descartes, as I understand it, goes beyond Scotus in holding the controversial and, according to many critics, unintelligible view that

the nonexistent possibles themselves—like actually existing things—are created and hence dependent on God as an efficient and total cause. AT I 147, 151. See Alanen and Knuuttila, "The Foundations of Modality and Conceivability in Descartes and His Predecessors," pp. 33, 36, and the texts there quoted. See also Lilli Alanen, "Descartes, Duns Scotus and Ockham on Omnipotence and Possibility," *Franciscan Studies* 45 (1985): 157–188, 173–174.

48. See the excellent presentation by Gabriel Nuchelmans of later developments of the notion of objective being in the commentaries on the *Sentences* by Durandus a Sancto Porciano (written between 1307 and 1327) and by Petrus Aurelous (between 1313 and 1318), who are called exponents of the "objective existence theory" of proposition, which together with the Thomistic doctrine (and unlike Ockham's "mental act" theory and Rimini's "logical realism") survived in various forms as late as the beginning of the early modern period. Nuchelmans, *Judgment and Proposition,* pp. 17–35.

49. AT VII 166, CSM II 117; AT VIII-1 25–26, CSM I 210–211. Compare Normore, "Meaning and Objective Being," p. 226.

50. Compare AT VII 41 ll. 18–29, CSM II 28; AT VII 165, CSM II 116.

51. Spinoza writes: "So clearly, there can be no other first cause of ideas except that which (as we have just shown) everyone understands clearly and distinctly by the natural light: viz., one in which there is contained either formally or eminently the same reality which the ideas have objectively." ("Expositor of Descartes' 'Principles of Philosophy,' " in E. Curley, ed., *The Collected Works of Spinoza,* vol. 1 (Princeton, N.J.: Princeton University Press, 1985), pp. 244–245). Spinoza illustrates it by two examples, one of which is as follows: consider two books, composed by different, unequal authors (a great philosopher versus a trifler), but written by the same hand. One who attends not to their meaning or content, but only the text and the order of letters, has no reason to assume they have different causes. But if one attends to the meaning, one will find great inequality between them. "And so he will conclude that the first cause of the one book was very different from the first cause of the other, and really more perfect than it in proportion to the differences he finds between the meaning of the discourses of each book, or between the words considered as images" (ibid., p. 245).

52. I do not wish to enter into a discussion of Descartes's version of the ontological proof. I mention it here merely to bring out the close connection between Descartes's use of the notion of objective reality and his theory of modality. See The First Set of Replies: "[P]ossible existence is contained in the concept or idea of everything that we clearly and dis-

tinctly understand; but in no case is necessary existence so contained, except in the case of the idea of God. Those who carefully attend to this difference between the idea of God and every other idea will undoubtedly perceive that even though our understanding of other things always involves understanding them as if they were existing things, it does not follow that they do exist, but merely that they are capable of existing" (AT VII 116–117, CSM II 83).

53. Compare Normore, "Meaning and Objective Being," p. 238. Given that true essences of physical things are mathematical, the details of this story, if it is at all applicable to Descartes, has of course to be spelled out somewhat differently.

54. Kenny, *Descartes,* pp. 114, 116. Compare Gaston Berger, who takes Descartes to have "upheld the theory of ideas as copies." G. Berger, *The "Cogito" in Husserl's Philosophy* (Evanston: Northwestern University Press, 1972), p. 110. For recent criticisms of the attribution of the copy theory to Descartes, see Cook, "Descartes's Alleged Representationalism," pp. 179–193; Nadler, *Arnauld and the Cartesian Philosophy of Ideas,* pp. 9 ff.

55. Kenny, *Descartes,* p. 116.

56. Compare Donagan, *Spinoza,* p. 40.

57. The same point is made by Ayers, "Ideas and Objective Being," p. 1067.

58. We read in Thomas Aquinas: "Even in sensible things we observe that the same form can be in different sensible objects in different ways; . . . Furthermore, the same is true of the form of the sensible object; it exists in a different way in the thing outside than it does in sense knowledge, which receives sensible forms without their matter—for instance, the color of gold without gold itself. Similarly, the intellect receives material and changeable species of material things in an immaterial and unchanging way, in accord with its nature; *for things are received in a subject according to the nature of the subject.*" ST, vol. 12, 1a. 84, art 1. This is also, as we have seen above in section 1, the doctrine Brentano refers to in accounting for the origins of his notion of intentionality.

59. "*Ma'qul, ma'na* or *intentio* [in Al-farabi and Avicenna] is that which is immediately before the mind, whether the object of intention is outside the mind (in which case it is a *first* intention) or itself an intention (in which case the intention is a *second* intention)" (Christian Knudsen, "Intentions and Impositions," in N. Kretzmann, A. Kenny, J. Pinborg, eds., *The Cambridge History of Later Medieval Philosophy* (Cambridge: Cambridge University Press, 1982), p. 479). Katherine Tachau notes that Avicenna's use of this term, which he never defines, "has a built-in ontological ambivalence. On the one hand an 'intention'—particularly a second intention—is very nearly a concept. On the other, the 'inten-

tion' is some thing *(res)* given off by the object; thus it is the foundation of the concept's content, and has an extramental existence, qualified as having 'less being than that from which it intends.'" Tachau, *Vision and Certitude in the Age of Ockham* (Leiden: E. J. Brill, 1988), p. 14.

60. For instance, by Richard Rorty, *Philosophy and the Mirror of Nature* (Princeton: Princeton University Press, 1979), pp. 50–51; and Ian Hacking, *Why Does Language Matter to Philosophy* (Cambridge: Cambridge University Press, 1975).

61. Compare Martin M. Tweedale, "Mental Representation in Scholasticism," in J.-C. Smith, ed., *Historical Foundations of Cognitive Science* (Dordrecht: Kluwer Academic Publishers, 1990), p. 37 and the references there given.

62. Forms, according to Aquinas, are received in a subject according to its nature. See note 58. Aquinas, in addition, admits of two sorts of changes in the senses: natural (or physical) and spiritual. ST, 1a. 78,3. For his discussion of how the intellect can know corporeal things, see ST, vol. 12, 1a. 84, 2–7.

63. ST, vol. 12, 1a. 84, 2. See also Norman Kretzmann, "Philosophy of Mind," in Norman Kretzmann and Eleonore Stump, *The Cambridge Companion to Aquinas* (Cambridge: Cambridge University Press, 1993), pp. 128–159.

64. *"Sed species sensibilis non est illud quod sentitur, sed magis id quod sensus sentit. Ergo species intelligibilis non est quod intelligitur, sed id quo intelligit intellectus."* (ST, Ia. 85, 2).

65. A consequence of this theory of cognition is that the thing known can be known by the intellect only in its universality, not in its concrete individuality, because the intellect understands only by abstracting from the individuating material conditions that constitute the particular thing. ST Ia. 86, 1.

66. For an excellent account of the late medieval theories of visual representation and their philosophical problems, on which I rely here, see Tachau, *Vision and Certitude in the Age of Ockham.*

67. For instance, by Descartes in his *Optics* (AT VI 85, CSM I 153–154).

68. The likeness is taken for granted, as what makes representation possible. The species is a likeness of the object because it shares the same nature: it is, as it were, the object, but in another form of being. Because the relation between the object and species is, by virtue of their shared nature, natural or innate, the species are also taken to be *natural signs (signa naturalia)* of their objects. This natural relation of signification is taken as providing the basis for conventional, linguistic meaning. See Tachau, *Vision and Certitude in the Age of Ockham*, pp. 16–20.

69. Durandus explains why the species were introduced in the first place as follows: "For colour seems to effect its species in the medium and the [sense] organ, just as it appears sensibly . . . when reflected in a mirror. And if it were not for this, perhaps mention would never have been made of species required for cognition. But because some believe that the species of color in the eye represents to sight the color of which it is the species, they therefore posit, both in our and in angelic intellects, certain species for the purpose of representing things, that they may be known both by us and angels." Durandus of St. Porçiano, in *Sententias* II, dist. 3, q. 6, translated by Tachau, *Vision and Certitude in the Age of Ockham*, p. 4. Durandus, who according to Normore had an enormous influence, seems also to have been among the first who, following Francis de Mayronne, applied the term "idea" to the contents of the human mind—a move that conventionally is credited to Descartes and described as a Cartesian innovation. See Normore, "Meaning and Objective Being," pp. 234–235 and the references there given.

70. Katherine Tachau notes that Peter Olivi certainly "merits a place in the history of epistemology as the first of Bacon's readers to recognize the central problem faced by representational theories of perception." Tachau, *Vision and Certitude in the Age of Ockham*, p. 44 n. 3.

71. See the account in ibid., pp. 58 ff.

72. Though the term is found in Augustine, and also in Alhazen, subsequent medieval readers credited Scotus for inventing the notion of intuitive cognition. Ibid., p. 70. I have discussed Scotus's distinction between intuitive and abstractive cognition briefly in Chapter 1, section 2. The question for Scotus, as Tachau points out, was never whether certain knowledge of existents could be had, because he held that to be uncontroversial, but rather how it could be explained, since it cannot (as Henry had shown) be obtained through the process of abstraction. Instead of the supernatural illumination that Henry relied on to solve the problem, Scotus posits a natural capacity of discerning the true from the false: intuitive cognition. The intellect is certain both of propositions known *per se* and of those perfect acts lying within its power— that one understands, hears, is awake. Evidence from one sense can be checked against evidence from another, and when the judgments of the external senses themselves diverge, certitude can still be had by appeal to the ultimate independence of the intellect from the senses: the intellect can compare sense experience to propositions that it knows *per se*, which are "more certain than any judgement from the sense . . . such that the intellect always corrects the acts of the senses with such a proposition." Thus when to the sense of sight a stick partly submerged in wa-

ter appears broken, the truth can be arrived at by the intellect's recourse to the proposition "nothing that is harder can be broken by the touch of something softer yielding to it." Deception of the sense does hence not on Scotus's view inevitably lead to deception of the intellect. See Tachau, *Vision and Certitude in the Age of Ockham,* pp. 76–79. Compare also Descartes's distinction of grades of certainty in the senses, discussed in Chapter 3, section 3 and Chapter 5, section 5.

73. See Normore, "Meaning and Objective Reality," p. 234 and the references there given.

74. For the difference between Ockham's and his predecessors' account of representation, see Tweedale, "Mental Representation in Later Medieval Scholasticism," pp. 35–52. See also the account in Nuchelmans, *Judgment and Proposition,* pp. 26–28. Ockham also thinks it a contradiction to claim that an extramental thing would have merely "intentional and spiritual existence, because every entity outside the soul is a true substance or accident." Light and color are present in themselves, in the medium (*per se* and not *per accidens*), and the sense of vision thus perceives its proper substantial object directly. For difficulties in Ockham's view, see Tachau, *Vision and Certitude in the Age of Ockham,* pp. 135 ff. Compare Tweedale, "Mental Representation in Later Medieval Scholasticism."

75. See Fransisco Suárez, *Disputationes metaphysicae* II.1.1 (*Opera omnia,* vols. 25–26); reprint, Hildesheim: Olms, 1965. See also Ayers, "Ideas and Objective Being," pp. 1062–1074 and literature there quoted.

76. Compare section 3.

77. Using contemporary terms, objective being is best described as the content or object of thought—the thing represented, which, in being thought of, individuates a particular thought: my actual thought of the cat, for instance, as opposed to my thought of the mat on which it is presently lying. Neither Descartes, nor any of his Scholastic predecessors, ever believed that the thing itself, in being thought of, was in the mind. But they all had to face this difficulty, which Aquinas inherited from Aristotle, of accounting for how something external to, and different in nature from, the mind or the intellect could somehow be "in" the mind or its immediate object.

78. Quoted from Steven Nadler, *Malebranche and Ideas* (New York: Oxford University Press, 1992), p. 27 n. 17.

79. Ibid., pp. 44–45.

80. Nadler writes: "The universal failure of seventeenth century Cartesians to elaborate a positive and forthright answer to the problem leads one to believe that this is the case." The representativeness or image-like-

ness of ideas seems to constitute "an unanalyzable, 'self-evident' datum of consciousness." Ibid., p. 50.

81. Antoine Arnauld and Pierre Nicole, *La logique, ou l'art de penser* (1662) (Paris: Flammarion, 1970), p. 65.

82. Donagan, *Spinoza*, pp. 40–41.

5. Sensory Perceptions, Beliefs, and Material Falsity

1. According to Descartes's wide sense of idea, sensations are ideas. Compare the introduction to Chapter 3, notes 1–3, and the discussion in Chapter 4, section 1. See also the discussions in L. J. Beck, *The Metaphysics of Descartes: A Study of the Meditations* (Oxford: Clarendon Press, 1965), pp. 150–161; Anthony Kenny, *Descartes* (New York: Random House, 1968), chap. 5; Margaret Wilson, *Descartes* (London: Routledge and Kegan Paul, 1978), pp. 156–158. See also M. Wilson, *Ideas and Mechanism* (Princeton: Princeton University Press, 1999), pp. 26–40.

2. The clearest statement of a traditional representationalist interpretation of Descartes's general theory of ideas is found in Anthony Kenny's influential book, *Descartes*, pp. 114–116, discussed in Chapter 4, section 6. The "veil-of-ideas" reading is defended in Richard Rorty, *Philosophy and the Mirror of Nature* (Princeton: Princeton University Press, 1979), pp. 50–51; and Ian Hacking, *Why Does Language Matter to Philosophy* (Cambridge: Cambridge University Press, 1975), p. 33. One of its earliest proponents was Thomas Reid, who presents it as a "generally received view" among his contemporaries and charges Descartes and his followers (Malebranche and Arnauld) for having developed the philosophical theory of perception of which the British empiricists were to draw the ultimate epistemological consequences. See *The Philosophical Works of Thomas Reid*, W. Hamilton, ed., 2 vols. (Edinburgh: James Thin, 1896), vol. 1. The representationalist reading has been questioned recently by, for instance, B. E. O'Neil, *Epistemological Direct Realism in Descartes's Philosophy;* John W. Yolton, *Perceptual Acquaintance from Descartes to Reid* (Minneapolis: University of Minnesota Press, 1984); and, by the same author, "Ideas and Knowledge on Seventeenth-Century Philosophy," *Journal of the History of Philosophy* 13 (1974): 145–166; "On Being Present to the Mind: A Sketch for the History of an Idea," *Dialogue* 14 (1975): 373–389. For criticisms of Kenny's interpretation, see, e.g., Thomas Lennon, "The Inherence Pattern and Descartes' *Ideas,*" *Journal of the History of Philosophy* 12 (1974): 43–52; see also the literature quoted in Chapter 4 note 54.

3. For a representationalist reading of Descartes's theory of sense perception, see, e.g., Nancy Maull, "Cartesian Optics and the Geometrization of Nature," in S. Gaukroger, ed., *Descartes: Philosophy, Mathematics and Physics* (Brighton: Harvester Press, 1980), pp. 23–40. A direct realist reading of Descartes's earliest version of this theory is defended by John Schuster, "Descartes' *'Mathesis Universalis'*: 1619–28," in Gaukroger, ed., *Descartes: Philosophy, Mathematics and Physics*. Compare also the discussion in Robert McRae, "'Idea' as a Philosophical Term in the Seventeenth Century," *Journal of the History of Ideas* 26 (1965): 176–190, esp. 178–179.

4. A problem with this whole discussion is the unclarity about what "representationalism" and "direct realism" are supposed to mean in this context, and the lack of consensus concerning the differences between them. Compare the discussion in Monte Cook, "Descartes' Alleged Representationalism," *History of Philosophy Quarterly* 4 (1987): 179–193. Margaret Wilson questions whether Descartes had any philosophical theory of perception at all (*Descartes,* p. 203), whereas Roland Arbini argues that he did have a consistent causal but nonrepresentationalist theory. See R. Arbini, "Did Descartes Have a Philosophical Theory of Sense Perception?" *Journal of the History of Philosophy* 21 (1983): 317–337. One may also ask to what extent the kind of questions raised concerning direct and indirect realism in contemporary debates on sense perception are at all relevant for the kind of theory Descartes defended. See Thomas M. Lennon, "Representationalism, Judgement and Perception of Distance: Further to Yolton and McRae," *Dialogue* 19 (1980): 151–160. For a recent defense of reading Descartes's theory of sense perception as direct realism, see Tom Vinci, *Cartesian Truth* (New York: Oxford University Press, 1998), pp. 116–121.

5. Their only difference, actually, is their organs and bodily location. In his first version of Rule Eight, as in the *Studium bonae mentis,* the memory is not treated as a third faculty independent from the intellect and the imagination, while the second version of Rule Eight, as the Rule Twelve, mentions four modes of knowing. Cf. Geneviève Rodis-Lewis, *L'oeuvre de Descartes* (Paris: Vrin, 1971), vol. 1, p. 93.

6. See Schuster, "Descartes' *'Mathesis Universalis,'*" pp. 62 ff.

7. See Norman Kemp Smith, *New Studies in the Philosophy of Descartes* (London: Macmillan, 1966), pp. 51–52; and Schuster, who writes: "There is no doctrine of representative perception in rule 12, no postulation that physical entities can be known only through mental duplicates" ("Descartes' *'Mathesis Universalis,'*" pp. 60–61). Ideas, whether they are sensory impressions traced in the brain, or purely mental concepts, are, ac-

cording to this reading, the direct object of consciousness or cognitive awareness. I agree that there is no doctrine of representative perception, taken as involving the postulation of mental duplicates intervening between the mind and physical objects, for such a view can be found neither in Rule Twelve nor elsewhere in Descartes.

8. Compare Rodis-Lewis, *L'oeuvre de Descartes*, vol. 1, pp. 94–95.

9. The truth of the operations of universal mathematics, as well as "the ontological reference of its objects," would, according to Schuster, be based on what he calls the "optics-psychology-physiology nexus." Schuster, "Descartes' *'Mathesis Universalis,'*" p. 62.

10. "So we can conclude with certainty that when the intellect is concerned with matters in which there is nothing corporeal or similar to the corporeal, it cannot receive any help from those faculties . . . *If, however, the intellect proposes to examine something which can be referred to the body, the idea of that thing must be formed as distinctly as possible in the imagination.* In order to do this properly, the thing which this idea is to represent should be displayed to the external senses" (AT X 416–417, CSM I 43; my emphasis). Compare AT X 414–415, CSM I 41.

11. To *conceive* more distinctly, here, is not the same as to *know* more distinctly. "Conceive" in the *Rules* seems to be used interchangeably with "imagine" (AT X 414, CSM I 42). Cf. note 20.

12. See Schuster, "Descartes' *'Mathesis Universalis,'*" pp. 62 ff.

13. A person suffering from jaundice, for instance, will see yellow-looking things around him (AT X 423, CSM I 47), and although Descartes does not say much about it in this connection I assume he holds that normal visual perception presents us with variously colored and shaped ordinary objects and things at various distances. This, certainly, is the case in the Sixth Replies discussion of grades of certainty in the senses: there the direct object of visual perception is a bent-looking stick half immersed in water, not sensations or brain movements caused by the refraction of light emitted from the stick (AT VII 437–438, CSM II 295). Cf. Arbini, "Did Descartes Have a Philosophical Theory of Sense Perception?" p. 330.

14. See, e.g., Kemp Smith, *New Studies in the Philosophy of Descartes*, pp. 51–52; Schuster, "Descartes' *'Mathesis universalis,'*" pp. 60–61.

15. The various sensations or passions that the mind immediately perceives are *the effects* of these cerebral movements on the mind, not the movements as such. See AT XI 141, CSM I 81; AT XI 338, CSM I 333; Schuster, "Descartes' *'Mathesis Universalis.'*"

16. See AT VI 130; compare the passage quoted in note 34 below.

17. See Rule Three (AT X 365, CSM I 14), Rule Nine (AT X 400, CSM I 33),

Rule Twelve (AT X 419–420, CSM I 44–45). See also, e.g., John Cottingham, *Descartes* (Oxford: Basil Blackwell, 1986), pp. 25 f., and Gary Hatfield, "The Senses and the Fleshless Eye: The *Meditations* as Cognitive Exercises," in A. Oksenberg Rorty, *Essays on Descartes' Meditations* (Berkeley: University of California Press, 1986), pp. 45–80.

18. AT X 416–417, CSM I 43. See also Rule Fourteen (AT X 438, CSM I 56). Descartes, it should be noted, uses both conceive *(concipere)* and imagine *(fingere)* in this context as distinguished from the act of intellection *(intelligere),* which is reserved for the intellect alone (AT IX 414–416), as in the passage quoted above. Cf. Rodis-Lewis, *L'oeuvre de Descartes,* vol. 1, p. 94.

19. Descartes's new method, in fact, requires abstraction from the senses and the imagination. For an instructive account of the very abstract and general nature of Cartesian algebra, as opposed to ancient arithmetics and geometry, see Stephen Gaukroger, "The Nature of Abstract Reasoning: Philosophical Aspects of Descartes's Work in Algebra," in J. Cottingham, ed., *The Cambridge Companion to Descartes* (New York: Cambridge University Press, 1992), pp. 91–114.

20. I take "imagination" in this passage to mean not the corporeal imagination, but the intellect insofar as it "applies itself" to whatever figures are impressed in the corporeal imagination.

21. See *Discourse on the Method* (AT VI 39–40); and the discussion of the grades of certainty of sense perception in the Sixth Replies (AT VII 436–437, CSM II 294). Spatial qualities, such as distance, size, shape, and location—that is, the qualities Locke calls primary and that are supposed to be the only true properties of bodies—are not, as is made clear in the Sixth Replies, perceived by the senses strictly speaking, but require mostly unnoticed inferences depending on the intellect. Cf. Gary Hatfield and William Epstein, "The Sensory Core and the Medieval Foundations of Early Modern Perceptual Theory," *Isis* 70 (1979): 362–384.

22. Schuster, in "Descartes' *'Mathesis Universalis,'* " pp. 63–64, admits that it is not much we can know through the senses, but takes it that the fact that some aspects of physical things are delivered for direct inspection in the brain is sufficient to ground Descartes's optimism in his method. He writes: "[A]ll that is delivered . . . are patterns of disturbance impinging on sense organs and ultimately derived from objects in the outside world. What those objects are really like, what their complete natures or 'forms' are, cannot be shown with certainty, for we know them only in respect of their geometrical-mechanical patterns of effect upon us . . . On the other hand, in sensation we *are* in touch with some di-

rectly registered aspects of the external corporeal world and not with some 'spiritual' object . . . It may seem that on this basis we know desperately little of the corporeal world for certain, but the little we can know—along with the machinery of imagination—will prove sufficient to ground universal mathematics" (ibid., p. 94).

23. Charles Larmore, "Descartes' Empirical Epistemology," in Gaukroger, ed., *Descartes: Philosophy, Mathematics and Physics,* pp. 12 ff.; see also the *Optics* (AT VI 112, CSM I 165).

24. For instance, "the closer to red in the spectrum a colour is, the faster, according to Descartes, the corresponding rotational velocity of the light-corpuscles." Larmore, "Descartes' Empirical Epistemology," p. 15.

25. To Charles Larmore this indicates that the generalized notion of representation was discovered by Descartes after having first defended (or considered) some form of direct realism in the *Rules* and the *Treatise on Man.* Ibid., p. 15 n. 22. See also Arbini, "Did Descartes Have a Philosophical Theory of Sense Perception?" p. 335.

26. Compare Alquié, vol. 1, p. 450 n. 2. The same kind of inconsistency in the use of "idea" is also found in the *Optics,* written, presumably, around the same time, although published only in 1637. See AT VI 85, 109, 112, 114, 130. See also *Discourse* V (AT VI 55, CSM I 139).

27. "And note that by 'figures' I mean not only things which somehow represent the position or the edges and surfaces of objects, but also anything which, as I said above, can give the soul occasion to perceive movement, size, distance, colours, sounds, smells and other such qualities. And I also include anything that can make the soul feel pleasure, pain, hunger, thirst, joy, sadness and other such passions" (AT XI 176, CSM I 106). The analogy in the *World* and the *Optics* between sensory ideas and linguistic symbols, introduced mainly to illustrate the lack of resemblance between the sign and the signified, can also be seen as another application of an extended concept of representation (AT XI 3 ff., CSM I 81–82; AT VI 113–114, CSM I 165–166). See also *Meditations* (AT VII 88, CSM II 60), and *Passions of the Soul,* where there are numerous references to a sign theory. Cf. Yolton, *Perceptual Acquaintance,* pp. 22 ff.

28. See, e.g., *Optics* (AT VI 112, CSM I 165). A very instructive account of earlier theories of visual perception is given by Hatfield and Epstein, "The Sensory Core and the Medieval Foundations of Early Modern Perceptual Theory."

29. Schuster, "Descartes' *'Mathesis Universalis,'*" p. 60, and n. 90.

30. See, e.g., R. J. Hirst, "Realism," in Paul Edwards, ed., *The Encyclopedia of Philosophy* (New York: Macmillan, 1967), vol. 7, p. 80. This picture is

oversimplified. Compare the medieval discussions referred to in Chapter 4, section 7. Recent research has also questioned the attribution to Locke of any straightforward or simple "representationalism."

31. Compare Margaret Wilson, "Descartes on the Perception of Primary Qualities," in Wilson, *Ideas and Mechanism,* pp. 26–40. See also Alison Simmons, "Spatial Perception from a Cartesian Point of View," unpublished manuscript.

32. See the Sixth Meditation (AT VII 80 ff.; CSM II 55 ff.).

33. See, e.g., the discussion in Yolton, "On Being Present to the Mind," pp. 378, 382 ff.; and the literature referred to in note 2. But see also McRae, who finds features of such a theory in Locke and thinks it can be traced back to the doctrine of the *Rules* ("'Idea' as a Philosophical Term in the Seventeenth Century," p. 178). See also his reply to Yolton, R. McRae, "On Being Present to the Mind: A Reply," *Dialogue* 14 (1975): 664–666. The only uncontroversial candidate for an object theory of ideas as here outlined seems to be the one developed by Malebranche, who did not, however, apply it to sensations!

34. He writes: "Thus it is not only the images depicted in the imagination which I call 'ideas.' Indeed, in so far as these images are in the corporeal imagination, that is, are depicted in some part of the brain, I do not call them 'ideas' at all; I call them 'ideas' only in so far as they inform the mind itself, when it is directed towards that part of the brain" (AT VII 160–161, CSM II 113). Cf. also Descartes's reply to Hobbes concerning the idea of God (AT VII 181, CMS II 127); and Chapter 4, section 2.

35. See, e.g., *Treatise on Man* (AT XI 143–144, CSM I 102–103); the Sixth Meditation (AT VII 80–88, CSM II 56–60); *Passions of the Soul* I, art. 34–50 (AT XI 354–369, CSM I 341–348).

36. These are, as Arnauld clearly saw and insisted, inseparable aspects or features of thought or perception. Compare the quotation from Arnauld on page 122, and the references there given.

37. See Chapter 4. For a crisp and clear summary of Descartes's theory of ideas, basically in agreement with the reading here defended, see Michael Ayers, "Ideas and Objective Being," in D. Garber and M. Ayers, eds., *The Cambridge History of Seventeenth Century Philosophy,* 2 vols. (Cambridge: Cambridge University Press, 1988), vol. 2, pp. 1066–1069.

38. Cf. Chapter 4, sections 3–4.

39. For example, sensations of temperature: Is the sensation of cold merely one of absence of heat? See the discussion in AT VII 44, CSM II 30; AT VII 232–235, CSM II 162–164.

40. Calvin Normore agrees with Margaret Wilson that "we must distinguish

the representative character of Cartesian ideas from their objective reality." All ideas purport to be or are taken to be about something and hence have a representative character. All ideas, however, would not in fact have objective reality: materially false ideas are ideas of nonthings that lack objective reality altogether and hence fail, in spite of their representative character, to represent anything real. C. Normore, "Meaning and Objective Being: Descartes and His Sources," in Rorty, ed., *Essays on Descartes's Meditations,* p. 226. Compare the discussion in Wilson, *Descartes,* pp. 102–119. Margaret Wilson, however, defends a more nuanced position in her essay "Descartes on the Representationality of Sensations," in J. A. Cover and M. Kulstad, eds., *Central Themes in Early Modern Philosophy* (Indianapolis: Hackett Publishing, 1990), pp. 1–22, 13 ff. Wilson now distinguishes two senses of *represent* and argues that those thoughts, like sensations, which do not represent *presentationally* can nevertheless be said to represent *referentially.*

41. *"Jam quod ad ideas attinet, si solae in se spectentur, nec ad aliud quid illas referam, falsae proprie esse non possunt"* (AT VII 37, CSM II 26; AT VII 232, CSM II 163). Compare Chapter 3, section 2.

42. I have found the writings of Margaret Wilson, as well as a recent paper of Jean-Marie Beyssade on this difficult topic, very helpful, even on the points where I differ from them. Beyssade and Wilson base their readings on a distinction between two different ways in which Cartesian ideas can refer to or represent things, although they seem to draw the distinction in quite different ways and terms. See Jean-Marie Beyssade, "Descartes on Material Falsity," in P. Cummins and G. Zoeller, eds., *Minds, Ideas, and Objects* (Atascadero, Calif.: Ridgeview Publishing, 1992); Margaret Wilson, "Descartes on the Representationality of Sensation."

43. It should be noted that Descartes makes a distinction between knowing a thing completely and having an adequate knowledge or understanding of it. Having a complete understanding of something is understanding "something to be a complete thing," that is, "a substance endowed with the forms or attributes which enable me to recognize that it is a substance." I can know that a thing is complete, that is to say, a substance, without having a "wholly adequate" knowledge of it. It is "adequate enough" if we are able to perceive that we have not rendered it "inadequate by an abstraction of the intellect" (AT VII 221–222, CSM II 156). But even so, complete knowledge is not necessarily knowledge of actual existence, except in the privileged cases of my knowledge of the existence of my mind as a thinking thing—revealed in the Cogito—or the knowledge of the existence of God, whose idea contains that of necessary existence.

44. To Mersenne, July 1641 (AT III 392–395, CSMK 185–186). As Gabriel Nuchelmans observes, Descartes does not show much interest in the question of how ideas are expressed—his real concern is the distinction between imagination and the pure intellect. Thus although he clearly was aware of "the difference between concepts as elements of propositions and propositional concepts," he nevertheless "used the word *idea* for both kinds of concepts and thereby made a crucial distinction less clearly recognizable." And although he "sometimes contrasts an idea with a proposition, or a notion which does not involve affirmation or negation with a prejudice, the very fact that he occasionally speaks of ideas which do not involve any affirmation or negation indicates that for him there are also ideas that do involve predication." This lack of explicitness certainly is confusing. G. Nuchelmans, *Judgment and Proposition: From Descartes to Kant* (Amsterdam: North-Holland Publishing, 1982), p. 43.

45. Wilson, *Descartes*, pp. 140–141.

46. Ibid., p. 141.

47. In Scholastic terminology, between apprehensive and judicative notions. I can think of the pope as sleeping, without judging that "the pope is sleeping" or not. A judgment or judicative notion requires assent or dissent from a notion that is merely apprehended (actually entertained proposition). See, e.g., Alexander Broadie, *Notion and Object: Aspects of Late Medieval Epistemology* (Oxford: Clarendon Press, 1989), pp. 125 ff. A natural source for Descartes's use of these notions is undoubtedly Francisco Suárez's *Disputationes Metaphysicae,* and Descartes seems to follow Suárez in insisting on the lack of falsity of simple apprehensive notions or concepts. See Norman Wells, "Objective Reality of Ideas in Arnauld, Descartes and Suárez," in E. J. Kremer, ed., *The Great Arnauld and Some of His Philosophical Correspondents* (Toronto: University of Toronto Press, 1994), pp. 138–183, 143–144, and the references there given. See also Nuchelmans, *Judgment and Proposition,* chap. 2. Again, it is useful to take note of the terminology here. Descartes can use for the act of judgment both "to judge" or "to believe (that something is true)," "to assent," and so forth, and for the object of judgment expressions like "that which is understood," or "the thing that is conceived by the mind," meaning thereby a complex idea or propositional concept. Ibid., p. 44.

48. See Chapter 7 and the references there given.

49. See the letter to Regius, May and December 1641 (AT III 372 and 454–455); letter to Mesland, May 2, 1644 (AT IV 113); letter to Hyperaspistes, August 1641 (AT III 432); *Principles* I, 32; and *Passions of the Soul* I, 17 ff.

50. Compare Jill Vance Buroker, "Judgment and Predication in the Port-

Royal Logic," in Kremer, ed., *The Great Arnauld and Some of His Philosophical Correspondents,* pp. 3–27, 4–5.

51. Alan Donagan argues that although Spinoza's proof for this is "one of his rare aberrations," it contains an important insight and constitutes an emendation of Descartes's theory. See A. Donagan, *Spinoza* (New York: Harvester Wheatsheaf, 1988), chap. 3, section 3.3.

52. See Spinoza, *Ethics* II, Prop. 43, Sch. 3.

53. Compare Jonathan Bennett, *A Study of Spinoza's Ethics* (Indianapolis: Hackett Publishing, 1984), p. 162.

54. Compare Chapter 1 note 40, and this chapter note 47. See also the discussion in Donagan, *Spinoza,* p. 45.

55. AT VI 39, CSM I 130; AT VII 36 ff., CSM II 25 ff.; AT VIII-1 16, CSM I 203.

56. It is because it has a power not to assent that the will is free and constitutes our main perfection. See *Principles* I, art. 37 (AT VIII-1 18–19, CSM I 205); Chapter 8.

57. AT VII 116. Cf. Donagan, *Spinoza,* p. 51; McRae, "On Being Present to the Mind," p. 82.

58. This means that assent or denial, and hence judgment, is involved in at least two distinct levels, that of essence or nature (Is it a real, that is, clearly and distinctly conceivable—complete—thing?), and that of existence (Does it actually exist?).

59. Whether "simple apprehensions" can be true or not was a matter of discussion among the Scholastics, and Descartes seems to follow those who held that not only propositions, but simple ideas or apprehensions can be true. See Ayers, "Ideas and Objective Being," pp. 1069–1070.

60. Compare above section 2. Three ways of composing ideas are distinguished in Rule Twelve of the *Rules:* by impulse (spontaneously, as it were), by conjecture, and by deduction. The first category includes all the cases in which we are "caused to believe something," without reflecting on it or using our own reason, either supernaturally, by our own free will (in this case, I gather, unreflectingly), or by the disposition of our corporeal imagination (AT X 424, CSM I 47–48).

61. Cf. Beyssade, "Descartes on Material Falsity."

62. Arnauld writes: "For an idea is called 'positive' not in virtue of the existence it has as a mode of thinking (for in that sense all ideas would be positive) but in virtue of the objective existence which it contains and which it exhibits to our mind. Hence the idea in question may perhaps not be the idea of cold but it cannot be false" (AT VII 207, CSM II 145).

63. The contrast made earlier was on the one hand between ideas taken materially (or formally), as actual modes of thought, and ideas taken

objectively as representing something (AT VII 41, CSM II 28), and on the other hand between the objective being of ideas and the actual or formal being or reality of their causes (AT VII 41–42, CSM II 29). "Formal" in this connection is used of an existing thing, as interchangeably with "subjective"—for what actually exists in a subject of predication. It is not to be confounded with "formal" as used about the form or essence of particular things that can be thought of in abstraction from the thing, and that hence can have objective being. (Compare Chapter 4, section 7.) The terminology—and Descartes's use of it—is bewildering, though not necessarily inconsistent, as suggested by the comments of Marjorie Grene, *Descartes* (Minneapolis: University of Minnesota Press, 1985), pp. 177, 189. See also Norman Wells, "Material Falsity in Descartes, Arnauld and Suárez," *Journal of the History of Philosophy* 22 (1984): 25–30, and the debate between Norman Wells, "*Esse cognitum* and Suárez Revisited," and Jorge J. E. Gracia, "Suárez and Metaphysical Mentalism," *American Catholic Philosophical Quarterly* 17 (1993): 339–354. In his "Objective Reality of Ideas in Arnauld, Descartes, and Suárez," *Journal of the History of Philosophy* 28 (1990): 33–61, and more recently, "Suárez on Material Falsity" (unpublished manuscript), Wells catalogues all the misunderstandings he has found of these topics. I share the honor of being listed, with Arnauld and a number of recent scholars, among those who have failed to understand Suárez's and hence Descartes's positions on objective reality and material falsity. Wells refers to my earlier published unsuccessful "efforts" on this subject, parts of which are reproduced here. But as far as I can make out, his reading of what Suárez says about material falsity seems to support, rather than undermine, the one I defend in Alanen, "Sensory Ideas, Objective Reality and Material Falsity," in J. Cottingham, ed., *The Cambridge Companion to Descartes* (Cambridge: Cambridge University Press, 1992). See Wells, "Suárez on Material Falsity." For a clear and more helpful account of Descartes's usage of the terms and its possible philosophical ancestry, see Nuchelmans, *Judgment and Proposition,* pp. 39–41. But see also Alan Nelson, "The Falsity in Sensory Ideas: Descartes and Arnauld," in E. J. Kremer, ed., *Interpreting Arnauld* (Toronto: University of Toronto Press, 1996), pp. 13–32, for a challenging reading that goes against all interpretations taking Descartes's commitment to his Scholastic heritage seriously.

64. Descartes writes: "Confused ideas which are made up at will by the mind such as the ideas of false gods do not provide as much scope for error *(erroris occasione)* as the confused ideas arriving from the senses such as the ideas of colour and cold (if it is true as I have said that these

ideas do not represent anything real). The greatest scope for error is
provided by the ideas which arise from the sensations of appetite. Thus
the idea of thirst which the patient with dropsy has does indeed give
him subject-matter for error since it can lead him to judge that a drink
will do him good when in fact it will do him harm" (AT VII 234, CSM II
163–164).

65. "If I considered just the ideas themselves simply as modes of thought
without referring them to anything else, they could scarcely (*vix*) give
me material for error" (AT VII 37, CSM II 26).

66. "*Illam materialiter falsam appello, quod, cum sit obscura et confusa, non possim
dijudicare an mihi quid exhibeat quod extra sensum meum sit positivum, necne*"
(AT VII 234, ll. 14–17). I do not see, as Beyssade does, a change of emphasis or position here, but take this as a mere repetition of the point
made in the Third Meditation: the obscurity and confusion of the ideas
of sensory qualities hinder me from seeing whether they are true or
false, that is, whether they are of things or not (AT VII 43, ll. 23–26).
The reality they exhibit, Descartes there explains, is so slight that I cannot even distinguish it from a nonthing (AT VII 44, l. 15, CSM II 30).
This, as Beyssade rightly stresses, is a phenomenological problem—not
a scientific one: phenomenologically, the reality they contain objectively, whatever it is, is confounded with their material or formal reality
as modes of thought. Beyssade, "Descartes on Material Falsity."

67. See, e.g., *Principles* IV, art. 197–198, AT VIII-1 321–322, CSM I 284–285.

68. See Chapter 2, section 6. Compare Beyssade, "Descartes on Material
Falsity."

69. The distinction suggested here seems to be one between the sensation
as a pure experience (qualia?) and sense perception in a broader and
more familiar sense of the term as perception of sensory objects. The
former is the directly experienced sensory response to external or internal stimulation; the latter involves beliefs immediately and automatically generated by that response, which have not been but can be made
subject for criticism. For a similar account of sensations, see Wilfrid
Sellars's lectures in Pedro Amaral, ed., *The Metaphysics of Epistemology*
(Atascadero, Calif.: Ridgeview Publishing, 1989), pp. 95–120. Descartes's account is *not*, though it is often taken in that way, a genetic or
descriptive one, but epistemological: the purpose of the distinction of
grades of sensation is to determine the scope and certainty of sensory
knowledge. The sensations in the strict sense (second-level sensations),
I take it, are *not* given as such; rather, they are identified or categorized
as sensations or sensory states only as an outcome of a critical analysis of
what exactly is given in sensory perception in the broader, commonsense meaning of the term.

70. Differently from ideas of size, shape, and so on, which Locke called "primary qualities" and which, insofar as they can be clearly and distinctly perceived, are, for Descartes, ideas of the intellect, the sensory, "secondary" qualities cannot, because they are incommensurable with the former, be distinctly conceived as properties of real, extended things.

71. "Descartes on the Perception of Primary Qualities," in Wilson, *Ideas and Mechanism*, pp. 26–40.

72. Compare Hatfield, "The Senses and the Fleshless Eye," pp. 56–60.

73. Alan Gewirth, "Clearness and Distinctness in Descartes" (1943), reprinted in Willis Doney, ed., *Descartes: A Collection of Critical Essays* (Garden City, N.Y.: Doubleday, 1967), pp. 250–277; cf. Grene, *Descartes*, p. 177. If we apply Gewirth's distinction between what he calls the direct and the interpretive content of an idea to the example discussed above, we could say that the sensations involved in the perception of a stick immersed in water constitute its direct content—what is immediately or directly perceived. The interpretive content here would be the taking of what is immediately perceived or seen as a true representation of what is in the water: a stick that is bent in the way it appears because of the reflections of light in water. This interpretive content, as I understand it, is what would normally or naturally present itself to an uncritical observer. It is what is *first* perceived, whereas the direct or what I would also call the *immediate* content is what is left after the critical reflection on this primary perception. (Because what is directly perceived is the only thing of which I can have *immediate* certainty.)

74. Contrary to Gewirth, who does not think that the act can be judgmental, because there is no volitional act involved. Cf. "Clearness and Distinctness in Descartes," p. 264. What is needed here is a concept of assent that is not volitional, and indeed Descartes provides one in talking of beliefs by natural impulse. We are as it were compelled, by nature, to beliefs suggested by vivid sensory impressions.

75. Cf. the interesting discussion by Jean-Claude Pariente, *L'Analyse du langage à Port-Royal* (Paris: Les Éditions de Minuit, 1985), pp. 72–77.

76. Pariente argues that Arnauld, in his later work (the *Art of Thinking*, in 1662), seems to have adopted the Cartesian doctrine, without, however, using the term "material falsity," because he there claims that complex ideas can be false because they contain (unnoticed) judgments. What Arnauld has realized, according to Pariente, is that "the level of the idea and that of judgement should not be opposed as two rigid levels," and that one must admit, in between them, "relations which are not reducible to the simple anteriority of the idea before the judgement" (Pariente, *L'analyse du langage,* p. 73). The judgments involved are not

to be understood as actual, explicit judgments, but rather as preju-
dices—beliefs or opinions already formed that are accepted without
scrutiny. There is hence, as it were, a layer or sediment of old judgments within the false idea (ibid., pp. 76–77).

77. As ideas, sensations (in the strict sense) may belong to the bottom level
of represented perfections—representations of what is such that, to
speak in Platonist terms, we do not know if it is or is not. But, I want to
insist, even though they can be said to have in this sense their share of
nonbeing or nothingness, they are *not* nothing—they are not nonideas.
There is clear difference between a nonidea—that is, a contradictory
idea—and a sensory idea. The latter is of something, though we know
not what; the former is of a nonthing—that is, of a thing so specified
that we see, as soon as we try to conceive or think of it, that it is unthink-
able. The sensory idea, *qua* mode of the mind caused by mechanical
movements in the body, fulfills the two features characteristic of "idea"
or "thought" in Descartes's large sense of the word: it is an act of the
mind, and it comes with some content whereby it points to something
mind-independent even when we do not know what reality it points to.
A contradictory idea, on the other hand, represents nothing at all,
since it is the idea of a thing the existence of which is impossible. A contradictory idea—the idea of a nonthing—excludes the reality of its object because its object is inconceivable—it can neither be represented
nor exist. A sensory idea, by contrast, does not by itself exclude all objective reality, but we need other ideas and critical judgment to determine what formal reality it contains objectively. The case of chimeras is
worth special mention. As Descartes understands it, they are fictitious
beings that, insofar as they are composed of elements that can be
clearly and distinctly conceived, are possible, and hence, real (although
unexistent) beings. The idea of a chimera, in itself, is thus a true idea.
See AT VII 362, CSM II 250; *The Conversation with Burman* (AT V 160,
CSMK 343); letter to Clerselier, April 23, 1649 (AT V 354, CSMK 376).
Spinoza, however, takes "Chimera" to mean something that "of its own
nature, cannot exist," and which as such is a contradictory entity, on the
par with the (non) idea of a round square, which is inconceivable. "Expositor of Descartes' 'Principles of Philosophy,'" in *The Collected Works of
Spinoza,* ed. and trans. E. Curley (Princeton: Princeton University Press,
1985), pp. 299, 307.

78. See, e.g., Hatfield, "The Senses and the Fleshless Eye"; Wilson, "Descartes on the Perception of Primary Qualities." Wilson's careful discussion also shows that Descartes's view of the relation of sense perception
and the intellect in the knowledge of external bodies is ambiguous and

remains, ultimately, problematic. See also her "Descartes on the Representationality of Sensation."

79. I borrow this expression from Wilfrid Sellars, quoted in Amaral, ed., *The Metaphysics of Epistemology,* pp. 133–134. For recent helpful discussions of Descartes's positive account of sensory perception, see Alison Simmons, "Are Cartesian Sensations Representational?" *Nous* 33:3 (1999): 347–369; and Simmons, "Descartes on the Cognitive Structure of Sensory Experience," forthcoming in *Philosophy and Phenomenological Research.* See also Paul Hoffman, "Descartes on Misrepresentation," *Journal of the History of Philosophy* 34 (1996): 357–381.

6. Passions and Embodied Intentionality

1. See Elisabeth's letter of July 1, 1643. She writes: "I find too that the senses show me that the soul moves the body; but they fail to teach me (any more than the understanding or the imagination) the manner in which it does it. And therefore I think that there are properties of the soul unknown to me, which might perhaps reverse what your Metaphysical meditations, with so good arguments, have persuaded me" (AT IV 2).

2. For a different reading where Descartes is seen as another Platonist taking a pure disembodied reason or intellect to be the essence of the human mind and nature, see Stephen Voss, "Descartes: The End of Anthropology," in John Cottingham, ed., *Reason, Will and Sensation: Studies in Descartes's Metaphysics* (Oxford: Clarendon Press, 1994). I hope to show in this and the following chapters the grounds I have for being strongly opposed to that reading of Descartes.

3. While agreeing, in a letter to Chanut, June 15, 1646, on the great importance for morals of a true philosophy, Descartes admits not only that he neither pretends nor promises that "everything I've written would be true," but moreover that there is a very great gap "between the general notion of heaven and earth, that I have tried to give in my *Principles,* and the particular knowledge of the nature of man, of which I have not yet dealt with" (AT IV 441, CSMK 289).

4. Descartes's early notes and correspondence give ample evidence of how emotive he was himself—prone to strong feelings or emotions, from enthusiasm, admiration, and generosity, to fear, suspicion, and irascibility. His earliest writings, as we have seen, contain interesting remarks on emotions and passions, which show that the subject matter was important for him. See "Early Writings" (AT X 213–219, CSM I 2–5), and the references given in Chapter 1, and in G. Rodis-Lewis's re-

cent introduction to the English translation by Stephen Voss of Descartes, *The Passions of the Soul* (Indianapolis: Hackett Publishing, 1989). Yet it would be some twenty-five years until he took up the subject for detailed examination, and the way he deals with it is to a large extent determined by the correspondence with Elisabeth, in the context of which he starts to think seriously about the role of emotions in human life.

5. "If I thought joy were the supreme good, I should have no doubts one ought to try to become cheerful *(joyeuex)* at any price, and I should approve the brutishness of those who drown their sorrows in wine, or dull themselves with tobacco" (AT IV 305, CSMK 268).

6. Virtue for the Stoics, as Tad Brennan points out, cannot consist merely in a good will, for it is not compatible with false beliefs. T. Brennan, "The Old Stoic Theory of Emotions," in J. Sihvola and T. Engberg-Pedersen, *The Emotions in Hellenistic Philosophy* (Dordrecht: Kluwer Academic Publishers, 1998), pp. 21–70. Descartes on the contrary thinks it resides in the "firm and constant resolution" to use one's free will or judgment (Fr. *libre arbitre*) as well as possible and to undertake and carry out only what one judges, having used one's reason as well as possible, to be best. A virtuous will in Descartes's sense is compatible with lack of knowledge. See *Passions of the Soul* III, art. 152–154 (AT XI 445–447, CSM I 384).

7. See Descartes's letters to Elisabeth in August and September, 1645 (AT IV 263–266, 273–277, 281–286, 290–296, CSMK 257–267).

8. Indeed (as argued in the next chapter), he comes out in the end as an extreme voluntarist. For Augustine's stoicism and criticism of Stoic psychology and ethics, see Gérard Verbeke, "Augustin et le stoicisme," *Recherches Augustiniennes* (Paris: Études Augustiniennes, 1958), vol. 1, pp. 67–89; Marcia L. Colish, *The Stoic Tradition from Antiquity to the Early Middle Ages* (Leiden: E. J. Brill, 1990), vol. 2. For a clarifying account of the voluntarist tradition and the debates between intellectualists and voluntarists on the role of the will, see Bonnie Kent, *Virtues of the Will: The Transformation of Ethics in the Late Thirteenth Century* (Washington: Catholic University of America Press, 1995).

9. As André Gombay has pointed out in a conversation.

10. Compare the joy Descartes experiences in overcoming his fear and nausea during a boat trip on a stormy sea in an early letter to Beeckman (AT X 158).

11. This also explains, I believe, many of the tensions in Descartes's moral therapy between on the on hand the Stoic ideal of detachment and submissive acceptance, and on the other his own technological and re-

formist approach. (I return to this in Chapter 7. Compare the notes of Alquié, vol. 3, pp. 1061–1063.)

12. AT IV 310, CSMK 270. This principle of interaction is announced for the first time in the *Treatise on Man* (AT XI 143 ff., CSM I 102 ff.) to explain sensory perceptions primarily, but also feelings and emotions (AT XI 176, CSM I 106), and it now becomes the basis of his therapy of passions (*Passions* I, art. 34–44).

13. For earlier applications of it in the context of a psycho-physiological theory of emotions, see, e.g., the sources quoted by James Hankinson, "Actions and Passions: Affection, Emotion, and Moral Self-Management in Galen's Philosophical Psychology," in J. Brunschwig and M. Nussbaum, eds., *Passions and Perceptions* (Cambridge: Cambridge University Press, 1993), pp. 184–222.

14. See G. Rodis-Lewis's introduction and notes in her edition of Descartes, *Les passions de l'âme* (Paris: Vrin, 1955); and F. Alquié's introduction to *Les passions de l'âme*, in Alquié, vol. 3, pp. 942–943. A brief summary of some of the precedents to Descartes's treatment of passions is given also by Stephen Gaukroger, *Descartes: An Intellectual Biography* (Oxford: Clarendon Press, 1995). Although no detailed study, to my knowledge, has been made of the background of Descartes's views (apart that of Rodis-Lewis), the question whether Descartes had anything new to offer has been raised many times. Alquié seems to think the novelty of his treatment of passions resides mainly in his monistic conception of the soul. But that conception, I want to argue, is at best a new application of a doctrine found already in the Stoics. A good recent overview of the precedents of Descartes's theory is given by Deborah Brown, "What Was New in the *Passions* of 1649?" in T. Aho and M. Yrjönsuuri, eds., *Norms and Modes of Thinking in Descartes. Acta Philosophica Fennica* 64 (1999): 211–232.

15. That thought includes emotions is emphasized in the French translation of the *Meditations,* where loving and hating are added to the list of acts of thinking: *"Je suis une chose qui pense, c'est-à-dire qui doute, qui affirme, qui nie, qui connaît peu de choses, qui en ignore beaucoup, qui aime, qui hait, qui veut, qui ne veut pas, qui imagine aussi, et qui sent"* (AT IX 27).

16. See Chapter 5, section 4.

17. As noted by Annette Baier and Lisa Shapiro in their paper "Why Do All the Passions of the Cartesian Soul Get Expressed in the Cartesian Body," presented at the Descartes Workshop, University of Toronto, October 1994. See also Amelie Oksenberg Rorty, "Cartesian Passions and the Union of the Mind and the Body," in A. Oksenberg Rorty, ed., *Essays on Descartes' Meditations* (Berkeley: University of California Press, 1986).

18. Cf. this chapter, section 7.

19. Many contemporary discussions of emotions are based on a more or less explicit dichotomy between propositional, ergo cognitive, cultural, mental states, and natural, nonpropositional, ergo blind or brutish feelings or sentiments. This dichotomy underlies, to mention just one example, much of the discussion in Martha Nussbaum's *The Therapy of Emotions* (Princeton: Princeton University Press, 1994). It is often granted that emotions, in order to be rational or cognitive, must be reducible to propositional states, and that if they are not, they must be mere feelings or affective states, having no cognitive value or function at all. A useful survey of recent theories is given by John Deigh, "Cognitivism in the Theory of Emotions," *Ethics* 104 (1994): 822–854. In being himself committed to this dichotomy, as if there were no other alternatives, Deigh badly misconstrues the classic theories he mentions. Descartes's theory of emotions, notably, is mentioned, together with Locke's and Hume's, as representative of "feeling-centered" theories assimilating emotions to nonintentional bodily sensations (pp. 825–826). Descartes's theory, as I will try to show, cuts across such dichotomies in more than one way, which is also why I think it to be so interesting.

20. Galen makes the same distinction in his influential account of passions, although he uses the terms *energeia* and *pathos,* and applies it in a different framework: to the parts of the tripartite soul. An *energeia* or active motion is defined as one coming from the moving object itself, "while *pathos* is a motion in one thing that comes from something else," and they "can often be combined in one and the same basic situation, differing not in reality but in definition." One of Galen's examples is the cutter and the thing divided by the cutter: "In the same way anger is an *energeia* of the thumoeides, but a *pathema* of the other two parts, indeed of our whole body, when our body is forcibly driven to act by anger." Quoted by Hankinson, "Actions and Passions," p. 196. See the other senses of the terms *energeiea* and *pathos* discussed by Galen. See also Susan James, *Passions and Action: The Emotions in Seventeenth-Century Philosophy* (Oxford: Clarendon Press, 1997).

21. It is often but need not be associated with that of the immortality of the soul, to which we find Descartes referring in some of his letters to Elisabeth.

22. See, e.g., *Discourse* IV (AT VI 36, 45); *Principles* I, art. 21 (AT VIII-1 13).

23. Compare *Passions* I, art. 42–43 (AT XI 360–361, CSM I 341–342). Descartes distinguishes two kinds of imaginations—those caused by the soul and those caused by the body. The first depend on its own activity and are caused by the will (art. 20 (AT XI 344, CSM II 336)). The sec-

ond are mostly caused by the fortuitous course of the animal's spirits in the nerves and the brain, when this movement is not caused and directed by any particular determinate cause or volition. Such are our dreams and also our daydreams when our mind is idly wandering "without applying itself to anything of its own accord" (art. 21 (AT XI 345, CSM I 336)).

24. Paul Hoffman deserves credit for having brought the largely ignored difficulty this creates to the fore in his essay "Cartesian Passions and Cartesian Dualism," *Pacific Philosophical Quarterly* 71:4 (1990): 310–331.

25. See Aristotle, *Physics* III.3, 202a22 ff., and *De Anima* II.3.429 ff.

26. Hoffman, "Cartesian Passions and Cartesian Dualism," pp. 311–313.

27. Compare note 20.

28. The idea of straddling modes presupposes that of the mind–body union as a third kind of substance that Hoffman defends in "The Unity of Descartes's Man," *Philosophical Review* 95 (1986): 342–349. See also Hoffman's "Cartesian Passions and Cartesian Dualism."

29. As recognized also by Hoffman, "Cartesian Passions and Cartesian Dualism," p. 323.

30. See, e.g., *Principles* IV, art. 190, 198 (AT VIII-1 317, 322, CSM I 281, 285).

31. Descartes notes, in article 2, that "we are not aware of any subject which acts more directly upon our soul than the body to which it is joined. Consequently we should recognize that what is a passion in the soul is usually an action in the body. Therefore there is no better way of coming to know about our passions than by examining the difference between the mind and the body and of the functions attributable to each" (AT XI 328, CSM I 328).

32. *"Mon dessein n'a pas été d'expliquer les passions en orateur, ni même en philosophe moral, mais seulement en physicien,"* prefatory letter to *Les passions* (AT XI 326, CSM I 327). See also ibid., I, art. 1 (AT XI 327, CSM I 328); art. 68 (AT XI 379); Chapter 7, section 4. Compare F. Alquié, "Introduction to Les passions de l'âme," Alquié, vol. 3, pp. 943–944.

33. See *Passions* I, art. 4–8 (AT XI 329–333, CSM I 329–331). It is remarkable that Descartes on this point sided with the ancients against the moderns. A correct explanation of the circulation of the blood by muscle contractions in the heart had already been given by William Harvey. Descartes could not accept it because it was not mechanistic enough: it presupposed some hidden, unexplained force in the heart muscle. He explained it instead by using the old Aristotelian principle according to which there is some continuous heat source in the heart, which he describes as "a kind of fire that the blood of the veins maintains there"

and which he takes to be "the corporeal principle underlying all the movements of our limbs" (art. 8 (AT XI 333, CSM II 331)). He also explains with great detail how, through the rarefaction of the blood by this "fire without light"—which he postulated without explaining—in the heart, the liveliest and finest particles of blood, the so-called animal spirits, are created in the brain. "For what I am calling 'spirits' here are merely bodies: they have no other property than that of being extremely small bodies which move very quickly, like the jets of flame that come from a torch. They never stop in any place, and as some of them enter the brain's cavities, others leave it through the pores in its substance. These pores conduct them into the nerves, and then to the muscles. In this way the animal spirits move the body in all the various ways it can be moved" (AT XI 335, CSM II 332). The subsequent articles contain a summary of the account given in the unpublished and incomplete *Treatise on Man,* of the movements of the muscles and the nerves, of the action of external objects on the sense organs, and how the animal spirits are directed into the muscles, causing various movements in the brain, and through these, appropriate reactions of the body.

34. See Gary Hatfield, "Descartes' Physiology and Its Relation to His Psychology," in John Cottingham, ed., *The Cambridge Companion to Descartes* (Cambridge: Cambridge University Press, 1992), pp. 335–370, and the references there given.

35. See also *Treatise on Man* (AT XI 201–202, CSM I 108); and the exchange with Arnauld concerning the mechanical sheep (AT VII 229–230).

36. He writes in the unfinished "Description of the Human Body" he worked at during the winter of 1646–1647 that his aim was "to give such a full account of the entire bodily machine that we will have no more reason to think that it is our soul which produces in it the movements which we know by experience are not controlled by our will than we have reason to think that there is a soul in a clock which makes it tell the time" (AT XI 226, CSM I 315).

37. For Descartes's sense of "mechanism" and the limitations of his mechanistic physiology, see Geneviève Rodis-Lewis, "Limitations of the Mechanical Model in Descartes's Conception of the Organism," in Michael Hooker, ed., *Descartes: Critical and Interpretive Essays* (Baltimore: Johns Hopkins University Press, 1978); and "Limites du modèle mécanique dans la 'disposition' de l'organisme," in G. Rodis-Lewis, *L'anthropologie cartésienne* (Paris: Presses Universitaires de France, 1990). See also Gary Hatfield, "Descartes's Physiology and Its Relation to His Psychology"; Gaukroger, *Descartes.* It is not far-fetched to presume that it was this insufficiency of his mechanistic model of explanation that hindered

him from ever completing the treatise on animals he worked on for so long. An interesting account of Descartes's notion of mechanism is given in Lisa Shapiro, "The Union of Soul and Body: Descartes' Conception of a Human Being," Ph.D. diss., University of Pittsburgh, 1997.

38. See the notes by Stephen Voss to art. 22–25 in his English translation of *The Passions of the Soul* (Indianapolis: Hackett Publishing, 1989).

39. See this chapter, section 8, p. 189.

40. How this all comes about is explained with more detail in articles 32–39.

41. It is awkward to talk of the neural motions as causes, as Descartes does, since if they constitute the actions in the body of which the passions felt in the soul are, as it were, another side, they must be the same event, as Spinoza saw. It is awkward also to talk, as Descartes often does, about those motions representing things to the mind. With regard to the action-passion identity, this is of course all right: the actions on the level of the body are representations on the mental level. But the mind does not perceive those motions, and the corporeal patterns do not represent: representing, for Descartes, is a thoroughly mental *affaire*. Hence the occasionalist talk: the bodily motions give "occasion" to the mind to represent . . .

42. Although Descartes holds that the soul is really joined to the *whole* body and to the *whole* assemblage of its organs (because the body constitutes, through the assemblage of its organs, a whole that is said to be "in a sense one and indivisible," and the indivisible unextended soul can be united only to the functional unity of the body as we read in article 30 (AT XI 351, CSM I 339)), there is nevertheless one organ in which it is said to "exercise its functions more particularly than in all the others," namely, the pineal gland. Descartes thinks it is particularly suitable for the mind–body interaction because it is "situated in the middle of the brain's substance and suspended above the passage through which the spirits in the brain's anterior cavities communicate with those in its posterior cavities," so that the slightest movements on the part of this gland may alter very greatly the course of these spirits and conversely any change, however slight, taking place in the course of the spirits may do much to change the movements of the gland (art. 31–32 (AT XI 351–353, CSM I 340)).

All this is presented as an empirical hypothesis backed up by some observations (dissections of animal brains) and considerations of various sorts (as, for instance, unity of the body, or symmetry, developed in article 32). The purpose is to explain both how the mechanisms through which the body functions work, and how they could be related to their perceived mental causes and effects, in particular, the affections or emotions.

43. William James, quoted in Cheshire Calhoun and Robert Solomon, eds., *What Is an Emotion?* (New York: Oxford University Press, 1984), pp. 128–129.

44. I say that James *seems* to identify them—I am not in a position to take any stand on how James should be interpreted and what his theory exactly says. This is how the passage from which I quoted begins: "My thesis on the contrary is that *the bodily changes follow directly the* PERCEPTION *of the exciting fact, and that our feeling of the same changes as they occur* IS *the emotion*" (ibid., p. 128; my emphasis).

45. For a comparison of Descartes's view with the James–Lange theory, see, e.g., the introduction to Calhoun and Solomon, eds., *What Is an Emotion?* p. 9.

46. In the Scholastic account of sense perception, they would normally coincide: the object I see (the whiteness of Socrates) is the (efficient) cause of my seeing it. Not so with Cartesian emotions. And whether they exist or not, their objects are rarely as represented or perceived by the person emotionally affected by them.

47. As argued by Deborah Brown, who takes the most interesting contribution of Descartes's account of passions to consist in his new notion of representing in terms of referring introduced in the Fourth Replies to explain how sensory ideas lacking objective reality could have a content. See Brown, "What Was New in the *Passions* of 1649?"

48. Compare the discussion in Chapter 5, section 3, of the famous passage on the judgments involved at the second grade of sense perception in AT VII 436–437, CSM II 294–295.

49. The example is given in Descartes's letter to Chanut, June 6, 1647 (AT V 56–57, CMSK 322), to illustrate how we can fall in love with persons without knowing their merits. I discuss Descartes's definition of the passion of love and the difference between love as a passion and love as a merely intellectual judgment in sections 8 and 9 of this chapter.

50. Susan James seems to take this to be case, see James, *Passion and Action*, p. 94.

51. See Spinoza, *Ethics* II, Prop. 28, Proof, in *Collected Works*, ed. and trans. E. Curley, vol. 1 (Princeton: Princeton University Press, 1985).

52. Or think of a person suffering from bipolar depression; her evaluation of herself, her possibilities, and the world around her varies to a dramatic degree depending, according to contemporary medical expertise, on the level of certain chemicals—serotonin for instance—in her brain. While she thinks she has reasons for feeling depressed or overjoyed, as the case might be, it is all a matter of the production of these

chemicals in her brain, or in the case of deficiency, on her intake of prescribed drugs supposed to restore the balance of those chemical substances.

53. In the first part of the *Passions* Descartes distinguishes the functions of
the body from those of the soul in order to define the passions as states
of the soul or mind caused by movements in the body, and thus to distinguish the passions from other kinds of body-dependent thoughts.
Now, in classifying the passions in Part II according to their function,
the perspective has changed—the point of view that prevails here is that
of the mind–body union. So when Descartes talks of nature here, of
what nature dictates, he is talking of the nature of the union as instituted by God. Thus, when he speaks of utility and harm, he speaks of
what is useful or harmful for the union. On this natural knowledge—
the teachings of nature—its use and limitations, see *Meditation* VI (AT
VII 80–90, CSM II 56–62). See also the comments of Rodis-Lewis, "Limitations of the Mechanical Model."

54. See letter to Chanut, February 1, 1647 (AT IV 607–610, CSMK 308–
314).

55. Compare also the definition of passions given in the letter to Elisabeth:
one can call "passions" "all the thoughts which are thus aroused in the
soul without the assistance of its will, and hence, without any action on
its part, by the cerebral impressions alone, for whatever is not an action
is a passion" (AT IV 310, CSMK 270).

56. To what extent does this account undermine the power of pure reason
to counteract emotions? See the discussion of whether one can love
God by the natural light, that is, by rational consideration alone, in the
letter to Chanut (AT IV 607–610, CSMK 308–310).

57. The judgment or belief that something is agreeable and worth joining
oneself to is thus presupposed in the very definition of love, so that all
forms of love, as Alquié notes, have to contain this intellectual element.
Alquié, vol. 3, p. 1013. See also the account of different kinds of love in
the letter to Chanut, February 1, 1647, discussed below. But this is no
more or less intellectual than the unnoticed judgments involved in
sense perception (the third-level judgments), as Paul Hoffman justly
has pointed out to me.

58. "It seems to me that it is always the same movement that inclines one to
seek the good, and thereby to avoid the evil which is its contrary" (art.
87 (AT XI 393)).

59. *Passions* I, art. 50. Compare John Yolton, *Perceptual Acquaintance from
Descartes to Reid* (Minneapolis: University of Minnesota Press, 1984),
pp. 26 ff.; see also below, quote from letter to Chanut.

60. Thus we can we feel sad or joyful "without being able to observe so dis-

tinctly the good or evil which causes this feeling. This happens when the good or evil forms its impression in the brain without the intervention of the soul, sometimes because it affects only the body and sometimes because, even though it affects the soul, the soul does not consider it as good or evil but views it under some other form whose impression is joined in the brain with that of the good an evil" (*Passions* II, art. 93).

61. They do as a matter of fact constitute important weapons in the struggle to master the passions on which they depend. See, e.g., art. 147 (AT XI 440–441, CSM I 381).

62. "[O]ur soul and body are so linked that once we have joined some bodily action with a certain thought, the one does not occur afterwards without the other occurring too" (art. 107 (AT XI 407, CSM I 365)). See also letter to Elisabeth, May 1646 (AT IV 408, CSMK 286).

63. The same principle explains individual variations and idiosyncracies. See the letter to Elisabeth, May 1646 (AT IV 408, CSMK 286).

64. *Passions* I, art. 44 (AT XI 361–370, CSM I 344–348). See also the letter to Chanut (AT IV 604 ff., CSMK 307 ff.).

65. See the example of the two different evaluations of joy discussed in section 1. From article 139 on, Descartes deals with the value and ordering of the passions from the point of view of the soul, which, as indicated, does not necessarily coincide with their value for the body and the mind–body union, and which will therefore not detain us here.

66. The objects causing passions are always described by Descartes as being represented to the mind in different ways—for instance, joy and sadness arise from the consideration of some good or evil "which is represented to us as belonging to us" (Fr. *"qui nous est représenté comme nous appartenant"*) (AT XI 376), a formulation that recurs in the *Passions* but that the translation of CSM often obscures, as in CSM I 351. Whether and to what extent the representations or their propositional contents, in the case of passions, are in fact properly described as assented to is not quite clear. They do seem to involve (unnoticed) assent as long as they are allowed to play a role in our behavior and emotional life. That assent, often, is triggered as it were against or in spite of our will, although, as argued in the next chapter, Descartes, like the Stoics, thinks that assent could always be withheld.

67. Susan James deserves credit for emphasizing, in her recent account, their double character of psycho-physical states and hence for avoiding such distortions. See James, *Passion and Action,* chap. 5.

68. See also articles 42–44.

69. *"Comme il n'y a aucun bien au monde, excepté le bon sens, qu'on puisse*

absolument nommer bien, il n'y a aussi aucun mal, dont on ne puisse tirer avantage, ayant le bon sens." To Elisabeth, June 1645 (Alquié, vol. 2, p. 579). See also the subsequent letters to Elisabeth in the summer and fall of 1645 (AT IV 251–317, CSMK 255–273).

70. In Chapter 7, section 9, I return to the conflict between the Stoic theme of controlling ourselves and themes related to the technical domination of the world. Compare Alquié, vol. 2, p. 52 n. 1.

71. At least, that is, when they are in full possession of their power of reasoning. See the letter to Elisabeth, September 1, 1645 (AT IV 281–287, CSMK 262–265).

72. See also the letter to Huyghens, January 1646 (AT III 658, wrongly dated in AT V 262).

73. AT VI 23, CSM I 122. Descartes does not apply this strictly to himself, but it follows from the doctrine here examined that this must apply in our own case as well.

74. We are also often most moved by them when events of life give us no time for reflection, as Elisabeth testifies when complaining to Descartes about the difficulty of practicing his advice always to examine the true value of things in the light of reason and not to let oneself be misled by passions. See the correspondence of Elisabeth and Descartes during 1645–1646. For Elisabeth's contributions, see my "Descartes and Elisabeth. A Philosophical Dialogue?" (forthcoming).

7. Free Will and Virtue

1. Art. 41 (AT IX 359). Cf. the questions raised by Ferdinand Alquié's notes to article 47, Alquié, vol. 3, pp. 990 n. 1, 991 n. 1.

2. See Plato, *Republic* IV, 436b8.

3. Art. 49. Descartes seems to think that also false judgments, if firm, can be considered as the soul's "proper weapons." But he also notes that there is "a great difference between the resolutions which proceed from some false opinion and those which are based solely on the knowledge of the truth." Only those who follow the latter can be assured of never having to regret their actions (AT XI 368, CSM I 347).

4. Plato presents at least two different, equally influential models. One is that of the tripartite soul outlined in the *Republic,* which Aristotle develops into his doctrine of three different souls or psychic powers; the other is that of the *Phaedo* and the *Phaedrus,* where the emphasis is even more on the opposition between the rational and the irrational forces operating in the human soul. But to the extent that the distinction between rational versus nonrational desires plays a central role in both,

the Aristotelian and Platonist theory can, for the purposes of the comparison here undertaken, be treated as different forms of basically dualist models.

5. I am using dualism versus monism in the way Brad Inwood uses these terms in characterizing the psychology of the Stoics as opposed to the Platonic and Aristotelian model. The dualism is internal to the soul, and does not refer to mind–body dualism. Both the Stoic and the Cartesian psychologistic monism go hand in hand with their respective body–soul (Stoics) and mind–body (Descartes) dualisms. See B. Inwood, *Ethics and Human Action in Early Stoicism* (Oxford: Clarendon Press, 1985); and "Seneca and Psychological Dualism," in J. Brunschwig and M. Nussbaum, eds., *Passions and Perceptions: Studies in Hellenistic Philosophy of Mind* (Cambridge: Cambridge University Press, 1993), pp. 150–183.

6. It is not difficult to find many echoes of and also explicit references to Stoic moral ideas in Descartes's exchange with Elisabeth and in the *Passions,* for instance, to their view of passions as obstacles to virtue, which Descartes emphatically rejects.

7. As we saw, he characterizes as purely "fictitious" *(imaginaires)* the battles *(combats)* that are "customarily" supposed to take place between the lower and the higher part of the soul, between the part called "sensitive" and the one called "raisonnable," or, as he also describes them, between the natural appetites and the will. See *Passions* I, art. 47 (AT XI 364); and the account in, for example, Seneca discussed below. Compare also the passage from Plutarch about Chrysippus from H. von Arnim, *Stoicorum veterum fragmenta,* vol. 3 (Leipzig, 1924), p. 459, quoted by Julia Annas, *Hellenistic Philosophy of Mind* (Berkeley: University of California Press, 1992), p. 117, where the conflict is described in terms strikingly similar to those Descartes uses in art. 48 (AT XI 367), quoted above, with the interesting difference that where the Stoics see a conflict opposing reason to itself, Descartes talks of the will as being opposed to itself.

8. For the Stoic view, see the account in Annas, *Hellenistic Philosophy of Mind,* pp. 75 ff., 117; for more thorough discussions of the early Stoic view, see Inwood, *Ethics and Human Action in Early Stoicism,* chap. 5; Tad Brennan, "The Old Stoic Theory of Emotions," in J. Sihvola and T. Engberg-Pedersen, *The Emotions in Hellenistic Philosophy* (Dordrecht: Kluwer Academic Publishers, 1998), pp. 21–70.

9. Compare Inwood, *Ethics and Human Action in Early Stoicism,* p. 144.

10. Thus pain is described by Cicero as "an opinion about a present evil, and in this opinion there is this element, that it is right to feel pain." This opinion is often described as fresh, but that does not necessarily

mean recent or actual in a temporal sense. The opinion is fresh as long as it is assented to, and as long as, by virtue of this assent, it remains active. *Tusculan Disputations* quoted by Inwood, *Ethics and Human Action in Early Stoicism,* pp. 148 ff.

11. Is the affective reaction with concomitant physiological changes produced by the evaluative judgment or is it a (partial) cause of it? There obviously are, as the critics of Stoics have not failed to point out, affective reactions that even a Stoic sage seems unable to control, such as pallor, trembling, blushing, and so on. They are described in an often quoted passage by Aulus Gellius, based on a (lost) fragment of Epictetus, as involuntary presentations (impressions) striking the mind at some unexpected event, before any evaluative opinion is formed of it. "Therefore, when some frightening sound from the sky or a collapsing building or the sudden announcement of some danger, or something else of the sort, occurs it is inevitable that even a sage's soul be moved for a short while and be contracted and grow pale, not because he has formed an opinion of anything evil, but because of certain rapid and unreflective movements which forestall the proper functioning of the intellect or reason. Soon, though, the sage in question does not give assent . . . to such presentations . . . but he rejects and refuses them and judges that there is nothing in them to be feared. And they say that the difference between the mind of the sage and the fool is that the fool thinks that the violent and harsh presentations which first strike the mind *(primo animi sui pulsi)* really are as they seem; and he also confirms with his own assent these initial reactions, just as though they were to be feared." See Aulus Gellius, *Noctes Atticae* 19.1.14–20, quoted by Inwood, *Ethics and Human Action in Early Stoicism,* p. 177. These involuntary motions have a counterpart in Descartes's theory: the physiological reactions and the involuntary inclinations of the will that are the immediate mental effects of the perceptions causing the passion (Chapter 6, section 6).

12. He writes: "Emotion is not a matter of being moved by impressions received, but of surrendering oneself to them and following up the chance movement . . . So the first mental agitation *(agitatio animi)* induced by the impression of wrong done *(species iniurae)* is no more anger than the impression itself. The impulse that follows, which not only registers but confirms *(adprobavit)* the impression, is what counts as anger, the agitation of a mind proceeding by its own deliberate decision to exact retribution." This last movement is described as "really out of control, wanting retribution not just 'if it is right' but at all costs, it has completely overcome reason." Seneca, *De Ira* 2.3, quoted in Seneca, *Moral*

and Political Essays, ed. and trans. John M. Cooper and J. F. Procopé (Cambridge: Cambridge University Press, 1995), pp. 44–45.

13. Seneca, *Moral and Political Essays,* p. 45. The doctrine of propassions seems to be a later development and one can ask whether it does not constitute a change of the original Stoic doctrine, bringing it closer to the Platonic than to Chrysippus's position. As Simo Knuuttila points out, it presents the Stoic sage with the challenge to master not only his own rational judgments but also the inclinations and changes related to the involuntary propassions. See S. Knuuttila, *Emotions in Ancient and Medieval Philosophy,* chap. 1 (forthcoming, Oxford University Press).

14. Brad Inwood has argued that Seneca here introduces a specific (new?) sense of rationality, which presupposes a mere possibility of change by rational deliberation, yet does not require that such deliberation has taken place. See Inwood, "Seneca and Psychological Dualism," pp. 167, 175 ff. For a very instructive more general discussion of the early Stoic notions of rationality, see also Brennan, "The Old Stoic Theory of Emotions."

15. For instance, in Justus Lipsius, Montaigne, and in particular in Guillaume du Vair's *Philosophie morale des Stoiques* (1585). See Anthony Levi, *French Moralists* (Oxford: Clarendon Press, 1964), chaps. 4 and 9. Spinoza too notes the resemblance between Descartes's view of the will and the Stoic view of mind's absolute control over affects, see *Ethics* V, Preface.

16. It is somewhat surprising that so little attention has been paid to the parallels between Descartes's and Seneca's views—in spite of the common streak of voluntarism so prominent in both theories. According to Stephen Gaukroger, Renaissance and early modern discussions of passions are dominated by what he broadly terms a polarity between Stoic and Augustinian conceptions of the passions. But there is no discussion of in what ways or forms such bipolarity would be found in Descartes. Gaukroger draws on William J. Bouwsma, "The Two Faces of Humanism: Stoicism and Augustinianism in Renaissance Thought," in H. Oberman and T. Brady, eds., *Itinerarium Italicum* (Leiden: Brill, 1975); Albrecht Dihle, *The Theory of the Will in Classical Antiquity* (Berkeley: University of California Press, 1982); and Levi, *French Moralists.* Stephen Gaukroger, *Descartes: An Intellectual Biography* (Oxford: Clarendon Press, 1995), pp. 395–398.

17. See the clarifying account of Michael Frede, "The Stoic Doctrine of the Affections of the Soul," in M. Schofield and G. Striker, eds., *The Norms of Nature* (Cambridge: Cambridge University Press, 1986), pp. 93–110, 95 ff.

18. See NE VII, 3, 1146a1–24, 1147b9–18, and 1147a24–1147b1.
19. Inwood, *Ethics and Human Action in Early Stoicism,* p. 11.
20. Cf. Aristotle, *De Motu Animalium* 3.11, 434a16–21. Inwood also draws attention to ibid. 3.7., 431a8–14, where Aristotle compares the information provided to desire by perception with a verbal report. Inwood, *Ethics and Human Action in Early Stoicism,* pp. 15–16.
21. Inwood, *Ethics and Human Action in Early Stoicism,* p. 17. The notion of assent, which in the Stoic account may be said to take the place of deliberation in Aristotle's account, presupposes that the information embedded in the presentations of the *phantasia* can be formulated in terms of *lekta* and *axiomata.* Assent is given to *lekta* and is therefore possible only in rational animals (that is, adult humans in full possession of language)—in fact assent comes with reason (language) and is what distinguishes a rational animal from brutes. See also Annas, *Hellenistic Philosophy of Mind,* p. 96. Annas also points out that the Stoics downplay the role of deliberation and that they make little use of the Aristotelian concept of deliberated choice *(prohairesis).* They are also said to substitute the Aristotelian broad concept of desire in general *(orexis)* with their term impulse *(horme),* and this latter became established philosophical usage. Ibid., p. 92 n. 8.
22. According to Stobaeus's account of Zeno, in Inwood, *Ethics and Human Action in Early Stoicism,* p. 30, and the same phases are mentioned also by Seneca.
23. The passions, *pathe,* which are false beliefs concerning the good or bad presented by involuntary impulses and appearances, lead to irrational actions and may, as we have seen, be called irrational in this sense. However, to the extent that the mind could have, even when it did not, refused assent, they should be seen as products of reason itself, and the acts they lead to are acts for which the agent is fully responsible. See the references given in Inwood, *Ethics and Human Action in Early Stoicism,* chap. 3; Michael Frede, "Stoics and Skeptics on Clear and Distinct Ideas," in M. Burnyeat, ed., *The Skeptical Tradition* (Berkeley: University of California Press, 1983); Annas, *Hellenistic Philosophy of Mind,* whose accounts I basically have followed here.
24. "[T]he appearance that moves the impulse is of something as being then and there 'appropriate'" (Annas, *Hellenistic Philosophy of Mind,* p. 96). Compare also note 21.
25. As Annas puts it, given the appearances I have, "I cannot help desiring my bringing about the satisfaction of certain predicates and not others. But what I can help is assenting to the corresponding statements of 'I ought to F': for without such an assent there may be a mere desire to

bring about a certain state of affairs, but there will not be the full impulse to bring it about, and so there will not be the action" (ibid., p. 98).

26. Yet, as Annas understands it, assents do occupy "the conceptual room taken up by *basic* actions in some modern theories." See the discussion in ibid., pp. 98–100. Such internalization of the concept of (basic) action seems problematic in more ways than one, and is likely to mislead as a reading of the Stoics. That it suggests itself is, however, noteworthy, and deserves a fuller discussion than can be given here.

27. See Frede, "Stoics and Skeptics on Clear and Distinct Ideas," p. 67, and "The Stoic Doctrine of the Affections of the Soul"; but see also Inwood, who expresses some reservations about this, *Ethics and Human Action in Early Stoicism,* p. 76.

28. See the discussion in Inwood, *Ethics and Human Action in Early Stoicism,* pp. 46–52, and the sources there quoted. However, what matters for Chrysippus, for instance, is not, as one commentator argues, whether assent is necessarily caused, but whether what ultimately determines the action is an internal (and hence voluntary) as opposed to external cause. See Richard Sorabji, "Causation, Laws and Necessity," in M. Schofield, M. Burnyeat, and J. Barnes, eds., *Doubt and Dogmatism: Studies in Hellenistic Epistemology* (Oxford: Clarendon Press, 1980); see also Inwood, *Ethics and Human Action in Early Stoicism,* p. 69. For a thorough discussion of the problem, see Suzanne Bobzien, *Determinism and Freedom in Stoic Philosophy* (Oxford: Clarendon Press, 1998), and the textual references there given.

29. Inwood, *Ethics and Human Action in Early Stoicism,* p. 83.

30. Ibid., p. 83, and the sources on pp. 83–84.

31. See the account of Bobzien, who mentions early Christian apologists like Justin Martyr as both strongly influenced by Stoic thought of his time and sternly opposed to Stoic determinism. In his work one can find what one misses in earlier texts (for example, Epictetus), "the introduction of *eleutheros* into the discussion of the compatibility of the Fate Principle with that which depends on us." Justin is reported to have claimed that human beings and angels have a power *(dynamis)* of free choice *(eulethera prohairesis)* and this, according to Bobzien, is "the first time, perhaps, where the two terms are associated," although it is not clear what precisely he took this freedom to involve. The notion of "that which depends on us" and "free" are found closely related also in Alexander Aphrodisias, in Nemesius, and in Plotinus. See Bobzien, *Determinism and Freedom,* pp. 344 ff., and the references there given.

32. See, for instance, Dihle, *The Theory of the Will in Classical Antiquity;*

Charles Kahn, "Discovering the Will: From Aristotle to Augustine," in
J. M. Dillon and A. A. Long, eds., *The Question of "Eclecticism": Studies in
Later Greek Philosophy* (Berkeley: University of California Press, 1988),
pp. 234–260; T. H. Irwin, "Who Discovered the Will?" in J. E. Tom-
berlin, ed., *Philosophical Perspectives 6, Ethics* (Atascadero, Calif.: Ridgeview Publishing, 1992), pp. 453–474. I touch briefly upon this discussion in section 6.

33. Compare Frede, "The Stoic Doctrine of the Affections of the Soul,"
p. 101; Kahn, "Discovering the Will," pp. 239 ff. Aristotle is often read,
notably by Aquinas and his followers but also by contemporary commentators, as holding that deliberation is always about means, not
about ends, and that the intellect is somehow primary in the process of
deliberation. These assumptions are not straightforwardly supported by
the texts. His use, in the *Nicomachean Ethics*, of expressions that are
translated as "deliberate (reasoned) desire" or "desiderative reason" indicates that there is really no order of priority between reason and desire: both are necessary constituents of choice or decision. And as other
passages indicate, the action toward the end (the virtuous action), being a constituent of the end, cannot be considered as a simple means to
an end—it is also an expression of the end. In deliberating about the
means, one deliberates about the end: about the action that best real-
izes the end. So there seems, arguably, to be a sense in which it is, for
Aristotle, also a matter of deliberation and decision (or choice)
whether the end pursued is good or bad. See David Wiggins, *Deliberation
and Practical Reason*, reprinted in D. Wiggins, *Needs, Values, Truth* (Oxford: Clarendon Press, 1998), pp. 215–238.

34. Charles Kahn, "Discovering the Will," p. 241.

35. Ibid., p. 242. According to Kahn, "this notion of willing as a purely spiritual, incorporeal activity points ahead to the Cartesian notion of volition as a mental event causing bodily motion" (ibid., p. 243). For a
more recent survey of various developments in the prehistory of the notion of the will, see Richard Sorabji, *Emotion and Peace of Mind: From
Stoic Agitation to Christian Temptation* (Oxford: Oxford University Press,
2000), pp. 320–321. Whatever the actual agents of the change involved
here were, Kahn seems right in seeing the Stoic notion of assent—the
decisive role attributed by them to assent as the cause of voluntary action—as an important early step toward later developments of the notion of will. It is not, he points out, the act of an immaterial mind, but
"occurs as some kind of change in the tension of the soul-*pneuma* located in the heart." But, he argues, "once the Stoic concept of 'assent' is
taken over into Neo-platonic and Christian views of the soul as an im-

material entity, Chrysippus's doctrine of assent will become the focal point of the concept of volition or 'willing' that we find in Augustine, Aquinas and Descartes. For *sunkatathesis* in the Stoic theory of human action plays exactly the same role that *concensus* and the 'command of the will' play for St. Thomas" (Kahn, "Discovering the Will," pp. 245–246).

36. As I read Aristotle, his account remains Socratic in the sense that the weakness he criticizes Socrates for not admitting is in the end analyzed as a failure of the intellect, which for one reason or another is unable to pay full attention to the better reason. See NE XVII.

37. For Descartes's use of the terms *bona mens, lumen naturalis, bon sens, sagesse,* and so on, see René Descartes, *Discours de la Méthode: Texte et commentaire,* ed. É. Gilson (Paris: Vrin, 1925, 1967), pp. 81–82.

38. The will, it is true, is not mentioned as a separate faculty. But the strategy recommended by Descartes in the *Rules,* as in the later rules of the *Discourse,* presupposes that the intellect is in control of its own acts, that it can direct its attention and determine whether to consent or not to what is presented to it. The unity of the mind or reason, here described also as a "purely spiritual" power of cognition, which is now active, now passive, is stressed already in Rule Twelve (AT X 415–416).

39. Everyone can perceive/see by intuition that she exists, that she is thinking, "and similar things, which are far more numerous than most people realize, disdaining as they do to turn their mind to so simple matters" (AT X 368, CSM I 14).

40. God's will, recall, is itself infinite and unrestrained in its power: by willing something God makes it true and not the other way around, as Leibniz and many other rationalists would have it. See Chapter 1, section 12, and the references there given. I return to this point below in section 9.

41. For this point, beyond the passages from the Fourth Meditation quoted at the end of the last section, see also AT VIII-I 19–20, and conversation with Burman, April 16, 1648 (AT V 159).

42. B. Kent, *Virtues of the Will: The Transformation of Ethics in the Late Thirteenth Century* (Washington, D.C.: Catholic University of America Press, 1995), pp. 94–95.

43. AT VII 57. We also read in the *Principles* I, 35: "The will . . . can in a certain sense be called infinite since . . . its scope extends to anything that can possibly be an object of any other will—even the immeasurable will of God" (AT VIII-I 18, CSM I 204). I have discussed the interpretation of this doctrine elsewhere (see Chapter 1, section 7, note 51 and the references there given). I claim that Descartes's radical conception of God's power is significant for his doctrine of freedom in that the infini-

tude he ascribes to the latter presupposes the former, namely, the idea that nothing can be prior to or restrain the divine will.

44. Letter to Mersenne, April 15, 1630 (AT I 146, CSMK 23); G. F. W. Leibniz, *La Monadologie*, art. 43–46.

45. See the discussion by Michelle Beyssade cited in note 57.

46. But a few paragraphs later, at the end of the same letter, he agrees to the dictum that *omnis peccans est ignorans.* Cf. also AT VII 57–58, 59, ll. 2–3.

47. The *locus classicus* for this hypothesis is Étienne Gilson, *La liberté chez Descartes et la théologie* (Paris: Alcan, 1913, reprint, Paris: J. Vrin, 1987). Gilson's reading is strongly colored by his own Thomist bias, shown in his eagerness to present Descartes as in total agreement with Aquinas, and in his misunderstanding of the freedom of indifference advocated by the critics of Aquinas's position. Gilson, *La liberté chez Descartes,* Part 2, chaps. 1–3, for instance, p. 311.

48. Harry G. Frankfurt, "Concerning the Freedom and Limits of the Will," in H. Frankfurt, *Necessity, Freedom and Love* (Cambridge: Cambridge University Press, 1999), p. 71.

49. See Frankfurt, "Concerning the Freedom and Limits of the Will," pp. 71–72, 80–81, and the references there given.

50. Spinoza, *Ethics* III, Prop. 2, p. 497.

51. For textual evidence, see section 4.

52. August Dihle, for instance, has argued that the concept of will as distinct from intellect or reason, on the one hand, and from desire or emotion on the other emerges in the Christian tradition: it presupposes the theological doctrine of the divine will as the source of moral norms and authority, on which the notion of the human will is modeled, and it gets its full philosophical articulation in Augustine. See Dihle, *The Theory of the Will in Classical Antiquity.* Richard Sorabji reports that the terminology of *libera voluntas* appears in the first century A.D. in Lucretius, followed by Cicero (who translates Aristotle's *boulesis* with *voluntas*). Tertullian, who wrote shortly after A.D. 200, uses *libera arbitrii potestas* and *arbitrii libertas,* which sometimes are used as translations of the Greek term *to autexousion.* See Sorabji, *Emotion and Peace of Mind,* pp. 320–321.

53. Kahn, "Discovering the Will," p. 238.

54. Quoted from R. A. Gauthier, *Aristotle: L'Éthique à Nicomaque* I.1, 2nd ed. (Louvain: Publications Universitaires de Louvain, 1970), p. 259, by Kahn, "Discovering the Will," p. 238. See also T. H. Irwin, "Who Discovered the Will?" Simo Knuuttila points out that since Augustine's conception of the will not only is connected to a Platonist division of the human soul but also to a special theological theory of corruption

and grace, there are good reasons to be hesitant in calling him, as Dihle does, "the inventor of our modern notion of the will." S. Knuuttila, "The Logic of Will in Medieval Thought," in G. Matthews, ed., *The Augustinian Tradition* (Berkeley: University of California Press, 1999).

55. *De libero arbitrio* I, 16. I have used the translation by T. Williams, *On the Free Choice of the Will* (Indianapolis: Hackett Publishing, 1993), pp. 27, 104–105. The second thesis is the answer given in Book III to the question concerning the first cause of sin, and hence of the will itself (p. 104). The question seems to lead to an infinite regress. If there is a cause of the will, shouldn't one ask what causes this cause, and what causes the cause of the cause of the will to sin, and so on, *ad infinitum?* There is no point, Augustine says, to search any further than the root of the issue. The root cause of sin is a perverse will, and we can go no further. He asks: "And besides, what could be the cause of will before the will itself? Either it is the will itself, in which case the root of all evils is still the will, or else it is not the will, in which case there is no sin" (p. 105).

56. I here rely on the work of D. Odon Lottin, *Psychologie et morale aux XII et XIIIe siècles,* vol. 1, *Problèmes de psychologie* (J. Duculot, S:A. Éditeur, Gembloux, 1957); and Kent, *Virtues of the Will.* The Latin *arbitrium* with its legal connotations is perhaps better translated as decision than choice, at least in the earliest discussions before 1277. Among the issues debated before that date was whether free decision is an act (William of Auxerre) or a power of reason and will (as suggested by Peter Lombard), or whether it was a distinct faculty, or perhaps a habit. Related issues were the status of reason and will themselves: whether they were separate faculties or not, and how they were related—what role they played respectively in deliberation and decision. While the early Franciscan masters did not see them as necessarily opposed, and often identified free decision with reason and will—the latter providing the motive force and the former the rational apprehension—Bonaventure and his followers put more emphasis on the will, which was taken to command the other faculties. "Decision belongs to reason, freedom to will, for the other powers in us have to be moved at the nod *(nutus)* of the will" *(Dicitur enim liberum et dicitur arbitrium; et arbitrium est ispius rationis, liberats, vero ipisius voluntatis)* (Bonaventure, *Sent.,* cited in Kent, *Virtues of the Will,* p. 101). Free decision begins in reason but is completed in and by the will, which according to Bonaventure is essentially active. He leans on Anselm citing his remark that "the will is a self-moving instrument." This obscure idea of Anselm's of a self-moving instrument was frequently repeated by later Franciscans. See the account in Kent, *Virtues of the Will,* pp. 99–101 and *passim.*

57. Somewhere along the way choice becomes what seems a more natural translation of *arbitrium* than decision. On changes in Descartes's uses of the terms *voluntas, liberum arbitrium,* see Michelle Beyssade, "Descartes's Doctrine of Freedom: Differences between the French and Latin Texts of the Fourth Meditation," in J. Cottingham, ed., *Reason, Will and Sensation: Studies in Descartes's Metaphysics* (Oxford: Clarendon Press, 1994), pp. 191–208.

58. See Kent, *Virtues of the Will,* chap. 2, for an interesting account of the discussions of the will in the aftermath of the condemnations in Paris in the 1270s and the transformations of the notion of virtue in this context.

59. "Just as the intellect necessarily adheres *(inhaeret)* to the first principles of thought, or the will necessarily adheres to the pursuit of our ultimate goal, which is happiness; as Aristotle says in Physics II, the goal has the same role in practical reasoning as premises have in theoretical reasoning" (ST Ia.82.1).

60. "We are masters of our own acts in that we can choose this or that. But we choose, not the end, but *things for the sake of the end,* as we read in the Ethics. Hence our desire for the ultimate end *(appetitus ultimi finis)* is not among the things we are masters of" (ibid., Ia. 82, 1,3).

61. See Calvin Normore, "Picking and Choosing: Anselm and Ockham on Choice," *Vivarium* 36 (1998): 23–39, where a sharp contrast is drawn between two different ways of thinking about choice with respect to the question of ends: on the one hand, the intellectualist, Aristotelian model (that is, *roughly* Aristotelian, since the debate was precisely about whether Aristotle defended this model—yet it does capture central claims of a model widely attributed to him in medieval discussions), and on the other, the alternative model emerging in the voluntarist tradition.

62. I rely in particular on studies by Allan Wolter and John Boler on Scotus's conception of the will. The texts here quoted are from Duns Scotus, *On the Will and Morality,* sel. and trans. A. B. Wolter (Washington, D.C.: Catholic University of America Press, 1986).

63. Scotus writes: "The *affectio justitiae* is nobler than the *affectio commodi,* understanding by 'justice' not only acquired or infused justice, but also innate justice, which is the will's inborn liberty *(libertas ingenita)* by reason of which it is able to will some good not oriented to itself." *Ordinatio* III, suppl., dist. 4 (quoted from *On the Will and Morality,* p. 153). John Boler notes that this contrast is not a traditional one; I shortly return to this point.

64. *Ordinatio* III, dist. 17 (*On the Will and Morality,* p. 155). For Scotus's dis-

tinction between nature and will, see *Quaestionem in Metaphysicam* IX, q. 15 (ibid., pp. 136–137).

65. David Hume, *A Treatise of Human Nature,* ed. L. A. Selby-Bigge, 2nd ed. (Oxford: Clarendon Press, 1978), Book II, Part III, Section II.

66. "Descartes on the Will," in A. Kenny, *The Anatomy of the Soul* (Oxford: Basil Blackwell, 1973).

67. *Ordinatio* II, dist. 17 (*On the Will and Morality,* p. 155; my emphasis). On Scotus's analysis, freedom consists in the fact that for any act of willing *W,* if the will freely elicits or refuses to elicit *W,* it must at the same instant of eliciting or refusing to elicit *W* be actively capable of eliciting the opposite. This means, as Boler explains: "No finite agency or natural conditions operating upon the will, in particular nothing internal to the rational agent (e.g., the intellect), determines a free will to move itself to will or refrain from willing." See John Boler, "Transcending the Natural: Duns Scotus on the Two Affections of the Will," *American Catholic Philosophical Quarterly* 67, no. 1 (1993): 109–126.

68. *Ordinatio* IV, suppl., dist. 49, qq. 9–10, art. 2 (*On the Will and Morality,* p. 161). Rega Wood has pointed out in correspondence that Wolter's translation of the line inserted in Latin is misleading. Scotus never says the will can *nill* happiness; on the contrary, he says that it cannot nill happiness. The construction, however, is awkward, so I have rendered the translation as Wolter renders it. But I agree that the argument does not establish anything else than that we can fail, or omit, to will happiness. This point is clearly stated also from *Opus Oxoniense* 4.49.10, where he says: *"voluntas respectu cuiuscumque actus est libera et a nullo obiectio necessitatur, non tamen potest voluntas nolle aut odire beatitudinem."* (Rega Wood translates: "the will with respect to any act whatever is free and it is necessitated by no object. Yet the will cannot reject or hate beatitude, nor [can it] will misery" (Lyons 1639—or Hildesheim—10:514)). According to Wood, Ockham is the first to claim we can hate the good as such.

69. See *Ordinatio* IV, suppl., dist. 49, qq. 9–10, art. 2 (*On the Will and Morality,* pp. 161–162).

70. *Quaestionem in Metaphysicam* IX, q. 15 (*On the Will and Morality,* pp. 136–137). Scotus connects it to his ideas on logical possibility and synchronic alternative possibilities: there is a sense in which at any time of eliciting an act *Z* of the will, the will is actively capable of not eliciting it: to elicit and not elicit cannot both be actual at once, but they are nonetheless both possible at one and the same instant. See *Lectura* I, 39, intro., trans., and commentary by A. Vos Jaczn, H. Velcus et al. (Dordrecht-Holland: Kluwer Academic Publishers, 1994), pp. 117 ff.

John Boler does not discuss the connection between these two doctrines—the metaphysical doctrine of contingence and the doctrine of logical possibility and Scotus's notion of free decision. He insists that while the freedom of the will does presuppose independence in voluntary action from other causal processes (efficient as well as final), its proper autonomy is "that of a moral agent." "Transcending the Natural," p. 110. There are also, he argues, good reasons to keep the idea of dual inclinations of the free will distinct from the claim of superabundant sufficiency or inborn liberty, which is its metaphysical presupposition. It is the latter that counts for the Scotian notion of free agency. An agent can have two inclinations and always follow the stronger one, hence never act freely—she can have one inclination, and because of superabundant sufficiency, she can be free—free not to follow the present inclination of her will. The crucial thing is not the ability to choose between two affections but "the capacity of the will to refuse to act no matter what the antecedent conditions." Boler takes Scotus's thought experiment about a fictional agent in *Ordinatio* III, dist. 26—he calls it the Amoral Angel—to support this. See ibid., pp. 113–115, and the references there given. This latter capacity, to refuse to act no matter what the antecedent conditions, as I understand it, presupposes Scotus's idea of logical possibility: the idea that acting and not acting are both possible at one and the same point in time.

71. The natural desire of the highest part of the soul—the rational appetite or will, which in other rationalist accounts is the agent of moral action—is here reduced as it were to a merely *natural* inclination bound by its natural goal: it is necessarily tending to the self-realization of its intellectual nature. For as Boler points out, "while *affectio commodi* is said to be 'natural and necessary,' neither *affectio justitiae* nor the combination of the two *affectiones* is so described." The affection for justice is not another appetite tending to the realization of a higher kind of nature. As Boler explains: "Scotus is not saying just that the rational will has a higher and a lower appetite; he is saying that the normal (Aristotelian) scheme, in terms of appetite and proper object, for explaining how an agent comes to move itself is not appropriate for will." The rational will transcends it and operates in a way radically different from any natural appetite. Ibid., pp. 116–118.

72. I borrow this expression from Wilfrid Sellars. See his "Fatalism and Determinism," in Keith Lehrer, ed., *Freedom and Determinism* (New York: Random House, 1966), p. 145; and *Science, Perception and Reality* (London: Routledge and Kegan Paul), pp. 6, 16–17, 39.

73. Spinoza, *Ethics* III, Prop. 2, and V, Preface; Leibniz, *Monadology*, art. 80.

74. For instance, in the letter to Elisabeth, November 3, 1645 (AT IV 332–333, CSMK 277).
75. See the texts quoted in section 5.
76. Descartes's radical doubt can be seen as an expression of the freedom he attributes to the will in his main work.
77. Compare Leibniz, *Monadology*, art. 78–79.
78. Paul Hoffman argues persuasively in a recent paper that Descartes, far from being a libertarian, is in fact a compatibilist, and moreover, that he is a kind of Super-compatibilist. See P. Hoffman, "The Passions and Freedom of Will," unpublished manuscript, 1999, section 1.
79. Note that Descartes's correspondent, a Jesuit, apparently defended the more radical doctrine. For he continues: "And so, since you regard freedom not simply as indifference but rather as a real and positive power to determine oneself, the difference between us is merely one of names—for I agree the will has such a power" (AT IV 116, CSMK 233–234). But, as noted earlier, a few paragraphs down in the same letter he adheres to the dictum that *omnis peccans est ignorans*.
80. Kenny, "Descartes on the Will," in A. Kenny, *The Anatomy of the Soul* (Oxford: Basil Blackwell, 1973), p. 109.
81. See Kent, *Virtues of the Will*.
82. See Calvin Normore, "Picking and Choosing: Anselm and Ockham on Choice," *Vivarium* 36 (1998): 23–39.
83. See Ferdinand Alquié, *La découverte métaphysique de l'homme* (Paris: Presses Universitaires de France, 1950), chap. 14; Kenny, "Descartes on the Will," pp. 105 ff.
84. Descartes uses these very terms in the letter to Mesland, February 9, 1645 (AT IV 173, l. 17), in a passage that is discussed at the end of section 9.
85. If it were the case that clear and distinct ideas determine assent necessarily, why then did God make our will such that it so easily fails to attend with sufficient care to the clear and distinct ideas He also provides the mind? Why were our minds created with such a deficient power of attention? This kind of worry does indeed come up in the *Meditations* (see note 86), and not without reason, for the intellect, after all, is a passive power of the mind: it receives whatever ideas it has, and all its actions depend on the will. (See, e.g., AT III 372, CSMK 182; AT IV 113, CSMK 232.) Now if the will were determined by some ideas, the source of the ideas must determine the will. It is not our will that makes those ideas clear and distinct: it finds them so. If on the other hand it is because "the nature of the soul is such that it hardly attends for more than a moment to a single thing" (AT IV 116, CSMK 233)—if it is a failure of

attention—it follows, in the end, that we sin by the imperfection of our nature and our will. But this goes against what Descartes says elsewhere about the will being our highest perfection. It also contradicts what he says in the second Mesland letter (AT IV 174, CSMK 245), to be considered shortly.

86. This leads to the troubling question why God, as a perfect craftsman, did not give him a perfect nature, to wit, "a nature such that I was never mistaken." Perhaps there is some reason—perhaps it is better that "I should make mistakes than that I should not do so." We cannot understand the reasons for all God's actions, and there would be considerable "rashness" in thinking oneself capable of investigating the purposes of God (AT VII 55, CSM II 38–39).

87. For Spinoza's criticism of Descartes's theory of judgment, see the discussion in Chapter 5, section 3.

88. AT VI 25, CSM I 123. None of the other passions lead us to action except by means of the desire they produce (AT XI 436, CSM I 379), for desire is the only passion that concerns the future, whether its object is to acquire (or preserve) some good or avoid some present or future evil (AT XI 375, CSM I 350; AT XI 392–393, CSM I 358–359).

89. Any particular desire makes the whole body "more agile and ready to move than it normally is" without it, and this condition of the body reinforces it, rendering the desires of the soul "stronger and keener" (AT XI 411, CSM I 367).

90. See also AT VI 25–26, CSM I 123–124.

91. We could use this knowledge, Descartes writes in advertising his new philosophy in Part VI of the *Discourse,* as artisans use theirs, "for all the purposes for which it is appropriate, and thus make ourselves, as it were, the lords and masters of nature," which, he continues, "is desirable not only for the invention of innumerable devices which would facilitate our enjoyment of the fruits of the earth and all the goods we find there, but also, and most importantly, for the maintenance of health, which is undoubtedly the chief good and the foundation of all the other goods in this life" (AT VI 143, CSM I 62). This is not a matter of individual salvation but a shared, public endeavor for the common good.

92. See the letter to Reneri for Pollot, April or May 1638 (AT II 36–37, CSMK 97–98). But see also the comments of Alquié on that passage. Where others see a conflict between the Stoic idea of self-mastery through mastery of our thoughts and technical mastery of the world, Alquié sees the former as a presupposition of the latter: "Thus, to understand that nothing depends on us except our thoughts, prepares us,

in fact, to the technical mastery of the physical reality." Alquié, vol. 2, pp. 52–53 n. 1.

93. See also the letter to Queen Christina, November 20, 1647 (AT V 85, CSMK 325–326).

94. Compare Aristotle in NE X, 1179a.

95. See Stephen Voss's translation of *The Passions of the Soul* (Indianapolis: Hackett Publishing, 1989), p. 103, note.

96. See articles 154–155 (AT XI 446–447, CSM I 384–385) and articles 158–161 (AT XI 449–454, CSM I 386–388).

97. The outward appearance, the gestures, the gait, and so on vary, we are told, with the better or worse opinion a person has of herself (AT XI 446, CSM I 384).

Index

abstraction, 35, 133, 307n19
action(s), 48, 50, 53, 74, 75, 94, 102, 109, 110, 168, 170, 213, 222, 225, 229, 234, 240, 241, 243, 249, 251, 252, 254, 256; of soul/mind, 51, 167, 170, 182, 190, 202, 203, 208, 209; natural action, 52; of animal spirits, 80; and passion, 102, 151, 170, 172–180, 211, 216; of external objects on the sense organs, 119, 120, 133, 140, 146, 159, 171, 186; actions in/of the body, 178, 182, 183, 190, 201, 203, 210; belief-desire model of, 220. *See also* acts of thinking; will
act(s)/activity of thinking, 101, 112–118, 128, 134, 135, 209, 224; activity of the mind, 174
Adams, Marilyn McCord, 267nn25,26
Adams, Robert M., 260n9
admiration. *See* wonder
affection(s), 60, 89, 92, 176, 185, 219; two affections of the will, 236–239
agency: rational, 99, 209, 211, 240; Stoic account of, 216–218, 220–224; conditions of, 256–257
agent(s), 51, 74
Aho, Tuomo, 264n14
Alanen, Lilli, 267n26, 268n27, 272nn51,52, 274n66, 277n10, 280n32, 297n34, 299n47, 313n63, 327n74
Albritton, Rogers, 232
Alexander Aphrodisias, 332n31
Al-farabi, 300n59

algebra, 18, 32, 33, 269n31, 271n48, 272n49, 307n19
Alhazen, 302n72
Almog, Joseph, 275n3, 276n10
Alquié, Ferdinand, 242, 243, 246, 261n3, 262n7, 269nn31,33, 272n51, 274n63, 296n25, 298n41, 308n26, 319nn11,14, 321n32, 325n57, 327n70, 327n1, 340n83, 341n92
anaclastique line, 19, 271n45
analysis, 18; configurational, 33; conceptual, 71
analytic history of philosophy, 2–4. *See also* historiography
angel, 58; fallen, 256
anger, 180, 203, 210, 218, 222, 320n20
Anglo-American philosophy of mind, 45
animal(s), 84, 108, 200, 282; spirits, 50, 80, 90, 182, 183, 190, 191, 200, 211, 321n23, 323n42; and thinking, 85–88, 90, 287n17; movements of, 141
Annas, Julia, 221, 328nn7,8, 331nn21,24,25, 332n26
Anscombe, Elisabeth, and Geach, Peter, translation of *Meditations,* 286n5
Anselm of Canterbury, 236, 243, 336n56
anthropology, Descartes's, 46, 166, 278n7, 317n7
appetite(s), 65, 203, 206, 211, 222, 235, 236, 239, 246
apprehensive notions, 17; apprehension, 267n27

343

Deigh, John, 320n19
deliberation, 189, 223, 236, 330n13,
  331n21, 333n33; means-end, 243,
  337n59
depression (bipolarity), 324n52
"Descartes's myth," 56. *See also* Cartesian, Ghost-in-the-Machine myth
Description of the Human Body, 46
desire, 194, 215, 220, 222, 223, 236, 249
determinism, 233, 240, 241; ethical, 209,
  231, 234
development, Descartes's intellectual,
  2–9, 34
Dihle, Albrecht, 330n16, 332n32,
  335n54
Dioptrique, La. See *Optics*
Discours de la méthode. See *Discourse on the
  Method*
Discourse on the Method, 24, 29, 32, 33, 37,
  41–42, 44–47, 86, 96, 225, 272n51
distinction: of reason, 29; arguments for
  real distinction of mind and body, 44,
  276n10; conceptual, 45, 71; real, 47,
  55, 70, 125, 166
Donagan, Alan, 100, 129, 137, 275n6,
  290n49, 297n32, 300n56, 312n51
dualism, ix-xi, 1, 43, 44, 45, 46, 48, 98,
  117, 166, 168, 171, 201, 241, 281n46,
  328n5; substance, 70, 80, 173, 276n6,
  283n63, 284n64; Platonic, 70, 165;
  anomalous, 72, 177; Aristotelian, 80,
  215, 216.
Duns Scotus, John, 16, 117, 125, 126,
  133, 230, 235–241, 267n25,
  268nn28,29, 298nn45,46,47,
  337nn62,63,64, 338nn67,68,69,70,
  339n71
Durandus of St. Pourcain, 133, 302n69
duration, 28

Elisabeth, Princess (of Bohemia), 48, 50,
  51, 59, 60, 61, 63, 72, 74, 76, 165, 166,
  167, 168, 169, 191, 201, 202, 207, 218,
  240, 317n1, 327n74, 328n6
emotion(s), 11, 61, 65, 66, 70, 90, 113,
  165, 166, 171, 181, 183, 186, 187, 188,
  200, 216; and music, 11; emotional
  state, 55, 67; and confused thoughts,
  64, 92, 159; "cognitivist" accounts of,

166; interior, 169, 182; as cognitive or
  intentional states, 171, 172;
  intentionality of, 171–177, 180, 184–
  197; intellectual, 190, 194, 195, 196.
  See also passion(s)
ens per se and *ens per accidens*, 280n39
Epictetus, 329n11, 332n31
epistemology, 8, 18, 22, 24, 33, 266n19
Epstein, William, 307n21, 308n28
error(s), 18, 30, 59, 60, 92, 99, 150, 153,
  156, 158, 162, 226, 242, 247, 249, 253,
  313n64
Essays (accompanying the Discourse),
  24, 41
essence(s)/nature(s) of things, 39, 40,
  57, 107, 119, 124, 144, 154
eternal truths(s), 8, 37–41, 56, 61, 104,
  123, 231; creation of eternal truths, 8,
  36, 37, 39, 273nn55,57, 291n68
evidence, 14–16, 74; self-evidence, 14;
  evident cognition, 15; self-evident
  principles, 70
evil, 225, 235, 245
evil demon hypothesis, 36, 37
existence, 28, 58, 150; arguments for
  God's, 44, 127; necessary and possible, 127, 130, 299n52; of God, 246
ex nihilo, 39, 108, 122, 231
experience, 30, 35, 50, 57, 58, 73, 75, 76,
  77, 177, 197, 200, 206; of mind-body
  union, 60, 61, 62, 63, 65, 72, 74, 84,
  176; private, 81, 83; Descartes's notion
  of, 266n21
expression(s) of feelings or emotions,
  85, 86, 210
extension, 25, 27, 48, 51, 59–63, 71, 74,
  75, 80, 97, 134, 143, 155, 160, 175,
  176; notion of, 48, 59, 60, 64; modes
  of, 66. *See also* body

faculties, 57, 79; of knowledge, 20–23,
  26, 29, 42
faculty psychology, 26, 79, 139, 233, 235
fallibility, 77, 252, 253
falsity, 27, 28, 160, 246; formal vs. material, 149, 156–164
fear, 183, 187, 214
feeling(s), 57, 58, 70, 86, 166, 180, 181,
  183, 184, 192; of animals, 85

irrationalism, 41, 209
Irwin, T. H., 333n32
iudicio. See judgment(s)

James, Susan, 320n20, 324n50, 326n67
James, William, 184, 324nn43,45
joy and sadness, 167, 168, 195, 198, 206,
  253, 318n10, 326n65
judging, power of, 82
judgment(s), 13, 29, 30, 31, 55, 64, 149,
  151, 152, 153, 158, 180, 182, 185, 187,
  191, 192, 224, 242, 267n27; of pure
  understanding, 37; precipitated, 66,
  106, 162, 248; perceptual, 88, 90, 92,
  93, 157, 289n32; unnoticed, 154, 160–
  162; explicit judgments, 185; evaluative, 188, 190; as weapons against excessive passions, 204; Descartes's doctrine of, 226–228, 246–249

Kahn, Charles, 333nn34,35, 335nn53,
  54
Kant, Immanuel, 109, 110, 291n66
Kenny, Anthony, 114, 129, 237, 242, 243,
  244, 277n17, 293n55, 295n20,
  297n37, 300n54, 304n2, 338n66,
  340nn80,83
Kent, Bonnie, 230, 235, 261n11, 318n8,
  334n42, 336n56, 337n58, 340n81
Kepler, Johannes, 139
knowledge, 20, 22, 30, 31, 55, 59, 63, 64,
  66, 76, 106–107, 125, 139, 143, 144,
  148, 167, 175–177, 178; abstractive,
  15; evident/intuitive, 17, 143, 144;
  foundations of, 20; order of, 22, 27,
  56, 61, 143; objects of, 22, 27–30, 60,
  63, 64, 132; a priori, 30; and nature of
  mind, 46, 54–56; self-knowledge, 48,
  49, 251; domains or kinds of, 48, 50,
  51, 59–63, 64, 71, 73, 74, 77; tacit, 74;
  limits of rational, 75; perfect or absolutely certain, 103, 106, 282n48; role
  of sensation in, 148, 150, 159–160; adequate vs. complete, 150, 151, 152,
  162, 310n43; of passions and their
  causes, 178–182
Knudsen, Christian, 300n59
Knuuttila, Simo, 297n34, 298n47,
  330n13, 335n54
Kretzmann, Norman, 301n63

Langston, Douglas C., 267n25
language. *See* thought, and language
Larmore, Charles, 308nn23,24,25
laws of nature, mechanical, 77, 241
Leibniz, Gottfried Wilhelm, 10, 40, 67,
  83, 231, 240, 273nn53,54, 283n56,
  334n40, 335n44, 339n73, 340n77
Lennon, Thomas M., 304n2, 305n4
Levi, Anthony, 330n15
libertarianism, 208
liberty of indifference. *See* indifference
life, 41, 41, 84, 86; as a mechanical phenomenon, 88, 93; principles of, 178
light: action of, 120, 121; refraction of,
  306n13. *See also* natural light of reason
Lipsius, Justus, 330n15
Locke, John, 105, 133, 286n3, 307n21,
  309n30, 320n19
logic, 33, 265n16, 267n64, 272n48; syllogistic, 33, 271n48
logical truths or principles, 67, 123
Lombard, Peter, 336n56
Lottin, Odon, 336n56
love, 187, 194, 196, 197, 198, 199, 253
Lucretius, 335n52
Lullus, Raymundus, 9

machine(s), 70, 124, 175, 177, 179; and
  thinking, 93–97; Turing machine, 98
Mäenpää, Petri, 271n48
Malcolm, Norman, 70, 76, 85, 87, 89, 90,
  278n20, 283n62, 284n64, 285n79,
  287n13, 288n20, 289n29
Malebranche, Nicholas, 122, 135, 136,
  286n3, 304n2, 309n33
Man, Treatise on, 18, 35, 41, 42, 169
Marion, Jean-Luc, 264n15, 268n29,
  272n53
material falsity of ideas. *See* falsity, formal vs. material; idea(s)
materialism, 98
mathematics, 19, 21, 31, 32, 33, 34, 41;
  and Cartesian physics, 32
mathesis universalis, 19, 268n31
matter, 53, 75, 98, 117, 146, 155, 174,
  278n21, 292n2; metaphysical, 71, 135;
  powers of, 79, 81, 91; as extension, 80,
  140. *See also* form: form and matter
Mattern, Ruth, 277n11, 284n66
Matthews, Gareth B., 289n33

psycho-physiology, 72; psycho-physiological state, 69
Putnam, Hilary, 290n47

qualia, 81, 99, 286n8
quality(ies), 52, 67, 139, 141, 142, 145, 149, 154, 156, 158; real qualities, 51, 158. *See also* primary vs. secondary qualities

Radner, Daisie, 284n66, 290n51
rationality, 98, 221, 224, 245; principles or norms of, 40, 153, 291n66; standards of, 41, 99
real distinction, 47, 166; arguments for, 44, 47, 276n10
realism, direct vs. representational, 124, 139, 141, 145–147, 304n2, 305nn3,4,7, 306nn8,13,15, 307n22, 308nn25,30, 309n33
reality: formal/actual vs. objective/intentional, 122–125, 130, 131, 186, 187; degrees of, 128
reason, 13, 77, 105, 106, 166, 167, 210, 218, 221, 245, 246; light of, 13; human, 19, 94; for every thing, 40, 103; power of reason to control passions, 212, 254; classic notion of, 222; order of reason vs. order of causes, 239
Rees, Rush, 290n58
reference, causal, 122, 187
referring, 180, 186
reflection, 132, 192, 200
reflexive reaction(s), 193
reflexivity, 100
refraction, law of, 41
Regius (Henry le Roy), letter to, 52, 174, 280n39, 281n41
Regulae ad directionem ingeni. See Rules for the Direction of the Mind
regulation of passions, 253. *See also* general remedy to excesses of passion; passions, mastery of
Reid, Thomas, 304n2
relations: contingent, 29; necessary, 29, 30, 31
represent, 27, 104, 122, 187, 188, 310n42
representation, 27, 35, 84, 95, 96, 112,

113, 116, 128, 130, 134–137, 140, 141, 144, 145, 148, 149, 183, 184, 187, 188, 192, 193, 194, 195, 202, 295n18; representational, 82, 128, 173; causal theory of, 146; representative, 305n7, 310n40. *See also* idea(s); objective reality/being
responsibility, moral, 233, 244, 255, 256
Richardsson, Robert C., 275n6, 278n23, 280n38, 284n67
Rodis-Lewis, Geneviève, 278n20, 305n5, 306n8, 307n18, 317n18, 319n14, 322n37, 325n53
Rorty, Amélie Oksenberg, 319n17
Rorty, Richard, 259n1, 301n60, 304n2
Rozemond, Marleen, 69, 275n3, 276n10, 279n26, 281n, 283n61
Rules for the Direction of the Mind, 7–8, 12–38, 47, 263n8, 265nn16,17,19, 266nn19,20,21, 269nn31–38, 271nn45,48, 306n11, 312n60
Russell, Bertrand, 116, 260n8
Ryle, Gilbert, 45, 49, 53, 54, 66, 275n4, 279n29, 290n50

sadness, 167, 195
sapientia, 7
Schmalz, Tad M., 277n11, 281n44
scholastic(s), 45, 46, 51, 52, 56, 71, 72, 115, 117, 118, 121, 124, 126, 127, 131, 134, 139, 146, 151, 158, 214, 224, 251; terminology, 45; scholasticism, 124
Schuster, John A., 145, 263n8, 268n31, 269nn32,33, 271n45, 272n49, 296n24, 305n3, 306nn9,12,15, 307n22, 308n29
science, 9–10, 63, 73, 76, 130, 158, 179; mechanistic science of nature, 36; vision of unitary, 36; cognitive, 81
scientia, 7–8, 13, 17, 18, 31, 34, 73, 76, 77, 103, 143, 261n1
scientific vs. manifest image, 8
seal-wax metaphor, 24, 25
Searle, John, 115, 293n9
Secada, Jorge, 260n10, 264n15
Second Meditation, 48, 55, 56, 57, 249
Second Replies, 110, 119, 131, 268n27, 286n1, 290n49
self, 42, 56, 215; self-knowledge, 48, 57, 251, 280n37; nature of, 57; self-deter-